Innovations in Inter
to Address Intimate
Violence

Innovations in Interventions to Address Intimate Partner Violence: Research and Practice speaks to what can be done to effectively intervene to end intimate partner violence against women. Including contributions from both researchers and practitioners, chapters describe service innovations across systems in large urban and remote rural contexts, aimed at majority and minority populations, and that utilize a range of theoretical perspectives to understand and promote change in violence and victimization. Reflecting this range, contributions to this volume are organized into five sections: legal responses to domestic violence, intervention with men who have perpetrated domestic violence, responses to women who have experienced domestic violence, restorative approaches to intimate partner violence, and a section on integrating intervention for domestic violence across systems. The book highlights advances in practice that will be of interest to researchers, practitioners, policy makers, and students.

Tod Augusta-Scott, MSW, RSW, is the executive director of Bridges, a domestic violence counseling, research, and training institute in Truro, Nova Scotia, Canada. He was awarded the Distinguished Service Award from the Canadian Association of Social Workers in 2013.

Katreena Scott, PhD, holds the Canada Research Chair in Family Violence Prevention and Intervention at the University of Toronto.

Leslie M. Tutty, PhD, is professor emerita in the Faculty of Social Work at the University of Calgary.

"This exciting new edited volume on domestic violence represents perspectives from a wide range of regions and cultures across Canada. Through the lens of restorative justice, it describes approaches with victims and perpetrators, as well as coordinated community approaches that promote accountability, personal transformation, and reconciliation. The editors shine a light on domestic violence in an innovative and hopeful manner."—**Daniel Sonkin, PhD**, author, *Learning to Live Without Violence: A Handbook for Men;* Independent Practice, Sausalito, California

"The authors provide one of the most comprehensive volumes to date on progress and innovation in the prevention of intimate partner violence in Canada. Recognizing the breadth of responses required to reduce this type of violence, leaders across a variety of fields/disciplines provide up-to-date knowledge about legal and social responses and their potential for addressing intimate partner violence. A must-read for both new and established practitioners, researchers, and scholars."—**Myrna Dawson**, professor, Canada research chair in Public Policy in Criminal Justice, University of Guelph

"This book takes a holistic approach to IPV intervention, recognizing that any approach that does not involve researchers and practitioners from multiple systems is bound to fail. The contributors to this volume convincingly demonstrate that the way forward in reducing IPV must be collaborative and interdisciplinary."—**Claire M. Renzetti, PhD**, Judi Conway Patton Endowed Chair for Studies of Violence Against Women; professor, chair of Sociology, University of Kentucky

"This collection is a major contribution to the vision of ending intimate family violence in Canada and throughout the world. I've been in practice for 40 years working with men who use violence. The respectful, collaborative, and creative approach shown in these articles will assist therapists, volunteers, researchers, policy makers, and agencies as we work together to bring peace, justice, and healing to families and communities."—**Dale Trimble, MA** (psychology), AEDP Institute, faculty; private practice, Vancouver, BC

Innovations in Interventions to Address Intimate Partner Violence

Research and Practice

**Edited by
Tod Augusta-Scott,
Katreena Scott, and
Leslie M. Tutty**

 Routledge
Taylor & Francis Group

NEW YORK AND LONDON

First published 2017
by Routledge
711 Third Avenue, New York, NY 10017

and by Routledge
2 Park Square, Milton Park, Abingdon, Oxon, OX14 4RN

Routledge is an imprint of the Taylor & Francis Group, an informa business

Library of Congress Cataloging in Publication Data
A catalog record for this book has been requested

ISBN: 978-1-138-69226-8 (hbk)
ISBN: 978-1-138-69227-5 (pbk)
ISBN: 978-1-315-53277-6 (ebk)

Typeset in Baskerville
by Florence Production Ltd, Stoodleigh, Devon, UK

Contents

List of Illustrations   viii

Notes on Contributors   ix

Introduction by Tod Augusta-Scott, Katreena Scott, and Leslie M. Tutty   xi

PART I
Responses to Women Abused by Intimate Partners   1

1   "A Place To Go To When I Had No Place To Go To": Journeys of Violence Against Women's Emergency Shelter Residents   3
Leslie M. Tutty

2   Rethinking Safety Planning: A Self-Directed Tool for Rural Women Who Are Abused   18
Deborah Doherty

3   "If They Can Get Through It, So Can I": Women's Perspectives of Peer-Led Support Groups for Intimate Partner Violence   33
Leslie M. Tutty, Cindy Ogden, Karen Wyllie, and Andrea Silverstone

PART II
Intervention with Men Who Have Perpetrated Intimate Partner Violence   51

4   Justice-Linked Domestic Violence Intervention Services: Description and Analysis of Practices across Canada   53
Katreena Scott, Lisa Heslop, Randal David, and Tim Kelly

5   Complex Trauma and Dominant Masculinity: A Trauma-Informed, Narrative Therapy Approach with Men Who Abuse Their Female Partners   75
Tod Augusta-Scott and Leland Maerz

6 Co-Constructing Meaning: Women and Men Define Taking
Responsibility and Making Amends 93
Yoshiyuki Takano

7 A Continuum of Services for Men Who Abuse: Developing a
Small-City Coordinated Community Response Model 108
Rosanna Langer

PART III
Legal Responses to Domestic Violence 123

8 The Nova Scotia Domestic Violence Court Pilot Project:
Lessons Learned from Evaluation 125
Diane Crocker and Robert Crocker

9 Shifting Toward a Trauma-Informed, Holistic Legal Service
Model for Survivors of Violence: The Calgary Legal Guidance
Family Law Program 139
Kayla Gurski and Tiffany Butler

PART IV
Restorative Justice 155

10 Creating Safety, Respect, and Equality for Women: Lessons from
the Intimate Partner Violence and Restorative Justice Movements 157
Tod Augusta-Scott, Pamela Harrison, and Verona Singer

11 Restorative Justice, Domestic Violence, and the Law: A Panel
Discussion 174
Tod Augusta-Scott, Leigh Goodmark, and Joan Pennell

12 Preparing Men to Help the Women They Abused Achieve
Just Outcomes: A Restorative Approach 191
Tod Augusta-Scott

PART V
Broadening the Lens: Integrating Interventions for
Domestic Violence Across Systems 205

13 Strengthening Families: An Evaluation of a Pilot Couples Program
for Situational Intimate Partner Violence and Substance Abuse 207
Leslie M. Tutty and Robbie Babins-Wagner

14 Men Who Abuse Intimate Partners: Their Evaluation of a
   Responsible Fathering Program   227
   Joan Pennell and Erika Brandt

15 Preventing Homelessness for Women Who Leave Abusive
   Partners: A Shelter-Based "Housing First" Program   244
   Monique Auffrey, Leslie M. Tutty, and Alysia C. Wright

   Index   259

Illustrations

Figures

2.1   Step One—Deciding Who to Tell About the Abuse in My Life   22
2.2   Step Two—Identifying My Lived Reality   23
2.3   Step Three—Making My Safety Plan While Living with Abuse   24
7.1   Sudbury Domestic Violence Continuum   114

Tables

3.1   Demographics for Growth Circle Respondents   38
4.1   Domestic Violence Courts and Court Processes in Canada   56
6.1   Male and Female Participants' Themes in Taking Responsibility 96
8.1   Characteristics of Offenders, Victims, and Charges (June 2012 to
      December 2013)   131
8.2   Relationship between Program Level and Characteristics of
      Offenders   132
8.3   Comparison of Outcomes for Charges Pre- and Post-Pilot   133
13.1 Comparison of Demographics of Non-Completers and
      Completers   213
13.2 Comparison of Measures for Non-Completers and Completers
      at Pretest   215
13.3 Comparison of Pretest/Posttest Scores   217
13.4 OQ-45 Comparison of Non-Completers and Completers   219
14.1 Demographic and Program Information of Research
      Participants   231
14.2 Participant Satisfaction Ratings   233
14.3 Self-Reported Motivations and Outcomes   235

Contributors

Monique Auffrey, BA, BSW, MSW—Discovery House Family Violence Prevention Society, Calgary, Alberta.

Tod Augusta-Scott, MSW—Bridges, a domestic violence counseling, research, and training institute, Truro, Nova Scotia.

Robbie Babins-Wagner, PhD, MSW, RSW—Calgary Counselling Centre, Calgary, Alberta.

Erika Brandt—Center for Family and Community Engagement, Raleigh, North Carolina.

Tiffany Butler, BPAPM, JD—Calgary Legal Guidance, Calgary, Alberta.

Diane Crocker, PhD—Saint Mary's University, Halifax, Nova Scotia.

Robert Crocker—Memorial University, Corner Brook, Newfoundland.

Randal David—University of Toronto, Toronto, Ontario.

Deborah Doherty, BA, MA, PhD—Public Legal Education and Information Service of New Brunswick, Fredericton, New Brunswick.

Leigh Goodmark, JD—University of Maryland Frances King Carey School of Law, Baltimore, Maryland.

Kayla Gurski, BHJ, BSW, RSW—Calgary Legal Guidance, Calgary, Alberta.

Pamela Harrison—Transition House Association of Nova Scotia, Halifax, Nova Scotia.

Lisa Heslop—London Police Services, London, Ontario.

Tim Kelly, HBSW RSW—Changing Ways, London, Ontario.

Rosanna Langer, BA, LLB, LLM, PHD—Laurentian University, Sudbury, Ontario.

Leland Maerz, MMin, MEd, RCT—Bridges Institute, Truro, Nova Scotia.

Cindy Ogden, MSW, PhD(c)—University of Calgary, Calgary, Alberta.

Joan Pennell, PhD—Center for Family and Community Engagement, North Carolina State University, Raleigh, North Carolina.

Katreena Scott—University of Toronto, Toronto, Ontario.

Andrea Silverstone, WT, Q.Med, RSW—Sagesse, Calgary, Alberta.

Verona Singer MCA, PhD—Halifax Regional Police, Halifax, Nova Scotia.

Yoshiyuki Takano, PhD—John Howard Society of Grande Prairie, Grande Prairie, Alberta.

Leslie M. Tutty, PhD—University of Calgary, Calgary, Alberta.

Alysia C. Wright, MSW—University of Calgary, Calgary, Alberta.

Karen Wyllie, MSW, BSW, BA—Alternative Support Services, Calgary, Alberta.

Introduction

Tod Augusta-Scott, Katreena Scott, and
Leslie M. Tutty

Intimate partner violence (IPV) is a critical issue for families, communities, and for social service providers across North America. In the recent US National Intimate Partner and Sexual Violence Survey, an estimated 22.3 percent of women and 14 percent of men reported having been severely physically abused by a partner in their lifetimes (Breiding, 2015). In Canada, intimate partner violence accounts for approximately one-quarter of all violent crime reported to police services, and for one in five solved homicides (Sinha, 2013). In the five years preceding the 2009 national Canadian General Social Survey, 6 percent of both men and women reported having been physically or sexually victimized by their current or previous spouse (Statistics Canada, 2011).

Although the public generally thinks of intimate partner violence as severe physical abuse, abuse also entails sexual violence and emotional abuse, including harassment, stalking, and threats to kill (Breiding, 2015; Johnson, 2006). Emotional or psychological abuse includes denigrating comments and threats to either harm or to take custody of the children should she leave (Ansara & Hindin, 2010). Stalking can be as seemingly insignificant as multiple phonecalls or texts, repeatedly checking her whereabouts or can entail dedicated following, spying, and harassing threats (Burgess, Harner, Baker, Hartman, & Lole, 2001). Sexual assaults are also common (Bergen & Bukovec 2006; Gorman, 2012).

Across all forms of IPV, women are the more severely affected (Arias & Corso, 2005; Breiding, 2015; Johnson, 2006). For example, of Canadian women who reported that their partners had acted violently in the previous five years, 34 percent had been sexually assaulted, beaten, choked, or threatened with a gun or a knife by their partner or ex-partner in the past five years compared to about 10 percent of men (Au Coin, 2005). Sexual assaults and stalking are also perpetrated predominately by men against women. In 2011 in Canada, women were victims of sexual assault eleven times more than men and of stalking three times more than men (Sinha, 2013). While the numbers of individuals murdered by spouses is relatively small in relationship to the total number of IPV victims, women remain more likely to be killed by abusive spouses, often followed by the suicide of the male partner (Campbell, Glass, Sharps, Laughon, & Bloom, 2007; Dawson, 2005). Still, in cases where women are abusive to their male partners, this violence is important to acknowledge and address.

It is also important to recognize that the end of an intimate relationship does not necessarily denote the end of abuse and violence. Women are also abused after they leave the partners; in fact, many women are at heightened risk of further violence after leaving (Brownridge, 2006; Fleury, Sullivan, & Bybee, 2000). Further, women often have continued contact with abusive ex-partners through systems such as child welfare, custody arrangements, or divorce proceedings. While some have referred to this experience as "paper abuse" (Miller & Smolter, 2011), others suggest that this term minimizes the pain experienced by the victims in having to continually cope with their abusive ex-partner' actions.

Overall, the costs of IPV are profound. Recent estimates place the cost of intimate partner violence to Canadian society at 6.9 billion dollars per year (Arias & Corso, 2005; Varcoe et al., 2011). The impact in terms of human suffering is even greater. Intimate partner violence victimization has been associated with increased risk for all major mental health disorders, social problems (e.g. unemployment, criminal behavior) and chronic physical health conditions (e.g. cardiovascular disease, cancer, gastrointestinal problems) (Anda et al., 2006; Currie & Widom, 2010; Gilbert et al., 2009).

Children, as well, often pay the price for violence in adult relationships with exposure to intimate partner violence associated with behavioral difficulties (both withdrawal and aggression) and trauma symptoms (Hungerford, Wait, Fritz, & Clements, 2012; Wolfe, Crooks, Lee, McIntyre-Smith, & Jaffe, 2003). Children exposed to IPV between their fathers and mothers, whether directly witnessing, hearing incidents, or seeing the effects such as bruises, account for about a fifth of the 235,842 cases of substantiated child maltreatment opened each year in Canada (Trocmé et al., 2010). In the United States, an estimated 15.5 million children live in families where IPV has occurred at least once in the previous year, with about 7 million of these living in homes with severe partner violence (McDonald, Jouriles, Ramisetty-Mikler, Caetano, & Green, 2006). Beyond simple "exposure," children also physically intervene in efforts to protect their mothers, effectively putting themselves in harm's way (Gewirtz & Medhanie, 2008).

Intersections of IPV with other social identities and systems of oppression and discrimination are also important to recognize. Some populations are more impacted by intimate partner violence than others. In the US, individuals of Black and Hispanic racial background report higher rates of intimate partner violence (Field & Cataneo, 2005). These findings suggest the need for increased programming for these groups to both prevent and offer assistance to those affected by IPV (Lipsky, Caetano, Field, & Larkin, 2006). In Canada, Aboriginal families are an important group. According to Brownridge (2008), Aboriginal women are at three times higher risk of being abused by intimate partners than non-Aboriginal Canadian women (21 percent compared to 7 percent).

Sexual orientation is another important intersection. Although the incidence and prevalence data are not yet reliable, some argue that abuse in same-sex relationships occurs more often than in heterosexual partnerships (Allison,

Thoennes, & Tjaden, 1999) and others report that the incidence does not differ (Blosnich & Bossarte, 2009). While the nature of the abusive acts is similar, including psychological, physical, and sexual assaults, the dynamics in same-sex couples also include, for example, threats of "outing" the other partner as gay or lesbian (Baker, Buick, Kim, Moniz, & Nava, 2013; Frankland & Brown, 2014; Ristock, 2003).

At times, the scope, range, and impact of IPV may seem daunting. Yet, grass roots organizations, service providers, researchers, and policy makers have been working rapidly to develop, implement, and examine interventions to address this issue. Significant developments include women shelters specific to intimate partner violence (Hughes, Cangiano, & Hopper, 2011; Tutty, 2015), indicator-based assessment of intimate partner violence in medical settings (MacMillan, et al., 2006; Nelson, Bougatsos, & Blazina, 2012), and group counseling and support to assist both adult women (McWhirter, 2011; Tutty, Babins-Wagner, & Rothery, 2015) and child victims (Graham-Bermann & Miller, 2013; Pepler, Catallo, & Moore, 2000). The criminal justice system has also created important strategies such as specialized domestic violence courts (Tutty & Koshan, 2013), groups for both mandated men (Augusta-Scott & Dankwort, 2002; Scott, King, McGinn, & Hosseini, 2011) and women charged with perpetrating intimate partner violence (Tutty, Babins-Wagner & Rothery, 2009) and legislation to more effectively provide emergency protection orders for victims (Burgess-Proctor, 2003; Koshan & Wiegers, 2007). Policies to address the potential harm to children of exposure to IPV have been developed across North America (Cross, Mathews, Tonmyr, Scott, & Ouimet, 2012; Nixon, Tutty, Weaver-Dunlop, & Walsh, 2007).

The current volume of work explores some of these innovations in addressing IPV with women, men and in systems. It grew from contributions made to the Canadian Domestic Violence Conference held biannually in Toronto and co-sponsored by Bridges Institute in Truro, Nova Scotia and the Hincks-Dellcrest International in Toronto since 2009. The conference brings together internationally recognized researchers and practice leaders to develop and share innovations in intimate partner violence service. The result has been a growing body of knowledge about how to best intervene to address intimate partner violence. Through this edited collection, we invited these scholars to share their innovation and knowledge on responses to women who have experienced domestic violence, men who have perpetrated IPV, in legal responses to IPV, in restorative justice, and in the breadth of IPV interventions across systems.

We recognize that many of the issues and ideas that we are exploring in this volume are controversial. There are longstanding tensions in the intimate partner violence field, touching many areas of service. We struggle, for example, to appreciate the profound impacts of violence while at the same time recognizing the resilience of women who are "survivors." We need our justice and social systems to recognize that assault of an intimate partner is a serious crime, but we know that punishment itself is unlikely to lead to long-term change. We recognize the need to explore new and potentially more effective ways to intervene with men and women around IPV issues including those that recognize the impact of childhood trauma and the helpfulness of conjoint work for some cases, and we want to ensure these explorations always incorporate the lessons learned through the intimate partner violence movement about issues of safety, power, and control.

Yet despite these controversies, we believe that it is often through open dialogue precisely in these controversial areas that knowledge grows, practice improves, and more effective services are developed. As an editorial team, we were not free from these controversies. In fact, one of the best parts of curating this collection of chapters was the associated debates about what and how innovations might best be profiled. It is our hope that readers will also be similarly provoked and will end up gaining similar knowledge and understanding.

We also found much common ground. As an editorial team, we shared a number of underlying values and beliefs that guided our decisions and therefore, this volume of work. First, as both researchers and clinicians, we share a passion for supporting the most effective interventions available and promoting novel approaches to dealing with what is a pernicious and sometimes life-threatening issue. As a fundamental commitment, we believe that intervention for IPV should have, as its primary aim, promoting the safety of past and potential victims of abuse, including children exposed to IPV. Women and men both need to be involved. Victims of IPV need supportive, empowering, protective, and healing interventions. We also need to work with those who have perpetrated violence to help them end their use of violence, be accountable for their actions, and develop values, skills, and strategies that will prevent future violence perpetration. Although violence may be preceded by many factors—childhood trauma, substance use, provocation—those who perpetrate violence need to take responsibly to stop it. This is even the case when violence is mutual (Augusta-Scott, 2007). While men need to take responsibility to stop their own abuse, when women perpetrate abuse, women also must take responsibility to stop their abuse.

Second, we recognize that there is heterogeneity of violence and that consideration of this heterogeneity is critical to advancing intervention. Intimate partner violence perpetration varies in severity and intensity of abuse (Johnson, 2008; Kelly & Johnson, 2008). Not all abuse is high risk for lethality; for example, not all women are terrorized by their partners in intimate partner violence cases. There is also violence that is moderate and low-level risk of lethality. Making such distinctions is often important in all spheres. For example, such distinctions can be a contributing factor to why many women want to flee and others to stay and try to restore the safety, equality, and respect in the relationship. Further, recognizing the differences in the effects and intensity of the abuse may open the door to a broader range of interventions for men who have perpetrated violence, some focused on monitoring and containing risk, others on restorative and repairative actions.

Third, while we agree that women are more often the victims of severe abuse, we recognize that some women do abuse their male or female partners. In some cases, this is "resistance" violence, where women defend themselves in the context of an abusive male partner (Fanslow, Gulliver, Dixon, & Ayallo, 2015; Johnson, 2008; Neilson, 2014), while in other cases, women's violence is unilateral or is mutual to some degree in the relationship. While most professionals acknowledge that men can be abused by female intimate partners, the extent and seriousness have been much debated (Dragiewicz & DeKeseredy, 2012). Some argue that patriarchal expectations on men not to appear as victims or vulnerable in any way prevent them from seeking help and result in few resources that are specific to their needs, in contrast to the national network of women's shelters (Mann, 2008; Tutty, Babins-Wagner, & Rothery, 2006). We agree that it is important to consider the needs of all those affected by interpersonal violence, without resorting to a stereotypical gender lens.

Finally, as an editorial team, we believe in the value of empirically examining our work and in using lessons learned from research to create better systems of response. Victims of violence, as well as society as a whole, have the right to expect that decisions on programming for intimate partner violence are based on the best possible evidence around "what works." Such a commitment does not constrain us to any specific methodology, world view, or definition of success, but it does require us to clearly articulate our assumptions and ideas, put them to the test with the best available evidence, and then be open to critical appraisal of the robustness of the evidence presented.

Overview of the Book

Despite the controversies, numerous programs, policies, and legislation impacting most of society's major institutions such as the legal system and courts, mental and physical health and child welfare, have been developed to address the safety and well-being of victims and to hold perpetrators accountable for their behaviors. Examples of innovations to prevent and assist all those affected by IPV represent the core of this book. While this volume is focused primarily on men's violence against women, the editors recognize it is also important to address other conversations concerning women's violence, violence in same-sex relationships as well as intimate partner violence that is particular to other cultural contexts.

Included in this volume are contributions from researchers and practitioners working in a range of systems and community contexts. Authors describe service innovations across systems in large urban and remote rural contexts, aimed at majority and minority populations, and that utilize a range of theoretical perspectives to understand and promote change in violence and victimization. Reflecting this range, contributions to this volume are organized into five sections: responses to women who have experienced intimate partner violence, intervention with men who have perpetrated domestic violence, legal responses to domestic violence, restorative justice responses, and integrating interventions for domestic violence across systems.

Responses to Women Who Have Experienced Intimate Partner Violence

A strong system of services and supports to empower victims of abuse is a foundational component of societal response to intimate partner violence. This edited volume includes contributions from a number of researchers and practitioners at the forefront of developing more effective and compassionate ways to meet the needs of women whose partners have abused them. In the first chapter, Leslie Tutty presents research about women's experiences of violence against women shelters, providing a voice to women to identify how they access shelters, what they need and want from their shelter residence, and how they fare six months to a year afterwards. In the next chapter of this section, Deborah Doherty focuses on assisting women living in rural communities in being safe. Recognizing that in rural communities, staying in the relationship is often the norm, her work offers a strategic means for women to assess and mitigate their personal risk while remaining in a relationship with a partner who has been abusive. In the final chapter of this section, Leslie Tutty, Cindy Ogden, Karen Wyllie, and Andrea Silverstone examine community-offered peer-led support groups for women, listening to the members' perspectives on what the group sessions offer women whose partners have abused them and how effectively they work.

Intervention with Men Who Have Perpetrated Intimate Partner Violence

Every region of the United States and Canada offers intervention services to men who have perpetrated intimate partner violence. As a beginning point in exploring innovations in services to men, Katreena Scott, Lisa Heslop, Randal David, and Tim Kelly outline the results of the first national research project to document and describe justice-linked interventions across Canada. This chapter is useful for informing who receives service, what intervention they receive, how court-linked services are (or are not) integrated across other justice system responses, and for considering major similarities and differences in service across Canada.

Following from this broad overview, the next three chapters explore recent innovations in practice with men who have perpetrated violence against their female partners in the area of responsibility, trauma, substance use, and racism. For men who abuse and have been traumatized themselves, Tod Augusta-Scott and Leland Maerz illustrate the importance of attending to both men's experiences of trauma and dominant masculinity in efforts to stop their violence. In the next chapter, Yoshiyuki Takano expands the definition of taking responsibility to include men finding ways of becoming socially and emotionally self-reliant rather than relying solely on their partners for these things. Takano explores how men can take care of themselves in ways that are not self-absorbed but, rather, increase their female partners' sense of well-being. Finally, Rosanna Langer contributes a chapter describing the development of a multiagency coordinated community response that provides a continuum of preventative and intervention service to men who are at risk of intimate partner violence.

Legal Responses to Intimate Partner Violence

Canada has a robust justice system response to intimate partner violence that includes specialized police training, dedicated courts, and justice-linked services for both perpetrators and victims of domestic violence. This section of the book explores innovations in how the legal system deals with intimate partner violence. To begin, two chapters examine the courts as a locus for intervention. Diane Crocker and Robert Crocker evaluate a new specialized domestic violence court in Nova Scotia, comparing the outcomes from the innovative procedures to the pre-court processes. The lessons learned may be transferable to other specialized courts across North America. Their work is followed by a contribution from Kayla Gurski and Tiffany Butler who elaborate on a trauma-informed legal response to those who have experienced domestic violence. Their agency's model of client-centered, community engaged, trauma-informed, and interdisciplinary practice helps "set the bar" for good practice.

Restorative Justice

In the next section, three chapters explore an emerging approach to intimate partner violence, restorative justice, which draws on many of the values and practices that have existed in the IPV movement for decades. This approach seeks to restore women's safety, equality, and respect, while inviting the men who did the harms and the wider community to become part of the solution of achieving just outcomes for women. First, Tod Augusta-Scott, Pamela Harrison, and Verona Singer explore how restorative justice can center women's definitions of just outcomes in community and legal responses to intimate partner violence. In this model, women can be empowered to name the harms and solutions to these harms; men and the wider community can be empowered to both stop the violence and repair the effects of it. The next chapter is a transcription of a panel by Tod Augusta-Scott, Leigh Goodmark, and Joan Pennell that explores the distinctions between the traditional legal approach to domestic violence and a restorative approach. The panelists discuss their own work in the field of intimate partner violence and the concerns they continue to address as they seek out alternative forms of justice that are not based on punishment and retribution. In the final chapter of this section, Augusta-Scott elaborates on one aspect of a larger restorative justice process: preparing men to take responsibility in a restorative process. The chapter underscores that men can be positioned to engage restoratively, to take responsibility to repair the harms they have created, even if there is no contact with their partners or ex-partners.

Broadening the Lens: Integrating Interventions for Intimate Partner Violence Across Systems

Intimate partner violence interventions are no longer restricted to specialized agencies and service providers. In the final section of this edited volume, we explore responses that broaden the ways in which we can integrate services across sectors and thereby improve our interventions to end domestic violence. In the first chapter of this section, Leslie Tutty and Robbie Babins-Wagner present an evaluation of a unique program entitled "Strengthening Families" that provides counseling to couples in relationships with both situational intimate partner violence and substance abuse. In the next chapter, Joan Pennell and Erika Brandt focus on promising work with fathers. Based on men's reports, they examine fathers' motivations to attend intervention, what they see as the effects of participating, and suggestions they have for improved services. In the final chapter, Monique Auffrey, Leslie Tutty, and Alysia Wright explore the relationship between intimate partner violence and homelessness, reporting on a community housing program to prevent women whose partners have abused them from becoming homeless.

Overall, the contributions in this section encourage us to widen our perspectives on how, when, and in what contexts intervention for intimate partner violence might be possible. We trust that you will enjoy these thought-provoking contributions and that they will prompt, for you and your community, some of the same controversies and explorations that they have for us.

References

Allison, C. J., Thoennes, N., & Tjaden, P. (1999). Comparing violence over the life span in samples of same-sex and opposite-sex cohabitants. *Violence and Victims, 14*(4), 413–425.

Anda, R. F., Felitti, V. J., Bremner, J. D., Walker, J. D., Whitfield, C., Perry, B. D., . . . & Giles, W. H. (2006). The enduring effects of abuse and related adverse experiences in childhood. *European Archives of Psychiatry and Clinical Neuroscience, 256*(3), 174–186. doi:10.1007/s00406–005–0624–4

Ansara, D. L., & Hindin, M. J. (2010). Formal and informal help-seeking associated with women's and men's experiences of intimate partner violence in Canada. *Social Science & Medicine, 70*(7), 1011–1018. doi:10.1016/j.socscimed.2009.12.009

Arias, I., & Corso, P. (2005). Average cost per person victimized by an intimate partner of the opposite gender: A comparison of men and women. *Violence & Victims, 20*(4), 379–391. doi:10.1891/0886–6708.20.4.379

Au Coin, K. (Ed.) (2005). *Family violence in Canada: A statistical profile 2005* (85-224-XIE2005000). Ottawa, ON: Canadian Centre for Justice Statistics. Online at: www.statcan.gc.ca/pub/85–224-x/85–224-x2005000-eng.pdf.

Augusta-Scott, T. (2007). Conversations with men about women's violence: Ending men's violence by challenging gender essentialism. In C. Brown, & T. Augusta-Scott (Eds.), *Narrative therapy: Making meaning, making lives* (197–210). Thousand Oaks, CA: Sage Publications.

Augusta-Scott, T., & Dankwort, J. (2002). Partner abuse group intervention: Lessons from education and narrative therapy approaches. *Journal of Interpersonal Violence, 17*(7), 783–805. doi:10.1177/0886260502017007006

Baker, N. L., Buick, J. D., Kim, S. R., Moniz, S., & Nava, K. L. (2013). Lessons from examining same-sex intimate partner violence. *Sex Roles, 69*, 182–192. doi:10.1007/s11199-012-0218-

Bergen, R. K., & Bukovec, P. (2006). Men and intimate partner rape: Characteristics of men who sexually abuse their partner. *Journal of Interpersonal Violence, 21*(10), 1375–1384. doi:10.1177/0886260506291652

Blosnich, J. R., & Bossarte, R. M. (2009). Comparisons of intimate partner violence among partners in same-sex and opposite-sex relationships in the United States. *American Journal of Public Health, 99*(12), 2182–2184. doi:10.2105/AJPH.2008.139535

Breiding, M. J. (2015). Prevalence and characteristics of sexual violence, stalking, and intimate partner violence victimization—National Intimate Partner and Sexual Violence Survey, United States, 2011. *American Journal of Public Health, 105*(4), e1–e12. doi:10.2105/AJPH.2014.302321

Brownridge, D. A. (2006). Violence against women post-separation. *Aggression and Violent Behavior, 11*(5), 514–530. doi:10.1016/j.avb.2006.01.009

Brownridge, D. A. (2008). Understanding the elevated risk of partner violence against Aboriginal women: A comparison of two nationally representative surveys of Canada. *Journal of Family Violence, 23*(5), 353–367. doi:10.1007/s10896–008–9160–0

Burgess, A. W., Harner, H., Baker, T., Hartman, C. R., & Lole, C. (2001). Batterers' stalking patterns. *Journal of Family Violence, 16*(3), 309–321. doi:10.1023/A:1011142400853

Burgess-Proctor, A. (2003). Evaluating the efficacy of protection orders for victims of domestic violence. *Women & Criminal Justice, 15*(1), 33–54. doi:10.1300/J012v15 n01_03

Campbell, J. C., Glass, N., Sharps, P. W., Laughon, K., & Bloom, T. (2007). Intimate partner homicide: Review and implications of research and policy. *Trauma Violence & Abuse, 8*(3), 247–269. doi:10.1177/1524838007303505

Cross, T. P., Mathews, B., Tonmyr, L., Scott, D., & Ouimet, C. (2012). Child welfare policy and practice on children's exposure to domestic violence. *Child Abuse & Neglect, 36*(3), 210–216. doi:10.1016/j.chiabu.2011.11.004

Currie, J., & Spatz Widom, C. (2010). Long-term consequences of child abuse and neglect on adult economic well-being. *Child Maltreatment, 15*(2), 111–120. doi:10.1177/1077559509355316

Dawson, M. (2005). Intimate femicide followed by suicide: Examining the role of premeditation. *Suicide and Life-Threatening Behavior, 35*(1), 76–90. doi:10.1521/suli.35.1.76.59261

Dragiewicz, M., & DeKeseredy, W. (2012). Claims about women's use of non-fatal force in intimate relationships: A contextual review of Canadian research. *Violence Against Women, 18*(9), 1008–1025. doi:10.1177/1077801212460754

Fanslow, J. L., Gulliver, P., Dixon, R., & Ayallo, I. (2015). Hitting back: Women's use of physical violence against violent male partners, in the context of a violent episode. *Journal of Interpersonal Violence, 30*(17), 2963–2979. doi:10.1177/0886260514555010

Field, C. A., & Caetano, R. (2005). Intimate partner violence in the U.S. general population: Progress and future directions. *Journal of Interpersonal Violence, 20*(4), 463–469. doi:10.1177/0886260504267757

Fleury, R. E., Sullivan, C. M., & Bybee, D. I. (2000). When ending the relationship does not end the violence: Women's experiences of violence by former partners. *Violence Against Women, 6*(12), 1363–1383. doi:10.1177/10778010022183695

Frankland, A., & Brown, J. (2014). Coercive control in same-sex intimate partner violence. *Journal of Family Violence, 29*, 15–22. doi:10.1007/s10896-013-9558-1

Gewirtz, A. H., & Medhanie, A. (2008). Proximity and risk in children's witnessing of intimate partner violence incidents. *Journal of Emotional Abuse, 8*(1–2), 67–82. doi:10.1080/10926790801982436

Gilbert, R., Widom, C. S., Browne, K., Fergusson, D., Webb, E., & Janson, S. (2009). Burden and consequences of child maltreatment in high-income countries. *The Lancet, 373*(9657), 68–81. doi:10.1016/S0140-6736(08)61706-7

Gorman, K. (2012). *The intersection of domestic and sexual violence: A review of the literature.* Calgary, AB: Alberta Association of Sexual Assault Services. Retrieved from: http://aasas-media-library.s3-us-west-2.amazonaws.com/AASAS/wp-content/uploads/2015/08/Intersection-of-Domestic-and-Sexual-Violence-AASAS-Review.pdf.

Graham-Bermann, S. A., & Miller, L. E. (2013). Intervention to reduce traumatic stress following intimate partner violence: An efficacy trial of the Moms' Empowerment Program (MEP). *Psychodynamic Psychiatry, 41*(2), 329–349. doi:10.1521/pdps.2013.41.2.329

Hughes, H. M., Cangiano, C., & Hopper, E. K. (2011). Profiles of distress in sheltered battered women: Implications for intervention. *Violence and Victims, 26*(4), 445–460. doi:10.1891/0886-6708.26.4.445

Hungerford, A., Wait, S. K., Fritz, A. M., & Clements, C. M. (2012). Exposure to intimate partner violence and children's psychological adjustment, cognitive functioning, and social competence: A review. *Aggression and Violent Behavior, 17*(4), 373–382. doi:10.1016/j.avb.2012.04.002

Johnson, H. (2006). *Measuring violence against women: Statistical trends 2006.* Ottawa, ON: Minister of Industry. Retrieved from: www.unece.org/fileadmin/DAM/stats/gender/vaw/surveys/Canada/2006_Publication_VAW.pdf.

Johnson, M. (2008). *A typology of domestic violence: Intimate terrorism, violent resistance, and situational couple violence.* Lebanon, NH: Northeastern Press University.

Kelly, J. & Johnson, M. (2008). Differentation among types of intimate partner violence: Research update and implications for interventions. *Family Court Review, 46*(3), 476–499.

Koshan, J. & Wiegers, W. (2007). Theorizing civil domestic violence legislation in the context of restructuring: A tale of two provinces. *Canadian Journal of Women & the Law, 19*(1), 145. doi:10.3138/cjwl.19.I.145

Lipsky, S., Caetano, R., Field, C. A., & Larkin, G. L. (2006). The role of intimate partner violence, race, and ethnicity in help-seeking behaviors. *Ethnicity & Health, 11*(1), 81–100. doi:10.1080/13557850500391410

McDonald, R., Jouriles, E. N., Ramisetty-Mikler, S., Caetano, R., & Green, C. E. (2006). Estimating the number of American children living in partner-violent families. *Journal of Family Psychology, 20*(1), 137–142. doi:10.1037/0893-3200.20.1.137

MacMillan, H. L., Wathen, C. N., Jamieson, E., Boyle, M., McNutt, L., Worster, A., Lent, B., & Webb, M. for the McMaster Violence Against Women Research Group. (2006). Approaches to screening for intimate partner violence in health care settings: A randomized trial. *Journal of the American Medical Association, 296*(5), 530–536. doi:10.1001/jama.296.5.530

McWhirter, P. T. (2011). Differential therapeutic outcomes of community-based group interventions for women and children exposed to intimate partner violence. *Journal of Interpersonal Violence, 26*(12), 2457–2482. doi:10.1177/0886260510383026

Mann, R. M. (2008). Men's rights and feminist advocacy in Canadian domestic violence policy arenas: Contexts, dynamics, and outcomes of antifeminist backlash. *Feminist Criminology, 3*(1), 44–75. doi:10.1177/1557085107311067

Miller, S. L., & Smolter, N. L. (2011). "Paper abuse": When all else fails, batterers use procedural stalking. *Violence Against Women, 17*(5), 637–650. doi:10.1177/1077801211407290

Neilson, L. (2014). At cliff's edge: Judicial dispute resolution in domestic violence cases. *Family Law Review, 52*(3), 529–563. doi:10.1111/fcre.12106

Nelson, H. D., Bougatsos, C., & Blazina, I. (2012). Screening women for intimate partner violence: A systematic review to update the 2004 US Preventive Services Task Force Recommendation. *Annals of Internal Medicine, 156*(11), 1–4.

Nixon, K. L., Tutty, L. M., Weaver-Dunlop, G., & Walsh, C. A. (2007). Do good intentions beget good policy? A review of child protection policies to address intimate partner violence. *Children and Youth Services Review, 29*(12), 1469–1486. doi:10.1016/j.childyouth.2007.09.007

Pepler, D. J., Catallo, R., & Moore, T. E. (2000). Consider the children: Research informing interventions for children exposed to domestic violence. *Journal of Aggression, Maltreatment & Trauma, 3*(1), 37–57. doi:10.1300/J146v03n01_04

Ristock, J. (2003). Exploring dynamics of abusive lesbian relationships: Preliminary analysis of a multisite, qualitative study. *American Journal of Community Psychology, 31*(3/4), 329–341. doi:10.1023/A:1023971006882

Scott, K. L., King, C., McGinn, H., & Hosseini, N. (2011). Effects of motivational enhancement on immediate outcomes of batterer intervention. *Journal of Family Violence, 26*(2), 139–149. doi:10.1007/s10896-010-9353-1

Sinha, M. (2013). Measuring violence against women: Statistical trends. *Juristat*. Retrieved from: www.statcan.gc.ca/pub/85-002-x/2013001/article/11766-eng.pdf.

Statistics Canada (2011). *Family violence in Canada: A statistical profile.* Ottawa, ON: author. Retrieved from: www.statcan.gc.ca/pub/85-224-x/85-224-x2010000-eng.pdf.

Trocmé, N., Fallon, B., MacLauren, B., Sinha, V., Black, T., Fast, E., . . . & Holroyd, J. (2010). *Canadian Incidence Study of Reported Child Abuse and Neglect—2008: Major Findings.* Retrieved from: www.phac-aspc.gc.ca/cm-vee/public-eng.php.

Tutty, L. M. (2015). Addressing the safety and trauma issues of abused women: A cross-Canada study of YWCA shelters. *Journal of International Women's Studies, 16*(3), 101–116. Retrieved from: http://vc.bridgew.edu/jiws/vol16/iss3/8.

Tutty, L. M., Babins-Wagner, R., & Rothery, M. A. (2006). Group treatment for aggressive women: An initial evaluation. *Journal of Family Violence, 21*(5), 341–349. doi:10.1007/s10896-006-9030-6

Tutty, L. M., Babins-Wagner, R., & Rothery, M. (2009). A comparison of women who were mandated and non-mandated to the "Responsible Choices for Women" Group. *Journal of Aggression, Maltreatment and Trauma, 18*(7), 770–793. doi:10.1080/10926770903249777

Tutty, L. M., Babins-Wagner, R., & Rothery, M. A. (2015). You're not alone: Mental health outcomes in therapy groups for abused women. *Journal of Family Violence, 31*(4), 489–497. doi:10.1007/s10896-015-9779-6

Tutty, L. M. & Koshan, J. (2013). Calgary's specialized domestic violence court: An evaluation of a unique model. *Alberta Law Review, 50*(4), 731–755. Retrieved from: www.albertalawreview.com.

Varcoe, C., Hankivsky, O., Ford-Gilboe, M., Wuest, J., Wilk, P., Hammerton, J., & Campbell, J. (2011). Attributing selected costs to intimate partner violence in a sample of women who have left abusive partners: A social determinants of health approach. *Canadian Public Policy—Analyse de Politiques, 37*(3), 359–380.

Wolfe, D. A., Crooks, C. V., Lee, V., McIntyre-Smith, A., & Jaffe, P. G. (2003). The effects of children's exposure to domestic violence: A meta-analysis and critique. *Clinical Child and Family Psychology Review, 6*(3), 171–187. doi:10.1023/A:1024910416164

Part I

Responses to Women Abused by Intimate Partners

1 "A Place To Go To When I Had No Place To Go To"

Journeys of Violence Against Women's Emergency Shelter Residents[1]

Leslie M. Tutty

Emergency shelters for women are often seen as society's major resource to address intimate partner violence (IPV). Although shelters are commonly used as sites to access women to study the nature and consequences of IPV, little research has focused more holistically on women's experiences in shelter. Canadian evaluations support the importance of violence against women's (VAW) shelters in providing safety and assisting the transition to a life separate from an assaultive partner (Tutty, 2015a; Tutty, Weaver, & Rothery, 1999). Similarly, American studies generally conclude that shelters are helpful (Bennett, Riger, Schewe, Howard, & Wasco, 2004; Chanley, Chanley, & Campbell, 2001; Grossman & Lundy, 2011; Ham-Rowbottom, Gordon, Jarvis, & Novaco, 2005).

In Canada in the year ending March 31, 2014, 60,341 women were admitted to 627 shelters (mostly VAW specific), according to Statistic Canada's Transition House Survey (Beattie & Hutchins, 2015). Different forms of shelters provide services for various lengths of time: the 281 first stage emergency shelters described in Beattie and Hutchins have residency of from one day to eleven weeks, with an average limit of about three to six weeks; 123 were second stage shelters with occupancy from three to twelve months.

While VAW shelters are available across Canada, most are clustered in urban areas. Many VAW shelters provide additional services such as crisis phone-lines, outreach support for women who are not shelter residents and follow-up programs for former residents who have moved into the community (Burczycka & Cotter, 2011; Tutty, 1996; Wathen, Harris, Ford-Gilboe, & Hansen, 2015). In 2010, 64 percent of all shelters reportedly offered culturally sensitive programs for Aboriginal women and their children while thirty-nine shelters were located on mostly rural Aboriginal reserves (Burczycka & Cotter, 2011).

The majority of women abused by partners do not use VAW shelters. In their study on what abused women wanted from health care providers, Chang and colleagues (2005) found that many women did not want to be told simply to "go to a shelter." According to Statistics Canada (Brzozowski, 2004), 11 percent of women abused in the past five years had used a shelter, only 7 percent as residents. A thirty-year-old comment that holds true today is that shelters are serving those who need them most, providing, "options for women who have few options" (Weisz, Taggart, Mockler, & Streich, 1994).

Shelters are complex organizations and coping with the rules and structures needed to function within a communal setting can be challenging for both residents (Dewey & St. Germain, 2014; Glenn & Goodman, 2015; Tutty et al., 1999; Tutty, 2015a) and staff (Burnett, Ford-Gilboe, Berman, Wathen, & Ward-Griffin 2016). Although primarily positive about their shelter experiences, some residents have raised concerns about the behaviors of a few other residents, some staff not being helpful, feeling under the watchful eyes of staff, and not receiving sufficient help to access housing or other basic needs (Dewey & St. Germain, 2014; Tutty et al., 1999). Staff concerns are with respect to the complex nature of the women's needs, including some women with mental health concerns, structural issues such as poverty (Goodman, Smyth, Borges, & Singer, 2009), and the short time-frame within which to assist women. Glenn and Goodman (2015) posit that women with post-traumatic stress disorder (PSTD) could be hypersensitive and misread staff behaviors as judgmental; Tutty (2006) speculated that shelter staff are at risk of vicarious traumatization (McCann & Pearlman, 1990), caused by repeatedly hearing traumatic stories in one's professional capacity.

Considering the structural complications and limitations of VAW shelters and, given their central place in society's response to intimate partner violence, it is important to understand how women get to shelters, what they need for themselves and their children and how they fare afterwards—the focus of this research. This chapter presents narratives from twenty women who resided in emergency VAW shelters from across Canada documenting the nature of the abuse from which they sought shelter, their supports prior to going to shelter, their experiences while in shelter and what happened two to six months afterwards. Especially in the early research (Aguirre, 1985; Cannon & Sparks, 1989), women whose partners abuse them have been described as returning to abusive partners an average of about eight times and as returning to the VAW shelters repeatedly (in the latest Canadian Transition House Survey (Beattie & Hutchins, 2015), one-quarter of the residents had stayed in the same shelter before). While using any resources for safety reasons is entirely appropriate and does not indicate failure on either the woman or the shelter, it is of interest to examine what has happened to a group of former shelter residents to identify whether such patterns remain prevalent.

The Context of the Current Study

The current qualitative research supplemented a quantitative study that described the needs, trauma symptoms, and safety issues of 368 women as they entered and left emergency shelters in ten Canadian VAW emergency shelters; nine operated by the YWCA and a private shelter in Nova Scotia (Tutty, 2015a).

The results captured the nature of the abuse, what the women wanted from shelter residence, the services they received, and their plans for afterwards.

On shelter entry, on the Danger Assessment (Campbell, Webster, & Glass, 2009), over 75 percent of 305 women residents who completed the scale fell in the range of Extreme or Severe Danger of risk of lethality from partners. Factors on the Danger Assessment are with respect to the partner, so these would not likely change on shelter exit and were not assessed. On exit, although still in the clinical range, total and subscale scores on a trauma scale (Impact of Event Scale—Revised) (Weiss, 2004) significantly improved from shelter entry. These results suggest both the need for safety and the positive impact of shelters. Finally, on leaving the shelter, the majority of the 225 residents (about 90 percent) who answered the Exit Survey were not planning to return to their partners; about 4 percent planned to return to their partner and 5 percent were undecided.

The qualitative interviews were conceived as one way to assess how a small portion of the 368 women fared from two to six months after they had left the emergency shelters. Except for the few residents who return to the shelter and those who use shelter follow-up programs, staff typically know little about whether or how the shelter stay was useful, or how the women are doing post-shelter, questions that this research sought to address. A semi-structured interview schedule, developed in consultation with the YWCA Canada Research Advisory Team, asked women about the nature of the abuse, what they wanted and expected from the shelter, and how they were doing afterwards. The research protocol was approved by the University of Calgary Conjoint Ethical Review Board to ensure that issues such as informed consent, confidentiality, and permission to withdraw from the study were addressed.

The Demographics of the Shelter Residents

The twenty women were interviewed from two to six months after their shelter stay and were from all of the shelter sites involved in the study (Kamloops, BC-3; Calgary, AB-1; Regina, SK-1; Brandon, MB-1; Sudbury, ON-4; Peterborough, ON-4; Halifax, NS-1; Yellowknife, NWT-1), with the exception of the Toronto Arise shelter, which had fewer residents since their average stay is six months. Half of the twenty women had been in a shelter previously (at least once), although one of these was a homelessness shelter, not one for violence against women.

With respect to the racial backgrounds of the women, thirteen were Caucasian (65 percent), six (35 percent) were of Aboriginal/Métis background, and one was African-Canadian (5 percent). The majority (75 percent or fifteen) had younger children living with them. Two had adult children (10 percent) and three (15 percent) had no children. Before going to the shelter, nine of the twenty were working (45 percent), eight were not (40 percent), mostly stay-at-home mothers, and employment status was unclear for three women (15 percent).

The women were primarily abused by intimate partners: eight common-law partners (40 percent), eight married spouses (40 percent), two live-in boyfriends

(10 percent), and one boyfriend with whom the respondent was not cohabiting (5 percent). The one remaining interviewee sought shelter because of abuse by her adolescent daughter who had been sexually abused by her father for years. Of the twenty, nine (45 percent) described the worst abuse as psychological, seven described physical abuse (35 percent) and four, sexual abuse (20 percent). One woman whose partner had physically abused her mentioned, "I don't even remember what he beat me up about. We were drinking, and my face was out like a balloon and I had to show up on a job interview the next day." Another noted, "He had me by the neck, and he had a few knives close to my neck and he said he was going to kill me. That was in front of his mom."

Several women whose partners had sexually abused them commented on their experiences. In one woman's case, "He pushed himself on me quite a bit until I finally caved, sexually. I'd tell him I didn't want to do it; he just started doing it even though I would say no." Another recounted:

> New Year's Eve, he slipped me drugs so I would succumb to certain sexual things he wanted. I knew right away but he kept denying it so I went through a paranoid state. It became clear that I really needed to get out.

As well, psychological abuse is inherent when one has been physically or sexually abused. Most of the women described upsetting psychological abuse such as being called degrading names or told they were "crazy." One woman commented, "Oh my Lord, he would start calling me names. He would call me a whore, a cunt. He would say I'm spending all the money, when I didn't have my card, he did." Another stated:

> He told me that I had a borderline personality disorder and that's why I thought he was cheating. Really the whole time it wasn't me. Telling me I was mentally ill and almost making me believe it is probably the worst thing.

The psychological abuse was often of a serious nature such as threats to kill or to commit suicide, sometimes with firearms, which has been long known by violence women advocates and researchers as a risk factor to homicide (Campbell et al., 2009; Tutty, 2015b).

> I went to bed without saying, "Are you coming to bed now," because I had a cold. The next day it was harsh words. It was "What kind of a wife are you?" He went into this violent rage and, "I'm going to kill myself if you leave." He threatened suicide.
>
> He was raging. He was never physically abusive. I never threatened to leave him, ever, but he said if I left he might as well take a gun to his head and shoot himself. He said this in front of my kids. That was the final straw. He's talking about shooting my daughter, he's bought bullets and put them beside me, and now he's talking about shooting himself. That said he's going to shoot my kids, shoot me, and then he's going to shoot himself.

The women were asked what strategies they had used to deal with the abuse before going to shelter. Many had used informal supports, although seven mentioned not talking to anyone outside their immediate families. Seven others spoke with friends, but three did not find this particularly helpful. Three others commented on their friends as a valuable support in dealing with and acknowledging the abuse. Eleven women had not used formal services to assist them, while nine had. The formal programs included addictions counselors (two), generic crisis phone-lines (two), a YWCA counselor (one), Victim Services (associated with police units) (one), and a Native Friendship Centre (one). Two had used more than one formal agency. Notably, though, only two had spoken with representatives from VAW-specific services.

Of the twenty former shelter residents, two-thirds (fifteen) had previous involvement with the police because of the abuse. Eight respondents had called the police themselves, but in two cases, the neighbors had called and, in another situation, the partner had called the police as a strategy to stop himself from behaving abusively. Three women were unhappy that the police had not criminally charged their partners, the outcome they had wished for at the time. As one commented, "I called the police. [*Was he charged?*] No, because I couldn't say for sure whether it was accidental or on purpose." Four other women described the police actions as helpful. Several partners were charged with assaults and/or the police provided safety to the women and their children. In two instances, police officers had been the ones to suggest that the woman go to the VAW shelter.

Reflecting on Their Shelter Experiences

In thinking about their time in the emergency VAW shelters, the majority of the comments were positive, although one woman had nothing good to say about her shelter residency, with the staff as her primary concern (see below). Many of the comments simply endorsed the fact that their shelter stay was valuable and assisted them in a number of ways. Overall, the comments about shelter strengths are with respect to the same issues as were identified as concerns. Notably, none of the concerns was with respect to any one shelter and, in fact, residents in the same shelter often perceived issues differently, one noting staff approachability as a problem, another seeing the staff in the same shelter as caring and supportive.

In describing what benefits the shelters offered, the most commonly mentioned positive was emotional support (seventeen of nineteen women), followed by providing basic needs (fourteen of nineteen) and safety (eleven of nineteen). Comments about emotional support referenced counseling and information about IPV including, "They were there to listen to me and a shoulder to cry on" and "Probably the most helpful thing was advice . . . it's not your fault, you didn't do anything wrong, you didn't create it." A woman of Aboriginal background commented: "We had good talks. There was a lady there who does the traditions and she took me on a sweat and that helped a lot."

Safety was explicitly mentioned as essential by eleven of nineteen interviewees, noting, "I was hoping it would provide a safe place and it did"; "I felt secure there, no one was allowed in, so the security, the emotional, the fact that I had a place to sleep without having to worry—I had food and I had shelter." And, "They cared about you. My priority was safety, and what they provided for me was great."

Another five women commented on the other shelter residents. Three had positive experiences, commenting, "Other women there were going through the same thing so it was very helpful to talk to them" and, "I realized that there are many other people in a very similar situation, so that was the one plus." Two relayed concerns about other residents. One commented, "I stayed for a month. One reason I chose to leave when I did was a woman who was a drug addict." Another mentioned:

> One woman, I really didn't get along with. She'd give me a dirty look once in awhile. It was a full house, beyond capacity. It was so uncomfortable with that many people; we were bumping into each other. You didn't have your own space, it was so chaotic.

Ten women commented about how the shelter staff and facilities had impacted their children. While two mothers mentioned that they had hoped for counseling for their children, both admitted that they had not pursued it while in shelter. All ten mothers noted the emotional support that their children received from the staff who sometimes went above and beyond to be supportive. Comments included, "They're as much concerned about my children's welfare as they are mine, they're concerned about whatever decisions we can make to make their visitation safer"; "He's special needs; they made him feel more relaxed. He enjoyed himself there"; and, "They were so good to my daughter. She wanted a Dora doll and before we left one of the workers bought one and she got to take that home with her."

Some shelters offer group meetings either daily (or in the evenings) or weekly. Sometimes attendance is mandatory, but this becomes difficult with the many demands on women's time to prepare a new home in the community. Six women commented on the utility of the shelter group meetings, although one of these wished for additional meetings with resources from the community in attendance. One women noted, "We had weekly group sessions and that to me was very good therapy. I attended every one." Another mentioned, "The group sessions made me feel really comfortable. They helped me through it."

Twelve of the twenty former residents shared concerns or made suggestions that could have improved their shelter stays. With regard to shelter staff members:

> I find them lax in some areas. They are available to talk to; some are and some aren't, some are more helpful, are more available to listen. Others are just straight work-orientated; they never seem to have time.

> If they had more staff it would've been easier for them to meet my expectations. When it was a bad time and there was only one staff on and the office door was closed, it was hard waiting for them. It seemed like it was closed way too often.

Five concerns were with respect to having the shelter provide more help to address basic needs such as assistance with housing and childcare:

> They weren't very supportive when it came to finding shelter. In fact, I did that for all the girls; I would phone rental management and have them fax over the rentals every day. The shelter had the newspaper, but we found shelter on our own.
>
> I had lawyer's appointments and would have to work late the odd time because I went to an appointment, while there's no day care, nobody to look after the kids other than somebody else at the shelter. Babysitting was a real problem.

After the Shelter

One of the primary reasons for interviewing the twenty women was to discover how they were faring several months after having resided in the shelter. Once back in the community, seven of the twenty were working, and one was a university student. Two more who were not currently working were planning to go to school. Of those without income from employment or school support, five were receiving social assistance, three were on disability benefits, and another was a widow who received survivor benefits. Three received some support from their ex-partners (one who was also employed) but two had no current means of support. With respect to housing, five had moved home to live with their parents at some point. Except for three women, most had safe and affordable accommodation. One of the three had moved repeatedly between friends and family and had no stable residence.

Were They in Contact with Their Partners?

Except for the woman abused by her adolescent daughter, seventeen interviewees were separated from partners and many were in the process of obtaining a divorce. Of these, eight had no contact with their former partners, three had contact but their partner is no longer being abusive and six described continuing abuse, often over custody and access or divorce proceedings.

> [*Is your partner continuing to be abusive?*] Not so badly in the last month, but he would call me every other day and, the pity trip and the crying, "Look what you've done to us, you messed us all up." Last week I had the first normal conversation with him in five months because he has a girlfriend.

He tries to engage me once in awhile, because I've gone through court and tried to get allowance from him. I did contribute to the relationship with money and I worked. So I thought I might be entitled to a little money while I went to school. That keeps a tie, but I'm a different person. I know when he's engaging me, and why, so I trust myself even when I have contact with him.

One woman had reconciled with her partner:

I went to see my boyfriend. It started out calm and cool, but the girlfriend that I moved out with didn't like him, so that's why I have to move. [I was] back out on the street. So what does every bright person do? They head back to what they know. Now, I'm back with him. But I don't put up with it anymore. [*You're not being abused now?*] No.

Another exception was a woman who was planning to reconcile in future since the separation was based on what appeared to be a false allegation of child abuse against her partner by a third party. The other party had been discredited and the family was hoping to reconcile shortly.

Three mothers had contact because of custody and access visits of the children with their fathers. All of these visits were unsupervised. The visits went well for one family:

[*Does he have access to your children?*] Yes he does. Unsupervised, because it didn't come up in court about his physical [abuse of her]. [*How is that going?*] Actually good. He is a good dad; has good qualities and bad qualities, but overall he loves his kids.

However, unsupervised exchanges can be upsetting for children, as in the following example:

They aren't eager to go with him. The first visitation that was unsupervised, my five year old wouldn't go. She was screaming, she was crying, she wouldn't have gone.

Were the Women Still Being Abused?

The women were asked whether any individual, including a new partner, was abusing them since the shelter. Fourteen women simply replied "no." One interviewee had a new boyfriend whose behavior was sometimes concerning, but she confronted his behavior directly:

The boyfriend jokes around, but sometimes it's not funny. But with him, what I say means something so when I tell him, he said, "Okay, if I do that again, make sure you tell me." When he finds out that something offends me he doesn't do it anymore.

One former shelter resident spoke eloquently about her realization of her lack of power to remove herself from his influence and that, even if they are not living together, he can continue controlling her through the children.

> I've tried to disengage from him. I had the restraining order for the first few months. He's still abusive; he still thinks he has control over me. He's constantly threatening that he'll force me to move back to [another province]. Of course, he threatens to take the kids away. I thought by moving I would be free of this abuse, but I don't think I ever will 'cause he's gotten no help. I have the children so I will forever have a connection with him. I don't know how I'm going deal with him for the rest of my life.

A second woman commented:

> He's been great at paying child support, but if I need anything extra, he removes some of the child support. He shut off my hydro one time, 'cause he didn't like that I had the air conditioner on. But my son has asthma, and we had that really hot spell.

Another type of abuse that women often experienced was their partner lying to the authorities about them. This was an issue for three interviewees whose partners had called child welfare authorities to complain about their behavior with the children:

> He called Children's Aid when I was in the shelter. I don't know what he said, but they told me it was extreme and they don't believe it. They've been supportive. In the court papers he's lying and saying I'm an unfit mother, and it's just because he's angry. [*Is he paying support?*] No, we're still in the process of that in court.
>
> He's tried that a few times but he has no guardianship and they pretty much ruled that he—he's not allowed access, he's not allowed to see her at all, he's got nothing. [*So he has made false complaints against you?*] Yeah.

Used Services Post-Shelter?

The women were asked what services, if any, they had used since leaving the shelter and whether these were helpful. Five women have followed up with their shelter for support. One noted, "They have follow up. One of the ladies there will call me occasionally, check to see how I'm doing financially, physically, emotionally, so yes there is a good program there." Another mentioned:

> I was having a really rough time with child welfare, and I talked to one of my old counsellors at the [shelter]. There was an outreach worker in the office, and I made a decision to go back and see her again.

Nevertheless, a number of women that had been staying at shelters that do offer follow-up and support groups were not aware of these services. Two mentioned that their shelters have follow-up programs, but they have not used them. Three former residents had intended to use the shelter follow-up programs when more settled. One woman was involved with a support group for woman abuse afterwards, commenting, "Every Wednesday night we had group meetings, and that was good therapy."

Nine former residents had counselors or programs from community agencies, noting, "I've had some appointments through mental health. I'm learning that if I need more I will seek it." And, "The YW has a counselor I talked to a couple of times. [*Was that helpful?*] Yes." Another former resident commented:

> I have an [addictions] counselor that I see weekly and I do relapse prevention. I've done treatment and I'm going back for a phase three (IPV group) and I have a sponsor and go to meetings. [*Do those provide enough support?*] Definitely.

Life in General: Better or Worse?

The women were asked in what ways their lives are better or worse since they had left the shelter (and their abusive partners). With respect to ways that their lives are more difficult, ten did not describe their lives as worse in any way: nine women commented about at least one way that their lives were more challenging. Several were with respect to helping their children cope with their changed circumstances:

> The worse part was the kids, even though they're adults. It was rough for a couple of months because my husband puts them on the pity/guilt trip, same as he did me. But all three [children] are very much aware of the situation, and they're behind me 100 percent. That meant a lot, the fact that they're not going to disown me.
>
> The only difficult thing is starting over again. I left with nothing. We have four plates, four forks, but we will get those things again. The only worse thing is not having enough for the kids. My son keeps asking about hockey. He played on an AAA team and cannot do so now. He often asks me to call my ex-partner for the money and I tell him that I can't do that, say he will understand better someday, try to reassure him.

Several women spoke tersely about how difficult it was to live with fewer financial resources. "Bills. I have more bills now, because I'm on my own than, I had before." Two others spoke of feeling lonely. "I'm lonelier. I live on my own now with the babies whereas at the shelter there's always women around to talk to and stuff, but no, I don't think anything is better or worse." And "I miss [the shelter] terribly. It's been lonely. I'm anxious to get into my place 'cause I've never been alone."

With few exceptions, and considering the above noted concerns, most described many more improvements than problems in their lives. With respect to what was going well for them:

> I'm free from that abuse, my children are free from abuse. I recognize just how devastating abuse is. Three people's lives were affected in the positive, and I still pray one day, my husband sees the light and turns his life around so he can have a healthy relationship with his kids. Staying in the marriage wouldn't have helped my husband. There's nothing I can do to fix him, but, in the process of leaving, maybe.
>
> It's been awesome! My life is totally changing. I'm staying clean and sober. I have a new apartment that's beautifully furnished. My son has come home and things are really different. Everything is better, my self-esteem, my finances, my way of living. My hope is a lot stronger and I have no desire to ever go back to my ex.
>
> My self-esteem is a lot better, I'm not crying as much; I still cry but for different reasons now. It's nice not being scared all the time, 'cause I never knew how he was going to be that day, like, is he going to kill me today or how's he going to wake up, is he going to come home slamming or breaking stuff today. Not being afraid, that's a good thing.

Several mothers commented on seeing positive improvements in their children. One noted, "I see a big difference. There's no more tension. Sometimes they sensed the fighting. Now they're much happier." Another commented:

> I've lost 285 pounds of stress (laughs). We can relax, we can breathe, we can laugh, we can have fun, and nobody is judging us, nobody is yelling at us, it's peaceful. My daughter said to me, "I don't even miss daddy." Well, I'm not surprised.

A final interview question was about what advice they would give to a friend in an abusive relationship. Fifteen respondents would tell their friend that it only gets worse and to leave the relationship. One woman would say, "Get out and go to a shelter, just for safety and protection. It is a good place and [gives you] time to make some comprehensive plans, where do you want to go from here." A final respondent was even more succinct, "Call [shelter's name], for God's sake! Don't do what I did and stick it out for thirty-one years. Things will never get better."

Discussion

To briefly summarize, their partners had abused the women in multiple ways. However, unlike the stereotype of abused women as passive and helpless, most had sought assistance or advice from family and friends as well as formal supports such as counselors and the police before seeking shelter, although these were not necessarily seen as helpful. Once in shelter, the most useful aspects for the majority were the emotional support from staff and other residents, safety, and the assistance with basic needs both while in shelter and in preparation for leaving.

Some mentioned difficulties with staff being available for counseling or support. The residents' comments need to be put in the context of the everyday life within a shelter, however. As mentioned earlier, Canada shelters are mostly funded by the provincial/territorial governments. Each province has different standards and funding structures, making comparisons across the country difficult. Most shelters are funded only for the in-house residential care they provide, not additional programs such as outreach or follow-up. In general, the funding to pay salaries of shelter staff is minimal and staffing is at a "bare-bones" level. One consequence of this is that many shelters have only a single front line worker and most night shifts are single-staffed (Tutty, 2006).

Shelters are busy places. Residents often need to take immediate action to secure social assistance and housing, since these two basic needs are central to re-establishing themselves. Often, women must start the process of getting social assistance and finding new accommodations before any final decision about separating from their partners, simply because these take time to put into place. If she was injured in the incident that led to shelter, she may have medical appointments: if the police charged her partner, she may have to make a statement about the events. If she is working, she needs to continue working to ensure that she remains employed.

One primary reason for interviewing the twenty former shelter residents was to discover how they were faring several months after having resided in the shelter and what they thought of their shelter stay in retrospect. Yet these women may have been different from those who chose not to agree to a follow-up interview. They may have had more stable community supports (and so could provide us the name of a relative or family member to contact) or were returning to their own residence, so could provide us a working phone number. Nevertheless, their narratives provide valuable feedback about their experiences post-shelter that is seldom captured by researchers. Some women now use shelters strategically, as their first step in leaving an abusive partner, rather than only in reaction to an assault or other emergency. This is confirmed by recent research in New Mexico (Krishnan, Hilbert, McNeil, & Newman, 2004), in which some residents went to shelter for respite from the abuse and others for a planned transition to a new life.

On exit, the majority of women interviewed (nineteen of twenty or 95 percent) had not reconciled with their partners, congruent with 90 percent of the larger sample of the YWCA study (Tutty, 2015a) and the Canadian Transition Home Survey, which reported that about 90 percent of the women did not plan to return to their partner post-shelter (Sauvé & Burns, 2009).

Nevertheless, on leaving the shelters, women are often faced with inadequate housing and financial support that leaves them with a choice between homelessness and returning to abusive partners. Previous Canadian research has drawn links between being abused, leaving the relationship, and becoming homeless. Homeless women are not uncommonly former shelter residents who failed to find adequate and/or safe housing (Auffrey, Tutty, & Wright, 2017, Chapter 15, this volume; Tutty, Ogden, Giurgiu, & Weaver-Dunlop, 2013). A number of the twenty women interviewed endured housing instability. Five had moved home to live with their parents at some point. Except for three women, most had safe and affordable accommodation. One of the three had moved repeatedly between friends and family and had no stable residence. But even after having been established in the community for a while, if the housing or finances are not adequate, women may return to an abusive partner to sustain themselves and their children with better housing and financial support than they could manage on their own.

In summary, the twenty former shelter residents provided revealing glimpses of how their lives were progressing, as well as important feedback about their shelter stays. Comparable with the open-ended comments from the 368 shelter residents in the quantitative aspect of the research (Tutty, 2006), the women strongly endorsed the shelter in assisting them with safety, support, and access to essential basic needs.

While these endorsements are welcome, with relatively few staff, shelters provide substantial services both to women in residence and without, through crisis phone-lines, counseling for children exposed to IPV, outreach and follow-up services. Similarly, shelters provide much to the community at large through prevention programs in schools and being advocates for keeping society's focus on the serious consequences of IPV. While shelter funding is always a central point of negotiation between provincial shelter associations and their respective governments, the current research provides important additional evidence of the importance of shelters in protecting the lives of women and children.

Note

1. This research was funded by Status of Women Canada, Homelessness Secretariat, and the Department of Justice Canada. Jenny Robinson was invaluable as the YWCA representative that secured the funding and led the project from within. Paulette Senior, CEO of YWCA Canada, was an important supporter. The Internal Research Advisory Team consisted of (in alphabetical order): Kristine Cassie, Lyda Fuller, Carolyn Goard, Susan Logan, Sheila Loranger, Colette Prévost, Joan White, Jill Wyatt. A number of shelter directors and staff assisted in the survey design: Lise Armstrong, Melanie Demore, Lori De Pourcq, Barb Dewalt, Ruth Doucette, Suzanne Fedorowich, Doreen Healy, Kathleen Lee, Donna McDougall, Colette Perkin, Lisa Quinlan, Michele Anne Robbins, Sylvia Samsa, Michele Walker, and Kathryn Waugh. The External Research Advisory Team was: Diane Delany, Kim Dreaddy; Anita Olson Harper, Giselle Lalonde, Carol MacLeod, Jackie Mathews, Verna McGregor, Anna Pazdzierski, Jan Reimer, Elaine Smith, Karen Stone, and Marie-Guylda Thélusmond. Thanks especially to Janie Christensen of the YWCA Calgary Sheriff King Home who conducted the interviews.

References

Aguirre, B. E. (1985). Why do they return? Abused women in shelters. *Social Work, 30,* 350–354.

Auffrey, M., Tutty, L. M., & Wright, A. C. (2017). Preventing homelessness for women who leave abusive partners: A shelter-based "Housing First" program. In T. Augusta-Scott, K. Scott, & L. Tutty (Eds.), *Innovations in interventions to address intimate partner violence: Research and practice.* New York, NY: Routledge.

Beattie, S., & Hutchins, H. (2015). *Shelters for abused women in Canada, 2014.* Retrieved from: www.statcan.gc.ca/pub/85–002-x/2015001/article/14207-eng.htm.

Bennett, L., Riger, S., Schewe, P., Howard, A., & Wasco, S. (2004). Effectiveness of hotline, advocacy, counseling, and shelter services for victims of domestic violence: A statewide evaluation. *Journal of Interpersonal Violence, 19*(7), 815–829. doi:10.1177/0886260504265687

Brzozowski, J. E. (2004). *Family violence in Canada: A statistical profile 2004.* Ottawa, ON: Canadian Centre for Justice Statistics Retrieved from: www.canadiancrc.com/PDFs/PHAC_2004_family_violence_profile_e.pdf.

Burczycka, M., & Cotter, A. (2011). Shelters for abused women in Canada 2010. *Juristat, Catalogue no. 85–002-X.*

Burnett, C., Ford-Gilboe, M., Berman, H., Wathen, N., & Ward-Griffin, C. (2016). The day-to-day reality of delivering shelter services to women exposed to intimate partner violence in the context of system and policy demands. *Journal of Social Service Research, 42*(4), 516–532. doi:10.1080/01488376.2016.1153562

Campbell, J., Webster, D. W., & Glass, S. (2009). The Danger Assessment: Validation of a lethality risk assessment instrument for intimate partner femicide. *Journal of Interpersonal Violence, 24*(4), 653–674. doi:10.1177/0886260508317180

Cannon, J. B., & Sparks, J. S. (1989). Shelters—an alternative to violence: A psychosocial case study. *Journal of Community Psychology, 17,* 203–213.

Chang, J. C., Cluss, P. A., Ranieri, L., Hawker, L., Buranosky, R., Dado, D., McNeil, M., & Scholle, S. H. (2005). Health care interventions for intimate partner violence: What women want. *Women's Health Issues, 15*(1), 21–30. doi:10.1016/j.whi.2004.08.007

Chanley, S. A., Chanley, J. J., & Campbell, H. E. (2001). Providing refuge: The value of domestic violence shelter services. *The American Review of Public Administration, 31*(4), 393–413. doi:10.1177/02750740122065018

Dewey, S. C., & St. Germain, T. S. (2014). Social services fatigue in domestic violence service provision facilities. *Affilia: Journal of Women and Social Work, 29*(4), 389–403. doi: 10.1177/0886109914528700

Glenn, C. & Goodman, L. (2015). Living with and within the rules of domestic violence shelters: A qualitative exploration of residents' experiences. *Violence Against Women, 21*(12), 1481–1506. doi:10.1177/1077801215596242

Goodman, L. A., Smyth, K. F., Borges, A. M., & Singer, R. (2009). When crises collide: How intimate partner violence and poverty intersect to shape women's mental health and coping? *Trauma, Violence, & Abuse, 4,* 306–329. doi:10.1177/1524838009339754

Grossman, S. F. & Lundy, M. (2011). Characteristics of women who do and do not receive onsite shelter services from domestic violence programs. *Violence Against Women, 17*(8), 1024–1045. doi:10.1177/1077801211414169

Ham-Rowbottom, K. A., Gordon, E. E., Jarvis, K. L., & Novaco, R. W. (2005). Life constraints and psychological well-being of domestic violence shelter graduates. *Journal of Family Violence, 20*(2), 109–121. doi:10.1007/s10896-005-3174-7

Krishnan, S. P., Hilbert, J. C., McNeil, K., & Newman, I. (2004). From respite to transition: Women's use of domestic violence shelters in rural New Mexico. *Journal of Family Violence, 19*(3), 165–173. doi:10.1023/B:JOFV.0000028076.72706.4f

McCann, L. & Pearlman, L. A. (1990). Vicarious traumatization: A framework for understanding the psychological effects of working with victims. *Journal of Traumatic Stress, 3*(1), 131–149. doi: 10.1007/BF00975140

Sauvé, J. & Burns, M. (2009). Residents of Canada's shelters for abused women, 2008. *Juristat, 29*(2), 1–21. Retrieved from: www.statcan.gc.ca/pub/85-002-x/2009002/article/10845-eng.htm.

Tutty, L. M. (1996). Post shelter services: The efficacy of follow-up programs for abused women. *Research on Social Work Practice, 6*(4), 425–441. doi:10.1177/104973159600600402

Tutty, L. M. (2006). *Effective practices in sheltering women leaving violence in intimate relationships: Phase II. Final report to the YWCA Canada.* Retrieved from: http://ywcacanada.ca/data/publications/00000013.pdf.

Tutty, L. M. (2015a). Addressing the safety and trauma issues of abused women: A cross-Canada study of YWCA shelters. *Journal of International Women's Studies, 16*(3), 101–116.

Tutty, L. M. (2015b). "I didn't know he had it in him to kill me": Canadian women and non-lethal firearms involvement in intimate partner violence. *Journal of Forensic Social Work, 5*(1–2), 130–149. doi:10.1080/1936928X.2015.1092906

Tutty, L. M., Weaver, G., & Rothery, M. A. (1999). Resident's views of the efficacy of shelter services for abused women. *Violence Against Women, 5*(8), 869–925. doi:10.1177/10778019922181545

Tutty, L. M., Ogden, C., Giurgiu, B., & Weaver-Dunlop, G. (2013). I built my house of hope: Abused women and pathways into homelessness. *Violence Against Women, 19*, 1498–1517. doi:10.1177/1077801213517514

Wathen, C. N., Harris, R. M., Ford-Gilboe, M., & Hansen, M. (2015). What counts? A mixed-methods study to inform evaluation of shelters for abused women. *Violence Against Women, 21*(1), 125–146. doi:0.1177/1077801214564077

Weiss, D. S. (2004). The Impact of Event Scale-Revised. In T. M. K. J. P. Wilson (Ed.), *Assessing psychological trauma and PTSD: A practitioner's handbook* (2nd ed.) (pp. 168–189). New York, NY: Guilford Press.

Weisz, G., Taggart, J., Mockler, S., & Streich, P. (1994). *The role of housing in dealing with family violence in Canada.* Ottawa, ON: Canada Mortgage and Housing Corporation.

2 Rethinking Safety Planning

A Self-Directed Tool for Rural Women Who Are Abused

Deborah Doherty

Intimate partner violence (IPV) refers to the controlling, often violent behavior, of a current or former intimate partner. It is prevalent in society and victims/survivors, along with children exposed to it, often suffer serious emotional, physical, and sexual harm (Canadian Centre for Justice Statistics, 2013). Women are much more likely than men to be the victims of IPV and they are also more likely than men to experience emotional, health, and mental health consequences and even death (Beattie & Cotter, 2010; Doherty & Berglund, 2008). Over the past two decades, a significant body of research has emerged in Canada, the United States, and elsewhere, that informs our understanding of the risk factors associated with IPV and domestic homicide such as past history of domestic violence, separation, presence of weapons, threats of harm or suicide, isolation of the victim, addictions, jealousy, escalation of physical violence, choking and sexual violence, disputes about child custody, lack of community supports, and so on (Campbell et al., 2003; Websdale, 2003).

The presence of one or more of these domestic violence lethality risk factors signals the potential for serious harm and even death; and the more risk factors that are present, the more likely it is that the situation will turn deadly (Ontario Domestic Violence Death Review Committee, 2008). Several studies have confirmed that women's increased fear for personal safety and an escalation of IPV can best be understood within a strategic context that reflects women's cultural and geographic environment (DeKeseredy & Schwartz, 2009; Logan, Walker, & Leukefeld, 2001). For example, Dudgeon and Evanson (2014) found that, although rates of intimate partner violence are similar for rural and urban women, rural women face greater barriers accessing help and services. Indeed, rurality itself may be viewed as an indicator of increased strategic lethality risk for women experiencing IPV.

This body of research has supported the development of a number of domestic violence interventions, perhaps most notably efforts to provide effective safety planning options to women who are subjected to intimate partner violence. Safety planning has emerged as a critical component in helping women in crisis to achieve safer outcomes. Such crisis-oriented approaches understandably address the immediate safety needs of women. To a large extent, traditional safety planning interventions are provided through police and victim services, transition houses, and domestic violence professionals. Though these interventions are not premised on encouraging women to leave, in practice, their primary focus is supporting women to get safely out of the relationship.

However, it is not uncommon for women to choose to stay with abusive partners for personal, social, economic, and cultural reasons. Several studies have shown that sometimes women who are being abused by their partner cannot, or do not, access services from domestic violence specialists. These women may feel safest by addressing the abuse using a variety of strategies that may be effective for them, at least for a period of time (Lindhorst, Nurius, & Macy, 2005). They may learn to appease the abuser, they may take temporary reprieves by visiting family, or they may simply feel the best option for them at the time is to endure the abuse. Women who decide to return or stay with the abusive partner may feel ashamed to interact with domestic violence professionals for fear that their decisions will be viewed as a sign of failure. Thus, we must be careful not to assume that the most effective intervention for all abused women is leaving the relationship. This is clearly an important option, especially in crisis, but it could be a harmful option if we fail to recognize the complexity of women's choices in deciding whether to stay or leave (Goodkind, Sullivan, & Bybee, 2004).

Unfortunately, there is a paucity of research on the effectiveness of interventions for helping women to safely address the violence while still in their relationships. In fact, we know very little about whether danger and risk assessments, which often precipitate safety planning, are effective in reducing revictimization or lowering the rates of re-assault (Websdale, 2000). Most studies do not include an assessment of potential harm. What we do know is that safety planning will be most effective when women are supported to strategically contextualize their lived realities and balance the various harms that they face when making decisions about continuing or ending relationships (Wathen & MacMillan, 2003). Emergency safety planning should be but one tool available to women who are dealing with the complexity of their relationship with their abusive intimate partner.

This chapter presents a unique safety planning tool designed to address this gap in safety planning responses. The new tool is intended to help women living with intimate partner violence, especially outside of large urban areas, to assess their situation and strategically mitigate their risk of harm even if they have decided to stay or return to the abuse. The chapter summarizes the findings of a New Brunswick study to validate this tool by exploring the ways in which it resonates with local service providers and addresses the social, cultural, and economic realities of women living with an abusive partner.

The new tool was created as an evidence-based resource informed by three sources of data; namely, the findings of a "rural research team"[1] that conducted several studies on intimate partner violence in New Brunswick between 1995 and 2010 (Doherty & Hornosty, 2004, 2008; Hornosty & Doherty, 2004); the findings of a research initiative for the New Brunswick Silent Witness Project that examined about forty-five female domestic homicides in New Brunswick between 1990 and 2015 (Doherty, 2006, 2012); and the findings from a growing body of literature on risk assessment and safety planning for intimate partner violence and homicide, particularly in relation to the factors associated with risks in rural and isolated communities (Beattie & Cotter, 2010; Campbell, 2004; Johnson & Hotton, 2003; Kropp, 2008; Swanberg & Logan, 2005).

Although the risks associated with intimate partner violence and those related to domestic homicide are not identical, research in New Brunswick and elsewhere suggests a significant degree of overlap (Campbell, 2004; Doherty, 2006). These risk factors are found in both rural and urban environments, which may suggest that the elements of an effective safety plan are similar for urban women and rural women (Brownridge, 2006; Canadian Centre for Justice Statistics, 2011, 2013; Ontario Domestic Violence Death Review Committee, 2008). While there are more similarities than differences when comparing risk factors, it is the differences that are notable. Ignoring the differences is problematic to the extent that it promotes an urban-centric bias that is then built into services and programs for rural areas.

The New Brunswick Context

Doherty and Hornosty (2004, 2008) studied the dynamics of intimate partner violence in small towns and rural communities in New Brunswick and used a geographic lens to analyze variables associated with IPV such as firearms victimization, alcohol/drug misuse, threats of suicide, and harming family pets. They also investigated other factors such as seasonal unemployment, the homogenous nature of rural communities and pressure exerted on women by family and friends to stay. They found that physical and social isolation make it difficult for women in abusive relationships to seek professional help and learn about their options. This situation is exacerbated by systemic barriers to leaving abuse in rural regions, including poverty and low literacy, lack of employment opportunities, and limited access to transportation, housing, and daycare (Doherty & Hornosty, 2004, 2008; Hornosty & Doherty, 2003). Various other studies (Banman, 2015; Campbell et al., 2003; Lindhorst, Nurius, & Macy, 2005) have also found that women being abused by their partners in rural communities have limited access to services and few options for leaving, which impacts women's perception of whether they could leave partners (Campbell, 2004; Swanberg & Logan, 2005).

Doherty and Hornosty (2004, 2008) concluded that not only are services for victims of abuse absent or difficult to access in rural communities, rural women are often reluctant to call the police or involve social services for fear of starting a process that they are unable to control such as child protection or criminal proceedings. Women expressed concern that they might be forced to leave their relationships, homes, and communities. They were more likely to disclose their situations to family and friends, a physician or religious leader, or a community service provider such as public health nurse.

With respect to lethality risk (risk of homicide), separation from the partner is a well-documented and frequently encountered risk factor. The Ontario Domestic Violence Death Review Annual Report (2008) reported that over 80 percent of the women who had been killed by an intimate partner died at, or after separation. Mitigating the risk of harm at separation has become the shibboleth for action and the basis of considerable training, programing, and resource allocation with a view to helping avoid future deaths. The increased risk during separation underlies our risk assessment tools and our safety planning efforts (Ontario Domestic Violence Death Review, 2008). At the same time, domestic homicide research in New Brunswick did not find such a high degree of association of lethal DV with separation. Nearly two-thirds of the women killed by their partners had been living together in intact relationships at the time of death (Doherty, 2012). Although the New Brunswick sample size may not be considered statistically significant, the clustering of these factors has consistently shown that the types and frequency with which risk factors are associated with female domestic homicides differs from the patterns found at the national level or in more urban provinces.

Some of the most notable differences are that New Brunswick women killed by their partners are more likely to: live in rural communities as opposed to large urban centers; be assaulted or killed while living in an intact relationship as opposed to be killed at or after separation (30 percent compared to 80 percent in Ontario); and, be in a common-law relationship (66 percent compared to 48 percent of the victims in Ontario or nationally). There was also greater involvement of alcohol/drugs in the New Brunswick deaths (about 75 percent of the cases compared to 42 percent in the Ontario Report) and over 55 percent of the deaths were with firearms, mostly hunting rifles and shotguns (compared to 20 percent nationally where the most common cause of death was stabbing). As well, New Brunswick women are more likely than women in other provinces to be killed in domestic murder-suicides, mostly with firearms (Canadian Centre for Justice Statistics, 2011; Doherty, 2006). Finally, the New Brunswick victims were likely to be older. The average age of the women killed in murder-suicides over the past five years was 55 years while, in Ontario (Ontario Domestic Violence Death Review, 2015) the average age of victims is thirty-three years.

Given that New Brunswick is largely a rural province and nearly 70 percent of New Brunswick female victims of domestic homicide lived in small communities with populations of less than 10,000, it is important to question the relevance and effectiveness of existing safety planning tools which have traditionally focused on "emergency leaving" and/or staying safe after fleeing (Wilson & Websdale, 2006). Could safety plans be enhanced if they were more responsive to specific social and cultural contexts, including geography? Would this resonate with professionals who help victims of IPV if they reflected the lived realities of their clients? Would women living with abuse who have little access to professionals, use the safety planning tool by themselves? Would they feel empowered to identify risks and find ways to reduce the potential harm?

Developing a "Safety Planning Tool"

In order to explore these questions and expand efforts to support "safer staying" for women living in abusive relationships, the author developed a safety planning tool that incorporates the findings of the rural team and the silent witness research. It is intended to help women reflect on their situation and strategically identify and mitigate personal risks of harm by their partner. It is not intended to replace traditional Danger Assessments by professionals nor does it mitigate the need for safety plans for women experiencing abuse in emergency situations. In fact, the tool includes information and links to emergency safety planning tools. However, it is careful not to imply that women are a "failure at leaving" if they decide to stay in, or return to, the relationship.

The safety planning tool is written in plain language and contains three steps. It is intended to be self-administered. Women can complete it by themselves or with someone they trust. Step One explores whom to tell about abuse. It contains two columns, one explaining common fears that prevent women from reaching out for help, and the other that responds to each of those fears.

Step Two offers a "checklist of risk factors" that helps women assess their personal situation and possible risk for increased violence. Each risk factor has a brief description of what we know about this factor based on research in

---

STEP 1

Deciding Who to Tell About the Abuse in My Life

You can use this booklet alone or with someone else you trust to play a role in your plan. Although you will have to decide for yourself if and when you will tell others about the abuse, consider that friends, family, neighbours and even co-workers can help protect you if they know what is happening. Consider talking to a domestic violence specialist - someone who can help you assess your risk. Trust your intuition and make choices that you feel are best for your safety – don't be pressured into action. If you are reluctant to reach out for help, consider the following:

I don't want to start interventions in my life that I have no control over.	• It is understandable that you want to be in control and manage your risks how and when you need to. Seek out services and resources and that respond to your specific needs.
He has threatened to take the kids or harms the pets or property – and he has all the rights.	• Both parents have rights to custody and access so it is important to contact services that offer accurate information, advice and/or support.
I am committed to making my marriage work and being a good spouse. I love him and really just want the abuse to stop. He keeps promising he will change.	• You can't change your partner, but if he is willing, encourage him to find appropriate counseling and services that help him to become accountable for his actions and stop abusing you.

Figure 2.1 Step One—Deciding Who to Tell About the Abuse in My Life

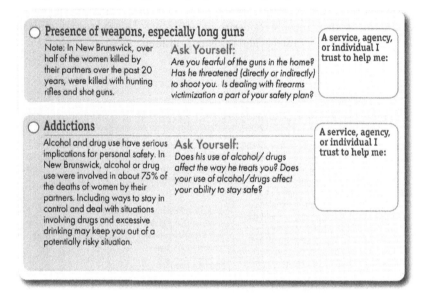

Figure 2.2 Step Two—Identifying My Lived Reality

New Brunswick. This information is intended to act as a reality check. Although women are the experts on their own lives, research shows that oftentimes women in abusive relationships become complacent to the risks that they face (Campbell, 2004; Doherty, 2012; Dudgeon & Evanson, 2014). This step encourages women to question their own perceptions of these risk factors and to identify services, agencies, or individuals they trust as sources of support.

In total, seventeen risk factors are incorporated into the tool, including personal supports, emotional responses, fear, increasing physical violence or choking, where the abuse occurs, and when abuse typically happens. The tool encourages the reader to ask herself if abuse increases at particular times, such as seasonal unemployment, payday, weekends, or at special events. Other factors in the tool include life events associated with abuse, threats of suicide, attitudes and values that condone the abuse, available resources and access to services, presence of children, legal actions (family and criminal), harm to pets or other family members, alcohol and drug use, physical and mental health issues, economic stressors (unemployment, financial worries), presence of weapons (especially long guns), and reaction to past attempts to leave.

Step Three provides a template for a woman experiencing abuse to create her own safety plan for living in the abusive relationship. In this section, she can identify specific concerns related to each of the risk factors and then craft a strategy for dealing with that factor. She may decide not to deal with all of the factors at once. If she prefers, she can create a plan that responds to those risk factors that she is most comfortable addressing. The plan starts with emergency leaving tips. It then encourages her to identify what she might do to mitigate her personal risk in a strategic and systematic fashion.

STEP 3
Making My Safety Plan While Living with Abuse

Your "Safety Plan" is a response to your checklist and notes from Step 2 where you identified the risk factors in your relationship. You have also identified agencies and people who you trust to help you. Include them in your safety plan. You may not be ready to take action in all areas of your life all at once. Deal with the ones that you know you can do something about – and work on the others over time. Nobody can predict every possible scenario, but if you plan and think ahead about what you might do in case your partner attacks you, the children, the pets, your property or others you love, you may be prepared to protect yourself. Each strategy you create may help to reduce risk and increase your safety.

Consider a code word that you can use with the special people and agencies you have told about your situation. That way, if you contact them, they will know you are in a dangerous situation and they will call the police to help you.

My code word is: _____

My Personal Safety Plan

Risk Factor:
Addictions

I will be alert to the situations where he might become more violent because he is using alcohol/drugs.

My strategy for dealing with abuse that tends to happen when he is drinking or taking drugs, is: _____

I will be alert to the situations where I am using alcohol/drugs and my ability to activate my safety plan might be put at risk.

My strategy for dealing with abuse that tends to happen when both of us are drinking or taking drugs, is: _____

Figure 2.3 Step Three—Making My Safety Plan While Living with Abuse

Validation Study Objectives and Method

In 2014, the Department of Justice Canada, Research and Statistics Division, contracted Public Legal Education and Information Service of New Brunswick to conduct a small-scale research study intended to validate the safety planning tool. The two objectives were: first, to consult with professionals, victims, and key family violence stakeholders in New Brunswick as to whether the safety planning tool resonated with them; and, second, to identify potential users of the tool and strategies to move the tool to completion and dissemination.

The study consisted of focus groups with crisis interveners, service providers, and community agencies in the rural communities of Miramichi in northern New Brunswick and Woodstock in the southwestern area. A third focus group was held in Fredericton and included six women from a support group for women who had disclosed or self-identified as having left an abusive relationship. The researcher also interviewed two key informants with expertise and knowledge on risk assessment and safety planning tools. One was an academic and professor emeritus who had conducted extensive research on the health impacts of domestic violence and the effectiveness of tools to help women who have been abused. The other interviewee was a senior police officer with extensive involvement in domestic violence research.

Results

The twenty-seven individuals who participated in focus groups and interviews reviewed the safety planning tool in advance. They were asked for feedback on its relevance for women in New Brunswick, as well as its accuracy and usefulness. Options for implementation and dissemination were also discussed. The following are the highlights of the responses starting with the feedback on the reasons that a rural woman might be reluctant to reach out for help.

Barriers to Leaving Abuse

The first component for discussion was the rural context of intimate partner violence, how it impacts women's help-seeking behavior, perceptions of risk, and whether the tool addresses these barriers. The participants quickly validated the factors that tend to keep rural women in abusive relationships. When talking about the lack of community support, a woman who had escaped an abusive relationship after many years explained, "I tested the waters with people and tried to tell them what was going on. But they went around and told him everything. You can image how that came down on me. No wonder women stay."

The participants went on to identify a range of situations that influence women who are considering leaving an abusive relationship. Some factors, such as a history of IPV, escalation of violence and choking, were considered universal risks for any woman experiencing abuse. Other factors were considered to have a stronger association with rural women such as the cultural and social values promoting victim blaming, the presence of firearms in the home, concerns that firearms may be used for suicide or turned on the women, her children, and/or pets, and the abuse of alcohol.

The service providers noted that many of their clients felt pressured to stay by family and friends, and were coping with feelings of hopelessness, shame and depression. Although this may not be a barrier unique to rural women, the ability of rural women to seek professional help may be further reduced by the lack of transportation and services in rural areas. Participants were pleased to see that the tool addressed all of these situations. For example, the tool refers to community attitudes and suggests that even professionals may hold patriarchal views that blame women. It encourages women to examine their personal, family, and community supports and to keep looking until they find someone supportive and non-judgmental.

Several participants commented that their favorite part of the tool was "Step One," where users review a list of reasons why women do not seek help. The service provider participants noted that they often heard these reasons when working with women. Reviewing this section of the safety plan would provide an opportunity to debunk each reason. Participants also appreciated the presentation of risk factors, which they thought were set out in a fashion that would be relevant to rural communities. They agreed that there is often tremendous pressure on women from community members who may not recognize a partner's behavior as abusive and encourage women to stay. One crisis worker spoke of the expectations placed on women to show loyalty to their family, "Loyalty is ingrained, and leaving is failure and failure isn't an option."

Responses to Step Two

The following are some responses to Step Two of the safety plan dealing with helping rural women to identify the risk factors in their own lives that may signal the potential for experiencing harm, in particular, the availability of firearms and victim's desensitization.

Many participants were pleased that the new tool addressed the danger of long guns in homes experiencing discord and violence. Although guns are present for hunting and shooting vermin, they contribute to the fear of personal harm, murder-suicide and intimidation when they are in the hands of a partner who is angry, jealous, controlling, depressed, or domineering. Several service providers were of the opinion that the safety planning tools they currently use do not place sufficient emphasis on firearm danger and certainly do not provide much advice on what a woman could do if she is fearful of firearms in the home. They attributed this to an urban-centric bias. As one person noted, "You just do not have this widespread access to firearms in urban centers. Hunting rifles are not the weapon of choice in domestic assaults in Toronto."

Further, several service provider participants noted that their clients suffer profound verbal and emotional abuse and that many present with very low self-esteem and self-worth. This was confirmed by the focus group with women who have been in abusive relationships. As one woman stated, "He always made me feel stupid and worthless." Five of the six women commented that they often dreaded certain behaviors, such as unwanted sexual activity, but they had never feared that their partner would kill them. As one woman noted, "I just wasn't worth killing."

Service providers saw this lack of self-esteem and minimization of risk as one of the reasons that women do not reach out for help or feel a need for safety planning. In fact, very few of the abused women focus group participants had created safety plans. In their view, safety plans typically tell women to call 911 in an emergency and leave, which is problematic for several reasons. First, women experiencing abuse often believe, "Seeing your house on fire or your child bleeding to death is an emergency. Being beaten by your partner is not an emergency—it's just another Saturday night." Second, there may be nowhere to go and no way to leave. Finally, in rural communities police may take over an hour to arrive so women know the importance of finding ways to resolve or de-escalate the situation themselves.

The Utility of the Safety Planning Tool

The study participants offered the following feedback on how and when the new tool could be used, liking the personalized approach, the inclusion of statistics, the tool's utility and suggestions for dissemination and usage.

The new tool is written in a non-judgmental fashion so that women are not made to feel guilty for their choices. Each woman is the expert on her own life and knows what makes her feel safe. As one experiential woman from the focus group noted, "I feel safer when I go back. I can read his moods and predict what he might do and deal with it. But if I leave, I haven't any idea what he will do." The strategic self-assessment approach in the new tool was praised for making it more accessible to women who can work on it with someone from a helping agency or by themselves. A police officer in the focus group noted its strength is, "Its repeated message that you have to make it unique for you and find a unique place to keep the safety plan."

Other service providers agreed that the tool would promote ownership and internalization of the plan because "each woman would customize it to their own needs." For these reasons, a number of the service providers thought the tool would help them explain to a woman that if her partner is choking her, pressuring her to have sex, threatening her with a firearm, or shooting a beloved pet, it's not just another Saturday night, but a serious emergency. The women in the study agreed that the tool would definitely have been "a wake-up call" while they were living with abuse. They also liked the fact that the tool is not a "one-time" assessment. Women are encouraged to review and strategically reassess their personal risks on a regular basis since exposure to risk factors and fearfulness clearly changes overtime.

Many of the participants commented that they especially liked the way in which the tool shared statistics about the risks for harm and clustering of factors specific to New Brunswick. They found the information enlightening and believed that it would help victims of intimate partner violence to "see themselves" in potentially risky situations. While the academic reviewer saw the specific data as important, she suggested that the research findings be clearly referred to as research or included in the introduction to give context to the statistics. She also noted that, "A lot of the research findings you present are actually supported throughout Canada, not just in New Brunswick, so you should include something to indicate the findings are widely supported."

Some of the service providers had experience with safety planning. Others were trained in detecting the risk for re-assault using risk assessment tools such as the Ontario Domestic Assault Risk Assessment (ODARA). Some had training using the Danger Assessment that identifies lethality risk (Campbell, 2004). However, there appeared to be little consistency in the types of safety plans used by community agencies, front line crisis workers and professionals. The participants agreed that the most common elements of their safety plans involve asking a woman questions and helping her to make an emergency leaving plan. Many of these service providers noted that there would be no conflict in using the new safety planning tool with their clients and indicated that they were anxious to have it available. One person commented, "The tool is amazing. I like it much better than the safety plans we have now. It actually gets women thinking as they read it."

Since most of the service providers had clients who were either living in an abusive home or planning to return, introducing a tool that does not imply that they are doing something wrong by staying is important. One person pointed out that it might seem counter-intuitive, but, "For many women who are fearful of their partners, it often seems safer to stay than to leave." Offering these clients a safety planning tool about leaving is not always productive. One service provider noted, "The brilliance of this new tool is that women can do it themselves even if they do stay." The tool does include a cautionary note to women on the importance of finding a safe place to keep the plan where their partner is not likely to find it.

The study participants voiced their appreciation for the value of the new tool, "It's very easy to understand. The tables are so useful and the language is plain"; "I really like the 'points to consider' section"; "This tool makes the plan unique to each woman. It's not general like so many of the others we have used"; "I don't see any gaps—you hit all the points appropriately given the intention of the tool"; and, "I love how it explains everything right at the start. She could do it by herself, or it's something we could go through together. It's great!"

There was a great deal of lively discussion of how to best disseminate the new tool. It could be widely available for women to discover in public places, or could be shared by service providers. Several participants reiterated that it needed to be a secretive tool so as to prevent abusive partners from finding out about it. To access the tool, women would have to be dealing with the police, mental health, a doctor, and so on. Ultimately, there was consensus that the tool should be widely available and promoted, perhaps even made accessible as a mobile device application (app) that women could scan from a poster and download onto their phone or tablet. Women could have the option of using it by themselves or with community helpers. As one service provider noted, when women come across the new tool in the doctor's office or at the gym, they might pick it up and start to read it which could promote help-seeking behavior. This was considered extremely positive because, "It's been my experience that the sooner in the relationship an abused woman has contact with a helping agency, the sooner she will make the decision to leave an abusive relationship." Clearly, telling women they should leave is not an empowering or acceptable approach to safety planning. The new tool does not infer that women should leave their abusive partners, but it does speak to the importance of recognizing the signals of personal danger. It encourages women to assess those personal risks and take steps to mitigate them. By presenting this assessment in a non-judgmental fashion, the tool becomes relevant for women who want to stay or leave.

The participants discussed the possibility of making the tool more generic so that it could be used across Canada. However, everyone agreed that this could lessen its impact. They liked the fact that it referred to seasonal unemployment in the fisheries, working in the woods, and hunting season. It was because of this content that the checklist of questions would resonate with women living in New Brunswick. They suggested that each province should adapt the tool and tailor it for rural women in their province. Indeed, the study participants agreed that the new safety planning tool could easily be adapted for use with marginalized populations, even those living in urban areas.

As for whether there is a need to offer professional training on the tool to helping agencies, while most felt this could be beneficial, they did not see it as necessary. One person stated, "I don't see any need for professional training. It's meant to be a do-it-yourself tool. Women may take it home with them. They may read it in the waiting room." However, several believed that training would be helpful. One police officer commented, "I think that all police officers should be trained to use this new tool. Just reading it, they would probably learn a lot."

Conclusion

The validation study on the new strategic safety planning tool for rural women living in abusive relationships shows that it strongly resonated with all participants. This has fuelled expectations among participants and others that the tool will move forward and eventually make a substantial contribution to the field of safety planning. The value of the new safety planning tool is the attention it focuses on the importance of including both the lens of geography and culture to account for different patterns of risk factors experienced by rural and urban women. The fact that it is an evidence-based resource predicated on intimate partner violence and domestic homicide research in New Brunswick suggests that it will be an effective resource in helping women, particularly those living in abusive relationships outside of large urban areas, to address their personal risks within meaningful social, cultural, and geographic realities (Doherty & Hornosty, 2004, 2008).

The new safety plan tool is also intended to make a contribution to the field in that it is designed to support a more collaborative approach to working with women by supporting informed self-determination. Traditional safety planning tools tend to focus on emergency leaving or staying safe after leaving. They are typically filled out by the woman while guided by the oversight of a crisis worker or professional. The new tool is one that a woman can chose to use on her own, or if she prefers, complete with the assistance of a professional or friend. It is personalized and can be used to mitigate risk even when a woman decides to stay or return to the relationship. Since a woman's exposure to risk and fear is not static, another contribution of the new tool is that it encourages women to review and strategically reassess their personal risks on a regular basis.

Perhaps one of the reasons that the new tool resonated with abused women and service providers is that it provided new insights into the dynamics of intimate partner violence and highlighted issues related to various specific social and geographical contexts. As Websdale (2000) notes: "Any thoughtful instrument has the potential to enlighten those who know little about the plight of battered women. They may also provide a touchstone for victims themselves as they seek to strategize about their futures and those of their children." In light of the potential for this tool to fill a gap in meeting the safety planning needs of rural women, efforts are under way to finalize the tool by incorporating the feedback from the validation study and moving into an implementation phase including the design of an evaluation framework for assessing effectiveness and outcomes.

Note

1. This research was undertaken by a team of the Muriel McQueen Fergusson Centre on Family Violence Research, established in 1994 to engage in participatory action research to understand and recommend actions to end violence against women. The team was one of the original four teams and was chaired by Dr. Jennie Hornosty. The team was comprised of academic researchers, community researchers, a farm woman, RCMP, and social service providers. Much of the research was co-authored by Doherty and Hornosty. However, the safety planning validation research presented in this chapter is solely the view of the author.

References

Banman, V. (2015). *Domestic homicide risk factors: Rural and urban considerations* (Master's thesis). Retrieved from: http://ir.lib.uwo.ca/etd/.

Beattie, S. & Cotter, A. (2010). *Homicide in Canada 2009* (Statistics Canada Catalogue No. 85–002-X). Ottawa, ON: Statistics Canada. Retrieved from: www.statcan.gc.ca/pub/85-002-x/2010003/article/11352-eng.htm.

Brownridge, D. (2006). Violence against women post-separation. *Aggression and Violent Behavior, 11*, 514–530. doi:10.1016/j.avb.2006.01.009

Campbell, J. C. (2004). Helping women understand their risk in situations of intimate partner violence. *Journal of Interpersonal Violence, 19*, 1464–1477. doi:10.1177/08862605 04269698

Campbell, J. C., Webster, D., Koziol-McLain, J., Block, C. R., Campbell, D., Curry, M. A., . . . & Wilt, S. A. (2003). Assessing risk factors for intimate partner homicide. *National Institute of Justice Journal, 250*, 14–19. Retrieved from: www.ncjrs.gov/pdffiles1/jr000250e.pdf.

Canadian Centre for Justice Statistics. (2011). *Family violence in Canada: A statistical profile 2011* (Catalogue No. 85–002-X). Ottawa, ON: Statistics Canada. Retrieved from: www.statcan.gc.ca/pub/85-002-x/2013001/article/11805-eng.pdf.

Canadian Centre for Justice Statistics. (2013). *Family violence in Canada: A statistical profile 2013* (Catalogue no. 85–002-X). Ottawa, ON: Statistics Canada. Retrieved from: www.statcan.gc.ca/pub/85-002-x/2014001/article/14114-eng.pdf.

DeKeseredy, W. S. & Schwartz, M. D. (2009). *Dangerous exits: Escaping abusive relationships in rural America.* New Brunswick, NJ: Rutgers University Press.

Doherty, D. (2006). Domestic homicide in New Brunswick: An overview of contributing factors. *Atlantis, 30*(3), 4–14. Retrieved from: http://journals.msvu.ca/index.php/atlantis/article/view/818/805.

Doherty, D. (2012). *Domestic homicide: The witnesses speak out.* Retrieved from: www.silentwitness.ca/swadmin/assets/documents/statistics%202012%20english%20updated.pdf.

Doherty, D. & Berglund, D. (2008). *Psychological abuse: A discussion paper.* Ottawa, ON: Public Health Agency of Canada (Cat.:HP20–121/2008E). Retrieved from: www.phac-aspc.gc.ca/sfv-avf/sources/fv/fv-psych-abus/index-eng.php.

Doherty, D. & Hornosty, J. (2004). Abuse in a rural and farm context. In M. L. Stirling, A. Cameron, N. Nason-Clark, & B. Miedema (Eds.), *Understanding abuse: Partnering for change* (pp. 55–81). Toronto, ON: University of Toronto Press.

Doherty, D. & Hornosty, J. (2008). *Exploring the links: Firearms, family violence and animal abuse in rural communities.* Retrieved from: www.legal-info-legale.nb.ca/en/uploads/file/pdfs/Family_Violence_Firearms_Animal_Abuse.pdf.

Dudgeon, A. & Evanson, T. (2014). Intimate partner violence in rural U.S. areas: What every nurse should know. *American Journal of Nursing, 114*(5), 26–35. doi:10.1097/01.NAJ.0000446771.02202.35

Goodkind, J. R., Sullivan, C. M., & Bybee, D. I. (2004). A contextual analysis of battered women's safety planning. *Violence Against Women, 10*, 514–533. doi:10.1177/1077 801204264368

Hornosty, J. & Doherty, D. (2003). Responding to wife abuse in farm and rural communities: Searching for solutions that work. In R. Blake & A. Nurse (Eds.), *The trajectories of rural life: New perspectives on rural Canada* (pp. 37–53). Regina, SK: Saskatchewan Institute of Public Policy.

Hornosty, J. & Doherty, D. (2004). Resistance and change: Building a framework for helping abused rural women. In B. Cheers, R. Clews, A. M. Powers, & L. Carawan (Eds.), *Beyond geographical and disciplinary boundaries: Human services in rural communities* (pp. 106–117) [Special issue of the Journal of Rural Social Work].

Johnson, H. & Hotton, T. (2003). Losing control: Homicide risk in estranged and intact intimate relationships. *Homicide Studies, 7*(1), 58–84. doi:10.1177/1088767902239243

Kropp, P. R. (2008). Intimate partner violence risk assessment and management. *Violence and Victims, 23*, 202–220. doi:10.1891/0886-6708.23.2.202

Lindhorst, T., Nurius, P., & Macy, R. J. (2005). Contextualized assessment with battered women: Strategic safety planning to cope with multiple harms. *Journal of Social Work Education, 41*(2), 331–352. Retrieved from: www.ncbi.nlm.nih.gov/pmc/articles/PMC2169137/.

Logan, T. K., Walker, R., & Leukefeld, C. G. (2001). Rural, urban influenced, and urban differences among domestic violence arrestees. *Journal of Interpersonal Violence, 16*, 266–283. doi:10.1177/088626001016003006

Ontario Domestic Violence Death Review Committee (2008). *Annual report.* Toronto, ON: Office of the Chief Coroner.

Ontario Domestic Violence Death Review Committee (2015). *Annual report.* Toronto, ON: Office of the Chief Coroner. Retrieved from: www.mcscs.jus.gov.on.ca/sites/default/files/content/mcscs/docs/ec165340.pdf.

Swanberg, J. E. & Logan, T. K. (2005). Domestic violence and employment: A qualitative study. *Journal of Occupational Health Psychology, 10*(1), 3–17. doi:10.1037/1076-8998.10.1.3

Wathen, C. N. & MacMillan, H. L. (2003). Interventions for violence against women. *Journal of the American Medical Association, 289*, 589–600. doi:10.1001/jama.289.5.589

Websdale, N. (2000, February). *Lethality assessment tools: A critical analysis.* Harrisburg, PA: VAWnet. Retrieved from: www.vawnet.org.

Websdale, N. (2003). Reviewing domestic violence deaths. *National Institute of Justice Journal, 250*, 26–31. Retrieved from: www.ncjrs.gov/pdffiles1/jr000250g.pdf.

Wilson, J. S. & Websdale, N. (2006). Domestic violence fatality review teams: An interprofessional model to reduce deaths. *Journal of Interprofessional Care, 20*, 535–544. doi:10.1080/13561820600959253

3 "If They Can Get Through It, So Can I"

Women's Perspectives of Peer-Led
Support Groups for Intimate
Partner Violence[1]

*Leslie M. Tutty, Cindy Ogden, Karen Wyllie,
and Andrea Silverstone*

The abuse of women by their intimate partners is a substantial problem in North America. Research on the effectiveness of interventions to hold offenders accountable and support victims has focused largely on treatment groups for batterers (Saunders, 2008) and protection for women in shelters (Hughes, Cangiano, & Hopper, 2011; Tutty, 2015). Considerably less research has evaluated community-based services such as support groups for women (Abel, 2000; Liu, Dore, & Amrani-Cohen, 2013; Tutty, Babins-Wagner, & Rothery, 2015). Further, the value of utilizing trained volunteers or peers to offer group support has rarely been investigated.

This chapter presents the qualitative narratives of ten women members of the Growth Circles program offered by Calgary's Peer Support Services for Abused Women (PSSAW) (recently renamed Sagesse). These support and psycho-educational peer-led groups provide women abused by intimate partners the opportunity to learn about the dynamics of intimate partner violence, to share their experiences and receive support from other women. Trained volunteers facilitate the programs, most of whom have a history of partner abuse. The chapter presents the in-depth perspectives of ten Growth Circle members with respect to their backgrounds, how they accessed the programs and their reflections on the value of the input from their peers, the group leaders and the groups.

The Nature of Intimate Partner Violence Against Women

Physical and sexual violence against women are serious problems that result in both injury and significant emotional harm (AuCoin, 2005). Intimate partner violence (IPV) is not marital conflict but the intentional, instrumental use of power to control women (Kimmel, 2002). While focusing on physical injuries is important, many women endure years of intense psychological abuse that can devastate their lives (Ansara & Hindin, 2011). Further, women can be at increased risk of abuse after having separated from their partners (Brownridge, 2006).

Chronic and ongoing abuse often leads women to be diagnosed with mental health issues such as depression and anxiety (Preston, 2002), although, in many cases, these are best seen as the consequences of IPV rather than as factors predisposing women to enter into abusive partnerships. While high rates of post-traumatic stress disorder (PTSD) are found in women abused by intimate partners, Walker (1991) cautioned that, "it is important to remember that not all battered women develop PTSD and even when they do, they may not need more than a support group with others in similar situations" (p. 28). Schlee, Heyman, and O'Leary (1998) support this, finding that women diagnosed with PTSD did well in group.

Though considerable research has documented the traumas and negative consequences for women who live with abusive partners, it can risk perceiving them as "helpless" victims, not seeing their strengths and coping abilities to resist the abuse whether they remain in the relationship or leave it. Acknowledging their resilience and finding ways to support their strengths is a critical aspect of any intervention (Tutty, 2006). Nevertheless, we must ask how we can most effectively assist women who live with or have left violent partners in the hope of creating new lives. Support groups are a common intervention usually offered in the community to women who may or may not have resided in shelters.

Group Intervention with Women Abused by Intimate Partners

Group intervention specific to women abused by intimate partners began in VAW shelters where the staff were often former residents with little formal counselor training. Since women were already living communally, it made sense to provide information about intimate partner abuse in feminist-informed groups that focused on the women's needs (MacLeod, 1990). The group format was later adopted by community agencies serving women who wanted to learn about abuse, women who were abused but wanted to stay and try to make things better, others who were considering leaving abusive partners, or those who had left but still felt the need for support.

Groups for women abused by intimate partners are often described as "support" groups, implying that although the results might be therapeutic the women were not necessarily perceived as having mental health problems or "needing therapy" (Tutty, Bidgood, & Rothery, 1996). The benefits of offering support in groups include the fact that groups reduce social isolation, one of the significant effects of being abused by an intimate partner (Fritch & Lynch, 2008). Members of support groups encourage each other, allowing women to see that their reactions to the abuse are common and understandable. Group members differ in terms of the risks to their safety and are often struggling to maintain their safety and dignity in the face of their partners' abusive actions. The women typically find it helpful to strategize with other group members about how to cope with their partner's abusive behaviors and may explore whether to remain in relationships. Opportunities to validate their experiences and learn from others are viewed as prime benefits of the group process (Abel, 2000; Moldon, 2002; Tutty et al., 1996).

Though professionally-led support groups for women abused by intimate partners are relatively common, little formal research on their effectiveness has been conducted. Tutty et al. (1996) and Abel (2000) reviewed nine and ten early studies conducted in the 1980s and 1990s respectively, most of which supported the groups as improving self-esteem, anger levels, attitudes toward marriage and the family, anxiety, and depression. Rinfret-Raynor and Cantin (1997) compared feminist group to feminist individual to non-feminist individual treatment for sixty women, finding no significant differences between the approaches with women improving, on average, in all three.

Several studies have focused on group process variables connected to outcomes. Tutty et al. (1996) found no consistently superior program outcomes that could be attributed to group characteristics, however did identify some advantages of two-leader groups over time. Larance and Porter (2004) observed the group process in support groups for women abused by intimate partners, noting the development of trust and interconnections.

Qualitative studies of professionally led groups for women abused by their partners support these benefits. In interviews with thirty-two groups, members all commented on the utility of the support they had received from fellow group members, the value of the information provided, and the competence of the group leaders (Tutty & Rothery, 2002). Interviews with eight support group members (Moldon, 2002) described their process of moving from the "lost self" to the "reclaimed self" with two key processes, safety and knowledge building. The women rewrote their personal narratives through a process of psychological and relational healing and change that was generated through the group connections.

Using Peers and Paraprofessionals to Support Women Abused by Intimate Partners

Peer support is often used in the context of substance abuse and mental health (Davidson et al., 1999). However, the current literature on groups for women abused by intimate partners is primarily with respect to professionals leading support or therapy groups.

There is some ambiguity about what constitutes a peer support group, with authors failing to specify whether the groups were, in fact, led by peers or by professionals. Shepard (1999) noted that self-help groups for women were offered as part of the Duluth Domestic Abuse Intervention Project, but provided no details about the leaders. Breton and Nosko (2005) described a "mutual aid" group for woman abuse; however the two co-leaders were apparently professionals. The co-leaders described by Ginter (2005) and Hartman (1983) were a professional and a peer.

Ginter (2005) and Hartman (1983) identified the benefits for group members as increased self-esteem or self-confidence and increased skills. Fearday and Cape (2004) described peer-led groups for traumatized women with co-occurring mental health and substance abuse diagnoses who had also survived violence. Service providers perceived the members of these peer-led groups as having benefited. However, overall, very little research about the effects and group process of peer-groups for women abused by intimate violence has been documented, especially hearing from the women themselves, providing a clear rationale for the current study.

Sagesse

Sagesse (formerly Peer Support Services for Abused Women) opened in 1988 in Calgary, Alberta, Canada in response to concerns that women leaving shelters often ultimately reunited with abusive partners because they were isolated and lonely. Sagesse is a feminist organization. As such, all programs include a feminist lens that addresses gender-based violence, systemic biases, and empowerment. The agency offers several programs for women abused by intimate partners. Growth Circles (twelve weeks in length) are peer support/psychoeducational groups led by trained volunteers and are a mainstay of the agency's programming. Through a support group, women can connect with others who had left abusive partners. The hope was also that women would build relationships that could be sustained outside the groups. The topics addressed in the Growth Circles include the dynamics of intimate partner violence including defining healthy and unhealthy relationships, the cycle of violence, boundaries, relaxation, self-esteem and dealing with anger, parenting, and family of origin issues.

Trained volunteers facilitate all of the agency programs, the majority of whom have a history of intimate partner abuse or abuse in their families of origin. As another aspect of the evaluation, we interviewed fourteen Growth Circle peer leaders, only three of whom had no history of abuse in their relationships (Tutty, Ogden, Wyllie, & Silverstone, 2017). Only two had been employed in counseling or support positions but the majority had volunteer experience with abuse-related services such as women's shelters and telephone distress lines.

Research Design and Procedures

As recommended by Kraemer Tebes and Tebes Kraemer (1991) in their evaluation of mutual aid support groups, the current research employed a qualitative process evaluation method to assess the perceptions of the "Growth Circle" group members. The research advisory team, all women professionals with feminist perspectives and considerable knowledge about intimate partner violence, created the interview guide for the leaders. The first two authors, primarily responsible for developing and carrying out the research, have decades of experience both leading and researching groups. The other three research advisory members have clinical and administrative experience with Sagesse and other clinical agencies.

The semi-structured interview guide included questions about how the women became Growth Circle members; their perceptions of the abuse that they experienced; the process by which they attended group; how they found the groups and the strengths and any challenges of being a group member. The first question about their pathways to the Growth Circles allowed them to narrate their stories using their own words. More specific questions, about their perceptions of the groups for example, were used as probes if the interviewees did not describe these themselves (Rogers & Bouey, 1996).

A mainstream qualitative approach was deemed appropriate (Marshall & Rossman, 2006; Patton, 2002). Mainstream qualitative methods use the practicality of the research question as the guiding principle, rather than the confines of qualitative traditions such as grounded theory or phenomenology. The research proposal was reviewed and approved by the University of Calgary Conjoint Research Ethics Review Committee. To ensure confidentiality, past clients of Growth Circles were initially contacted by staff members to ask about their willingness to be interviewed. The interviews, all conducted by the second author either in-person or by phone, lasted from one and half to two hours and were tape-recorded and transcribed. The transcripts were entered into ATLAS-ti to organize the analysis process, which follows accepted practices of mainstream qualitative research methods (Coleman & Unrau, 1996; Marshall & Rossman, 2006).

Results

Ten Growth Circle participants were interviewed. As can be seen in Table 3.1, five women had been married to their abusive partners and five were in common-law relationships. None were still partnered with these men. Three were in new non-abusive relationships. Six women had children living with them, two had adult offspring and two had no children. The women were predominately Caucasian (eight), one woman was Métis and one was of Chinese background, having immigrated to Canada as an adult. Four women were employed either part or fulltime. Six were not working and, of those, two were funded by provincial disability, one was on welfare, two lived with new partners and one was a college student.

The major themes that emerged from the women's narratives included the nature of the abuse from their ex-partners, their perceptions of the Growth Circle's structure, organization, and curriculum, interactions with other members and the group peer leaders and challenges.

Table 3.1 Demographics for Growth Circle Respondents

	Marital Status	Ages of Children	Racial Background	Employment/ Income Status	Most Significant Partner Abuse	Police Involved	Referred By
P1	Ex-Common-law	12	Caucasian	Seeking work, New partner	Forced prostitution	no	friend
P2	Ex-husband	13	Caucasian	On disability	Some physical, controlling	yes	Church mentoring program
P3	Common-law	none	Caucasian	Student	Stalking, controlling	yes	Internet
P4	Ex-husband	7, 9	Caucasian	Clerical work	Gun held to her head	yes	Shelter group worker
P5	Ex-common-law	Adults	Caucasian	welfare	Sexual, controlling	yes	Shelter
P6	Ex-husband/ other common-law partner	Adults	Métis	Not working. New partner	Stalking, controlling	no	Crisis phone-line
P7	Ex-common-law	6	Chinese	Clerical work	Strangling, controlling	yes	Colleague
P8	Ex-husband	10,11	Caucasian	Working	Physical, threats, controlling	yes	Poster in shelter
P9	Ex-husband	13	Caucasian	On disability	Some physical	yes	Friend
P10	Ex-common-law	none	Caucasian	Support worker	Strangulation, forced confinement	no	Transit advert

The Nature of the Intimate Partner Violence

The women described significant psychological abuse, including death threats and forced prostitution, and seven had been seriously physically abused by their partners. The police had been involved in seven cases and had charged four men for assaults on their partners. Comments from the women who had endured physical abuse include the following:

> He pushed me around, dragged me across the floor by my hair. The physical abuse was slower in escalating. In the beginning it wasn't there. Then it was pushing. It took a couple more years and then it was choking me. It was really rough!
>
> He felt more in power if I was naked so he'd always strip me naked, lock me in the basement all night. One night in the middle of winter he locked me on the balcony, naked. I huddled in a corner and pleaded for him to let me back in.

The partners of seven women had sexually assaulted them. Six men had threatened to kill their partners and/or had actually attempted to murder them. One woman commented, "My ex-husband held a gun to my head. He said that if he killed me, he'd only get ten years, he could do his business from prison and get out in five years for good behavior." Another disclosed:

> He had locked me in a room. I became quite upset and physically aggressive trying to leave. He put a pillow over my face and smothered me. I didn't think he would stop. I was almost at that point of succumbing and he stopped.

We asked the women what strategies they had used to deal with their partner's abusive behavior before coming to the agency. Consistent with other research, most either had not sought assistance or found that the support offered did not meet their needs. The women had considered asking for support from various sources including family, friends, informal support programs, formal support services, and violence against women shelters. However, ultimately, the women were hesitant to talk to others about the abuse.

> I didn't talk to anybody. One of the biggest problems is education. Even if they hear something on TV about a woman (whose) husband almost killed her, you hear women say, "I'd never stay in that relationship. I'm not that stupid." It's really hard to go, "I'm going to tell them and they're going to think I'm stupid."
>
> So many things you can't talk about with your family. I didn't feel comfortable and there's always repercussions. Once you've told them, it colors the way they interact with you. Besides, I'm the one in my family that everybody else comes to for help.

Group Structure and Organization

The participants commented about the structure and organization of the Growth Circles. Six women appreciated the efforts from the leaders and agency staff to ensure their physical and emotional safety. The leaders helped to ensure safety by stressing confidentiality, boundaries, and respect within the Growth Circles. In addition, the groups were closed to new members. As one interviewee mentioned, "They keep the door to the building locked so nobody can get in who's not supposed to be there. It's a safe environment." Another noted:

> They said, "Once we start we don't accept anybody else." That's important because you're scared to start sharing and once you start, you don't want new people coming in. Trust starts to build so, if anyone else comes in, everybody puts their walls up again.

Every participant perceived the group leaders as respecting their confidentiality, commenting, "We discussed how the group was confidential. Nothing was ever discussed about other individuals outside of group. So as far as I know, they took it seriously" and, "Things that I talked to (leader) about in private were never discussed in group. I never worried they were going to say something about me to anybody else."

Several described how the group leaders built emotional safety within the group. One woman mentioned, "At the first session there was a speech about boundaries and respect for people in group. It was safe. [Group leader] wasn't judgmental at all, which helps." Another noted:

> They're supportive, a safe environment. They keep your confidentiality. Anybody abused could learn a lot if they are willing to put in the time. We made up our own ground rules, and one was the right to say, "I don't feel like talking right now." It's very relaxed.

Group Curriculum

All ten Growth Circle members commented that they had learned useful information from the group leaders' presentations and exercises. While different women were drawn to various aspects of the curriculum, no one perceived this as a drawback, "Certain classes don't strike a chord, but for other women they might. Sometimes topics don't really relate to me and I let other women talk about it." Six women commented on the helpful nature of the information on abuse.

> They teach the different types of abuse; and every aspect of my life was abused, everything. I thought it was only married women in abusive relationships. I had no idea it went on in colleges. I thought kids these days knew better than to hit a girl.

He said I was going through the baby blues a couple of weeks ago. I said, "Our daughter is six. It can't be the baby blues." He was always trying to make it sound like I was crazy. He's so manipulative. Through Peer Support I've learned that's how a lot of them do it.

Five women commented that the exercise on family histories (genogram) was important. As described by one woman, "We did these charts. I still have mine. You do your mom and dad and if they had any abuse. It was an eye-opener to see how family history can affect you." Three women appreciated the discussions defining healthy and unhealthy relationships. One woman applied the information to a man she was dating.

Very, very possessive and I saw the red flags. I was going to the groups when I was dating him. Whoa. That one was scary. He was very argumentative. I said, "If you don't stop, I'm leaving." I don't think he believed me. I got up and took a cab home. I was getting stronger, whereas before, I probably would have stayed.

Women found the discussions about increasing self-esteem and dealing with difficult emotions, assertiveness, and the stages of grieving helpful, several of which are illustrated in these quotes:

A lot of things they talked about had never occurred to me, like the right to your own feelings. It turns your thinking around; validated you as a person. When you go through verbal abuse your self-esteem is so low. I learned that I didn't need to be with someone because I didn't want to be alone. I was worthy enough just myself.

The biggest part was learning that it's okay to say no; that you're allowed to have your own opinions and, if something doesn't feel right, it's okay to walk away. I have the power. I can leave, which is what I did.

They talked about the grieving process. It makes you think about what you've lost through a divorce; what you plan on doing to replace those losses.

One woman summarized what she learned in the Growth Circles, stating, "They've given me skills to make choices. I don't feel locked in anymore. If I had a dollar I could leave no matter what, get myself help and move ahead."

Eight women noted the importance of sharing their experiences of being abused by their partners with other group members. However, they were disappointed that the group format did not include enough time for women to tell their stories in detail rather than only disclosing the pieces that applied to a specific topic.

I wanted to talk about what happened to me and hear what happened to them. There's no class where we talk about what happened. It's good to hear women say, "My husband did this." Then I'm, "That happened to me too!" I appreciated those classes the most.

A number of women suggested that the curriculum be more flexible and that some issues be addressed in more detail. One comment specified, "I thought the curriculum would have more depth. We were getting the summary." Another woman would have liked to discuss dating and the potential risks of doing so:

> A lot of us thought about dating. You really have to watch out. If you have kids, with a lot of pedophiles, protect your kids. I've seen girls let their new boyfriend watch the kids while they go shopping. That's not a good idea.

Interactions among Group Members

When asked about their experiences with the other group members, all commented about the importance of talking with women who had similarly been abused. As one stated, "The women brought me back every week. We had so much in common. It's incredible. I thought, 'Now, somebody understands!' It was a huge weight lifted off my shoulders." Others noted:

> To know you weren't alone; that others experienced the same things. When you're talking out here [general public], people either trigger their own stuff, or don't understand. It was a place you could unload and feel supported.
>
> All these guys start the same. They are sweet talkers; fill your head with dreams. Some of the lines these guys were throwing were the same stuff I was told. I was, "Hey, there's something about these guys." I stopped blaming myself after the first day.

The women admitted that they were often in different places in their lives but saw these differences as a means of hope: "It makes you realize there are alternatives; you're not alone. It shows what trauma does. It leaves scars. It's happened to other women. If they can get through it, so can I," and, "Women [were at] different levels in the healing process. Some had found total peace, but it didn't happen overnight. I'm still in the beginning; there's lots I have to do."

However, several women recounted difficult experiences with some group members. One interviewee commented that, "Some people take over meetings. I don't like that. Lots of people have stuff to say, so, "Stop, you've had your time." Another noted:

> One group member was kind of whiney and grated on my nerves. We'd not get through our agenda; we'd be concentrating on her. I felt for her but I needed things from the group too. She was in crisis and needed a lot of help.

We asked whether the women had stayed in touch with other Growth Circle group members after the programs ended. Six women made friendships that endured past the group but four women had not. One of the latter commented, "I didn't make a huge connection on a friendship level with the women. It was

enough for me just to be in the group. I didn't need to make friends out of group."
Of the women who made long-term friends, one mentioned, "I still talk to one
of the girls. We've been friends for four or five years." Another noted:

> I still have contact with one woman. We've been friends since we met at
> Peer Support four years ago. Friendships are always important. Some
> people say when you're going through abuse you lose friends. That's true.
> You lose touch because he makes it hard and then you're embarrassed and
> ashamed. But it's nice to have one person that you can stay in touch with
> through the years.

Interactions with Growth Circle Group Leaders

The women saw the non-professional Growth Circles group leaders as an
integral part of their experiences; all mentioned some positive experiences,
describing qualities that made them good group leaders, including making the
groups interactive, the importance of good listening skills, and working collaboratively with group members. One woman noted, "Definitely a listening ear
and not pushy. When you related a situation [name would say], 'When I was a
kid this really helped.' That helps; it's not saying you 'should' do this."

> The facilitators are tremendous. [Name] is very upbeat. [Name] is quieter
> but upbeat too. It makes for a positive atmosphere. It's lively, interactive.
> They have a genuine concern for each of our stories. I like that the
> facilitators genuinely care.

The women all perceived the Growth Circle facilitators as knowledgeable
about IPV: "The amount of stuff we got through! She had a lot of information;
[could] change your mindset about things that are dragging you down."

> The facilitators were knowledgeable and supportive. It was nice that the
> group was based on peer support. It's more about being empathetic toward
> the situation and using the knowledge that they were trained with to work
> with [women in group].

The women also described the group leaders as respectful and responsive:
"She was concise, but elaborated when requested. She had compassion" and,
"If someone's not feeling comfortable they didn't force the issue. Listening and
being empathetic was huge. Showing respect. Not jumping in with their own
opinions or beliefs."

The participants mentioned that one way the group leaders showed their
respect and responsiveness to the group members was balancing the night's
agenda with women's needs or balancing the needs of a group member in distress
with the needs of other group members. As one woman mentioned, "Sometimes
one would go off with a woman to the side, and they would talk and the other

[leader] would continue. I thought they handled everything well." Another commented, "[Group leader] can tell you weren't paying attention. Then you can talk about it. With her, [we] got everything done but it definitely helped to talk about what was happening."

Nonetheless, several women described specific experiences with group leaders about which they felt uncomfortable. "I didn't feel she was genuine. She put on airs. She said she went through it [abuse] but it looked like she was pretending. She was a bit of a phony." A second group member mentioned, "I will compliment [leader] hugely. She read between the lines and offered more. The first gal, the flippant gal, was like check, check, check [tapping the table]."

The majority of women considered it helpful that a number of the group leaders had, themselves, been abused by intimate partners. As one woman noted, "They've gone through what we're going through so they know what we're feeling. That's important. Maybe it helps them heal, too, by helping other people." From another interviewee:

> There's a big difference between someone who has lived through something and someone who's read about it. They don't know the fear. Someone who has never been through an assault will never understand triggers, what it's like to live through it.

Nevertheless, three women were not concerned about whether the group leaders had been abused by their intimate partners:

> I don't think my group leaders had been abused but I don't think it would've added. Even if they haven't been, they were respectful, responsive, caring. They took confidentiality seriously. The group felt safe. The group leaders were great.

Organizational Challenges for Growth Circles

Although the women identified many benefits, they also mentioned challenges, most with respect to organizational issues such as the length of the program, having enough leaders and group members to start and complete Growth Circles in a timely manner, which significantly impacted the women's group experiences. Four women commented that, once the Growth Circle ended, they again felt isolated and struggled to rebuild their lives. They suggested adding another level of group:

> You need to talk about it but once that is over you need to move into a healthier realm of people. You have to learn how. One girl said, "You start to feel like there's freedom, but how do you live that freedom?"

Four were disappointed about having to wait months for a Growth Circle group to begin. As one woman stated, "I hate to think that someone is eager but has to wait months because they couldn't find facilitators. They want two; won't run the group with just one."

Four women were disappointed that their Growth Circles group did not start because of difficulty finding facilitators, when several leaders left mid-group. Once facilitators were found, there was a problem with the space.

> You start feeling comfortable with that group of people then, when the agency was trying to find facilitators, there was a long lapse. If somebody was still in crisis, they could fall back and maybe not reach out again for help. Even if one woman just needs some help, I think they've got to keep going because literally they restored my faith.

Three women perceived their groups as too small. One stated, "I like it small but I wonder if a larger group would add more diversity, more input." Another commented:

> More participants would be good. If there's more people you get more ideas. It's amazing how much you learn when you hear about other people's woes. Sometimes it makes yours not so bad. You realize you're not alone.

Discussion

The women in Growth Circles had experienced significant psychological abuse, including death threats or attempted homicide, and extreme physical violence from partners. Consistent with other research that examines whether women utilize family and friends as support (Ansara & Hindin, 2011), most had been reluctant to seek assistance or found that the informal support offered did not meet their needs. One woman was of the opinion that the fact that domestic violence is now more in the public eye is actually a barrier, since attitudes that women who stay with abusive partners must be somehow stupid or crazy have not shifted. As such, the shame of being victimized continues to be a barrier in women feeling comfortable seeking either formal or informal support. This also validates the need for the program, since the women that engaged in the Growth Circles program had little other support.

Perceptions of the benefits and challenges of offering peer support groups for women abused by intimate partners from the current study are consistent with the small body of quantitative and qualitative research conducted on professionally-led groups (Abel, 2000; Moldon, 2002; Tutty & Rothery, 2002; Tutty et al., 1996). Understanding the serious nature of the abuse and the common experiences with other women were significant learnings for Growth Circle group members as well as the volunteer groups facilitators (Tutty, Ogden, Wyllie, & Silverstone, 2017).

The group members saw using trained volunteers as group facilitators, a proportion of whom had been abused themselves, as an asset. Notably, three group members became volunteers after completing their own client work.

Nevertheless, several mentioned rare instances when group leaders had acted inappropriately, highlighting the importance of both screening and training in establishing that the group leaders had healed from their own abuse so that they could assist group members. Further, it supports authors such as Fearday and Cape (2004), MacLeod (1990), and Hartman (1983), all of whom affirmed that many women who have been abused can become empowered through taking leadership roles in groups.

The organizational challenges identified in offering the Growth Circle groups are common difficulties in professionally led groups as well, including finding enough participants to attend and maintaining group membership over time, and group members who monopolize or are in crisis, thus interfering in the group process for others (Moldon, 2002; Tutty & Rothery, 2002). The comments from the group members suggest that, for the most part, the leaders' training assisted them in addressing these issues constructively. Also challenging is the need to balance providing structure and information while still allowing time for the women to tell their stories in a safe and respectful setting, a factor identified by Moldon (2002) as central for the women. While the majority of the women valued the program curricula, several commented that they would have appreciated more time to discuss their own backgrounds and circumstances.

Agency Response to the Evaluation

In general, the women reported important, and for some, life-altering experiences that they attributed to the groups. The agency appreciated the women endorsing the Growth Circles, with most liking the general structure and content of the groups, the leadership skills of the non-professional group leaders, and the fellowship from the group members.

In addition, in response to some of the women's concerns, the agency implemented several changes. In reaction to concerns about the need for more women to access the program and requests for additional content, the Growth Circles were revised to create a continuous peer-led group that can be accessed in two different phases with no pre-requirements or specific entry points for either phase. The Growth Circle program was extended from twelve to fourteen weeks, focusing on the dynamics and effects of violence and self-exploration to address the root causes of domestic violence, including a deeper understanding of the role played by the family of origin, values and beliefs, reclaiming sexuality and mind-body connections. The training for volunteer facilitators was revised to include a more in-depth and supportive facilitator manual, greater experiential learning and more consistent and in-depth supervision from a staff social worker.

In conclusion, peer-led support groups offer a seldom-researched option that, according to the women in the current study, provide a high level of support and information to those abused by intimate partners. The group leaders represented exceptional role models and offer hope for change. While three group members also subsequently became leaders, all of the women respondents took part in the current study to assist other women survivors of intimate partner violence.

Note

1. This evaluation was funded by the United Way of Calgary and Area and Family and Community Social Services of Calgary. The Research Advisory Team for this project consisted of Ada Baxter from Sagesse (formerly Peer Support Services for Abused Women) and Naida Brotherston from Jewish Family Services. Website: www.sagesse.org.

References

Abel, E. (2000). Psychosocial treatment for battered women: A review of empirical research. *Research on Social Work Practice, 10*(1), 55–77.

Ansara, D. L. & Hindin, M. J. (2011). Psychosocial consequences of intimate partner violence for women and men in Canada. *Journal of Interpersonal Violence, 26*(8), 1628–1645. doi:10.1177/0886260510370600

AuCoin, K. E. (2005). *Family violence in Canada: A statistical profile 2005* (85-224-XIE2005000). Ottawa, ON: Canadian Centre for Justice Statistics. Retrieved from: www.statcan.gc.ca/pub/85-224-x/85-224-x2005000-eng.pdf.

Breton, M. & Nosko, A. (2005). Group work with women who have experienced abuse. In G. L. Grief & P. H. Ephross (Eds.), *Group work with populations at risk* (pp. 212–225). Oxford, UK: Oxford University Press.

Brownridge, D. A. (2006). Violence against women post-separation. *Aggression and Violent Behavior, 11*(5), 514–530. doi:10.1016/j.avb.2006.01.009

Coleman, H. & Unrau, Y. (1996). Analyzing your data. In L. M. Tutty, M. A. Rothery, & R. M. Grinnell (Eds.), *Qualitative research for social workers: Phases, steps and tasks* (pp. 89–119). Boston, MA: Allyn and Bacon.

Davidson, L., Chinman, M. J., Kloos, B., Weingarten, R., Stayner, D. A., & Tebes, J. K. (1999). Peer support among individuals with severe mental illness: A review of the evidence. *Clinical Psychology: Science and Practice, 6*(2), 165–187. doi:10.1093/clipsy. 6.2.165

Fearday, F. L. & Cape, A. L. (2004). A voice for traumatized women: Inclusion and mutual support. *Psychiatric Rehabilitation Journal, 27*(3), 258–265.

Fritch, A. M. & Lynch, S. M. (2008). Group treatment for adult survivors of interpersonal trauma. *Journal of Psychological Trauma, 7*(3), 145–169. doi:10.1080/19322880802266797

Ginter, C. (2005). Client confidentiality, anonymity, facilitator credibility, and contamination in rural family violence self-help groups. In K. Brownlee & J. R. Graham (Eds.), *Violence in the family: Social work readings and research from northern and rural Canada* (pp. 90–104). Toronto, ON: Canadian Scholars' Press.

Hartman, S. (1983). A self-help group for women in abusive relationships. *Social Work with Groups, 6*(3/4), 133–146. doi:10.1300/J009v06n03_13

Hughes, H. M., Cangiano, C., & Hopper, E. K. (2011). Profiles of distress in sheltered battered women: Implications for intervention. *Violence and Victims, 26*(4), 445–460. doi:10.1891/0886-6708.26.4.445

Kimmel, M. S. (2002). "Gender symmetry" in domestic violence: A substantive and methodological research review. *Violence Against Women, 8*(11), 1332–1363. doi:10.1177/107780102237407

Kraemer Tebes, J. & Tebes Kraemer, D. (1991). Quantitative and qualitative knowing in mutual support research: Some lessons from the recent history of scientific psychology. *American Journal of Community Psychology, 19*(5), 739–756. doi:10.1007/BF00938042

Larance, L. Y. & Porter, M. L. (2004). Observations from practice: Support group membership as a process of social capital formation among female survivors of domestic violence. *Journal of Interpersonal Violence, 19*(6), 676–690. doi:10.1177/0886 260504263875

Liu, S., Dore, M. M., & Amrani-Cohen, I. (2013). Treating the effects of interpersonal violence: A comparison of two group models. *Social Work with Groups, 36*(1), 59–72. doi:10.1080/01609513.2012.725156

MacLeod, L. (1990). *Counselling for change: Evolutionary trends in counselling services for women who are abused and their children in Canada.* Ottawa, ON: Health and Welfare Canada. Retrieved from: http://publications.gc.ca/collections/Collection/H72-21-77-1992E. pdf.

Marshall, C. & Rossman, G. B. (2006). *Designing qualitative research* (4th ed.). Thousand Oaks, CA: Sage.

Moldon, J. (2002). Rewriting stories: Women's responses to the Safe Journey group. In L. M. Tutty & C. Goard (Eds.), *Reclaiming self: Issues and resources for women abused by intimate partners* (pp. 81–97). Halifax: Fernwood Publishing and RESOLVE.

Patton, M. Q. (2002). *Qualitative research & evaluation methods* (3rd ed.). Thousand Oaks, CA: Sage.

Preston, S. L. (2002). Claiming our place: Women with serious mental health issues and support groups for abused women. *Canadian Journal of Community Mental Health, 21,* 101–113. doi:10.7870/cjcmh-2002-0008

Rinfret-Raynor, M. & Cantin, S. (1997). Feminist therapy for battered women: An assessment. In G. Kaufman Kantor & J. L. Jasinski (Eds.), *Out of the darkness: Contemporary perspectives on family violence* (pp. 219–234). Thousand Oaks, CA: Sage.

Rogers, G. & Bouey, E. (1996). Collecting your data. In L. Tutty, M. Rothery, & R. M. Grinnell (Eds.), *Qualitative research for social workers: Phases, steps and tasks* (pp. 51–87). Boston, MA: Allyn and Bacon.

Saunders, D. G. (2008). Group interventions for men who batter: A summary of program descriptions and research. *Violence and Victims, 23*(2), 156–172. doi:10.1891/0886-6708.23.2.156

Schlee, K., Heyman, R. E., & O'Leary, K. D. (1998). Group treatment for spouse abuse: Are women with PTSD appropriate participants? *Journal of Family Violence, 13*(1), 1–20. doi:10.1023/A:1022811331978

Shepard, M. F. (1999). Advocacy for battered women: Implications for a coordinated community response. In M. F. Shepard & E. L. Pence (Eds.), *Coordinating community responses to domestic violence: Lessons from Duluth and beyond* (pp. 115–126). Thousand Oaks, CA: Sage.

Tutty, L. (2006). There but for fortune: How women experience abuse by intimate partners. In M. Hampton & N. Gerrard (Eds.), *Intimate partner violence: Reflections on experience, theory and policy* (pp. 9–32). Toronto, ON: Cormorant Books and RESOLVE.

Tutty, L. M. (2015). Addressing the safety and trauma issues of abused women: A cross-Canada study of YWCA shelters. *Journal of International Women's Studies, 16*(3), 101–116.

Tutty, L. & Rothery, M. (2002). Beyond shelters: Support groups and community-based advocacy for abused women. In A. L. Roberts (Ed.), *Handbook of domestic violence intervention strategies Policies, programs, and legal remedies* (pp. 396–418). New York, NY: Oxford University Press.

Tutty, L. M., Babins-Wagner, R., & Rothery, M. A. (2015). You're not alone: Mental health outcomes in therapy groups for abused women. *Journal of Family Violence, 31*(4), 489–497. doi:10.1007/s10896-015-9779-6

Tutty, L. M., Bidgood, B. A., & Rothery, M. A. (1996). Evaluating the effect of group process and client variables in support groups for battered women. *Research on Social Work Practice*, *6*(3), 308–324. doi:10.1177/104973159600600303

Tutty, L. M., Ogden, C., Wyllie, K., & Silverstone, A. (2017). "When I'd dealt with my issues, I was ready to give back": Peer leader's perspectives of support groups for abused women. Advance Online publication. *Journal of Aggression, Maltreatment and Trauma*. doi:10.1080/10926771.2016.1241332

Walker, L. (1991). Post-traumatic stress disorder in women: Diagnosis and treatment of battered woman syndrome. *Psychotherapy*, *28*(1), 21–29.

Part II

Intervention with Men Who Have Perpetrated Intimate Partner Violence

4 Justice-Linked Domestic Violence Intervention Services

Description and Analysis of Practices across Canada

Katreena Scott, Lisa Heslop,
Randal David, and Tim Kelly

In Canada, as in other developed nations, an important component of the criminal justice system's response to domestic violence (DV) is intervention programming. The evolution of justice-linked intervention for domestic violence perpetrators across North America owes much to the Duluth model. Duluth offered the first community-based treatment model responsive to the need to work collaboratively with the justice system (Pence, Paymar, Ritmeester, & Shepard, 1993). Developed in the early 1980s, Duluth advanced a holistic model of how community-based interventions, women's advocacy services, and the criminal justice system might work together to prioritize and promote safety for women who are victims of men's violence and ensure that men were held accountable for their abusive behaviors. As one part of this accountability, men attend specialized DV intervention programs ordered by, and linked to, the courts or justice system. The justice system was informed of offenders' attendance and progress and this intervention was viewed as part of the overall justice response. Because of this linkage between the justice and intervention systems, these programs may be considered "justice-linked."

Inspired by the work of Duluth, as well as broader currents of support for problem-solving courts, justice-linked intervention programs for domestic violence quickly spread throughout North America. With this spread has come considerable development in both the intervention programs themselves and in models of connecting justice and intervention services. The original Duluth intervention program was based on the principles of adult education and was group-based, largely psychoeducational, and focused mostly on re-educating abusive men to be more respectful of women, hold less sexist attitudes and form more egalitarian relationships. Although many investigations (and critiques) assume or describe programs as relatively homogeneous "Duluth-based" re-education programs, surveys of practice reveal that there is a great deal of diversity in what is being offered (Hamilton, Koehler, & Lösel, 2013; Maiuro & Eberle, 2008). Some programs remain largely psychoeducational, while others have adopted cognitive behavioral, narrative, solution-focused or multicomponent/mixed methods of intervention. Innovations have also been made: Programs today vary in length, group size, composition, and structure. There is also considerable variation in the degree of integration between intervention programs and the justice system. Some programs function quite independently of the justice system with limited information sharing, and others work in close collaboration with frequent, open communication throughout the offenders' treatment.

In this chapter, we describe and analyze justice-linked intervention programs for DV offenders across Canada. We first consider various ways that individuals convicted of DV-related offenses access, or are mandated to attend, DV intervention and explore differing levels of coordination and communication between the justice system and intervention services. We then describe the programs themselves, considering issues of program length, modality, therapeutic orientation, content, and associated services to victims of men's abuse. Our aim is to provide an overview of justice-linked domestic violence intervention across Canada, identify core commonalities, and highlight the range of innovative responses being developed. Our hope is that this work will provide a foundation for national research and policy priorities in justice-linked DV perpetrator interventions.

Our review is based on data gathered from a review of online materials combined with interviews of approximately fifty key informants from police, justice ministries, and intervention services across Canada. Interviews took place over a six-month period in the spring of 2015 and covered issues of referrals, information sharing, models of service, and community collaboration. It is important to acknowledge that our review does not cover all DV intervention services. A continuum of DV intervention options is available in Canada, including preventative programs and early intervention/treatment services for men voluntarily seeking help for DV-related issues. These programs were outside the scope of our review though, as noted in the program descriptions, some of the justice-linked programs across Canada also serve men voluntarily seeking help.

Additionally, we concentrated our work on programming directed toward the majority of offenders; specifically, heterosexual men involved in the criminal justice system as a result of offending against women. Interventions specific to female offenders and lesbian, gay, bisexual, transgendered, and questioning (LGBTQ) offenders were not specifically reviewed. Services developed for specific language and cultural minority groups are reviewed and described when they are a key component of a justice-linked intervention response, but otherwise are not covered comprehensively. Finally, our review was limited to justice-linked responses that are community-based. We did not review programs offered to offenders while incarcerated.

Integration within a Justice Response to Domestic Violence

A first important consideration for describing justice-linked DV intervention is how such programs are integrated within the broader justice response to DV. Domestic violence cases present a distinct challenge to the justice system: The accused and the victim often have complex ties and there is considerable pressure from all parties to quickly find a solution that provides safety for the victim, holds the perpetrator accountable for his actions, and still allows for normal family functioning (e.g. parenting, mortgage payments). Moreover, such solutions must take into account the fact that DV crimes vary greatly in severity, context (e.g. among couples intending to remain together, in the process of separating, and who have separated), have a high likelihood of recurrence, and are among the most dangerous to women victims in terms of risk for lethality (Buzawa & Buzawa, 2003; Hanmer & Itzin, 2013).

Specialized problem-solving DV courts and court processes are viewed as one promising way to address these challenges. Problem-solving courts differ from traditional courts in many ways including enhanced training and dedicated time of court personnel; increased collaboration with community service providers; greater capacity to quickly respond to minor offenses; and focus on addressing underlying problems that lead to criminal behavior, generally through justice-linked interventions (Casey & Rottman, 2005; Eley, 2005; Tutty & Koshan, 2013). A growing trend is the implementation of problem-solving courts as a response to domestic violence. Over 350 domestic violence courts are now operating in Canada, Australia, the United Kingdom, and the United States (BC Ministry of Justice, 2014).

In Canada, ten of the thirteen provincial and territorial jurisdictions have a specialized DV court or DV court process (see Table 4.1). In most areas, these courts only operate in larger urban centers (Ontario is an exception, with coverage throughout the province). Nunavut has an alternate justice stream where a range of socially complex offenses are addressed including, but not limited to, domestic violence.

In Canadian regions without DV courts, offenders are typically ordered to attend DV intervention programs following a conviction for a DV-related offense as a condition of their probation order. In many jurisdictions, making an order for DV intervention is part of policy requirements or recommendations for prosecuting lawyers representing the government (Crown Prosecutors in Canada and State Attorneys in the US), with varying levels of specificity around the nature of the programs that must be attended. For example, in the province of Prince Edward Island, the Guidebook of Policies and Procedures for the Conduct of Criminal Prosecution published by the Crown Attorney's Office (2009) specifies that: "Whether or not incarceration is to be imposed, consideration should be given to probation as part of the sentence, with conditions obliging the offender to attend and participate meaningfully in a spousal violence program" (pp. 14–19). Programs typically report back to probation officers on whether the

Table 4.1 Domestic Violence Courts and Court Processes in Canada

Jurisdiction	Year Established	Locations	Aspects of Perpetrator Accountability Where DV Courts Exist		
			Differential Prosecution Streams	Differential Intervention Response	Level of Integration
Alberta	2000	Calgary, Edmonton, Lethbridge, Grand Prairie, Fort McMurray, Airdrie, Medicine Hat	Yes	No	High
BC	2009	Duncan, Nanaimo, Kelowna, Kamloops, Penticton	Some	Yes	Moderate
Manitoba	1990	Winnipeg	Yes	Yes	High
New Brunswick	2007	Moncton	Yes	Yes	High
Newfoundland	Until 2013	No current DV court	–	–	–
Northwest Territories	2011	Yellowknife	Yes	Yes	High
Nova Scotia	2012	Cape Breton Regional Municipality (Sydney)	Yes	Yes	High
Nunavut	*	Across Territory	No	No	Moderate
Ontario	1997	54 courthouses across Ontario and integrated criminal/family court in Toronto	Yes	No	Moderate
PEI		No DV court	–	–	–
Quebec		No DV court	–	–	–
Saskatchewan	2003	Regina, Saskatoon, North Battleford	Yes	No	High
Yukon	2000	Whitehorse, Watson Lake	No	No	Low

* There is no specific DV court process in Nunavut; however, an alternate prosecution model exists that shares many similarities to DV courts and processes many DV cases.

referred offender has successfully completed the program or not. When men fail to complete programs as ordered, they are subject to a potential breach of probation for failing to follow conditions.

Considerably more variation exists in the processes, procedures, and operations in regions where DV courts exist. DV courts vary in the criteria for inclusion, scope (e.g. criminal and/or family), degree of specialization of the justice partners, monitoring, and in the range of court processes that are involved. There are also differences in emphasis, with some courts focused primarily on more efficiently addressing low-risk, first-time offenders and others more focused on the need for differential prosecution of higher-risk offenders.

For the purposes of this chapter, we have highlighted two specific aspects of the DV court system that are most relevant to intervention: the existence of a differential court processing stream for lower- and higher-risk offenders and the extent to which differential prosecution is linked with differential intervention.

Differential Prosecution Streams

The most common model of prosecution for DV courts divides offenders into low and moderate/high-risk streams very early in the court process. Seven of the ten regions in Canada (see Table 4.1) have such a differential prosecution process. Although there are variations across courts, typically, courts running with this model consider high/moderate-risk offenders as those with previous DV charges and/or where the harm to the victim is determined to be too serious to be resolved outside of the traditional justice channels. For accused in this stream, the justice system precedes from charge to conviction to sentencing, with no opportunity for "fast tracking" or systematically delayed sentencing. Offenders are generally ordered to attend intervention as a condition of probation.

A second prosecution stream is reserved for "low-risk" offenders. Those considered low risk are generally first-time offenders accused of incidents where no major harm has come to the victim, where the offense did not occur in the presence of children and the offender did not criminally harass the victim. To enter this stream, offenders usually have to plead guilty to the offense and agree to attend an intervention program. Sentencing is typically delayed until after completion of the program, with reduced judicial consequences for compliance (most often a conditional discharge). A variation of this model makes use of peace bonds, instead of delayed sentencing. For example, in the Calgary DV court, first-time, low-risk offenders can enter a prosecution stream whereby they have their charges stayed and they are given a peace bond by accepting responsibility for the substantive offense and agreeing with the conditions of the bond (which most often includes participation in justice-linked DV intervention program). If the conditions of the bond are not met (e.g. if the DV program is not completed), the charges would be considered breached and the offender would be required to appear again in court.

Other DV courts in Canada have different procedures. For example, in DV courts in Kelowna, Penticton, and Kamloops, British Columbia, the focus has been placed mostly on ensuring greater training and expertise of court staff for DV cases and on improving efficiency of processing. Domestic violence courts expedite processing all but the most serious DV offenses but without any differential prosecution. Courts in the Yukon represent yet another variation. In this region, accused at all levels of risk can enter a domestic violence stream that links intervention and judicial monitoring so long as they plead guilty and agree to imposed conditions. The accused is assessed by probation to determine what services will best meet their needs and the court monitors their progress every two weeks.

Differential Intervention Response

The differential prosecution streams in DV courts are often aimed, in part, at facilitating timely access to intervention programs by processing lower-risk offenders more quickly (Moore, 2009). Differential prosecution steams also create an obvious opportunity for differential intervention, in other words, having different treatment programs for both higher- and lower-risk DV offenders. DV typology scholars have long argued for such differentiation. They advocate for longer and more intensive (e.g. a combination of group and individual versus group alone) interventions for generally violent, antisocial offenders (i.e. those with a history and range of prior offenses and who would be classified as high risk) as compared to low-level or family-only batterers who have a much less extensive and severe history of abuse (Cavanaugh & Gelles, 2005; Stewart, Flight, & Slavin-Stewart, 2013).

A leading model in criminal rehabilitation in general is the risk, needs, responsivity (RNR) model (Andrews & Bonta, 2006, 2010). One of the three core principles of RNR is that the intensity of intervention effort should match the offenders' level of risk to re-offend (RNR "risk principle"). Offenders at low levels of risk to re-offend should be offered less intervention, and those at high risk to re-offend should be offered more intense intervention. This principle of matching service intensity to level of offender risk has received a great deal of support in the empirical literature on general rehabilitation (Gendreau, Smith, & French, 2006; Hanson, Bourgon, Helmus, & Hodgson, 2009). As just one example, on the basis of a meta-analysis of over 13,000 offenders in ninety-seven correctional programs, Lowenkamp, Latessa, and Holsinger (2006) found that programs adhering to the risk principle of the RNR model were associated with up to an 18-percentage point reduction in recidivism rates relative to those that did not. There is a move within the field of DV intervention in general to align programs with the principles of RNR (Radatz & Wright, 2016) and in Canadian correctional services more specifically (Stewart, Gabora, Kropp, & Lee, 2014).

A review of justice-linked, domestic violence interventions across Canada identified that about half of the jurisdictions with differential prosecution also have differential intervention for offenders deemed to be lower or higher risk. Specifically, British Columbia, Manitoba, New Brunswick, the Northwest Territories, and Nova Scotia have at least one DV court that offers differential intervention. In the other half of jurisdictions with differentiated prosecution, the same DV intervention program is ordered for lower- and higher-risk offenders (though, of course, other aspects of judicial processing differ). Where court-linked differentiation in DV intervention does exist, there also tends to be tighter connections between the court and the service providers, so that men judged as being at various levels of risk are assigned to specific intervention programs funded with an understanding that the client group to be served has a defined profile of risk. These programs also tend to offer longer intervention (albeit sometimes only slightly longer) to offenders judged as higher risk.

Regions served by DV courts with differential intervention also have clear systems in place for information sharing and collaboration across justice and intervention services. Service providers in these places typically have full access to the offender's criminal and relationship history, the details of the substantive offense(s), and all risk assessments. The courts, in turn, have detailed information about the offender's attendance and progress at regular intervals through intervention.

The Domestic Violence Treatment Option Court (DVTO) in Yellowknife, Northwest Territories provides one example of court-linked differentiated intervention. In this jurisdiction, the police (RCMP) and the Crown determine the risk level (low or high) of offenders. Low-risk offenders receive a sixteen-hour, cognitive-behavioral program delivered by probation officers over an eight-week period. Offenders are brought back to the DVTO for an update during week four. If the low-risk offenders have not complied with the program requirements, they are sent back to court through the prosecution (i.e. high risk) stream. Offenders deemed at high risk and who are convicted of a DV-related offense receive a probation order to attend a community agency where they receive twenty weeks of group-based narrative therapy along with four individual sessions (forty-four treatment hours).

Another example of court-linked differentiated intervention is the DV court currently being piloted in Nova Scotia. In this program, a formal risk assessment (Ontario Domestic Assault Risk assessment (ODARA) and Spousal Assault Risk Assessment (SARA)) is conducted by the Department of Corrections in partnership with the police to determine which of three streams (low, moderate, or high) is most appropriate for the offender. The lowest-risk offenders participate in a five-week program (four open-group sessions and one individual session to develop a maintenance plan and reflect on learning) called *Second Chance*. Moderate-risk offenders participate in a ten-week, twenty-hour psychoeducational and cognitive behavioral program called *Respectful Relationships*. High-risk offenders are mandated to a seventeen-week, thirty-four-hour, cognitive-behavioral *Relationship Violence* program. The court monitors offenders' progress and participation. All offenders, even those still in the midst of treatment, must reappear in the court within three months. They may also be called to appear in court if the service provider reports that they have failed to attend programming. At sentencing, the judge receives the agreed statement of facts and the outcome of the treatment before passing sentence.

It is important to acknowledge that differentiated intervention can also occur independent of differential processing in court. In British Columbia for example, probation officers assess the level of risk among DV offenders on their caseloads (i.e. post conviction). Offenders assessed as low risk are offered the *Respectful Relationships* program, which is an open, ten-week (two hours per week), cognitive-behavioral group delivered by probation officers. Moderate- and high-risk offenders first complete the *Respectful Relationships* program, and are then referred to a community agency for the seventeen-week, closed, cognitive-behavioral *Relationship Violence* program.

Evaluations of differentiated programming are promising. For example, an evaluation of BC's *Respectful Relationships/Relationship Violence* program by the Research Division of Stroh Health found a 42 percent reduction in spousal assault offending over one year for individuals who completed the *Respectful Relationships* program (i.e. lower risk-offenders) as compared to a group of men who did not receive programming whose reduction in DV offending was between 4.5 percent and 2.4 percent. Similarly, there was a 53 percent reduction in DV offending over one year for individuals who completed the combined *Respectful Relationships/Relationship Violence* as compared to a comparison group of men who received community supervision only (14.6 percent versus 8 percent), despite their higher initial risk level. Effects persisted over a two-year follow-up period; men who completed both components of treatment where less likely to re-offend (BC Ministry of Public Safety and Solicitor General, 2009).

The Yukon DVTO court, which makes use of the same two DV intervention programs (i.e. *Respectful Relationships* and *Relationship Violence* programs) was evaluated by the Canadian Research Institute for Law and the Family (Hornick, Boyes, Tutty, & White, 2005). Overall, the evaluation was quite positive, concluding that this model, which combines a comprehensive justice-system approach with a treatment program for offenders, provided an excellent framework for dealing with spousal assault and abuse. More specifically, in the twelve months following the completion of intervention, 9 percent and 10 percent of the lower-risk and higher-risk offenders, respectively, assaulted their partners, at a rate considerably lower than might have been expected by an analysis of their prior history and in comparison to other evaluations of treatment outcomes. Finally, Stewart, Gabora, Kropp, and Lee (2014) reported that moderate- and high-risk DV offenders incarcerated by Correctional Services Canada and who received intervention matched to their risk level showed statistically significant pre- to post-treatment changes in a range of attitudes and were 69 percent less likely than untreated offenders to be involved in an spousal assault incident following release.

Intervention Programs for Domestic Violence

In addition to understanding how intervention is integrated within the broader court processing of DV cases, it is also important to consider what intervention programs themselves are offering. Programs vary by modality, length, and specialization, and in their use of different theoretical models of change. In the following section, we consider a range of program characteristics along with evidence from DV intervention and related literatures on these program differences.

Program Length

In regions of Canada without differentiated intervention programming for offenders at varying levels of risk (including Alberta, Quebec, Saskatchewan, the Yukon Territories, and regions within provinces not served by DV courts) are almost all between fifteen and twenty weeks in duration. The notable exception is Ontario, which recently shortened its program from sixteen to twelve weeks. Where differentiated services exist, program length generally correlates with the level of offender risk. Programs targeting low-risk men are likely to be eight to twelve weeks in length. One shorter option is the five-week *Second Chance* program currently being piloted in Nova Scotia for offenders assessed as the lowest risk to re-offend. Programs targeting offenders at moderate or high risk for re-offending are typically between sixteen and thirteen weeks in duration. For example, the combined *Respectful Relationships* and *Relationship Violence* programs take a total of twenty-seven weeks to complete. A few justice-linked interventions are of much longer duration. For example, the *Evolve* program in Winnipeg offers men services for ten to twelve months (forty sessions).

A major question for intervention providers, funders, policy makers, and courts is optimal program length. To date, there are no agreed-upon, empirically supported recommendations for the ideal length of treatment for domestic violence. In comparison to other countries, programs in Canada are relatively short. In the USA, most batterer intervention program standards require a minimum of twenty-four to twenty-six weeks of service (Maiuro & Eberle, 2008). In the UK, the *Respect* organization, a major DV intervention accrediting body, requires a minimum of sixty hours of group work and twenty-four hours of individual work over six months (Blacklock & Debbonaire, 2012). This is slightly longer than the average program across Europe; generally a minimum of twenty weeks (Koehler, Lösel, Akoensi, & Humphreys, 2013). In Australia, programs tend to be shorter (twelve to eighteen weeks) which, according to multiple national and international stakeholders testifying for a recent in-depth review, is too short to be effective (Neave, Faulkner, & Nicholson, 2016).

There is limited research in the area of DV intervention to bolster (or counter) these opinions and recommendations. One of the only studies that compared outcomes of varying lengths of treatment is Gondolf's (2001) multisite comparison of programs. He found that the majority of outcomes did not vary across programs according to their length (programs compared lasted between three and nine months). However, Gondolf did note that the shorter and longer programs he evaluated had very different levels of integration with the justice system and, therefore, *could not* be compared on the basis of treatment length alone.

Some information, though, can be gleaned from research on the length of time necessary to prompt changes with respect to other types of problems. Empirical examination of the length of time needed to prompt change in outpatient psychotherapy for voluntary clients experiencing problems such as depression, anxiety, and other common psychological problems find that twenty sessions of intervention are needed to achieve the maximum level of benefit for most people (Harnett, O'Donovan, & Lambert, 2010; Lambert, 2007). In the criminal rehabilitation literature, it is generally recommended that treatment be reserved for those who are at high risk to re-offend, research suggests that a minimum of 100 hours, or six months, of intervention is needed to make a significant difference in rates of recidivism for this group

(Abrams, Terry, & Franke, 2011; Bourgon & Armstrong, 2005; Lipsey, 1999; Makarios, Sperber, & Latessa, 2014; Sperber, Latessa, & Makarios, 2013).

Program Modality

The vast majority of justice-linked intervention programs offered to DV offenders in Canada are group-modality programs with a minimum of six and maximum of twelve offenders per group. Ontario, which has a recommended *minimum* group size of fifteen, is the exception. Couples therapy and individual therapy are offered by some agencies, but very seldom as a first point of access for offenders attending programs as a result of a court or probation mandate. A sizable minority of programs, and most narrative programs, also offer a few individual sessions as a standard component of their DV program (individual sessions are also often a non-standard part of intervention for men who cannot be served in a group, such as those with significantly compromised cognitive skills or those who deal with psychiatric issues). Programs that offer both group and individual therapy typically hold individual sessions before group to focus on issues of engagement. This integration of individual sessions with group work is increasingly recommended as a method for creating and maintaining change in areas including parenting (Lundahl, Nimer, & Parsons, 2006) and fathering (Bronte-Tinkew et al., 2007).

Programs in Quebec are most unusual within the Canadian context. In this province, justice-linked DV intervention begins with a telephone intake followed by at least two individual meetings to assess group readiness, needs, motivation, types of violent behavior, and other treatment needs. Men who need extra preparation to enter a group setting are then met individually to problem solve and set goals, and for assistance in addressing reluctance. These meetings range from two to eight sessions. After motivation and readiness are established, men attend group-based services (generally twenty sessions). This model of practice (i.e. individual sessions to establish readiness) is a component of service in some other agencies across Canada (e.g. *Calgary Counselling Center* in Alberta, *Bridges Institute* in Nova Scotia) but is not a standard component of the provincial/territorial response (and is not generally funded in the justice-linked intervention envelope). The Quebec model is also unique in its provision of post-group follow-up meetings at six-, twelve-, and eighteen-month intervals.

Some further variation in program modality is associated with programming provided in agencies serving First Nations, Métis, and Inuit clients. These agencies are most likely to offer flexible programming that includes a mix of individual, group, and dyadic marital therapy sessions as part of its services to DV offenders. For example, the *Rankin Inlet Spousal Abuse Program* in Nunavut provides programming based on a mixture of traditional knowledge and more conventional counseling. Men accessing this program receive six one-hour sessions of individual counseling and twenty-nine two-hour group sessions (held twice weekly). Elders are often invited to the group counseling sessions to talk about family life, and non-violent dispute resolution, and to instill pride in traditional practices. A parallel program is provided for victims of abuse and in some cases family members and couples also have the option of working together to resolve issues.

Program Theoretical Orientation

Reviews and commentaries on intervention programs for men who have assaulted their intimate partners typically describe programs as Duluth-based, feminist, psychoeducational (as opposed to therapeutic), and focused on challenging offenders' patriarchal and sexist views with the aim of replacing them with more egalitarian beliefs (e.g. Graham-Kevan, 2007). The current survey of programs offered across Canada reveals that this generalized description is inaccurate. Only about one-third of programs state that their primary mode of intervention is psychoeducational. The other two-thirds are about evenly divided between those that describe their theoretical orientation as cognitive behavioral and those that are narrative (as well as a smattering of other orientations mentioned, including solution-focused, strength-based, humanistic, group process-oriented, and mindfulness-based).

Many programs describe using a combination of perspectives. Agencies providing services to cultural minorities often indicate that programming has been adapted to the specific population being served. Programs specifically targeting lower-risk offenders are most likely to be psychoeducational or a mix of psychoeducation and cognitive-behavioral therapy (CBT) whereas programs targeting moderate- and high-risk offenders in Canada are somewhat more likely to report using narrative methods. It is also relevant to note that, although discussion of gender roles, male socialization, and a gendered-based understanding of violence are common, programs are generally not dominated by content on sexism, patriarchy, and men's use of power. Instead, a fairly broad range of potential contributors to men's abuse is discussed.

Although psychoeducational, cognitive-behavioral and narrative-therapeutic orientations share some fundamental assumptions about key mechanisms, or drivers, of change (e.g. the need for a respectful and collaborative relationship between therapist and client), each orientation also advances different ideas about the nature of dysfunction, the proximal causes of abuse, and the ways in which treatment can best be used to promote change. Detailed descriptions are available for narrative therapy in Augusta-Scott and Dankwort (2002) and Jenkins (1990), CBT in Murphy and Eckhardt (2005), response-based approaches by Todd, Weaver-Dunlop, and Ogden (2014), restorative justice approaches (Grauwiler & Mills, 2004; Augusta-Scott, Harrison, & Singer, 2017, Chapter 10; Augusta-Scott, Goodmark, & Pennell, 2017, Chapter 11; and Augusta-Scott, 2017, Chapter 12, all this volume), and strengths or solution-based therapy methods in Lehmann and Simmons (2009).

Evaluations of interventions using each of these specific intervention models have also been published. Canadian qualitative and/or quantitative evaluations have been conducted for the *Responsible Choices for Men* narrative program

(McGregor, Tutty, Babins-Wagner, & Gill, 2002; Tutty & Babins-Wagner, 2016) and the Ontario-based programs with a mix of psychoeducational, motivation enhancing, cognitive-behavioral, and process-oriented practice (Quann, 2006; Scott, King, McGinn, & Hosseini, 2011, 2013; Tutty, Bidgood, Rothery, & Bidgood, 2001), with generally positive results. Additionally, as described earlier, evaluations have been conducted on the psychoeducational and cognitive-behavioral *Respectful Relationships* and *Relationship Violence* programs (Hornick et al., 2005; BC Ministry of Public Safety and Solicitor General, 2009).

Although theorists and practitioners often debate the merits of one theoretical orientation over another, research comparing treatments continues to demonstrate that most produce positive effects. For example, Mills, Boracas, and Ariel (2013) recently compared outcomes of psychoeducational/cognitive-behavioral batterer intervention to restorative justice-based treatment and found no significant difference in DV re-offending over follow-up.

These findings are consistent with those in the psychotherapy and criminal-rehabilitation literature more generally (Marcus, O'Connell, Norris, & Sawaqdeh, 2014). Although not specific to programs for men who abused partners, the work of Lipsey (2009) is particularly relevant. Lipsey recently demonstrated that all interventions that embody "therapeutic" philosophies—including CBT but also other forms of counseling such as family therapy, group therapy, individual psychotherapy, and mentoring—more effectively prompt change among young offenders than interventions based on strategies of control or coercion such as surveillance, deterrence, and discipline. However, within the category of therapeutic programs, no specific type of therapeutic intervention emerged as superior; rather, programs implemented with high quality (e.g. with well-trained staff, a clear program manual, supervision) were more effective. Given these results, future research in the area of DV intervention might profitably turn to the examination of specific DV intervention components (e.g. extent to which program includes behavioral practice, relies on insight, etc.) and contexts (quality of training and supervision) that are most predictive of success, rather than continue to debate the correct, and incorrect, theoretical orientation for DV intervention work.

Program Content

The importance of examining program components and contexts (as opposed to theoretical orientation) is further underscored by our content review. Despite variations in the length, theoretical orientation, and modality, most justice-linked DV intervention programs in Canada cover much of the same basic content. Descriptions of virtually all programs include sessions devoted to defining and describing abuse in intimate partner relationships and raising awareness of the impact of this abuse on others. Most programs also include material that prompts offenders to take responsibility for past abuse. In addition to this abuse-specific material, virtually all programs include a session on recognizing and managing intense emotions and a session on some aspect of skill development/problem-solving for difficulties in relationships. Often this includes a discussion of warning signs for conflict or abuse, awareness of self-talk, and some material to prompt the development of healthier relationships. This broad consistency in intervention content suggests consensus on *core components* of DV intervention as awareness, impact, responsibility, emotion regulation, and skill development for abuse avoidance.

Other components of programming are common, but not universal. Narrative programs and programs targeted at higher-risk offenders often include material about aspects of men's inner experience of shame, trauma, grief, and loss. Material on healing and repair, stress-management/relaxation or self-care is also used in programs of longer length. More unusual is program content on brain functioning, habit formation, distraction, and defense mechanisms. Surprisingly, relapse prevention/strategies to avoid recidivism are *explicitly* mentioned as an intervention topic in only about half of programs, though it is quite possible that such discussions are included as part of other topics.

Two areas of program content that deserve specific attention are substance use and parenting/co-parenting. The misuse of substances, especially alcohol abuse, has been clearly identified as a major cofactor in the etiology of domestic violence (Foran & O'Leary, 2008; Livingston, 2011). Moreover, continued problematic use of substances is one of the best current predictors of DV recidivism (Jewell & Wormith, 2010; Jones & Gondolf, 2001). These strong associations between substance use and DV offending have led some to suggest that interventions aimed at reducing violent behavior will be only marginally effective if co-occurring substance misuse problems are ignored (Easton et al., 2007; Fals-Stewart & Kennedy, 2005; Stuart et al., 2013). Our review found that justice-linked DV intervention programs in Canada often cover substance use as a specific content area in one or two sessions. In addition, DV offenders with substance use problems are typically court-referred to attend treatment for addictions; generally, such treatment is delivered by separate agencies with specific expertise in addictions and with little communication between the DV and addictions services.

Although non-integration is the norm, a handful of agencies across Canada provide specialized integrated intervention for offenders with both DV and substance use issues. One example is the *Sobering Effect* program offered by the YWCA Sheriff King Home in partnership with the Alberta Alcohol and Drug Abuse Commission in Calgary. Men attending this program have open files in both agencies and make contact with the program three times a week for fourteen weeks (Tutty, Ogden, & Warrell, 2011). Agencies serving Indigenous populations also often offer services in both DV and addictions, with varying levels of integration across services.

A second major co-occurring issue is men's perpetration of child maltreatment. Rates of overlap of men's perpetration of domestic violence and child physical abuse are high (Edleson, 1999; Jouriles, McDonald, Smith Slep, Heyman, & Garrido, 2008). Moreover, domestic violence is a triggering or compounding factor in a majority of cases referred to child protective services

(Fallon et al., 2015; Trocmé et al., 2010; US Department of Health and Human Services, 2013). In other words, the families of many of the men involved with justice-linked intervention are also involved with child protection services due to concerns about men's ability to safely parent their children. In recognition of this overlap, about two-thirds of justice-linked DV programs in Canada include material on fathering, generally in one or two sessions. These sessions generally focus on the impact of domestic violence on children, the need to be accountable to children, and on the value of being a better role model. Very few programs, however, provide integrated intervention with respect to domestic violence and parenting (i.e. there is no evidence for specialized tracks, assessment of need for parenting intervention, or additional services within the context of justice-linked intervention for domestically violent men as fathers). Instead, a number of agencies across Canada are offering, or referring to, separate intervention services to meet the needs of domestically violent men as fathers, such as *Caring Dads* or a similar fathering program (see Pennell & Brandt, 2017, Chapter 14 this volume).

Group Composition

There is ongoing debate about whether DV offenders with varying risk profiles should, or should not, attend intervention groups together. As previously reviewed, some justice-linked programs in Canada stream lower- and higher-risk offenders into different programs. More often, offenders at varying levels of risk for re-offending are grouped with self-referred men and with men referred by other social services (e.g. child protection, addiction services).

Some evidence from the literature on general criminal rehabilitation suggests that mixing lower-risk and higher-risk men may be detrimental both to the offenders so grouped and to the service provider's budgets (Bonta, Wallace-Capretta, & Rooney, 2000; Marlowe, Festinger, Lee, Dugosh, & Benasutti, 2006). There are several suggested reasons for this finding. One is that placing low-risk offenders with those at higher risk creates an opportunity for modeling antisocial behavior and for creating new peer associates who are likely to support and reinforce attitudes and behaviors supportive of offending (e.g. partner blaming; Lowenkamp & Latessa, 2005). Social comparison may play a role, as lower-risk men in mixed groups may continue to rationalize and minimize their abusive behavior by comparing themselves to the higher-risk men. However, it is important to note that there have been no studies examining this issue for the treatment of DV; thus, the extent to which these findings are applicable is unclear (see Radatz & Wright, 2016, for further discussion).

Associated Services to Victims of Men's Abuse

From their inception, a primary aim of justice-linked DV intervention has been victim safety. Sharing information between professionals working with victims of DV and those working with perpetrators is seen as critical to victim safety.

At the beginning of the movement toward justice-linked DV intervention, programs for DV perpetrators were very closely aligned with women's advocacy services and there were high levels of information sharing and collaboration. Intervention with men always involved contact with victims of men's abuse for safety planning and often as a way to monitor men's change. Many agencies offered services directly to female victims or were closely partnered with agencies to provide this service. Current recommendations for best practice continue to emphasize the need for information sharing as part of DV services (Office of the Chief Coroner for Ontario, 2015).

In our current review of programs across Canada we found that agencies offering *both* interventions to men arrested for DV offenses and parallel treatment options for female victims are in the minority. *Turning Point* in PEI, along with a few larger, multiservice agencies (e.g. individual mental health services, family counseling in addition to DV) are exceptions. More commonly, justice-linked programs concentrate on providing intervention to men and include partner contact services to female victims during an offender's treatment. This contact is generally for the purpose of describing offender services and linking the victim to community resources for safety planning. Limited additional information is shared and feedback from victims is not systematically used to inform men's treatment or to monitor progress. A small number of agencies offering justice-linked DV intervention (in New Brunswick, Manitoba, Saskatchewan) have stopped partner contact altogether; and throughout Newfoundland, victim contact is not a standard component of service.

On the other end of the spectrum, some of the newer differentiated DV court models have comprehensive information-sharing agreements. Although victim and offender services are still typically offered by separate agencies, detailed protocols are in place to share risk-related information and respond collaboratively to higher-risk cases. Additionally, programs in the north and in First Nation communities often offer a holistic model of DV offender intervention that can include all members of a family. Services may include individual counseling for victims and family members and/or couples' therapy alongside individual and/or group work for DV offenders. Examples include services in Nunavut and the Northern Society for Domestic Peace in British Columbia. These agencies offer a variety of parallel services to women, men, children, and families using a "family wrap-around" philosophy of service that support intra-agency collaboration and information sharing.

Summary and Reflections

To develop national research and policy priorities in justice-linked DV perpetrator interventions it is useful to understand the currently available programming. In this review of Canadian programs we found variation in many aspects of services across (and often within) jurisdictions including: degree of integration with the justice system, length of intervention, associated services to victims of men's abuse, and the theoretical orientation of the program.

Other aspects of service, including program modality and content, were more broadly similar. In most Canadian communities, including Quebec and Ontario (Canada's most populous provinces), a "one-size-fits-all" model of intervention is the norm. However, a growing trend is for service intensity to vary according to level of risk, with longer services being offered to men at higher risk for offending and shorter services for those identified as being of lower risk to re-offend.

In consideration of these observations, a number of research priorities emerge. The first concerns program differentiation. Although most developed nations, including the US, Europe, and Australia, rely on a single program to serve the needs of all offenders, there is growing international consensus that differentiated services are needed. The question is, on what basis differentiation should proceed? Canada has focused on differentiation on the basis of offender risk. From the general literature on criminal rehabilitation, we can expect (but need to confirm) that length of intervention will interact with level of offender risk such that those men at high risk to re-offend will show change only when enrolled in longer and/or more intense interventions. Other potentially salient differences between offenders advanced by models of differentiation include offender neuropsychology (Bueso-Izquierdo, Hart, Hidalgo-Ruzzante, Kropp, & Perez-Garcia, 2015), type of violence (Aaron & Beaulaurier, 2016), personality typology (Cameranesi, 2016), and cultural/racial background (Spiropoulos, Salisbury, & Van Voorhis, 2014). It is not yet clear which, if any, of these dimensions may also be central to offering effective intervention.

A second area of research concerns the programs themselves. There is considerable debate about the most appropriate approach (e.g. CBT versus narrative versus feminist re-education) and content (e.g. whether to include self-care). However, considering the current landscape of interventions, along with emerging literature on predictors of success, suggests that examining specific intervention content and theoretical orientation is likely unprofitable. Programs across Canada are broadly similar in what they are offering and, considering past research, there is little reason to expect therapeutic orientation to carry much variance in terms of outcome. In light of these findings, consideration might be given to exploring the value of offering lower-risk men a range of choices for intervention, so long as they cover some core program content. Candidate services could include traditional cognitive-behavioral or narrative group therapy, appropriately targeted DV couples therapy (Tutty & Babins-Wagner, 2017, Chapter 13 this volume) or integrated DV and fathering intervention. An index of program quality, specific to DV intervention services, would also be a helpful addition to the literature and to studies of DV interventions. It would be interesting to determine if having a range of services available might lead to the greater engagement of clients and the improvement of connections overall between DV perpetrator services and other community social service resources.

Finally, careful attention needs to be paid to the changing models of information sharing and collaboration. It is also important to remember that justice-linked DV programs are embedded within a system that varies in terms of the extent of punitiveness, processing time, and the degree of integration between the courts and intervention programs. At the moment, some Canadian communities and systems have strong collaborative models of service provision that tightly link justice, violence against women, and men's intervention sectors. Other programs function much more independently of the justice system and/or from women's advocates, and are providing service outside of strong, collaborative partnerships with women's advocates. We need to develop a better understanding of the how varying degrees of integration between community treatment providers, justice, and victim-serving agencies contribute to the outcomes of intervention, and develop protocols and legislation that supports those models of service that contribute most to ensuring women's safety.

In conclusion, Canada has a diversity of justice-linked DV intervention programs and is fertile ground for researching and developing models of intervention that will ensure the future safety of women victimized by abusive men and effectively rehabilitate DV offenders. This review has helped describe the landscape of service and identify questions most likely to advance the field.

References

Aaron, S. M. & Beaulaurier, R. L. (2016). The need for new emphasis on batterer's intervention programs. *Trauma Violence & Abuse*. Advance Online Publication. doi:10.1177/1524838015622440

Abrams, L. S., Terry, D., & Franke, T. M. (2011). Community-based juvenile reentry services: The effects of service dosage on juvenile and adult recidivism. *Journal of Offender Rehabilitation, 50*(8), 492–510. doi:10.1080/10509674.2011.596919

Andrews, D. A. & Bonta, J. (2006). *The psychology of criminal conduct* (4th ed.). Newark, NJ: LexisNexis.

Andrews, D. A. & Bonta, J. (2010). Rehabilitating criminal justice policy and practice. *Psychology, Public Policy, and Law, 16*(1), 39–55. doi:10.1037/a0018362

Augusta-Scott, T. (2017). Preparing men to help the women they abused achieve just outcomes: A restorative approach. In T. Augusta-Scott, K. Scott, & L. Tutty (Eds.), *Innovations in interventions to address intimate partner violence: Research and practice*. New York, NY: Routledge.

Augusta-Scott, T. & Dankwort, J. (2002). Partner abuse group intervention: Lessons from education and narrative therapy approaches. *Journal of Interpersonal Violence, 17*(7), 783–805. doi:10.1177/0886260502017007006

Augusta-Scott, T., Goodmark, L., & Pennell, J. (2017). Restorative justice, domestic violence and the law: A panel discussion. In T. Augusta-Scott, K. Scott, & L. Tutty (Eds.), *Innovations in interventions to address intimate partner violence: Research and practice*. New York, NY: Routledge.

Augusta-Scott, T., Harrison, P., & Singer, V. (2017). Creating safety, respect and equality for women: Lessons from the intimate partner violence and restorative justice movements. In T. Augusta-Scott, K. Scott, & L. Tutty (Eds.), *Innovations in interventions to address intimate partner violence: Research and practice*. New York, NY: Routledge.

BC Ministry of Justice (2014). *Framework for domestic violence courts in British Columbia.* Retrieved from: www2.gov.bc.ca/assets/gov/law-crime-and-justice/criminal-justice/victims-of-crime/vs-info-for-professionals/public/dv-courts-framework.pdf.

BC Ministry of Public Safety and Solicitor General (2009). *Revealing research and evaluation: Relationship violence prevention program.* Retrieved from: www2.gov.bc.ca/assets/gov/law-crime-and-justice/criminal-justice/corrections/research-evaluation/issue-1.pdf.

Blacklock, N. & Debbonaire, T. (2012). *The respect accreditation standard* (2nd ed.). Retrieved from: http://respect.uk.net/wp-content/themes/respect/assets/files/accreditation-standard.pdf.

Bonta, J., Wallace-Capretta, S., & Rooney J. (2000). A quasi-experimental evaluation of an intensive rehabilitation supervision program. *Criminal Justice and Behavior, 27*(3), 312–329. doi:10.1177/0093854800027003003

Bourgon, G. & Armstrong, B. (2005). Transferring the principles of effective treatment into a "real world" prison setting. *Criminal Justice and Behavior, 32*(1), 3–25. doi:10.1177/0093854804270618

Bronte-Tinkew, J., Carrano, J., Allen, T., Bowie, L., Mbawa, K., & Matthews, G. (2007). *Elements of promising practice for fatherhood programs: Evidence-based research findings on programs for fathers.* Gaithersburg, MD: US Department of Health and Human Services, Office of Family Assistance, National Responsible Fatherhood Clearinghouse. Retrieved from: www.fatherhood.gov/content/nrfc-promising-practices.

Bueso-Izquierdo, N., Hart, S. D., Hidalgo-Ruzzante, N., Kropp, P. R., & Perez-Garcia, M. (2015). The mind of the male batterer: A neuroscience perspective. *Aggression and Violent Behaviour, 25,* 199–384. doi:10.1016/j.avb.2015.09.009

Buzawa, E. S. & Buzawa, C. G. (2003). *Domestic violence: The criminal justice response.* Thousand Oaks, CA: Sage.

Cameranesi, M. (2016). Battering typologies, attachment insecurity, and personality disorders: A comprehensive literature review. *Aggression and Violent Behavior, 28,* 29–46. doi:10.1016/j.avb.2016.03.005

Casey, P. & Rottman, D. (2005). Problem-solving courts: Models and trends. *The Justice System Journal, 26*(1), 35–56. Retrieved from: www.jstor.org.myaccess.library.utoronto.ca/stable/27977213.

Cavanaugh, M. & Gelles, R. (2005). The utility of male domestic violence offender typologies: New directions for research, policy, and practice. *Journal of Interpersonal Violence, 20*(2), 155–166. doi:10.1177/0886260504268763

Crown Attorney's Office. (2009). *Guide book of policies for the conduct of criminal prosecutions in Prince Edward Island.* Retrieved from: www.gov.pe.ca/photos/original/jps_crown conduc.pdf.

Easton, C. J., Mandel, D. L., Hunkele, K. A., Nich, C., Rounsaville, B. J., & Carroll, K.M. (2007). A cognitive behavioral therapy for alcohol-dependent domestic violence offenders: An integrated substance abuse–domestic violence treatment approach (SADV). *American Journal on Addictions, 16*(1), 24–31. doi:10.1080/10550490601077809

Edleson, J. L. (1999). The overlap between child maltreatment and woman battering. *Violence Against Women, 5,* 134–154. doi:10.1177/107780129952003

Eley, S. (2005). Changing practices: The specialised domestic violence court process. *The Howard Journal, 44*(2), 113–124. doi:10.1111/j.1468-2311.2005.00361.x

Fallon, B., Van Wert, M., Trocmé, N., MacLaurin, B., Sinha, V., Lefebvre, R., . . . & Goel, S. (2015). *Ontario Incidence Study of Reported Child Abuse and Neglect—2013* (OIS-2013). Toronto, ON: Child Welfare Research Portal.

Fals-Stewart, W. & Kennedy, C. (2005). Addressing intimate partner violence in substance-abuse treatment. *Journal of Substance Abuse Treatment, 29*(1), 5–17. doi:10.1016/j.jsat.2005. 03.001

Foran, H. M. & O'Leary, K. D. (2008). Alcohol and intimate partner violence: A meta-analytic review. *Clinical Psychology Review, 28*(7), 1222–1234. doi:10.1016/j.cpr.2008.05. 001

Gendreau, P., Smith, P., & French, S. (2006). The theory of effective correctional intervention: Empirical status and future directions. *Taking stock: The status of criminological theory, Volume 15, Advances in Criminological Theory* (pp. 419–446). Piscataway, NJ: Transaction.

Gondolf, E. W. (2001). Limitations of experimental evaluation of batterer programs. *Trauma, Violence, & Abuse, 2*(1), 79–88. doi:10.1177/1524838001002001005

Graham-Kevan, N. (2007). Domestic violence: Research and implications for batterer programmes in Europe. *European Journal on Criminal Policy and Research, 13*(3), 213–225. doi:10.1007/s10610-007-9045-4

Grauwiler, P. & Mills, L. G. (2004). Moving beyond the criminal justice paradigm: A radical restorative justice approach to intimate abuse. *Journal of Sociology & Social Welfare, 31*(1), 49–69.

Hamilton, L., Koehler, J., & Lösel, F. (2013). Domestic violence perpetrator programs in Europe, part I: A survey of current practice. *International Journal of Offender Therapy and Comparative Criminology, 57*(10), 1189–1205. doi:10.1177/0306624X12469506

Hanmer, J. & Itzin, C. (Eds.) (2013). *Home truths about domestic violence: Feminist influences on policy and practice—A reader.* New York, NY: Routledge.

Hanson, R., Bourgon, G., Helmus, L., & Hodgson, S. (2009). The principles of effective correctional treatment also apply to sexual offenders: A meta-analysis. *Criminal Justice and Behavior, 36*(9), 865–891. doi:10.1177/0093854809338545

Harnett, P., O'Donovan, A., & Lambert, M. (2010). The dose response relationship in psychotherapy: Implications for social policy. *Clinical Psychologist, 14*(2), 39–44. doi:10. 1080/13284207.2010.500309

Hornick, J. P., Boyes, M., Tutty, L., & White, L. (2005). *The domestic violence treatment option (DVTO), Whitehorse, Yukon: Final evaluation report.* Retrieved from: www.crilf.ca/ Documents/Domestic%20Violence%20Treatment%20Option%20-%20Final%20 Report%20-%20Oct%202005.pdf.

Jenkins, A. (1990). *Invitations to responsibility.* Adelaide: Dulwich Centre Publications.

Jewell, L. M. & Wormith, J. S. (2010). Variables associated with attrition from domestic violence treatment programs targeting male batterers. *Criminal Justice and Behavior, 37*(10), 1086–1113. doi:10.1177/0093854810376815

Jones, A. S. & Gondolf, E. W. (2001). Time-varying risk factors for reassault among batterer program participants. *Journal of Family Violence, 16*(4), 345–359. doi:10.1023/ A:1012268725273

Jouriles, E. N., McDonald, R., Smith Slep, A. M., Heyman, R. E., & Garrido, E. (2008). Child abuse in the context of domestic violence: Prevalence, explanations, and practice implications. *Violence and Victims, 23*(2), 221–235.

Koehler, J., Lösel, F., Akoensi, T., & Humphreys, D. (2013). A systematic review and meta-analysis on the effects of young offender treatment programs in Europe. *Journal of Experimental Criminology, 9*(1), 19–43. doi:10.1007/s11292-012-9159-7

Lambert, M. (2007). Presidential address: What we have learned from a decade of research aimed at improving psychotherapy outcome in routine care. *Psychotherapy Research, 17*(1), 1–14. doi:10.1080/10503300601032506

Lehmann, P. & Simmons, C. A. (2009). The state of the batterer intervention programs: An analytical discussion. In P. Lehmann & C. A. Simmons (Eds.), *Strengths-based batterer intervention: A new paradigm in ending family violence* (pp. 3–38). New York, NY: Springer.

Lipsey, M. W. (1999). Can intervention rehabilitate serious delinquents? *The Annals of the American Academy of Political and Social Science, 564*(1), 142–166. doi:10.1177/0002 71629956400109

Lipsey, M. W. (2009). The primary factors that characterize effective interventions with juvenile offenders: A meta-analytic overview. *Victims & Offenders, 4*(2), 124–147. doi:10.1080/15564880802612573

Livingston, M. (2011). A longitudinal analysis of alcohol outlet density and domestic violence. *Addiction, 106*(5), 919–925. doi:10.1111/j.1360-0443.2010.03333.x

Lowenkamp, C. T. & Latessa, E. J. (2005). Increasing the effectiveness of correctional programming through the risk principle: Identifying offenders for residential placement. *Criminology & Public Policy, 4*(2), 263–290. doi:10.1111/j.1745-9133.2005.00021.x

Lowenkamp, C. T., Latessa, E. J., & Holsinger, A. M. (2006). The risk principle in action: What have we learned from 13,676 offenders and 97 correctional programs? *Crime & Delinquency, 52*(1), 77–93. doi:10.1177/0011128705281747

Lundahl, B. W., Nimer, J., & Parsons, B. (2006). Preventing child abuse: A meta-analysis of parent training programs. *Research on Social Work Practice, 16*(3), 251–262. doi:10. 1177/1049731505284391

McGregor, M., Tutty, L., Babins-Wagner, R., & Gill, M. (2002). The long term impact of group treatment for partner abuse. *Canadian Journal of Community Mental Health, 21*(1), 67–84.

Maiuro, R. D. & Eberle, J. A. (2008). State standards for domestic violence perpetrator treatment: Current status, trends, and recommendations. *Violence and Victims, 23*(2), 133–155. doi:010.1891/0886-6708.23.2.133

Makarios, M., Sperber, K. G., & Latessa, E. J. (2014). Treatment dosage and the risk principle: A refinement and extension. *Journal of Offender Rehabilitation, 53*(5), 334–350. doi:10.1080/10509674.2014.922157

Marcus, D. K., O'Connell, D., Norris, A. L., & Sawaqdeh, A. (2014). Is the Dodo bird endangered in the 21st century? A meta-analysis of treatment comparison studies. *Clinical Psychology Review, 34*(7), 519–530. doi:10.1016/j.cpr.2014.08.001

Marlowe, D. B., Festinger, D. S., Lee, P. A., Dugosh, K. L., & Benasutti, K. M. (2006). Matching judicial supervision to clients' risk status in drug court. *Crime & Delinquency, 52*(1), 52–76. doi:10.1177/0011128705281746

Mills, L. G., Barocas, B., & Ariel, B. (2013). The next generation of court-mandated domestic violence treatment: A comparison study of batterer intervention and restorative justice programs. *Journal of Experimental Criminology, 9*(1), 65–90. 10.1007/s11292-012-9164-x

Moore, S. (2009). *Two decades of specialized domestic violence courts: A review of the literature.* Retrieved from: www.courtinnovation.org/sites/default/files/DV_Court_Lit_Review. pdf.

Murphy, C. M. & Eckhardt, C. I. (2005). *Treating the abusive partner: An individualized cognitive-behavioral approach.* New York, NY: Guilford Press.

Neave, M., Faulkner, P., & Nicholson, T. (2016). *Royal Commission into Family Violence: Summary and recommendations.* Retrieved from: http://files.rcfv.com.au/Reports/Final/RCFV-All-Volumes.pdf.

Office of the Chief Coroner for Ontario. (2015). *Domestic Violence Death Review Committee 2013–14 Annual Report.* Toronto, ON, Canada. Retrieved from: www.mcscs.jus.gov.on.ca/sites/default/files/content/mcscs/docs/ec165340.pdf.

Pence, E., Paymar, M., Ritmeester, T., & Shepard, M. (1993). *Education groups for men who batter: The Duluth model.* New York, NY: Springer.

Pennell, J. & Brandt, E. (2017). Men who abuse intimate partners: Their evaluation of a responsible fathering program. In T. Augusta-Scott, K. Scott, & L. Tutty (Eds.), *Innovations in interventions to address intimate partner violence: Research and practice.* New York, NY: Routledge.

Quann, N. (2006). *Offender profile and recidivism among domestic violence offenders in Ontario.* Department of Justice Canada, Research and Statistics Division. Retrieved from: www.justice.gc.ca/eng/rp-pr/csj-sjc/crime/rr06_fv3-rr06_vf3/rr06_fv3.pdf.

Radatz, D. L. & Wright, E. M. (2016). Integrating the principles of effective intervention into batterer intervention programming: The case for moving toward more evidence-based programming. *Violence, Trauma & Abuse, 17*(1), 72–87. doi:10.1177/15248380 14566695

Scott, K. L., King, C., McGinn, H., & Hosseini, N. (2011). Effects of motivational enhancement on immediate outcomes of batterer intervention. *Journal of Family Violence, 26*(2), 139–149. doi:10.1007/s10896-010-9353-1

Scott, K. L., King, C., McGinn, H., & Hosseini, N. (2013). The (dubious?) benefits of second chances in batterer intervention programs. *Journal of Interpersonal Violence, 28*(8), 1657–1671. doi:10.1177/0886260512468321

Sperber, K., Latessa, E., & Makarios, M. (2013). Examining the interaction between level of risk and dosage of treatment. *Criminal Justice and Behavior, 40*(3), 338–348. doi:10.1177/0093854812467942

Spiropoulos, G. V., Salisbury, E. J., & Van Voorhis, P. V. (2014). Moderators of correctional treatment success: An exploratory study of racial differences. *International Journal of Offender Therapy and Comparative Criminology, 58*(7), 835–860. doi:10.1177/0306624X13492999

Stewart, L. A., Flight, J., & Slavin-Stewart, C. (2013). Applying effective corrections principles (RNR) to partner abuse interventions. *Partner Abuse, 4*(4), 494–534. doi:10.1891/1946-6560.4.4.494

Stewart, L. A., Gabora, N., Kropp, P. R., & Lee, Z. (2014). Effectiveness of risk-needs-responsivity-based family violence programs with male offenders. *Journal of Family Violence, 29*(2), 151–164. doi:10.1007/s10896-013-9575-0

Stuart, G. L., Shorey, R. C., Moore, T. M., Ramsey, S. E., Kahler, C. W., O'Farrell, T. J., . . . & Monti, P. M. (2013). Randomized clinical trial examining the incremental efficacy of a 90-minute motivational alcohol intervention as an adjunct to standard batterer intervention for men. *Addiction, 108*(8), 1376–1384. doi:10.1111/add.12142

Todd, N., Weaver-Dunlop, G., & Ogden, C. (2014). Approaching the subject of violence: A response-based approach to working with men who have abused others. *Violence Against Women, 20*(9), 1117–1137. doi:10.1177/1077801214549638

Trocmé, N., Fallon, B., MacLaurin, B., Sinha, V., Black, T., Fast, E., . . . & Holroyd, J. (2010). Characteristics of children and families. In L. Milner (Eds.), *Canadian Incidence Study of Reported Child Abuse and Neglect—2008: Major Findings.* Ottawa: PHAC. Retrieved from: http://cwrp.ca/sites/default/files/publications/en/CIS-2008_Child_Family_Characteristics.pdf.

Tutty, L. M. & Babins-Wagner, R. (2016). Outcomes and recidivism in mandated batterer intervention before and after introducing a specialized domestic violence court. *Journal of Interpersonal Violence*. Advance Online Publication. doi:10.1177/0886 260516647005

Tutty, L. M. & Babins-Wagner, R. (2017). Strengthening families: A pilot couples program for intimate partner violence and substance abuse. In T. Augusta-Scott, K. Scott, & L. Tutty (Eds.), *Innovations in interventions to address intimate partner violence: Research and practice*. New York, NY: Routledge.

Tutty, L. M. & Koshan, J. (2013). Calgary's specialized domestic violence court: An evaluation of a unique model. *Alberta Law Review*, *50*(4), 731–755.

Tutty, L. M., Ogden, C., Warrell, J. G. (2011). *Paths of change: A follow-up qualitative evaluation of men mandated to the Sheriff King offender groups*. Retrieved from: www.academia. edu/24558301/Paths_of_Change_A_Follow-up_Qualitative_Evalution_of_Men_ Mandated_to_the_Sheriff_King_Offender_Groups.

Tutty, L., Bidgood, B., Rothery, M., & Bidgood, P. (2001). An evaluation of men's batterer treatment groups: A component of a coordinated community response. *Research on Social Work Practice*, *11*(6), 645–670.

US Department of Health and Human Services, Administration for Children and Families, Administration on Children, Youth and Families, Children's Bureau. (2013). *Child maltreatment 2012*. Retrieved from: www.acf.hhs.gov/programs/cb/research-data-technology/statistics-research/child-maltreatment.

5   Complex Trauma and Dominant Masculinity

A Trauma-Informed, Narrative Therapy Approach with Men Who Abuse Their Female Partners

Tod Augusta-Scott and Leland Maerz[1]

Rather than accepting responsibility for their choices to use abuse, men often blame their circumstances, their female partners, and their mental health and addiction problems to excuse or justify their abuse perpetration (Pence & Paymar, 1993). In doing so they can create a story about themselves that *implies* they are only victims. In many cases, men have felt like they are only victims prior to their relationships with their partners. Men who abuse their intimate partners often disclose that they themselves have been victims of various forms of abuse, neglect, and violence. They avoid dealing with past victimization in part because dominant social ideas about masculinity lead them to think of themselves as flawed for feeling vulnerable. Consequently, these men act as if they are under constant threat. The victim-only narrative associated with this sense of threat needs to be disrupted for men to take responsibility to stop their violence and work at healing and repairing the effects of it.

Working with men who are victims of abuse and men who perpetrate abuse has typically been seen as two different forms of therapeutic conversation. Attending to men's experiences of being abused is generally not thought to be appropriate with those who are also using violence or engaged in abusive behavior. There is the risk that men's stories of victimization can be used to reinforce the victim-only narrative and distract them from taking responsibility for violence and for establishing safer behavior. Yet, recent developments in understanding how trauma impacts men's sense of self in relationships has meant a growing recognition that to stop abuse, it is important to simultaneously attend to men's experiences of being victimized and perpetrating violence.

This chapter describes a trauma-informed narrative therapy approach to conversations with men that draws from the perspective of the feminist domestic violence field. We begin by exploring how men are recruited into the victim-only narrative through traumatic experiences and the influences of dominant masculinity. We describe how the victim-only narrative serves to undermine men's willingness and ability to take responsibility. The chapter then elaborates on five strategies for deconstructing the victim-only narrative: challenging dominant masculinity, attending to persistent hyper and hypo-arousal, establishing a collaborative relationship, separating the past from the present and challenging the victim/perpetrator binary. As a result of deconstructing the victim-only narrative men are able to re-author their identities in a manner that supports taking responsibility to stop the abuse and build respectful relationships.

Complex Trauma and Dominant Masculinity

Factors that contribute to men using abuse are being increasingly recognized as varied and complex (Bartholomew, Cobb, & Dutton, 2015). While many men who abuse have had adverse childhood experiences, others have not. One way of making sense of how some men get recruited into victim-only narratives is understanding the concurrent effects of trauma and the influence of dominant masculinity (Bartholomew et al., 2015; Berthelot et al., 2014; Dutton & Sonkin, 2013; Heyman & Slep, 2002). By the time most men talk with staff from an abuse intervention program, many have already been diagnosed (as children and/or adults) with various mental health conditions such as reactive attachment disorder, oppositional defiant disorder, post-traumatic stress disorder, borderline personality disorder, and narcissistic personality disorder. In keeping with the current trauma discourse, we have begun to acknowledge that the conceptual framework for the emergent diagnostic term complex trauma (also referred to as Complex PTSD or Developmental Trauma Disorder) is helpful in describing how much of the behavioral phenomena expressed in men presenting with the aforementioned disorders develops through childhood into adulthood (Herman, 1992; Luxenberg, Spinazzola, & van der Kolk, 2001). Accordingly, complex trauma has also provided a useful context within which to understand how men who have been abused and who perpetrate abuse are recruited into a victim-only narrative.

Complex trauma describes both exposure to ongoing traumatic events involving interpersonal relationships *and* the long-term impact of living with this exposure (Briere & Spinazzola, 2009; Cloitre et al., 2009; Perry, 1997; van der Kolk, 2014; van der Kolk & McFarlane, 2012). People who suffer through childhood experiencing ongoing abuse and neglect can experience persistent states of hyper-arousal (fight or flight) in which their autonomic nervous system produces in them a psychological and physiological state of threat or ongoing alarm (Haskell, 2003; Poole & Greaves, 2012). When men grow up in a persistent hyper-aroused state they may begin to internalize the idea that they are always under threat of being harmed or taken advantage of by others (also referred to as hypervigilance). Individuals may also respond to ongoing abuse or to their own hyper-aroused states by entering into states of hypo-arousal. Hypo-arousal is also a state managed by the autonomic nervous system that promotes lethargy, avoidance, and dissociation. Men often describe feeling "checked out," "numb," and feeling as if they do not occupy their bodies. Over time, men can internalize that they are not able to feel connected or close to anyone (Bedout & Fallout, 2012).

The second defining aspect of complex trauma that supports developing a victim-only narrative results from the impacts of people living in traumatized states. Complex trauma not only accounts for the ongoing physiological impacts of traumatizing events and traumatic memories but can be the result of trying to adapt to and cope with the effects of living through time with induced states of hyper and hypo-arousal. When experiences of past traumatic injury are "triggered" in the present, a person's body sensations, ideas and emotions can be involuntary (Haskell, 2003); however, the adaptive coping strategies that people adopt in their struggle to make meaning of these painful experiences and how they choose to act in relation to them are voluntary.

Men's voluntary responses to the effects of trauma are heavily influenced and supported by the social norms of dominant masculinity. Dominant masculinity demands that men never show vulnerability, which can lead men to normalize or even valorize their maladaptive coping strategies. Men are encouraged to withdraw from others and be the "strong, silent types." Men are expected to avoid or "numb" their feelings. They are encouraged to be suspicious of others by "looking out for number one" or "each man for himself." Men are supposed to mask their pain through alcohol (i.e. "the more you drink, the more the man you are"). Further, men are encouraged to control their female partners. Again, rather than invite men to acknowledge their experiences of victimization, these social expectations support men's voluntary maladaptive responses to trauma (Bedout & Fallout, 2012).

In efforts to deconstruct the victim-only narrative, we find it helpful for counselors and men seeking help to distinguish between the involuntary *effects* of trauma expressed in hyper and hypo-arousal and a person's voluntary *responses* to these effects (Todd, Wade, & Renoux, 2004; Wade, 1997). Voluntary responses to trauma are often not intentional nor are they ones that people are aware they have chosen. For example, many men may adapt to the perceived threat from others by using violent or controlling behaviors, which they often only see as self-defense. These adaptations are a result of influences from socially determined ideas and behaviors (especially regarding dominant masculinity) that are considered "self-evident" or "the way things are." Such adaptive coping is often temporarily helpful in keeping someone emotionally or physically safe in relationships but also equally unhelpful and can, ironically, ruin relationships through abusive and self-harming practices (Berthelot et al., 2014; Dutton & Sonkin, 2013; Heyman & Slep, 2002; Perry, 1997). When men make meaning of coping with constant states of hyper and hypo-arousal that they are victims-only, this is a voluntary response that they are responsible to change.

In the complex trauma framework, being traumatized is more than simply being involuntarily triggered into a physiological state or merely the repetition of maladaptive behaviors. Rather, the framework makes visible the complex context of suffering in which these states and coping behaviors go on to influence a person's sense of agency and identity. Complex trauma describes how abuse and neglect have the potential to alter a person's inter- and intrapersonal development and their mental representation of themselves and others in relationship (Siegel, 2012). In the language of attachment theory this is referred to as a person's "internal working model." Applied insights from neuroscience have begun to establish correlative links between childhood trauma, insecure attachment, violent behavior, and mental illness (Dutton & Sonkin, 2013; Haskell, 2003; Poole & Greaves, 2012; Siegel, 2012; van der Kolk, 2014).

Victim-only narratives can thus be understood as a byproduct of complex trauma, supported by dominant masculinity, and expressions of a person's "internal working model." They are the enacted story of meaning that is chosen in the context of a person trying to adapt and cope with the involuntary effects of traumatic injury.

By acknowledging both involuntary effects and voluntary responses in complex trauma, counselors avoid inadvertently participating in and reinforcing victim-only narratives. When counselors primarily focus on the involuntary effects of trauma, they can diminish the importance of men's agency and responsibility and, therefore, reinforce the victim-only narrative. When counselors primarily focus on men's voluntary responses to trauma, they can lose compassion for men and the involuntary effects of trauma on them, thereby leaving men feeling further victimized. By acknowledging that there are both involuntary effects and voluntary responses in complex trauma, counselors can create a powerful means of deconstructing the victim-only narrative. They can help men, as victims of past trauma, to recognize that they are not to blame for being victimized or for the involuntary effects of the trauma. They are, however, responsible for how they choose to respond to the impact of these effects. Similarly, men are not responsible for the expectations of dominant masculinity that influences their maladaptive coping; however, they are responsible for how they choose to participate in it. They are responsible for how they allow dominant masculinity to define themselves and others through the victim-only narrative.

Responsibility for Abuse

Victim-only narratives are both a product of and are reflected in men being unable and unwilling to take responsibility. Taking responsibility requires men to both admit their abusive behavior and recognize their agency to end this behavior (Jenkins, 1990, 2009). Taking responsibility requires not only admitting perpetrating abuse but also stopping it and then repairing and healing the effects of the abuse. For many men, traumatic experiences and the influences of dominant masculinity lead them away from using their agency to take responsibility in a respectful and non-abusive way. For example, some boys were beaten, verbally abused, or ignored when they were young for making mistakes or for making poor choices. Dominant masculinity expects men to be perfect, know everything, and never be wrong. Men always need to be right and have solutions to fix other's problems and be able to solve their own problems. Men are encouraged not to ask for help. Under such influences they mature, learning to protect themselves by hiding mistakes and avoiding the responsibility to admit their mistakes. As a result, when talking with us, many men are not initially ready to acknowledge their mistakes and take responsibility.

Victim-only narratives manifest in different ways. Men sometimes refuse to admit that their behavior is abusive but still demonstrate agency by attempting to control others, while other men admit that their behavior is abusive but believe they have no agency (are powerless) to stop it. Still in other cases, men oscillate between both positions. Men who admit their behavior is abusive but feel powerless to stop it, often express being defeated and resigned to abuse and violence. Sometimes, as children, boys believe that they are responsible for being abused or neglected, yet are powerless to stop it. Often children infer that they were abused because they were bad and, as a result, they deserved it. Children conclude they were responsible for being abused, for not standing up to it, for not stopping it, or simply because there is something wrong with them. They also learn that while they are responsible for the abuse, paradoxically, they have no agency or power to stop the violence (Anda et al., 2006; Perry, 1997; Perry & Pollard, 1998; Perry, Pollard, Blakley, Baker, & Vigilante, 1995; van der Kolk, 2014; White, 2005).

Alternatively, the victim-only narrative is reflected in men recognizing their agency but not admitting that their behavior is abusive. These men fit the description of men described by the dominant domestic violence discourse: men who feel entitled to use violence against their partners to maintain power and control, while also not taking responsibility for their choices to abuse (Pence & Paymar, 1993). Men who are unwilling to accept blame often demonstrate their agency by enacting a policy of never being "pushed around" or "told what to do" and that they will avenge those that have hurt them. These men do not explicitly consider themselves victims or abusers but rather "survivors" and "fighters." These men confuse the past with the present and feel *entitled* to use violence while justifying and blaming their use of violence on others. Many of these men, however, excuse and justify their abuse to avoid facing the painful consequences of their choices and to keep hidden their feelings of failure, inadequacy, and the fear of vulnerability from past victimization (Bedout & Fallout, 2012).

Victim-only narratives can be disrupted by investigating *with* men how they have *learned* to feel that they have never had power or agency. The conversation can switch from equating the feeling of powerlessness with being a failure, to recognizing the power and agency they have as adults over their own choices. In recognizing their agency they can also learn how to use it responsibly without harming others. Over time, men can be more easily invited to consider the effects of the victim-only narrative on a person's willingness to take responsibility for the choices they make in relationships. Men can explore how these effects lead a person to take greater responsibility over time or less responsibility over time and how such ideas might lead someone to feel more empowered or less empowered to solve the problems they face in an assertive, non-abusive fashion (Jenkins, 1990, 2009).

In my earlier practice, when I (Leland) was only using a trauma-informed approach that focused on the involuntary effects of trauma, I often inadvertently reinforced the victim-only narrative. I thought that men blaming themselves and elaborating on the effects of their experiences of abuse was enough to create change. What I did not realize was that taking responsibility requires men to both admit to choosing abuse *and* recognizing they have the power to make other choices. As a result, while men sometimes admit to choosing to abuse, they also continue to deflect blame to their partners, traumatic childhoods, mental problems, and current circumstances for their violence and why they cannot change.

By focusing on psychological explanations for trauma without also attending with men to their victim-only narrative, I often contributed to men's justifications and excuses for their continued abusive behavior. To my surprise and dismay, I noticed that men would use these ideas to reinforce their excuses for abuse. Men would use psychological labels and explanations for their behavior as aspects of identity that abdicated them from knowing what kinds of responsible actions are possible (Jenkins, 1990). For example, one man told me:

> I got PTSD and there is nothing I can do to control my anger. I just black out and go crazy. She needs to know how traumatized I am. Without smoking a few joints a day there's no telling what could happen if I get pissed off.

Without recognizing how trauma affects men's sense of agency, men often felt defeated about being able to change—especially when they have admitted to using abuse. By focusing on men's childhood trauma without also focusing on how it affected their sense of agency, I inadvertently intensified men's hyper-focus on their victimization and the belief they cannot change.

In my (Tod) previous practice, despite my insistence that there is no excuse for abuse, I was implicitly afraid to acknowledge men's past victimization because I thought it might be used to excuse current abuse. As a result, I did not allow men to talk about their victimization. This left me and men unaware of how the meaning men make of past experiences of victimization (i.e. the victim-only narrative) often supports men being unwilling to take responsibility for stopping their abuse in the present.

By only focusing on the influences of dominant masculinity, I made the assumption that men were trying to manipulate me into thinking they wanted to change when they were not. While I recognized that some men admitted to their violence, I never understood how holding men responsible for their responses to the effects of trauma and the meaning they made of their past experiences (i.e. the victim-only narrative) is an important part of holding men responsible for stopping their abuse (Augusta-Scott, 2001). Alternatively, when men did not admit to their violence and abuse, I confronted and challenged them on their justifications and excuses in a such an oppositional manner that they perceived me as victimizing them and, in turn, I inadvertently reinforced their victim-only narrative about themselves.

Deconstructing the Victim-Only Narrative

To help men take responsibility, counselors need to collaboratively work with men to deconstruct their victim-only narrative. This deconstruction process involves helping men attend to the involuntary effects of trauma so that they can better examine the ideas they have adopted about themselves, others, and their own agency and responsibility. Deconstructing their victim-only narrative thus requires men to become aware of how the effects of trauma and the influences of dominant masculinity impact their body and brain as well as their sense of agency and identity. This process of deconstruction is (by definition) also a "re-authoring" process in which a renewed sense of self and agency can emerge in contrast to the problem-saturated identity associated with abuse and the victim-only narrative (Beaudoin & Zimmerman, 2011; White, 2007; Zimmerman & Beaudoin, 2015).

Challenging Dominant Masculinity

A helpful place to begin deconstructing the victim-only narrative is by addressing with men how dominant masculinity supports them to avoid being vulnerable (Augusta-Scott, 2008). It is important to engage men in this process of challenging dominant masculinity and disrupting the influence it has on how men define themselves and experience others. To challenge the influence of dominant masculinity leading men to avoid acknowledging pain and victimization, we often draw two circles: an inner circle and outer circle (Augusta-Scott, 2008). On the inside of the circle, men are invited to consider what feelings and issues men are expected not to talk about. Many men are clear that men are not expected to share problems, vulnerability, pain, and victimization. On the outside of the circle, men are invited to consider the ways in which men are supposed to avoid, hide from, escape these feelings.

Many men are aware of the social expectation on men to avoid these feelings by using violence, becoming angry, never being serious about anything emotional, etc. Then men are invited to consider the influence of these ideas on a man over time if he is not able to acknowledge to himself or others what is in the inner circle. Men readily identify that these ideas can lead to alcoholism, isolation, depression, and anxiety. Men are also asked how these ideas would affect a man's partner and their relationships? Men are often clear that the ideas would lead to distance in a relationship, pushing away a partner who wants to get close or wants him to share his vulnerable feelings.

Finally, dominant masculinity is subverted by simply asking men,

> Do you think it takes more courage to face the pain and victimization that is on the inside of the circle or to run from these feelings and avoid them by using the things on the outside of the circle: alcohol, violence, and anger?

Many men indicate that facing their pain and victimization would take more courage and might even make them feel stronger over time. Then we ask, "Would you respect yourself more for facing these feelings or for running from them?" The men are often clear that they would respect themselves more for facing their fears and pain rather than running from or trying to avoid them. They are asked if facing these fears would make them stronger or weaker over time. In this way, dominant masculinity is subverted and men conclude that in fact facing fear, pain, shame, and victimization actually takes more courage and strength than avoiding it and running from it. Men are given permission to respect themselves for the strength it takes to acknowledge their victimization. By accounting for how these ideas of dominant masculinity are associated with avoidance, men are able to face their victimization and, in turn, disrupt the influence it has on how they define themselves.

We find that men benefit more from therapeutic conversations if they can account for the various ways that dominant masculinity influences how men are expected to relate to others (Augusta-Scott, 2008). Men are invited to name the competitive, hostile, shaming, and violent practices that dominant masculinity encourages among men. Through this process, men can recognize how dominant masculinity can reinforce the voluntary maladaptive responses to trauma, namely, reinforce the idea that everyone is a threat. It is often in naming and resisting the expectations of dominant masculinity that men initially express how isolated they often feel and disclose (often for the first time) how they had been abused or neglected as children.

Attending to Persistent Hyper/Hypo-Arousal

When men live in a persistent hyper-aroused state they may internalize the idea that they are *always* under threat of being harmed or taken advantage of by others. This arousal can be inadvertently triggered during the therapeutic conversation or just being in a potentially vulnerable setting with a group of men. For example, during groupwork we have observed men suddenly become impatient, sarcastic, and interrupting of others, or they can become suddenly reserved; appear angry and sad, and cease to participate. Previously, we had assumed these were solely expressions of wanting to avoid taking responsibility; now we realize that sometimes these are also involuntary expressions of trauma.

In keeping with a trauma-informed approach, we help men attend to persistent states of hyper and hypo-arousal by inviting them to engage in practices that help them regulate their emotions and connect again with the feelings and sensations in their body. These processes help men better redirect their awareness to how they may be confusing the past with the present. When given the opportunity, men can develop in their own terms how they are affected by these alternating states of arousal. They can be invited to map and document for themselves the effects of these states but also develop for themselves practices that they find helpful when they get triggered.

If physiological activations are persistent and intrusive, we may even end the talk therapy. The involuntary effects of trauma cannot be reasoned with when they are dominating and depreciating men's ability to be intentional (Haskell,

2003; van der Kolk, 2014). Instead, we engage men in breathing and grounding exercises or safe visceral experiences such as creating art, or they may be referred elsewhere for therapeutic massage and yoga. Specialty therapies such as Eye Movement Desensitization and Reprocessing (Shapiro, 2001) or more physically focused activities (adventure therapy) may be helpful (and perhaps necessary in some cases) to draw out and manage the sensory information that has been disassociated by traumatic experiences. Men are invited in a collaborative manner to engage in these initiatives rather than such activities being prescribed or imposed on them. This collaboration is important in creating a safe relationship with the men so they are not unnecessarily triggered.

Collaboration

Deconstructing the victim-only narrative involves inviting men to challenge the ideas they have that support their feeling that they are always under threat and that they cannot change. Counselors can create safety while addressing men's fear of others and lack of agency through intentionally developing a collaborative relationship (Augusta-Scott, 2009; White, 2007).

Developing men's own sense of agency involves respecting their ideas about the problems they face and what solutions they think would be helpful. One way a trauma-informed narrative therapy approach develops this relationship is by using words and metaphors to define problems and solutions that men are familiar with (sometimes called experience-near language). While many therapeutic approaches value collaboration, not all make efforts to solicit and utilize the ideas and language of clients. Many want collaboration but inadvertently undermine this practice by still imposing clinical judgment, therapists' metaphors, therapists' language, diagnosis, and homework on clients in an un-collaborative manner. We encourage men to provide names and metaphors for their problems and use these to study the effects of these problems. For example, a client made use of the religious concept of "purgatory" to guide his own understanding of how stuck he was and how he felt he could not help himself anymore. Men are, thus, invited to evaluate and educate themselves about how these problems affect their lives and what solutions will be helpful to address these effects (Brown & Augusta-Scott, 2007; Duval & Beres, 2011).

Expert (or professional) ideas and language about how problems develop are offered tentatively to men with the understanding that they ultimately define what their experience has been, the meaning they have made of these experiences, and what may still be resonating in an unhelpful manner. For example, to invite men to consider how they may have been recruited into the victim-only narrative, we might ask,

> Some men indicate that their continuous experiences of violence in childhood led them to want to control others. What do you think might be a possible connection between these two experiences? Do you think that these experiences might be connected for you?

To invite men into considering solutions, we tentatively ask, "Some men say studying the effects of trauma is helpful in their efforts to stop the abuse and repair the effects of it. What do you think of this process? Do you think the process could be helpful to you?"

Previously, despite having built friendly rapport with men, I (Leland), unwittingly *imposed* psychological explanations on them. I confused the theory or the map of psychological concepts, for the territory or lived experience of men's lives. As a result, I easily adopted a reductionist attitude that encourages teaching or telling people explanations for their behavior. This assumption led me to erroneously think that I knew more about men and their experiences than they did. In feeling a sense of urgency to stop their violence I thought this practice would expedite the process. By focusing on my own professional ideas, I became distracted from utilizing the "knowledges" that men have about their own experiences. I now realize that imposing my ideas actually slowed the process or in some cases, stopped it altogether. I undermined my own efforts to help men take responsibility by robbing them of opportunities to build a respectful sense of self-agency.

Working with men who have both experienced and perpetrated abuse involves integrating scientific knowledge and psychological concepts tentatively while eliciting and respecting client's experiences, knowledge, and interpretations, however fragmented and contradictory. Such a therapeutic relationship accepts that men may continue defining themselves as unable or unwilling to change. Men help the therapist know what ideas may be useful for them but also *how* they are useful. The practice involves developing the same respectful, collaborative manner of relating with men that we are inviting them to create with their female partners (Augusta-Scott, 2001). By respecting men's ideas, acknowledging their agency, the therapeutic relationship is much better able to address the influence of complex trauma and dominant masculinity which supports the victim-only narrative and leads men to feel unsafe.

Separating the Past from the Present

Another strategy for deconstructing the victim-only narrative that leads men to feel constantly under threat, is to help men separate the feelings associated with their traumatic past from their present experiences in relationship. To separate the past from the present, we invite men to study recent incidents in relationship when they felt or acted threatened. We might ask him, "Does your current feeling of being scared or threatened remind you of feelings from the past? How might your need to withdraw and isolate, or your impulse to lash out aggressively be related to past traumatic experiences?" In this way, men can begin to explore how their past experiences in relationships may have "coded" in their minds and bodies to assume close relationships are essentially hostile—even when in the present they may not be hostile.

For example, during the process when I (Tod) was working with Frank to study a past incident of violence, he became animated as he described choking his partner on a bed. Emotionally engaged in his retelling of this experience, I asked Frank if he had ever felt a similar level of anger and hurt before? Frank blurted out, "My father, my father! I told myself I was never going to let anyone hurt me like that every again." Immediately, he realized that his partner was not his father. She was not abusing him. Frank then disclosed a history of being beaten by his father until the age of fourteen. At age fourteen, on Christmas Eve, he escaped from his family's house. He stayed the remainder of the winter in his friend's camp, going to school, while his mother snuck him food. Inviting him to contrast his partner with his violent father, Frank was able to clearly identify that she is trustworthy and she is not intent on hurting him. Frank continued to be emotionally triggered after this conversation, however, he became able to separate the past from the present; he was able to remind himself that his partner is not his father. Incidentally, Frank was also a man who swore he would never be like his father, yet could not identify that he was acting like his father. Upon identifying that he was acting like his father, he was unclear why. Now, Frank understood a significant explanation as to why and what he could do to interrupt it.

Men are invited to consider how their perceptions of safety and their partner's hostility may not reflect their partner's behavior and how they may be confusing the past with the present. In this way, men can examine their respective attachment patterns and styles in relationship in terms they can understand (Dutton & Sonkin, 2013; Haskell, 2003). In response, the men may need to work at interrupting how the past may be influencing them in the present, thereby deconstructing the victim-only narrative so they can actually be present to their partners. Some of the questions we ask in this process are:

1. How do the painful or unwanted experiences of the past make it difficult for you to contribute to the kinds of relationships you want with yourself and with others?
2. Do feelings of being threatened or attacked remind you of any feelings you may have had when you were younger?
3. How do you know when you might be confusing the past with the present, reacting to your partner as if she was someone else from your past? In those situations, what do you need to remind yourself to separate the past from the present?
4. What differences could this make to moving toward the kind of relationships you want?

By the time men explore the issue of confusing the past with the present, they are already clear that they are responsible for stopping their own abusive behavior, even if their partners do not do the same. While men cannot save their relationships by themselves, they can individually stop choosing to abuse (Augusta-Scott, 2007b). Throughout this process, we constantly remind men that in exploring how the past may be influencing their present decisions to abuse, they are still responsible for these choices to abuse. Men can develop clarity about their responsibility to understand the past as part of taking responsibility to interrupt their choices to abuse in the present.

Challenging the Victim / Perpetrator Binary

Deconstructing the victim-only narrative also involves moving away from thinking of men as either victims or perpetrators. In part, because I (Tod) did not see the effects of this either/or thinking or victim/perpetrator binary, I would often label men, totalizing their identity into one single story—the "power and control story" (Augusta-Scott, 2001). I used labels such as "perpetrators," "abusers," and "offenders," which served to define men as only-violent. As a result, also under the influence of the victim/perpetrator binary, men would cling to their victim-only narratives, thereby decreasing the possibility of them taking responsibility. Not until the victim/perpetrator binary was identified and challenged in our conversations did the men and I recognize that they are often both. One question we ask to make this binary visible is, "What is it like to be asked to take responsibility for how you have hurt others, when no one is taking responsibly for how they hurt you?" (Jenkins, 2009). Among other things, this line of inquiry has the effect of exposing the binary, while also affirming men are still responsible for their choices.

Once men begin addressing the influences of dominant masculinity, begin to regulate their emotions, and are able to clearly distinguish between the involuntary effects and voluntary responses to past trauma in their present lives, they can be invited to openly discuss their victim-only narrative. This process of deconstruction involves inviting men to name (acknowledge) the victim-only narrative and explore its effects on their relationship with themselves and others. Men adopt phrases such as "I'm a failure," "I'll never do anything right," "the force of resignation," "catastrophic forecasting," and "all or nothing mode" to describe their victim-only narratives. They can be further invited to study their victim-only narrative and the effects it has had on themselves, others and their relationships over time. Men can consider how the victim-only narrative has rendered invisible the power and agency they do have to shape their lives. The narrative leads them to mistrust everyone and to isolate themselves even when people are not actually threatening them. This process also allows men's pain to be acknowledged while at the same time not continuing to reinforce that they are only victims. By men naming the victim-only narrative they are better able to admit to their abusive behavior and at the same time begin to develop an identity separate from their experiences of being abused and separate from their experiences of perpetrating abuse.

When men can name and identify for themselves the effects of the victim-only narrative they no longer need to feel as compelled to excuse their abuse to protect themselves from feeling as if they are either only a victim or only a perpetrator. They can acknowledge the effects of both as expressed in their victim-only narrative and recover their agency toward an identity that fits with their values and hopes for relationship.

Re-Authoring Identity

Narrative therapists also offer the possibility of moving away from the victim-only narrative by giving men an opportunity to re-author their identities (Augusta-Scott, 2007c; White, 2004, 2005, 2007; White & Epston, 1990). Such a process allows men to develop alternative stories about themselves that are contrary to the victim-only narrative. These alternative stories often include stories of resistance to violence, stories about themselves where they did use their power to stand against abuse and stood up for fairness, justice, and respect. As men develop these stories about themselves, investigating their values and the skills and knowledge they already have for living these values, men are better able to perform these identities/stories about themselves. Identifying with stories about themselves, their identities, creates a foundation from which there is agency to confront their own use of violence in the present and build respectful, caring relationships.

This process involves therapists inviting men to identify what they value and how they prefer to be in relationships. Often men's values are contradictory: they feel the need for power and control while at the same time wanting fair, just, respectful, and caring relationships. While men often act irresponsibility, at the same time, they often value and prefer taking responsibility for their choices (Augusta-Scott, 2001). In efforts to stop abuse, the process of re-authoring identity can help to bring into focus men's values that are consistent with fairness and justice. Men are invited to name their value in the present and then trace the history of these values over time (Augusta-Scott, 2001, 2006, 2007c).

Often men's experiences of trauma include stories of resistance against injustice and violence that they have not noticed. Far from being passive recipients of violence, many men have resisted the abuse they and others have experienced (Wade, 1997; White, 2004). For example, a common childhood experience for many men we work with is trying to protect their mothers from their fathers' violence. We have worked with numerous men who, as children, have either directly confronted their fathers or helped their mothers escape. The re-authoring process involves asking these men what they think these incidents might say about what was important to them, what they valued as children (White, 2007). Many men identify the seeds of resistance and notice the seeds of their values for justice and fairness in these incidents. We can then ask these men, "How is that boy who was standing up to his father's violence, connected to the man who is sitting in front of me wanting to stand up for fairness, justice and against his own use of violence?" Through this line of questioning, men identify where these values may have developed and recognize they may also have a long history of living these values. Along with investigating other similar experiences men have of living up to these values, men leave the office with a sense of themselves as wanting and capable of stopping abuse and building fair, just, respectful relationships.

Men can also disrupt the idea that they have no power and agency by how they study their past experiences of violence. They can be invited to look at the various ways they may have actually resisted the violence done to them through staying silent, letting their bodies go limp or telling various people. Often men have not noticed these acts of resistance and they simply conclude that they let it happen and, as a result, are to blame.

While recognizing they were powerless to stop the person from choosing violence, they also can notice their resistance to the violence (Wade, 1997; White, 2004). As indicated earlier, men are often unaware of their resistance to the abuse. They can forget the different ways they sought to protect themselves and others. We ask men what values are implicit in their resistance. Men often talk about believing that violence is wrong and valuing fairness. Again, we invite them to consider how the child who was resisting violence is connected to the man we are speaking with in the present.

Through this process, we invite men to make distinctions between helpful guilt and unhelpful shame. Unhelpful shame is present when men equate making mistakes with their identity; when a man makes a mistake he concludes that he is a mistake. Often this shame and self-loathing make the process of men taking responsibly for mistakes or choices they are not proud of very difficult. The unhelpful shame continues to feed negative identity conclusions about themselves that the men continue to perform. In contrast, helpful guilt is related to feeling bad about one's practice—not one's identity. Helpful guilt informs men that they have transgressed their values. Helpful guilt allows men know when they have made a mistake.

In this process, we also invite men to make distinctions about who is responsible and, as a result, who needs to feel guilty (Jenkins, 2009). We invite him to consider who was responsible for choosing to abuse him as a child; it soon becomes clear that the person who chose to abuse him is responsible. We would also invite him to consider who needs to feel guilty for these choices. These lines of questioning further allow men not to blame themselves or take responsibility for being abused, thereby continuing to deconstruct the negative story about themselves.

At the same time, we invite men to have greater clarity about who is responsible for their abusing others. Men are often clear that they were not responsible for being abused, however, they are responsible for choosing to abuse others. They are asked to consider who needs to be feeling guilty for their choices to abuse? What are the values implicit in this guilt? What does their guilt over the effects of their violence imply about the kind of partner or father they want to be? What if they didn't feel guilty (Jenkins, 2009)?

Men often conclude that their guilt over the effects of their violence reflects their implicit value for peaceful, caring, just relationships (Jenkins, 2009). Again, this process connects men more to their power, agency, and responsibility in relation to their own use of violence. As well, this line of questioning aligns men more with the performance of an identity about them that is consistent with stopping violence and building respectful relationships.

Conclusion

This chapter has focused on disrupting the victim-only narrative that many men who use abuse have about themselves. Men are often recruited into a story of themselves being only victims through their experiences of abuse and the influences of dominant masculinity. There are various ways that the victim-only narrative can be deconstructed: challenging dominant masculinity, attending to persistent hyper and hypo-arousal, establishing a collaborative relationship, separating the past from the present as well as challenging the victim\perpetrator binary. The result of deconstructing the victim-only narrative allows men to re-author their identities in a manner that is consistent with stopping abuse and repairing the effects of it.

Typically, the trauma field has been focused on understanding and attending to the involuntary effects of trauma. Trauma-informed counselors appreciate how victims are not responsible for and left feeling powerless by states of hyper- and hypo-arousal. However, the trauma field has not always recognized the contributions of the intimate partner violence (IPV) field, which places emphasis on dominant masculinity, agency and responsibility. Similarly, the IPV field has been resistant to apply insights from the trauma field with respect to men because of how the involuntary effects of trauma can be construed to excuse or justify men's choices to use violence. Regretfully, in primarily focusing on dominant masculinity, agency, and responsibility, the IPV field has ignored the significance of the effects of trauma on men in their efforts to stop men's violence.

A trauma-informed narrative therapy approach works compassionately with men around their victimization and in a manner that allows them to take greater responsibility. Efforts to invite men to take responsibility must be collaborative and attend to both men's involuntary reactions and voluntary responses to trauma. Such an approach must also challenge masculinity and the influence it has on supporting traumatized men in their choices. Deconstructing the victim-only narrative helps men recognize that they can be both powerful and powerless, oppressors and oppressed, perpetrators and victims and still 100 percent responsible for their choices (Augusta-Scott, 2001, 2007a, 2007b). They can recognize that the traumatic and sexist\racist environment in which individuals live is responsible for fostering violence and, at the same time, individuals are responsible for their actions *despite* their environments.

Note

1. Authors' names are arranged alphabetically. We acknowledge the following for their valuable feedback on this chapter: Laura Boileau, The Tree of Peace Friendship Centre; Catrina Brown, Dalhousie University; Jim Duvall, JST Institute; as well as Janah Fair and Penny Gill, Colchester-East Hants Health Center.

References

Anda, R. F., Felitti, V. J., Bremner, J. D., Walker, J. D., Whitfield, C. H., Perry, B. D., . . . & Giles, W. H. (2006). The enduring effects of abuse and related adverse experiences in childhood. *European Archives of Psychiatry and Clinical Neuroscience, 256*(3), 174–186.

Augusta-Scott, T. (2001). Dichotomies in the power and control story: Exploring multiple stories about men who choose abuse in intimate relationships. *Gecko: A Journal of Deconstruction and Narrative Ideas in Therapeutic Practice, 2,* 31–54.

Augusta-Scott, T. (2006). Talking with men who have used violence in intimate relationships: An interview with Tod Augusta-Scott. *International Journal of Narrative Therapy and Community Work, 4,* 23–30.

Augusta-Scott, T. (2007a). Challenging anti-oppressive discourse: Uniting against racism and sexism. In C. Brown & T. Augusta-Scott (Eds.), *Narrative therapy: Making meaning, making lives* (pp. 251–268). Thousand Oaks, CA: Sage.

Augusta-Scott, T. (2007b). Conversations with men about women's violence: Ending men's violence by challenging gender essentialism. In C. Brown & T. Augusta-Scott (Eds.), *Narrative therapy: Making meaning, making lives* (pp. 197–210). Thousand Oaks, CA Sage.

Augusta-Scott, T. (2007c). Letters from prison: Re-authoring identity with men who have perpetrated sexual violence. In C. Brown & T. Augusta-Scott (Eds.), *Narrative therapy: Making meaning, making lives* (pp. 251–268). Thousand Oaks, CA: Sage.

Augusta-Scott, T. (2008). *Narrative therapy: A group manual for men who have perpetrated abuse: Facilitator's manual, participant's manual.* Truro, NS: Bridges Institute. Retrieved from: www.bridgesinstitute.org/?portfolio=narative-therapy.

Augusta-Scott, T. (2009). A narrative therapy approach to conversations with men about perpetrating abuse. In C. A. Simmons & P. Lehmann (Eds.), *Strengths-based batterer intervention: A new paradigm in ending family violence* (pp. 113–135). New York, NY. Springer.

Bartholomew, K., Cobb, R. J., & Dutton, D. G. (2015). Established and emerging perspectives on violence in intimate relationships. In M. Mikulincer, P. R. Shaver, J. A. Simpson, J. F. Dovidio, M. Mikulincer, P. R. Shaver, . . . & J. F. Dovidio (Eds.), *APA handbook of personality and social psychology, Volume 3: Interpersonal Relations* (pp. 605–630). Washington, DC: American Psychological Association.

Beaudoin, M. N. & Zimmerman, J. (2011). Narrative therapy and interpersonal neurobiology: Revisiting classic practices, developing new emphases. *Journal of Systemic Therapies, 30*(1), 1–13.

Bedout, R. & Fallout, R. (2012). Acknowledging and embracing "the boy inside the man": Trauma informed work with men. In N. Poole & L. Greaves (Eds.), *Becoming trauma informed* (pp. 165–174). Toronto, ON: Centre for Addictions and Mental Health.

Berthelot, N., Hébert, M., Godbout, N., Goulet, M., Bergeron, S., & Boucher, S. (2014). Childhood maltreatment increases the risk of intimate partner violence via PTSD and anger personality traits in individuals consulting for sexual problems. *Journal of Aggression, Maltreatment & Trauma, 23*(9), 982–998.

Briere, J. & Spinazzola, J. (2009). Assessment of the sequelae of complex trauma. In C. Courtois & J. Ford (Eds.), *Treating complex traumatic stress disorders: An evidence-based guide* (pp. 104–123). New York, NY: Guilford Press.

Brown, C. & Augusta-Scott, T. (2007). *Narrative therapy: Making meaning, making lives.* Thousand Oaks, CA: Sage.

Cloitre, M., Stolbach, B. C., Herman, J. L., Kolk, B. V. D., Pynoos, R., Wang, J., & Petkova, E. (2009). A developmental approach to complex PTSD: Childhood and adult cumulative trauma as predictors of symptom complexity. *Journal of Traumatic Stress, 22*(5), 399–408.

Dutton, D. & Sonkin, D. J. (2013). Treating assaultive men from an attachment perspective. In D. J. Sonkin & D. Dutton (Eds.), *Intimate violence: Contemporary treatment innovations* (pp. 104–134). New York, NY: Haworth.

Duvall, J. & Beres, L. (2011). *Innovations in narrative therapy: Connecting practice, training, and research.* New York: W.W. Norton & Company.

Haskell, L. (2003). *First stage trauma treatment: A guide for mental health professionals working with women.* Toronto, ON: Centre for Addiction and Mental Health.

Herman, J. L. (1992). Complex PTSD: A syndrome in survivors of prolonged and repeated trauma. *Journal of Traumatic Stress, 5*(3), 377–391.

Heyman, R. E. & Slep, A. M. S. (2002). Do child abuse and interparental violence lead to adulthood family violence? *Journal of Marriage and Family, 64*(4), 864–870.

Jenkins, A. (1990). *Invitations to responsibility: The therapeutic engagement of men who are violent and abusive.* Adelaide, AU: Dulwich Centre Publications.

Jenkins, A. (2009). *Becoming ethical: A parallel, political journey with men who have abused.* Lyme Regis, UK: Russell House.

Luxenberg, T., Spinazzola, J., & van der Kolk, B. A. (2001). Complex trauma and disorders of extreme stress (DESNOS) diagnosis; Part one—Assessment. *Directions in Psychiatry, 21*(25), 373–392.

Pence, E. & Paymar, M. (1993). *Education groups for men who batter: The Duluth model.* New York, NY: Springer.

Perry, B. D. (1997). Incubated in terror: Neurodevelopmental factors in the cycle of violence. In J. D. Osofsky (Ed.), *Children in a violent society* (pp. 124–149). New York, NY: Guildford Press.

Perry, B. D. & Pollard, R. (1998). Homeostasis, stress, trauma, and adaptation: A neurodevelopmental view of childhood trauma. *Child and Adolescent Psychiatric Clinics of North America, 7*(1), 33–51.

Perry, B. D., Pollard, R. A., Blakley, T. L., Baker, W. L., & Vigilante, D. (1995). Childhood trauma, the neurobiology of adaptation, and "use dependent" development of the brain: How states become traits. *Infant Mental Health Journal, 16*(4), 271–291.

Poole, N. & Greaves, L. (Eds.) (2012). *Becoming trauma informed.* Toronto, ON: Centre for Addictions and Mental Health.

Shapiro, F. (2001). *Eye movement desensitization and reprocessing: Basic principles, protocols and procedures* (2nd ed.). New York, NY: Guilford Press.

Siegel, D. J. (2012). *Pocket guide to interpersonal neurobiology: An integrative handbook of the mind.* New York, NY: WW Norton & Company.

Todd, N., Wade, A., & Renoux, M. (2004). Coming to terms with violence and resistance. In T. Strong, & D. Pare (Eds.), *Furthering talk: Advances in discursive therapies* (pp. 145–161). New York, NY: Springer.

van der Kolk, B. (2014). *The body keeps the score: Brain, mind, and body in the healing of trauma.* New York, NY: Penguin.

van der Kolk, B. A. & McFarlane, A. C. (2012). *Traumatic stress: The effects of overwhelming experience on mind, body, and society.* New York, NY: Guilford Press.

Wade, A. (1997). Small acts of living: Everyday resistance to violence and other forms of oppression. *Contemporary Family Therapy, 19*(1), 23–39.

White, M. (1995). Naming abuse and breaking from its effects. In M. White (Ed.), *Re-authoring lives: Interviews and essays* (pp. 82–111). Adelaide, AU: Dulwich Centre Publications.

White, M. (2004). Working with people who are suffering the consequences of multiple trauma: A narrative perspective. *International Journal of Narrative Therapy & Community Work, 2004*(1), 45–76.

White, M. (2005). Children, trauma and subordinate storyline development. International *Journal of Narrative Therapy & Community Work, 3*(4), 10–23.

White, M. (2007). *Maps of narrative practice.* New York, NY: WW Norton & Company.

White, M. & Epston, D. (1990). *Narrative means to therapeutic ends.* New York, NY: WW Norton & Company.

Zimmerman, J. & Beaudoin, M. N. (2015). Neurobiology for your narrative: How brain science can influence narrative work. *Journal of Systemic Therapies, 34*(2), 59–74.

6 Co-Constructing Meaning

Women and Men Define Taking Responsibility and Making Amends

Yoshiyuki Takano

The process of taking responsibility for violence is complicated, in part because its meaning can change depending on context (e.g. legal, therapeutic, intrapersonal, and interpersonal) and disciplines. From a legal perspective, the process of taking responsibility is sometimes reduced to simply stating, "I did it" followed by accepting a court's punishment designed to "fit the crime." From a feminist social advocate perspective, on the other hand, the focus of taking responsibility spans the personal and political realms. For example, Pence and Paymar (1993) propose a feminist approach that defines taking responsibility not only at the individual level, as in taking responsibility for one's actions, but also community responsibility to address the fundamental issues of unequally distributed power, culturally biased gender relational patterns, and patriarchal social patterns that influence men's choices to abuse. Still others focus on the damage done to victims, asserting that taking responsibility involves both ceasing violence and abuse, and fully understanding the harm caused to victims (Jenkins, 1990; Semiatin, Murphy, & Elliott, 2013).

Intervention programs for men who have perpetrated violence against their intimate partners often focus on the intrapersonal aspects of responsibility; in particular, on men's attributions of blame and their minimization and denial of abuse and its impact (Andrews & Bonta, 2006; Maruna & Mann, 2006; Scott & Wolfe, 2003). Men in these programs are typically invited and/or challenged to consider the extent to which they have made excuses, justified, blamed, and otherwise distanced and externalized responsibility for actions or harm to outside oneself (Holtzworth-Munroe & Hutchinson, 1993; Murphy & Eckhardt, 2005). Although the perspectives and possible experiences of women victims of abuse are typically raised by men and group facilitators in discussion of men's cognitive distortions (e.g. "how do you think that she might feel to hear you describe your assault of her as 'just a push'?"), focus remains on men's intrapersonal patterns of thinking.

In this chapter I explore an alternate perspective on responsibility-taking based on the context of an interpersonal relationship. Violence is a social event, in which at least two people interact (Coates & Wade, 2004) and thus, taking responsibility needs to be understood and be meaningful within this interpersonal context (McNamee & Gergen, 1999). With such a perspective, taking responsibility needs to move beyond individual men taking responsibility for their sexist ideas or "cognitive distortions" and instead take into account men consulting with women they have harmed about what men would do to meaningfully repair the harms they have created. In other words, taking responsibility needs to be an interpersonal process that includes women's perspectives on what men need to do to meaningfully repair the harms they have created.

As part of the responsibility-taking process, I was also interested in exploring interpersonal perspectives on making amends. As Radzik (2004) purports, making amends requires repentance, which means that one must "undergo a sincere change of heart" (p. 142). However, changing one's heart does not suffice because wrongdoing takes on a life of its own once it has been committed. Thus, making amends requires restitution. As such, "Wrongdoers have an obligation willingly to undergo pain, exertion or sacrifice in proportion to their wrongful acts" (p. 144). Such struggles often involve painful emotions of guilt and remorse and lead to creating restitution for the offense. In other words, "If a wrong is an insult and a threat that separates people from one another, then to right the wrong would be to repair this rupture" (p. 145). Making amends involves repairing the damage caused by one's behaviors and helping heal whatever hurts that one has caused (Gorski, 1989). Thus, the central meaning of making amends is not an apology and reconciliation, or alleviating guilt, but building trust and actively taking part in the healing process. Again, making amends needs to be viewed from intrapersonal perspective and it is critical to gain perspective from women how it is experienced.

In short, my study attempts to explore the additional dimensions of male offenders taking responsibility and making amends in domestic violence (DV) if women's voices were heard and made part of this process.

Methodology

To explore perspectives on responsibility, I conducted narrative inquiry with men who abused and women who were abused about their ideas about taking responsibility. Purposeful sampling (Schwandt, 2007) was used to select a sample of six DV male offenders (range twenty-three to sixty-six years, average forty-two years) who had made substantial change as evidenced by reports from men, partners, counselors, and men's involvement in group therapy and who were committed to continuing in their change process. All participants were assessed as being at low risk to re-offend on the *Spousal Assault Risk Assessment* (Kropp, Hart, Webster, & Eaves, 1995) and some were currently living with the partners whom they had abused. The interviews for the men started with a request to describe in general terms their experience of change, "Please share with me your stories of being away from violence and abuse. What do you call these stories? What do your stories mean to you?" Elaborating questions, such as "What does change mean to you and to your family?" and "How do you know that you are changing and/or have changed?" followed.

Four female victims of domestic violence (range thirty-six to sixty-three years, average fifty-three years) who were unrelated to the male participants were also recruited from victims' advocacy and support groups and interviewed. Two women were completely out of their abusive relationships and the other two were in the process of leaving. All had experienced their former male partners' physical violence, emotional abuse, and stalking. Interview questions included, "Please tell me about your experience of the substantial change that your [former] partner has made in his life with regard to his relational violence. What is this change, and what does change in your [former] partner mean to you?" and "How and when did you know that your [former] partner had changed?"

The research procedures followed a modification of the four steps of Arvay's (2003) collaborative narrative inquiry method: (a) setting the stage, (b) co-constructing the research interview, (c) engaging in six collaborative interpretive interviews and transcription processes, and (d) writing the narratives. The thematic analysis procedures have been outlined by several key qualitative research methodologies (Lieblich, Tuval-Mashiach, & Zilber, 1998; Polkinghorne, 1989; Riessman, 2008) to create an eclective approach to capturing self-contained units of meaning from participants' narratives.

Results

Taking responsibility and making amends were key themes in both men's and women's narratives. Men's stories of taking responsibility consisted of three subthemes: (a) being honest and open to oneself, (b) taking responsibility for one's life, and (c) being accountable to oneself. The theme of making amends consisted of five subthemes: (a) fully reflecting on and understanding one's own behavior and how it impacted and hurt one's partner(s), (b) making a peace with self and those people who hurt me, (c) if the victim desires, making an apology, reconnecting, and reconciling, (d) if the victim wants, rebuilding trust and nurturing, and respectful relationships, (e) if the victim wants, actively engaging in the healing process of their partners and children.

The female participants shared their ideas about men taking responsibility with four subthemes: (a) taking responsibility for his life, (b) acknowledging and taking responsibility for the impact of one's behavior on the lives of the women and children and the pain and suffering that it caused, (c) being accountable for what he has done, (d) being respectful of the women's and children's choice to live life independently. The first subthemes, about women wanting men to take responsibility for his own well-being has three further subthemes: (i) purpose for change, (ii) resolving his own issues, and (iii) becoming an independent, mature, and fair individual. These themes are laid out in Table 6.1 with comparison of male and female participants' sense of taking responsibility.

Table 6.1 Male and Female Participants' Themes in Taking Responsibility

---

Male Participants' Themes

---

1. Taking responsibility

    a. being open and honest with oneself;
    b. taking responsibility for one's life;
    c. being accountable to oneself.

2. Making amends with whom one hurt

    a. reflecting on and understanding one's own behavior and how it impacted and hurt one's partner(s);
    b. making a peace with self and those people who hurt me;
    c. apologizing, reconnecting, and reconciling;
    d. rebuilding trust and nurturing respectful relationships with those people whom one has hurt, if they allow;
    e. actively engaging in the healing process of their partners and children whenever possible.

Female Participants' Themes

---

1. Men's taking responsibility

    a. Taking responsibility for his life

        i.   purpose for change;
        ii.   resolving his own issues;
        iii. becoming an independent, mature and fair individual;

    b. acknowledging and taking responsibility for the impact of one's behavior on the lives of the women and children and the pain and suffering that it caused;
    c. being accountable for what he has done;
    d. being respectful of the women and children's choice to live life independently.

Male Participants: Taking Responsibility

The interviews with men revealed multiple components of taking responsibility. Male offenders and those affected by their violence and abuse concurred that taking responsibility is a critical element of the process of change. Men explained that taking responsibility includes being open and honest with oneself about their own internal experiences, such as emotions, thoughts, and behaviors. Part of taking responsibility involves men facing the shame of perpetrating abuse against their partners. The men who were interviewed identified that hurting their loved ones also hurt their own dignity and values. The men also defined taking responsibility as facing the pain of being victimized by others, such abuse they may have experienced in childhood. The men explained that facing such internal experiences openly and honestly is a critical process for taking responsibility.

One man, James, acknowledged that he abused his partner and was responsible for his choices to abuse, to stop the abuse, and to make amends for it. James also explained part of taking responsibility to stop his violence involved investigating the influence of experiences of childhood emotional hurt had on him avoiding pain. He was able to abuse his partner because he was so disconnected from her feelings and his own, but yet such feelings were overwhelmingly painful to him. Part of interrupting the abuse and making amends to his partner involved facing these feelings—hers and his. Through the process of taking responsibility, James recognized that a seed of his violent and abusive behavior was planted when he was two and a half years old, with a traumatic accident that resulted in severe burns to himself and his mother. The accident resulted in him being disfigured and subsequently being bullied by classmates, his father relapsing into addiction problems, the falling self-esteem of his mother, and the eventual separation of his parents. The family was broken into pieces. James commented, "When they separated, I was about seven. So, from the earliest times that I can remember, when I reflect back, I was already kind of disconnected within myself, emotionally, mentally." James was struggling. "I became very angry, frustrated with how my life kind of quickly . . . unravelled." These feelings of disconnection and frustration were the beginning of the violence and abuse that intruded into James' life.

As he became older, he experienced a sense of fear, shame, and guilt. James experienced intense negative emotions but could not comprehend them. This sense of confusion and emotional pain overwhelmed him. He disclosed,

> It was going back to that pain and suffering from within. I couldn't tolerate it or manage it. And feeling trapped a lot of times; feeling horrible because I'm this man that I just don't like. Didn't like him and I couldn't be accountable for him. Couldn't be responsible for him. So I just blamed everywhere. It was pure suffering.

James' depiction of himself was as a person in "survival mode." He was filled with painful emotions of shame, disappointment, and hurt that he did not know how to face. He used alcohol and drugs, and violence, to deny and avoid facing such internal experiences. It seemed as if aggression and violence helped him gain control in his life. James, who had been a victim of abuse, slowly transformed into a perpetrator himself and began to hurt his loved ones, just as others who were supposed to love him had hurt him deeply. James got himself into many legal problems and continued hurting his loved ones. Despite his desperate desire to survive and to feel better about himself, his life continued to fall into pieces. One day, he broke down in tears and felt that he could not go on any more. He believed that the only way to survive is to face such pain. Being open and honest with himself about the pain he was experiencing was difficult, but it was critical for taking responsibility for James. He commented,

> I think a lot of just the honesty; a lot of just being honest. Honest in the way of being able to identify with the characteristics or behaviors of an abusive person. Being able to say, "Yes, that was me. That was me. Yes, I reacted that way. Yes, I've been in that predicament or without

placing any blame on anybody, just saying that's me and being open and honest about it.'

James identified this honesty and openness as the critical step in taking responsibility.

In addition to being honest, the men emphasized that to take responsibility, it was necessary for them to be accountable to themselves; in other words, to move away from blaming violent and abusive behaviors on others or on past hurt. The men realized that their actions and choices are their own and that all behaviors have consequences. They began holding themselves accountable for their choices, behaviors, and emotions.

Another man, Dennis, admitted that he was verbally and emotionally abusive to his wife and that hurt his wife for many years. After a series of events that included receiving a peace bond and starting the divorce process, Dennis joined a men's treatment group for violent and abusive behavior. Attending such a group was challenging and he was quite reluctant at the beginning. He initially blamed his wife because she had instigated their fight with a physical assault. Dennis also often blamed others and external factors for his choices rather than taking responsibility. Dennis was a victim of childhood sexual abuse and described feeling stuck in the identity of being a victim for many years. While Dennis knew he was abusing others, he felt powerless to stop because he blamed his own childhood experiences of victimization rather than taking responsibility for his current choices.

Dennis stated that becoming accountable for himself was critical to taking responsibility process. He moved from blaming his abusive behaviors because he was victimized ("I was a victim, always a victim") to recognizing that, despite his past experiences of abuse, he needed to be the one responsible for his own action and change with regard to his abuse. He realized that he is responsible for his behaviors in spite of his past hurt and/or whatever situations he has encountered. His actions are his own. He explained that he asks himself a question every day, "What am I going to do differently?" rather than "to live— I am a victim, blame everything as abuse." Dennis continued to acknowledge his own victimization, while at the same time moving beyond the idea that he was only a victim, recognizing his agency and choices, attempting to create some positive change every day. Dennis found that attributing blame and responsibility to himself and his choices was necessary for his change process.

The other male participants similarly recognized that holding themselves accountable for their choices and emotional experiences—past and present— and realizing that all choices have consequences, is critical for taking responsibility. The men acknowledged the damage done to their partners and children and more importantly, they are more open to trying to understand their loved ones' experiences of being abused by the intimate partner or father whom they loved and trusted.

Finally, men's responsibility also extended to taking responsibility for their lives as a whole. Taking responsibility is not simply for a single action, but for the choices they make continuously about the direction and meaning of their lives consistently with their values and desires for life. One participant, Don, illustrated taking responsibility not only for the abuse, but also for his own well-being, by focusing on his life and pursuing how he would prefer to live his life. Don said,

> Try to change even if your wife don't come back. I'm doing for myself. I'm trying to relive myself here. I wasn't blaming my wife. I wasn't blaming anybody. I was just blaming myself. All I have to do is be responsible, figure out new ways, and live on with my life. The reason I am here and am doing is not because of them, it's because of me.

Male Participants: Making Amends

As the men began to take responsibility to face the pain they have experienced and caused others, they initiated making amends. The process helped them make sense of their anger and how their past manifested in their present lives, which in turn, created further compassion and empathy for those people whom they hurt. Making amends is a demonstration of responsibility and is an attempt to repair the harms with their partners and children.

The men emphasized that, in order to make amends, it was first necessary to reflect on and understand one's own behavior and how it impacted and hurt one's partner(s) by listening to her speak about the effects on her, acknowledging these effects, and asking her to generate possibilities for how to repair these effects. The process required men to develop an empathic understanding of their loved ones' pain and struggle. They needed to reflect on and understand what was wrong and why it was wrong. As Ryan explained, this process needed to include a full and detailed acknowledgment of past wrongs,

> Not just go up to her and say, "what I did in the past is wrong." I need to point out everything . . . to let her know I do know, not just saying what I did was wrong. I did know exactly what I did. I knew why exactly it was wrong. I tell her why it's wrong. It's not right for me to throw the table. It's not right for me to expect her to pick me up when I'm feeling crappy.

He also explained that he needed to understand *why* such behaviors were wrong:

> Just knowing it's not right is not good enough, at least not for me. Why was it not right? How she would have felt? How I would have felt if I was in her shoes? What? How? That really made her feel so relieved.

Second, along with reflecting on and understanding one's own behavior and how it impacted and hurt one's partner(s), making amends also meant that men started to actively reach out to themselves and to take better care of themselves at the same time. This process includes facing the shame involved in hurting others in a manner that leads them toward self-respect for having faced the abuse and stopping it. This process may also involve facing the pain of childhood violence in a way that releases them from self-loathing and, again, allows them to take greater responsibility for their present choices.

The men explained that holding those who abused them responsible for their choices also assisted them in taking responsibility for their own choices. For Paul, holding his parents accountable for their choices was a critical step in the healing process. Paul noted, "I talked to my parents. That's where it (abuse) all started. I knew that is where it started, so I had to go and talk to my parents." For Paul, as with other men, those that hurt them did not necessarily take responsibility, but the process of holding them accountable were still important. Paul's father maintained his denial of abuse and continued to blame and insult Paul. However, Paul reported that having the conversation was still important in his own process of taking responsibility. Paul explained,

> I finally stood up. That made me feel good that I could tell him that, "I don't care what you believe. I have my own beliefs. And I am not going to Hell." That was a revelation to me when I told him that. That was just such a feeling of being free. It was just a feeling of being free.

The process of holding those that harmed him responsible for their choices increased Paul's commitment to taking responsibility for his own choices.

Third, the men explained that making amends involves admitting one's wrong actions and may involve connecting with those people who were hurt by them. Some of those who have been harmed want to hear the men express sincere remorse and to apologize in respectful manners. Randy emphasized that making amends required a full reflection on the reasons why he was remorseful, what he did wrong, why he did everything that they did, and how he is facing their past violence and abuse now:

> An apology wasn't enough. There are some things that you do in life and you can go back and say you're sorry and you can tell them how much you wish you never did it, but it's just not going to mean anything, because what you did was very wrong and very hurtful. Saying sorry is not going to be enough. It took me about two months to really gather why I was feeling sorry, exactly what I did wrong, exactly why I did everything and exactly how I am facing it now. So the talk with her involved her knowing that I'm sorry; knowing that I understand exactly what I did wrong.

Fourth, the men reported that making amends involved maintaining non-abusive behavior and continuing to demonstrate responsibility-taking, so that men and their partners could gain trust and confidence in men's ability to make responsible choices. Paul commented, "I think because they trust me now; that if they phone me, I won't fly off the handle." They believed that it was essential to continue to have open communication, such as being willing to share their internal experiences with their partners in order to rebuild trust. Paul stated, "Just by being open with them; me being open with them and openly talking with them that I am trying to work on my life. I am responsible for myself and that will be ongoing."

If their partners were willing, the men tried to rebuild trust in the relationships with their families. In some cases, the families may have gone through separation and divorce, and in many occasions, their partners and children may want to have nothing to do with men. In such cases, the men accepted the consequences of their choices, respected their loved ones' choices and tried to build a safe environment for their ex-partners and children.

Finally, the men expressed hope that, by making amends and working to rebuild trust, they might be able to help break the cycle of violence and prevent their children from choosing to abuse their families when they are adults. As Paul explained:

> I try and talk to the kids about it, because I want to find out more what I did to them so that maybe we can work through it together. My dad refused to even acknowledge that he had done anything. I want to have my kids feel that I am trying to correct a hurt. I'm trying to change what it was that really really hurt them. If I did that and if I can find out what it was then I can work on it.

The men defined making amends in a manner that relied on not only men speculating about how others have been harmed but also involved consulting directly with those they have harmed about the effects of the violence on them. This process made the men more accountable and able to take greater responsibility.

Female Participants: Taking Responsibility

The female interviewees expressed similar sentiments as the men regarding the importance of taking responsibility to the change process. After having been abused and blamed for so long, the women explained that they often found it difficult to trust their own judgments and continued to blame themselves for the men's choices to abuse. Their male partners often made statements that degraded the women's self-worth and created self-doubt in the women's judgment and their experiences of their own reality. For example, Pam was abused by her partner for over ten years and described her partner blaming her for his choices as crazy making. While Pam initially knew she was not responsible for his choices, after her partner argued otherwise for years, she began to doubt herself and consider that perhaps she was responsible for his choices and perhaps she was the cause of his violent and abusive behaviors. Pam stated:

> I knew on an intellectual level that it (abuse) wasn't me, it was him. They (female victims) can intellectually know . . . but they need to know in their heart and soul that it's got nothing to do with them and then they can continue to live their lives. Otherwise they're always carrying the emotional baggage with them, until they get to that realization . . . and to try to get her to believe that her gut instincts and what she feels is correct, is a really hard job.

The women believed that men needed to take responsibility on the basis of their own values and ethics—responsibility-taking could not be done only because it was important to others as a means to reunite with their partners and children. Pam emphasized that men's motivation to change should not be, "To manipulate that so that he gets something else. So that he gets the relationship back." Rebuilding the relationship may be possible, but it requires a sincere responsibility taking and taking responsibility is not a "talking into" convincing women to give him a chance to trust him again.

The women also identified that taking responsibility required men to work on their own issues that are impacting their relationship. The women believed that their partners needed to work to resolve their own "unfinished business," which seemed to be expressed as violence and abuse. Their partners needed to be aware of, and face, their issues and understand how their behaviors impacted the women and children as a result. Ann commented, "Prior to getting married, I knew that he had some anger issues. I thought it had to do with his mother who would always be on his case." Marina shared a similar experience of her partner having his own issues:

> He has a problem. My ex also has ADHD. He has been suicidal in the past when he was a child, related to Ritalin. I know that mentally there may be some things . . . There was also drug use. He had to go through drug testing through the process to see the children. He was using cocaine and other drugs along the lines as well. I don't think that's an excuse for his behavior. I absolutely don't. But I do think there's something wrong with him.

The women believe that taking responsibility can be demonstrated by men looking closely at the roots of their own issues of violence and abuse and taking initiative by seeking appropriate help. They reported that part of the men's traumatic experiences led them to believe they needed to have power and control over their partners, which, of course is supported by dominant ideas about masculinity.

To fully take responsibility, the women also believed that their partners needed to respect women's and children's lives, become independent, and take responsibility for following up on the legal and financial obligations (e.g. child support) for which they were accountable. They perceived their male partners as depending on them emotionally. For example, the men relied on their partners to prop up their self-esteem and make them feel secure. The women wanted their partners to become more emotionally self-reliant, mature, and fair individuals. Ann noted, "If he were to come back and say, 'I changed,' he would have to show me that he could provide for our children; he has to be financially independent."

Most of the women's partners had been desperate to reunite after separation and, as a result, stalked the women. The women believed that taking responsibility includes men respecting women's choices about the distance and independence she wants. The women believed that if they actually took responsibility for creating their own sense of emotional security, self-worth, and well-being, their partners should leave them alone and wish them happiness. Ann commented that taking responsibility means a man,

> Accepting the idea that it is their partner and their children's decision as to whether or not they want to continue in a relationship with him. The ability of those individuals to let go of the relationship, and in an accepting, respectful manner, is key in recognizing if that individual does want to change.

The women recognized that men being able to respect women's and children's choices demonstrates taking responsibility.

For the women respondents, taking responsibility also involved men acknowledging the impact of their choices on the lives of the women and children and the pain and suffering that it caused. Pam commented, "acknowledging that he had hurt me. I want him to understand how much pain and suffering I went through because of his behavior." Marina said, "It [abuse] has an impact on my health, it has an impact on, definitely, on the children. It has an impact on so many things and he needs to take that responsibility. He has done these actions and it has a domino effect."

After reading through the male participants' themes, Ann commented, "It gives me some peace of mind that there are men that recognize the hurt that they have inflicted." Ann also shared how hurtful it was for her to receive shallow apologies repeatedly, "In the past I've had letters. When he'd blow up, there were notes and apologies and flowers and chocolate and I'd accept them and the same thing. I'm most afraid if he was to apologize to them in letter."

The women wanted their partners to fully face and acknowledge the extent of the pain and harm caused. It is not only about the "impact" of actual physical or emotional abuse, but also the impact of their actions to break down the resistance that those women and children had against violence. All of the women had tried repeatedly to resist violence and abuse to protect themselves, their children, and their family. They were not passive "victims," but active respondents to the violence and abuse being inflicted. They had sought out helping professionals for intervention. As Ann mentioned, "I look back and think, 'I don't know how we did it.' I was so exhausted on so many different levels." The men taking responsibility is to fully understand and acknowledge this level of impact on women and children.

Another important element for the women was for the community to take responsibility and hold the men accountable. The women did not want to have their partners go through extensive legal penalties, but wanted the men held accountable for their behavior in some way. Marina commented,

> I would like to see him be held accountable at some point, but the way the system is, I'm not expecting it truly to punish him. I don't want him to go to jail. That's not what I ever wanted for him, but I want him to get the help that I think he needs. And that is that this kind of behavior is not, it's not acceptable.

Discussion

Many therapeutic approaches with men who abuse define taking responsibility primarily by focusing on the offender's cognitive process of accurately identifying and acknowledging their violence and its causes. Such approaches focus primarily on reducing men minimizing the seriousness of the abuse, denying it, or blaming external factors. A definition of taking responsibility that relies on a process of co-constructing meaning between men and women is less commonly used. This form of constructing the meaning of taking responsibility involves the personal appraisal of events, as well as a process of gaining meaning through the interaction with others. To deepen appreciation of what responsibility-taking might mean under this perspective, abusive men who had made significant changes in their behavior and women who had been victims of abuse were interviewed about their experiences and perspectives on responsibility taking.

One of the contributions of this study is revealing the value of co-constructing the meaning of taking responsibility in the case of intimate relationship violence and abuse. The women and men defined taking responsibilities in similar ways. In particular, they saw taking responsibility as critical for men's change, for building trust, and for repair to take place. The men's and women's narratives made clear that taking responsibility is not a state of achievement, but an ongoing meaning-making process with a series of social interactions.

Both the men and women identified that taking responsibility needed to go beyond just the men's abusive behaviors. Contrary to what the researchers had postulated, it was clear from the men's and women's narratives that men's taking responsibility for their abusive and violent behaviors was not sufficient; they also needed to be responsible for their own emotional well-being, their relationships relation to others in the family and even with the larger community of people around them. This type of taking responsibility does not limit one's responsibility for the here and now, but anticipates the impact of own well-being on future relationships. Taking responsibility for themselves challenges men's desired ways of existence and the quality of our lives and relationships. This process of taking responsibility concerns how one might be, what one might be capable of, and what is possible, and men are not restrained by ideas of how one should live, but rather about expansiveness regarding the possibilities of life

(Jenkins, 2009). Women described the process of men taking responsibility for their own wellness as men needing to become more adjusted and mature as individuals, capable of being responsible. This type of taking responsibility challenges not just behavioral change, but the ways in which women and men wanted men to reclaim their authority over their lives and to become responsible for their lives.

Despite points of similarity, there were also notable differences in men's and women's narratives around responsibility taking particularly in meaning in accountability and making amends. For the male participants, holding themselves accountable involved "looking forward" to future choices, behaviors, and lives. In contrast, the female interviewees focused on the past harm that had been caused by the men and their need for restitution of this harm. The women emphasized that men themselves, as well as society in general, need to be held accountable for violence and abuse, and it needs to be acknowledged that violence and abuse are not acceptable. For the victims, being accountable meant creating justice in which "recognition and restitution—are necessary to rebuild the survivor's sense of order and justice" (Herman, 1997, p. 70). The male participants' notion of accountability is looking at the present and the future, and their focus is to admit they are wrong and "move forward." Once violence happens, it is a social fact that cannot be forgotten, erased, or compensated. Men may need to continue facing the effects of harm they caused throughout their lives. This involves continuing to be open and willing to listen and acknowledge how it impacted and hurt one's partner(s), and asking to generate possibilities for repairing these effects.

Other differences were with respect to the theme of making amends, which the men considered as one of the most important processes of change for putting their responsibility-taking into action. The role of making amends has been discussed in terms of recovery, especially in the field of addictions (Alcoholics Anonymous, 1981; Gorski, 1989). However, for the women, making amends was considered secondary to having their partners take full responsibility for their actions. Ann commented, "The men can try to 'make amends' but should not expect those that they viciously hurt to want to reconnect with them. Their victims are not responsible to them." Several women believed that their partners owed them a sincere apology and building trust by respecting their lives of separation and staying away from them, but they did not wish for "amends" beyond genuinely taking responsibility.

In conclusion, this narrative inquiry explored meanings of taking responsibility for male offenders and female victims. The study offers three main contributions. First, men taking responsibility is considered an important component of the change process for both male offenders and female victims, and co-constructing the meaning of taking responsibility is critical. Second, because the sense of what taking responsibility means is slightly different between the male offenders and female victims in this study, this discrepancy can be an important next step to promote further change with the men. Simply admitting one's wrongdoing differs from living genuinely and authentically with one's choices and consequences to rebuild trust and repair the harm that one caused. This process needs to be viewed co-constructively among offenders, victims, and others who are involved in violence and abuse, including the community. Such co-constructing process can be initiated by men by continuing to listen and understand what it means for women and children to be inflicted by violence and abuse by their loved ones. Third, the concept of taking responsibility for one's own well-being while also attending to the well-being of others is a critical aspect of offenders' taking responsibility and change process. Taking responsibility is not an end state, but an ongoing process that needs to expand beyond taking responsibility for choosing violence toward encompassing current relationships and life choices.

References

Alcoholics Anonymous. (1981). *Twelve steps and twelve traditions.* New York, NY: Author.

Andrews, D. A. & Bonta, J. (2006). *The psychology of criminal conduct* (4th ed.). Newark, NJ: LexisNexis.

Arvay, M. J. (2003). Doing reflexivity: A collaborative narrative approach. In L. Finlay & B. Gough (Eds.), *Reflexivity: A practical guide for researchers in health and social sciences* (pp. 163–175). Malden, MA: Blackwell.

Coates, L. & Wade, A. (2004). Telling it like it isn't: Obscuring perpetrator responsibility for violent crime. *Discourse and Society, 15*(5), 3–30. doi:10.1177/0957926504045031

Gorski, T. T. (1989). *Understanding the twelve steps: An interpretation and guide for recovering people.* New York, NY: Fireside.

Herman, J. (1997). *Trauma and recovery: The aftermath of violence—from domestic abuse to political terror.* New York, NY: Basic Books.

Holtzworth-Munroe, A. & Hutchinson, G. (1993). Attributing negative intent to wife behavior: The attributions of maritally violent versus nonviolent men. *Journal of Abnormal Psychology, 102*(2), 206–211. doi:10.1037/0021-843X.102.2.206

Jenkins, A. (1990). *Invitations to responsibility: The therapeutic engagement of men who are violence and abusive.* Adelaide, Australia: Dulwich Centre Publications.

Jenkins, A. (2009). *Becoming ethical: A parallel, political journey with men who have abused.* London: Russell House.

Kropp, P. R., Hart, S. D., Webster, C. D., & Eaves, D. (1995). *Manual for the Spousal Assault Risk Assessment Guide* (2nd ed.). Vancouver, BC: British Columbia Institute on Family Violence.

Lieblich, A., Tuval-Mashiac, R., & Zilber, T. (1998). *Narrative research, reading, analysis, and interpretation.* Thousand Oaks, CA: Sage.

McNamee, S. & Gergen, K. J. (1999). *Relational responsibility: Resources for sustainable dialogue.* Thousand Oaks, CA: Sage.

Maruna, S. & Mann, R. E. (2006). A fundamental attribution error? Rethinking cognitive distortions. *Legal and Criminological Psychology, 11*, 155–177. doi:10.1348/135532506X114608

Murphy, C. M. & Eckhardt, C. I. (2005). *Treating the abusive partner: An individualized cognitive-behavioral approach.* New York, NY: Guilford.

Pence, E. & Paymar, M. (1993). *Education groups for men who batter: The Duluth model.* New York, NY: Springer.

Polkinghorne, D. E. (1989). Phenomenological research methods. In R. S. Valle & S. Halling (Eds.), *Existential-phenomenological perspectives in psychology: Exploring the breadth of human experience* (pp. 41–60). New York, NY: Plenum.

Radzik, L. (2004). Making amends. *American Philosophical Quarterly, 41*(2), 141–154.

Riessman, C. K. (2008). *Narrative methods for the human sciences.* Thousand Oaks, CA: Sage.

Schwandt, T. A. (2007). *The Sage dictionary of qualitative inquiry* (3rd ed.). Thousand Oaks, CA: Sage.

Scott, K. L. & Wolfe, D. A. (2003). Readiness to change as a predictor of outcome in batterer treatment. *Journal of Consulting and Clinical Psychology, 71*(5), 879–889. doi:10.1037/0022–006X.71.5.879

Semiatin, J. N., Murphy, C. M., & Elliott, J. D. (2013). Observed behavior during group treatment for partner-violent men: Acceptance of responsibility and promotion of change. *Psychology of Violence, 3*(2), 126–139. doi:10.1037/a0029846

7 A Continuum of Services for Men Who Abuse

Developing a Small-City Coordinated Community Response Model

Rosanna Langer

Through vigorous advocacy by the battered women's movement and its supporters over the past thirty-five years, the criminal justice system and other public and social institutions have changed and broadened their responses to domestic violence (DV). Yet, often these initiatives remain fragmented, lack coordination, and fail to establish formal and informal relationships among agencies. Women may be placed at further risk when institutional authorities and service providers do not communicate regularly and coordinate their diverse interventions.

With a view toward improving coordination and maximizing effectiveness, coordinated community responses (CCR) to domestic violence have now become the norm (Pence & Shepard, 1999; Syers & Edleson, 1992), yet how best to develop these practices continues to be investigated. In particular, one wonders, how can smaller cities with limited resources create a coordinated approach? This chapter offers a description of a partial, yet promising, model for smaller jurisdictions, such as ours in Sudbury, Ontario, seeking to achieve synergies with limited resources. When numerous agencies brought their own resources to the table to initiate a new collaborative approach to addressing domestic violence, innovations were possible.[1]

Coordinated Community Responses to Domestic Violence

There is now a significant history of communities improving the coordination of their responses to male domestic violence. The Domestic Abuse Intervention Project originating in Duluth Minnesota in 1980 through the initiative of battered women's movement advocates and a few key legal officials has been adopted and adapted as a model across North America and other countries. Notable features of this model include expanded obligations to provide protection to abused women, to arrest abusive partners, to provide mandatory group batterer intervention programs to hold abusers accountable, and to generate coordination agreements among agencies (Pence & Shepard, 1999).

Much research supports a call for better collaborative links across sectors in order to address domestic abuse more holistically, however, best practices are still being developed (Laing, Irwin, & Toivonen, 2012; Murphy & Fanslow, 2012; Shepard & Pence, 1999). The following discussion reviews the academic and organizational literature for models or accounts of collaborative interagency models of practice in order to identify the key components and indicators for the success of such ventures.

Many communities have adopted coordinated or collaborative responses to domestic violence, and use the terms loosely to describe even limited short-term arrangements. Networks, partnerships, and coalitions are assumed to enhance the broader outcomes of victim safety and offender accountability by improving institutional and interinstitutional performance and creating synergies where the outcomes are greater than the sum of individual contributions. For example, arrest combined with completion of court-mandated counseling has been found to have a greater effect in reducing recidivism than arrest alone (Murphy, Musser, & Maton, 1998).

Murphy and Fanslow (2012) describe a spectrum of approaches ranging from *networks*, both relatively informal and more formalized, *cooperation* to improve communication and reduce duplication of services, more structured *coordination* over a longer term, with planning and some shared resources, and *collaboration* with well-defined relationships, comprehensive planning, and a commitment to at least some common objectives. The rationales behind these efforts are to change the nature of relationships among agencies, maximize the effectiveness of existing resources and avoid duplication in services such as risk assessment and victim support (Post, Klevens, Maxwell, Shelley, & Ingram, 2010). Further, these coalitions support a cross-fertilization of knowledge, experience, and ideas and they have the potential to develop a shared sense of their joint enterprise. In this sense, the primary goal of the collaborative project is to improve coordination among service providers (Worden, 2001). They are also based on the assumptions that a comprehensive approach to coordinated interventions will result in a "synergetic effect toward a 'tipping point' of change" (Gladwell, 2000, cited in Gondolf, 2004, p. 608).

Partnerships and program elements in providing direct and indirect services to reduce intimate partner violence vary, however a slight majority of US police department respondents to a national survey sponsored by the US Police Executive Research Forum (59 percent of 329 respondents) self-identify as participating in police partnerships which they referred to as coordinated community responses to domestic violence (Reuland, Schaefer-Morabito, Preston, & Cheney, 2006). The most frequently named activities include victim assistance or service, specialized domestic violence units, coalition or team participation, and education and outreach. The case studies reported by Reuland et al. refer to practices such as coordinated on-scene partnerships between police and volunteer victim service responders, crisis responders who also provide court advocacy, specialized police investigators stationed in social agencies to facilitate interagency information sharing and cooperation, and domestic violence arrest reports shared weekly with domestic violence coalition members.

Similarly, in Canada, local domestic violence coordinating councils or coalitions have also been widely established to bring together partners from the community, health, education, and justice sectors that provide responses and services to increase safety for victims of domestic violence. For example, in the Canadian province of Ontario, the Ministry of Community Safety and Correctional Services (MCSCS) developed the Policing Standards Manual, which contains advisory guidelines requiring police services to establish and maintain domestic violence coordinating committees. The partnership is to be formed with the local prosecutor's office, probation and parole services, Victim/Witness Assistance Program (VWAP), Victim Crisis and Referral Service (VCARS), local Children's Aid Societies, and other local service providers and community representatives responsible for issues related to domestic violence, including women's shelters. Forty-eight domestic violence community coordinating committees or coalitions in Ontario receive annual funding from the provincial government (Department of Justice Canada, 2015).

However, the specific focus of these coordinating councils also varies, ranging from increasing communication across systems, to policy development for improving criminal justice responses, for example, implementing practices to support evidence-based prosecutions that do not rely solely on victim testimony (Allen, 2006). In some communities, coordinated multiagency risk assessment committees also meet to discuss victim safety and offender accountability in individual high-risk local cases.

Enforcement and programming models differ across communities, with a similar variability as to the extent of coordination and collaboration. Service components typically include mandatory arrest policies, criminal prosecution of offenders, advocacy services for victims, and treatment services for offenders (Bouffard & Muftić, 2007). Some or all of the following services may be included: domestic violence hotlines, emergency shelters, support groups for women and child victims, safe housing for victims, criminal justice training, promotion of screening by health professionals, monitoring of probation and release compliance by offenders, court-mandated offender participation in rehabilitation programs, school interventions, and public education campaigns (Post et al., 2010). In addition, some collaborators are physically housed together, enhancing communication, training, and referrals among diverse multidisciplinary staff (Uchida, Putnam, Mastrofski, & Solomon, 2001).

Some combination of components ideally work together within what has come to be called a "coordinated community response" to reduce the incidence of domestic violence. CCRs are a required framework under the US *Violence Against Women Act* in order to access grants and funding from the Office on Violence Against Women (United States Department of Justice Office on Violence Against Women, 2010). A large-scale US study conducted by Klevens, Baker, Shelley, and Ingram (2008) reveals some common features of CCRs.

Beginning in 1996 and extended in 1999–2000, the US Centers for Disease Control and Prevention funded ten CCR project sites with the objective of documenting, evaluating, and enhancing the work of local coalitions. Each CCR site selected a neighboring community as a control site, to examine whether specific programming characteristics were associated with intimate partner violence rates. All ten CCRs had at least one fulltime staff member who was responsible for coordinating activities among the agencies. Eight sites had a central committee directing or overseeing activities; however, only half had based their goals or activities on a community-based needs assessment. Although the researchers found no significant impact of CCRs on rates of intimate partner abuse in the communities, this could be explained by the fact that those accessing CCR services would only comprise a sub-group of the population. They did find significant correlations between CCRs and women's contact with services, particularly in those communities where goals and priorities were based on identified community needs.

One particular and enduring challenge for models of coordinated community response is the tendency for service "silos" to be created in relation to criminal justice and community systems and support structures, with agencies developing separate goals, procedures, and understandings of the issues and problems to be addressed by them. "These silos have been the source of many barriers preventing services and agencies from meeting their intended outcomes, and together have created complex and inaccessible pathways . . . to navigate" (Wilcox, 2010, p. 1014).

In the realm of domestic violence services, coordination to address perpetrators of domestic violence has often been situated primarily within the criminal justice system and limited to men charged with domestic violence offenses (Hague & Bridge, 2008). This focus on coordination on domestic violence perpetrators identified by the justice system can create silos or separations between treatment services for men identified as "offenders" by the justice system and those experiencing similar problems, but who have not been charged with an offense.

Sudbury Pathways to Collaboration

The City of Greater Sudbury is a smaller city in northeastern Ontario with a population of roughly 160,000 residents, 30 percent of whom identify as francophone and 6 percent as Indigenous (First Nations/Métis/Inuit). It is the regional gateway to northeastern Ontario and has long been known as a center for the mining industry. In this local project, while financial resources and administrative capacity were not available for a "one-stop" centralized hub of services and programs, several agencies were able to work together to create and coordinate targeted interventions for particular populations or to meet particular needs including high-risk victim safety planning, post-charge crisis counseling, court-ordered abuser programming and an early intervention program aimed at men who have not been charged.

Until the establishment of a voluntary early intervention program for abusive men, few resources were available locally other than a single agency offering a six-week co-ed anger management course with a sliding scale fee and individual fee-for-service anger management counseling, both of which are regarded as inadequate to address the power and control issues prevalent within intimate partner violence. Furthermore, abusive men are often embarrassed and reluctant to discuss their violence, and many are uncertain about where to seek help (Campbell, Jaffe, & Kelly, 2009). When the Sudbury Coalition members conducted preliminary focus groups with men at a local residential recovery and treatment facility and at the Native Friendship Centre, they confirmed the need for prevention programming for self-identified abusive men who have not been criminally charged.

While Sudbury had strong community awareness of the local and well-established Partner Assault Response program (PAR), a court-mandated specialized counseling and education program for offenders, for many, these interventions come too late, after assaults have already occurred. Further, many women do not contact police to report their experiences of intimate partner abuse, and consequently, as Arias, Dankwort, Douglas, Dutton, and Stein (2002) have observed, post-charge batterer intervention programs are not the ultimate answer because the majority of abusive men do not become involved in intervention programs. A major issue is how to impact those men who abuse women but are never charged.

Thus, for our community, it became a priority for community agencies to coordinate their services to develop a continuum of services to address perpetrators of domestic violence. At the beginning of our project, collaboration on domestic violence among local service agencies was disjointed, with assumptions that other agencies were dealing with any gaps in service. An additional factor contributing to this disconnect was scarce funding, with individual agencies seeking to protect both funding and specialization of services. Some client-centered agency mandates gave rise perceived impediments to cooperation with agencies such as the police and child welfare, which have historically faced community mistrust. Similarly, regulatory and internal policies and investigative obligations not to reveal sensitive identifying information created barriers for information sharing by police and child protective services.

In an effort to overcome some of these barriers, a local group of agencies obtained funding to help the agencies work together and to pilot a new intervention program for identified, but not charged, abusive men. The result of the work of this committee was the Innovative Continuum of Services (ICS-DV) for abusive men. This interagency collaborative initiative formed to enhance communication and expertise and to identify, develop, and deliver a continuum of preventative intervention services for men at risk for perpetrating domestic violence. It is, therefore, unlike many coordinated community responses to intimate partner violence as it focuses on offering a range of services and programs to men who have been abusive in tandem with the existing systems supporting victims. Because of this limited agenda, the focus of the service continuum is two-fold; to illustrate the benefits of a greater diversity of targeted interventions to reduce male domestic abuse and violence and to establish the extent to which integration of these programs into a broader coordinated response to male domestic violence is feasible in the longer term.

The agencies also sought to strengthen their linkages and service provision in order to maximize the impact of the intervention along a continuum of services and programs. Through cooperation, information sharing, referrals, and commitment to a common project, this collaboration among community agencies in a small urban center enabled the establishment of new pathways for intervention with men at risk for repeated intimate partner violence. Without fully and explicitly realizing it, the local agencies were emulating a model that has now been promoted as a best practice in the effective provision of community responses to domestic violence—coordinated community responses.

The Innovative Continuum of Services for Domestic Violence (ICS-DV)

The continuum of programs that the group sought to create and unify includes three services: a promising early intervention pilot group program for men labeled "Before Everything Escalates" or BEEP; rapid individualized post-charge risk management counseling services to men arrested on a domestic violence incident; and the court-mandated post-charge, or post-conviction group PAR program. The Sudbury Innovative Continuum of Services for abusive men is presented in Figure 7.1.

As shown in Figure 7.1, this collaboration begins with identifying a man who has been, or is at risk of being abusive in his intimate partner relationship. The ICS-DV committee then helped to coordinate responses. A first pathway addressed men who came to the attention of the system as a result of domestic violence, but who have not been charged with an offense. Most often, these referrals were for men who had come into contact with police or the Children's Aid Society (CAS) for domestic violence but had not been criminally charged, or men who had self-identified to other agencies as needing assistance and support before a criminal offense occurs. These men were offered the opportunity to participate in the BEEP program.

BEEP is a thirteen-week group program designed to address prevention among a referred at-risk clientele. It begins with an intake assessment conducted by a local social service agency, while staff from another agency were trained to complete repeated partner contacts before commencement and throughout program attendance to ensure that victim safety issues have been addressed. BEEP groups are conducted with one male and one female facilitator from each of two social service agencies. Program content covers topics including male socialization, the abuse cycle, negative, irrational, and distorted thinking, effective communica- tion, managing emotions, problem-solving, healthy relationships, parenting, and self-care. Between 2013 and 2015, the BEEP program ran through three program cycles with fifty-six referrals and twenty-three participants completing the group

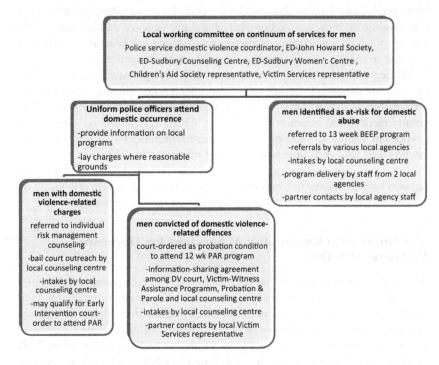

Figure 7.1 Sudbury Domestic Violence Continuum

and an additional ten clients receiving one-to-one counseling services as they had expressed an interest in the program between program cycles. Minimal funding was obtained for another program cycle in 2016.

Men might also come to the attention of the ICS-DV as a result of a DV charge. In cases where men come to the attention of the police service domestic violence coordinator as a result of police intervention, the case is reviewed for differential justice processing. Specifically, all criminal domestic incidents are reviewed by designated domestic violence Crown prosecutors who manage the prosecution of all domestic violence charges. The "Early Intervention" stream is a component of the local domestic violence court initiative that permits a justice to order a first offense accused who has exhibited a low level of domestic violence to complete the PAR program. The PAR program reports to the Ontario Ministry of Community Safety and Corrections Probation Office, and upon successful completion to the satisfaction of the Probation officer, the Crown will withdraw the charge and request the imposition of a section 810 Criminal Code recognizance or "peace bond" order or recommend a conditional discharge.

Alternately, offenders convicted of DV-related offenses may be ordered by the Court to attend PAR as a condition of probation. Repeat offenders are also frequently ordered to attend PAR. More serious offenders are sentenced to a custodial sentence and may receive institutional programming followed by PAR. In conjunction with the services for abusive men, partner contacts are made regularly while they attend the PAR program. The well-established PAR program is a Ministry of the Attorney General-funded twelve-week educational intervention for offenders. It aims to enhance victim safety and hold offenders accountable by adopting techniques, exercises, and skill-development from cognitive and behavioral therapies combined with a gender-based consciousness-raising approach. An information-sharing agreement is in place between PAR program providers and the Victim/Witness Assistance Program (V/WAP), the Crown Attorney's Office (Crown), and the Probation and Parole Service (P&P) (Department of Justice Canada, 2015). The local PAR program for men is run by a single social service agency, and is offered approximately nineteen times a year, with approximately 250 individuals court-ordered annually to attend and 106 completions (2014–2015).

In addition to BEEP and PAR, the community partner agencies initiated a local domestic violence bail court outreach program through the lead social service agency to offer crisis counseling and referral services for men arrested and facing domestic violence charges. The bail outreach risk management counseling service emerged organically, as a form of "bridging" intervention for those falling between program offerings. Intake for these participants is administered through routine client intake forms at the relevant agency. The year 2014–2015 saw thirty-one client intakes and six clients who received risk management counseling services.

Evaluation Methods and Results

The final focus of this chapter describes and assesses a snapshot of the collaborative process itself. A preliminary qualitative interview guide was developed to provide a snapshot of each agency's work in the field of domestic violence, constituencies and demand, familiarity with existing intervention and support programs in the community, and challenges to collaboration. Eight key representatives of each collaborative organization (including both senior managers and program staff) were interviewed to determine baseline information and indicators of partnership objectives. These interviews establish the collaboration historically and in relation to pre-existing programs in order to evaluate changes in local practice and identify and develop specific indicators. Six senior managers responded to a final survey posing a series of questions intended to measure collaboration effectiveness and satisfaction along a grid of indicators.

Members commented in the survey that the Continuum committee was appropriately focused on outcomes, information was readily shared (within the group), and decisions made promptly. Representatives had an opportunity to work with other agencies they were not ordinarily accustomed to partnering with and to learn more about each other's work. However, not all agency representatives agreed on what they perceived as necessary changes in the community's responses to domestic violence. Survey responses to questions about the accommodation of diverse viewpoints, and how disagreement and dissent were handled exhibited the most variation. This observation is not surprising, as this sector is well-known for strongly held views on the most pressing issues and appropriate responses to intimate partner violence. Respondents were also split on whether the collaboration stimulated policy changes within their own agencies.

Nevertheless, the majority of collaborators mentioned that members respected the context of each other's agencies and that consensus regarding the immediate project was the norm even when opinions differed. In working together, they were better able to collectively identify gaps in local practices so as to influence future changes. One member commented that, "The collaborative approach throughout this pilot project has been a unique and rewarding partnership . . . this process needs to be more the norm than not." This goodwill can be anticipated to produce sustainable longer-term outcomes for future local collaborative opportunities as well as providing a template for working with other agencies on similar projects.

Collaboration member agencies faced several challenges. Transitions in staffing and directorship of some agencies presented a challenge in achieving the orientation of new members to the working group and clear understandings of their roles within the project. While duplication of collaborative efforts was not mentioned as an explicit issue, agency representatives sit at multiple domestic violence "tables" which, in turn, multiplies agency commitments to collaborative partners without integrating knowledge and continuity from these other networks. In this sense, they fail to overcome the "silo" problem of adopting separate approaches to common problems.

A particularly thorny challenge is associated with agencies with specific policy mandates and confidential file management being cautious or restricted with respect to systematic or project-based data sharing or data reporting. Without formal institutional agreements, these limitations impede the centralization of referrals for an early intervention program and the tracking of program participants in order to monitor recidivism. In addition, statutory agencies such as police services and child welfare organizations create data management systems for their own reporting requirements, and find it difficult or impractical to respond to customized requests for specific data such as repeated police contacts, presence of children in the home, and individual recidivism histories. Similarly, community agencies may have differing intake processes depending on specific programs. In future collaborations, information-collection and data-sharing provisions for all partners should be addressed and resolved at the outset.

As reported by project participants, one positive outcome of the continuum is that having strong agency contacts makes it easier for agency staff to know whom to contact for information on available services in the community and to focus on giving clients current advice on local programs. Both women and men can learn of available services from a wider variety of sources. Local familiarity with the early-intervention BEEP program has grown among agencies, but recruitment was slow to build during the funding cycles. Significant staff resources were invested in recruitment, assessment, and intake, individual client and partner contacts and one-on-one counseling. In addition, the pilot program was co-facilitated by a bilingual Francophone facilitator from the Sudbury Counselling Centre and a staff member from the local Native Friendship Centre. However, in subsequent cycles, the committee was unsuccessful in reaching out to the local Indigenous communities for collaborative agency participation and program recruitment. More effective ways for working together with Indigenous communities must be explored in future local collaborations.

As a measure of collaborative success, more research needs to be conducted on drop-out and retention measures as well as wait times for program access. For example, several potential candidates for the BEEP program became ineligible when they were charged with offenses between recruitment and intake, illustrating the dynamic nature of domestic violence and the urgency for timely interventions. Several others expressed willingness to attend but the timing prevented their participation (e.g. away on a trade-school training program). Observing this gap, clients for risk management services were identified at Bail Court, and a number of individuals were serviced through one-on-one counseling, although these individuals were already facing criminal charges. Some BEEP clients and individual counseling clients were able to benefit from customized service provision tailored to a predominantly Indigenous cohort (in the pilot program) or francophone language requirements and this, in turn, impacted retention and program completion. However, unemployment, low employment, and low-income participants made the opportunity of a fee for service to recoup service delivery costs of these two programs unlikely. In addition, how to extend batterer programs to rural, Indigenous, and minority communities continues to be a challenge. Provincial PAR program protocols have changed from sixteen weeks to twelve weeks, in part to address wait list concerns, poor program completion rates, and cost containment. Although this program is the most well-established, only two PAR programs in the province have a specific Indigenous perspective and none developed for other cultural communities. While a systematic review of local PAR drop-out rates has not been conducted, there appears to be a significant need for programming alternatives.

Conclusions

This local initiative was intended to create a model continuum of services for men at risk for committing or repeating intimate partner abuse and to address identified gaps in local community responses to domestic violence. Those working in the community identified the need for an alternative to the PAR program for at-risk men who have come to the attention of the police or the local child welfare agency without charges being laid, men already on probation, or for those who have been charged with domestic-related summary (misdemeanor) offenses such as mischief. The results from the focus groups with men similarly voiced a need for such a resource. The post-charge risk management initiative responded to the dearth of available programming during the high-risk period after charges have been laid and prior to court-ordered PAR participation.

No one agency can meet all needs associated with domestic abuse, whether because of their mandate or due to limited funding. There is a great deal of interest in alternate models of service delivery in this field and in a very short time frame, the Sudbury CCR model attracted national and even international attention (Canadian Broadcasting Corporation, 2014). Community agencies that had not collaborated together before came together to establish a common objective that not only established positive working relations but also built local capacity for constructive future collaborations. One respondent observed that one of the biggest challenges is making a commitment to collaboration part of everyday practices.

Attributing impacts and accountability to a coordinated community response is not a straightforward task, especially with respect to a problem such as intimate partner violence, with multi-faceted factors and dimensions. Typically, studies have used the individualized outcome measure of offender recidivism, however, this fails to assess how the CCR may have affected the collective behavior of criminal justice and community service personnel or the community itself (Salazar, Emshoff, Baker & Crowley, 2007). We know little about how local political, social, and economic conditions are associated with particular combinations of structures, programs and policy responses to domestic violence (Worden, 2001). "There is a growing appreciation that collaboration requires a system of norms, relationships, processes, technologies, spaces, and structures that are quite different from the ways organizations may have worked in the past" (Barker Scott, 2014, p. 3). Policies and practices may develop over long periods of time, with some authors observing that as long as ten years is a reasonable timeframe within which to measure local improvements (Hague & Bridge, 2008). It may also be determined that different offenders respond to different intervention components resulting in cumulative program effects over time (Johnson, 2008; Scott, 2006).

Collaborative partnerships are dynamic, requiring frequent reassessment of program theory assumptions. They also have the potential to yield different costs and benefits at different stages of their development. Potential for the added value of collaboration tends to develop over time and experience and requires the provision of adequate sustained funding for development and support of programming. Nevertheless, significant measures of short-term success may include increased collaboration and communication among stakeholders, new pathways for exchange of information and resources, increased knowledge and access to resources, and stimulation of positive changes in community responses to domestic violence (Allen & Hagen, 2003).

The local Sudbury continuum can be characterized as a collaborative multi-agency initiative with common short-term objectives and the demonstrated ability to improve communication among agencies and implement a common agenda. However, more structured coordination over the long term would seem to require the types of changes in institutional commitment identified in much of the literature. Innovative local programs for men such as BEEP, high-risk crisis counseling and a proposed after-care group counseling program are designed to intervene to de-escalate male domestic abuse and to prevent recidivist behaviors. When we fail to intervene, violence repeats and escalates and criminal justice system costs rise. The Sudbury CCR model shows promise as a holistic, integrated, and ultimately cost-effective community response to men who abuse. The collaborative model is of particular usefulness for smaller communities where agencies must work together to create local synergies of expertise and scope across differing service sectors.

Note

1. These community projects were partially funded by the Ontario Trillium Foundation, an agency of the Government of Ontario, grant no. 136, 2014 and United Way/Centraide Sudbury & Nipissing Districts.

References

Allen, N. (2006). An examination of the effectiveness of domestic violence coordinating councils. *Violence Against Women, 12*(1), 46–67. doi:10.1177/1077801205277405

Allen, N. & Hagen, L. (2003). *A practical guide to evaluating domestic violence coordinating councils.* Harrisburg, PA: National Resource Centre on Domestic Violence. Retrieved from: www.vawnet.org/assoc_files_vawnet/nrcdv_evaldvcc.pdf.

Arias, I., Dankwort, J., Douglas, U., Dutton, M. A., & Stein, K. (2002). Violence against women: The state of batterer prevention programs. *Journal of Law Medicine & Ethics, 30,* 157–165.

Barker Scott, B. (2014). *Designing for collaboration.* Kingston: Queen's University Industrial Relations Centre. Retrieved from: http://irc.queensu.ca/sites/default/files/articles/designing-for-collaboration-by-brenda-barker-scott.pdf.

Bouffard, J. & Muftić, L. (2007). An examination of the outcomes of various components of a coordinated community response to domestic violence by male offenders. *Journal of Family Violence, 22,* 353–366. doi:10.1007/s10896-007-9086-y

Campbell, M., Jaffe, P., & Kelly, T. (2009). *What about the men? Finding effective strategies for engaging abusive men.* London, ON: Centre for Research & Education on Violence Against Women & Children. Retrieved from: www.changingways.on.ca www.changingways.on.ca/images/stories/MarcieCampbell/UnitedWayWrite-Up.pdf.

Canadian Broadcasting Corporation. (2014, August 21). *Abusive men get help in new program to prevent domestic assaults.* Retrieved from: www.cbc.ca/news/canada/sudbury/abusive-men-get-help-in-new-program-to-prevent-domestic-assaults-1.2742842.

Department of Justice Canada. (2015). *Making the links in family violence cases: Collaboration among the family, child protection and criminal justice systems.* Ottawa, ON: Author. Retrieved from: www.justice.gc.ca/eng/rp pr/cj jp/fv-vf/mlfvc-elcvf/vol2/p13.html.

Gondolf, E. (2004). Evaluating batterer counseling programs: A difficult task showing some effects and implications. *Aggression & Violent Behavior, 9,* 605–631. doi:10.1016/j.avb.2003.06.001

Hague, G. & Bridge, S. (2008). Inching forward on domestic violence: The "co-ordinated community response" and putting it in practice in Cheshire. *Journal of Gender Studies*, 17(3), 185–199. doi:10.1080/09589230802204134

Johnson, M. (2008). *A typology of domestic violence: Intimate terrorism, violent resistance, and situational couple violence.* Lebanon, NH: Northeastern University Press.

Klevens, J., Baker, C., Shelley, G., & Ingram, E. (2008). Exploring the links between components of coordinated community responses and their impact on contact with intimate partner violence services. *Violence Against Women, 14*(3), 346–358. doi:10.1177/1077801207313968

Laing, L., Irwin, J., & Toivonen, C. (2012). Across the divide: Using research to enhance collaboration between mental health and domestic violence services. *Australian Social Work, 65*(1), 120–135. doi:http://dx.doi.org/10.1080/0312407X.2011.645243

Murphy, C. & Fanslow, J. (2012). *Building collaborations to eliminate family violence: Facilitators, barriers and good practice.* New Zealand Family Violence Clearinghouse. Auckland, NZ: The University of Auckland. Retrieved from: https://nzfvc.org.nz/issues-papers-1.

Murphy, C., Musser, P., & Maton, K. (1998). Coordinated community intervention for domestic abusers: Intervention, system involvement and criminal recidivism. *Journal of Family Violence, 13*(3), 263–284. doi:10.1023/A:1022841022524

Pence, E. & Shepard, M. (1999). An introduction: Developing a coordinated community response. In E. Pence & M. Shepard (Eds.), *Coordinating community responses to domestic violence: Lessons from Duluth and beyond* (pp. 3–23). Thousand Oaks, CA: Sage.

Post, L. A., Klevens, J., Maxwell, C., Shelley, G., & Ingram, E. (2010). An examination of whether coordinated community responses affect intimate partner violence. *Journal of Interpersonal Violence, 25*(1), 75–93. doi:10.1177/0886260508329125

Reuland, M., Schaefer-Morabito, M., Preston, C., & Cheney, J. (2006). *Police-community partnerships to address domestic violence.* Washington, DC: US Department of Justice COPS Office. Retrieved from: http://ric-zai-inc.com/Publications/cops-p091-pub.pdf.

Salazar, L., Emshoff, J., Baker, C., & Crowley, T. (2007). Examining the behavior of a system: An outcome evaluation of a coordinated community response to domestic violence. *Journal of Family Violence, 22*, 631–641. doi:10.1007/s10896-007-9116-9

Scott, K. (2006). *Final report: Attitudinal change in participants of Partner Assault Response (PAR) programs:* Phase II, Province of Ontario. Ministry of the Attorney General. Retrieved from: www.oaith.ca/assets/files/Publications/ReviewPARSprograms.pdf.

Shepard, M. & Pence, E. (1999). *Coordinating community responses to domestic violence: Lessons from Duluth and beyond.* Thousand Oaks, CA: Sage.

Syers, M. & Edleson, J. (1992). The combined effects of coordinated criminal justice intervention in woman abuse. *Journal of Interpersonal Violence, 7*(4), 490–502. doi:10.1177/088626092007004005

Uchida, C., Putnam, C., Mastrofski, J., & Solomon, S. (2001). *Evaluating a multi-disciplinary response to domestic violence: The DVERT program in Colorado Springs, Final Report.* Silver Springs, MA: US Department of Justice. Retrieved from: www.ncjrs.gov/pdffiles1/nij/grants/188261.pdf.

United States Department of Justice Office on Violence Against Women. (2010). *Working together to end the violence.* Retrieved from: www.justice.gov/sites/default/files/ovw/legacy/2012/10/25/ctas-2010-report.pdf.

Wilcox, K. (2010). Connecting systems, protecting victims: Towards vertical coordination of Australia's response to domestic and family violence. *University of New South Wales Law Journal, 33*(3), 1013–1037.

Worden, A. (2001). *Models of community coordination in partner violence cases: A multi-site comparative analysis. Final Report.* Albany, NY: US Department of Justice. Retrieved from: www.ncjrs.gov/pdffiles1/nij/grants/187351.pdf.

Part III

Legal Responses to Domestic Violence

8 The Nova Scotia Domestic Violence Court Pilot Project

Lessons Learned from Evaluation[1]

Diane Crocker and Robert Crocker

Specialized domestic violence courts have been developing across Canada and the US since the early 1990s (Cissner, Labriola, & Rempel, 2015; Tutty, Ursel, & Douglas, 2008). The first such court in Canada, dealing broadly with family violence (FV), opened in Winnipeg in 1990 (Ursel & Hagyard, 2008). Since then, several provinces and territories have developed specialized courts that aim to improve the criminal justice system's response to various forms of family or domestic violence. While specialized courts operate differently, they generally work to ensure vigorous prosecution for domestic violence offenses; decreased re-offending among domestic violence offenders; and improved victim safety.

In this chapter, we describe the Nova Scotia Domestic Violence Pilot Project (referred to in this chapter as the Pilot Project or NSDVCPP) launched in Sydney, Nova Scotia in June 2012. The Pilot Project had broad goals including: (1) to break the cycle of violence; (2) to enhance safety; (3) to send the message, to the community, that domestic violence is a crime; (4) to improve the court's ability to respond to domestic violence; (5) to achieve justice for victims and offenders; and (6) to develop an integrated and holistic approach to domestic violence.

More specifically, the Pilot Project aimed to achieve several specific objectives related to helping victims, changing offender behavior and improving the criminal justice system response to domestic violence. In this chapter, we report findings from an evaluation that assesses whether the Pilot Project achieved these objectives. We demonstrate areas in which the Pilot Project succeeded and we highlight challenges associated with designing a program aimed to produce system change and support victims while working within the existing offender-focused court system.

Specialized Domestic Violence Courts

The current objectives of the Nova Scotia Pilot Project reflect those of many domestic violence courts across the continent. According to researchers, to work effectively, specialized domestic violence courts should balance three underlying principles: "(1) early intervention for low-risk-offenders; (2) vigorous prosecution for serious and/or repeat offenders; and (3) a commitment to rehabilitation and treatment" (Tutty et al., 2008, p. 76). Courts across the country balance these principles differently. Some, such as the Yukon domestic violence court process, have focused on early intervention and treatment for low-risk offenders but not vigorous prosecution. The specialized domestic violence court in Calgary offers treatment and intensive monitoring post-sentence for all domestic violence offenders. In Winnipeg, the family violence court provides pre-sentence treatment for low-risk offenders and rigorous prosecution, treatment and follow-up for high-risk offenders. The Nova Scotia Pilot Project focused on early intervention and pre-sentence treatment for offenders interested in participating and enhanced services and support for victims.

In Canada, specialized family/domestic violence courts have been evaluated extensively (Dawson & Dinovitzer, 2001; Gill & Ruff, 2010; Hoffart & Clarke, 2004; Hornick, Boyes, Tutty, & White, 2008; Johnson & Fraser, 2011; Moyer, Rettinger, & Hotton, 2000; Tutty, Koshan, Jesso, Ogden, & Warrell, 2011; Ursel & Hagyard, 2008). Overall, researchers have reported harsher sentences, increased conviction rates, less recidivism, and fewer cases dropped in the specialized courts than in the mainstream system (Hornick et al., 2008; Tutty et al., 2008; Ursel & Hagyard, 2008). While some questions remain, particularly in regards to victim safety (Johnson & Fraser, 2011), it appears that specialized domestic violence courts have achieved many successes.

The Nova Scotia Domestic Violence Court Pilot Project

The potential for offering specialized domestic violence courts has been debated in Nova Scotia for some time. In 2000, a highly publicized domestic homicide-suicide raised questions about the success of the existing Framework for Action on Family Violence. A subsequent evaluation of the Framework offered many recommendations, including the development of specialized courts for domestic violence (Russell & Ginn, 2001). In 2009, the Domestic Violence Prevention Committee delivered a report that led to a Domestic Violence Action Plan. The plan recommended that the Department of Justice pilot a specialized court in Sydney. The Action Plan did not recommend a specific model but suggested a court program with broad goals relating to offenders, victims, and community partnerships.

The Nova Scotia Domestic Violence Court opened in 2012 with several specific objectives related to helping victims, changing offenders, and improving the criminal justice system's response to domestic violence. To help victims, Victim Services, a Department of Justice agency with offices in the courthouse, provided enhanced opportunities for risk assessments and safety planning for victims. To change offender behavior, the Pilot Project expanded opportunities for those accused of domestic violence to participate in treatment programs. These interventions work with offenders to change their attitudes about relationships, provide them with tools to improve intimate relationships, and avoid further violence. In terms of the system, the Nova Scotia Pilot Project aimed to provide early, efficient, and effective intervention for domestic violence cases through collaboration between and among government and community agencies.

The domestic violence court sits one day a week. Dedicated staff, including duty counsel/legal aid, the Crown prosecutor (who plays a similar role as the District Attorney in the US), probation, and a Victim Services staff person, who works for the Department of Justice, attend the weekly court session. They all work exclusively on cases going through the Pilot Project and have training specifically related to domestic violence.

The process begins when the police lay a criminal charge that they believe constituted domestic violence. The Crown prosecutor decides whether the charge warrants an offer to the accused to proceed through the specialized court process. To be eligible for the program an accused must be over eighteen years old; live in, or have close ties to, the Sydney region; be willing to plead guilty; agree to participate in treatment; and, consent to allow community and government agencies to share information. Offenses such as murder, with mandatory terms of imprisonment, are ineligible.

After charges have been laid and before the first appearance of the accused, the Victim Services staff person contacts the complainant (similar to the plaintiff in an American court). The designated staff person encourages complainants to meet with her to complete a risk assessment and safety plan. Victim Services uses a risk assessment tool, the Danger Assessment, which measures the risk that a victim will be killed by an abuser (Campbell, 1995). As cases proceed through the system, Victim Services tries to remain in contact with complainants providing information and support or referrals to appropriate services as needed.

On the day of the first court appearance, but before the court session starts, the Crown prosecutor and defense lawyer (typically duty counsel or legal aid) present information about the Pilot Project to all accused individuals that the Crown prosecutor has deemed eligible. They detail conditions required for participation in the Pilot Project and inform potential participants that they may receive a reduced sentence upon successful completion of treatment. For individuals who express interest in the Pilot Project, the Crown prosecutor and defense lawyer recommend to the judge that cases be set over, typically for three months. During this time, the accused meets with a probation officer, allocated to the specialized court, who completes a Level of Service (LSI) risk assessment. The LSI measures various offender characteristics (such as criminal history, attitudes, family situation) to help service providers identify appropriate treatment and services (Andrews & Bonta, 1995). The probation officer may also administer the Ontario Domestic Assault Risk Assessment (ODARA) (Hilton et al., 2004), which measures likelihood of re offending.

Once assessments have been completed, a Case Management Team, which includes the court supervisor, probation officer, Victim Services staff, Crown prosecutor, a representative from the Department of Community Services (responsible for child protection and other social services), and duty counsel/ defense, meet to discuss each case and recommend an appropriate treatment program for each individual. Members of the team offer information from their perspective, sometimes based on contact with the complainant and/or accused. The Crown prosecutor describes the police report and provides background on any previous contact that the accused has had with the criminal justice system. The report also includes the results of the risk assessments completed by police and probation. If completed, the Danger Assessment is considered in the discussion. To avoid duplicating services, the representative from Community Services may provide information on services from his department being used by either the accused or the complainant. This person also advises on any relevant matters relating to child protection

Based on discussion, the Case Management Team recommends the level of treatment and whether other recommendations, such as addictions treatment, should be included. Higher-risk individuals participate in longer programs. The lowest-risk individuals participate in a five-week program. Higher-risk offenders attend a ten-week program. The highest-risk offenders complete a ten-week program followed by another program for seven weeks. Female offenders attend programming specifically designed for women. Community-based agencies deliver all the treatment programs.

Prior to the second court appearance, the defense lawyer, usually duty counsel/legal aid, meets with the accused to create an agreed statement of fact that provides details about the incident leading up to the charge. The Crown prosecutor also meets with the accused to provide information about the recommended treatment program and possible sentencing options upon its successful completion. This Pilot Project thus offers earlier intervention than available in the regular court process and the offender's sentence depends, at least in part, on successful completion of the treatment program.

At the next court session, prior to beginning treatment, those who have opted into the Pilot Project enter guilty pleas and agreed statements of fact. The court issues an order for them to enter the recommended treatment program and reappear in court within three months. After pleas have been entered, the probation officer refers each offender to the appropriate treatment program.

Depending on the duration of the treatment, several months may elapse before sentencing but all offenders reappear in court within three months even if not ready for sentencing. They may be called to appear in court at any time if the service provider reports that they have failed to attend programming. At sentencing, the judge receives the agreed statement of facts; a sentencing report written by the probation officer; and, the outcome of the treatment program, before passing sentence. The judge hears about whether the offender attended all treatment sessions and fully participated, which indicates whether the offender successfully completed the program. For the most part, offenders who have successfully completed treatment receive an absolute discharge. This means that while the offender has pleaded guilty, the court does not register a conviction or impose any conditions. The offender will not have a criminal record.

In practice, the process offered in the specialized court differs in several ways from the regular court:

- the probation officer begins working with individuals before they have entered a plea rather than after they have been sentenced;
- the treatment program is offered prior to sentencing rather than being part of a sentence;
- decisions about a case include input from the prosecution, Defense, Corrections, Victim Services and Community Services;
- a multidisciplinary Case Management Team reviews each case and recommends the appropriate treatment program;
- Victim Services aims to complete risk assessment with more victims;
- fewer victims need trial preparation because fewer cases go to trial;
- an offender's success in treatment determines, to a large extent, the sentence.

Research Methods and Data Sources

The research we report here includes data from various sources including minutes from meetings, case tracking forms, and judicial decisions. We conducted interviews with twenty-nine key informants who had been involved in the development or operation of the Pilot Project and seven program participants (two victims and five offenders). These conversations provided us with information about implementation and whether the court was working effectively.

We used several data sources to compare the situation before and after the implementation of the Pilot Project. We developed a questionnaire for victims whose cases went through the pilot and those whose cases proceeded prior to the development of the specialized court. Twenty-one victims returned these questionnaires (eleven post-pilot and ten pre-pilot). For official data, we relied on data collected by all Nova Scotia courts in the Justice Enterprise Information Network (JEIN). This database includes information about all court cases in the province and it allowed us to compare variables, such as final outcome, for domestic violence cases in Sydney before and after the implementation of the Pilot Project.

Using data from JEIN, Correctional Services, Victims Services, and the Case Management Team, we developed a master file of cases processed through the Pilot Project between June 2012 and December 2013. The file allowed us to describe cases going through the court and assess particular outcomes and compare characteristics of people and cases processed through the Pilot Project and those who opted out.

Finally, we received data from the local police on a sample of individuals who appeared in the Sydney court on a charge of domestic violence since the Pilot Project began. This data includes information on any contact that an individual has had with the police as a witness, suspect, or complainant. It also indicates whether the incident constituted domestic violence and whether charges were laid. We have manually linked a sample of cases in this file to cases in our master file that had a "final disposition" (i.e. the final outcome, pending appeal). This data allowed us to explore whether offenders who opted in to the Pilot Project re-offended less often than those who opted out.

We faced several challenges that limit the research in several ways. First, we interviewed substantially fewer victims and offenders than we had hoped. Even though almost everyone invited to participate in the research agreed to be contacted, we had a great deal of difficulty setting up appointments—phone numbers had changed, people did not return our calls or attend appointments. Like others researching specialized courts, we were therefore unable to provide much insight into issues relating to the experiences of anyone participating in the Pilot Project. Second, because individuals charged with domestic violence volunteer to participate in the project, those who opted out will likely differ in fundamental ways from those who opt in. In particular, those who opt in have agreed to plead guilty for reasons that may not be easily measured. In other words, we cannot be sure that the Pilot Project caused the differences between the groups, particularly in terms of re-offending. Third, several data sources, including JEIN, are not collected for research purposes. At times, this limited how we could measure the effects of the program.

Evaluation Findings

Between June 2012 and December 2013, the NSDVCPP processed 394 charges involving 153 individuals accused of domestic violence. Table 8.1 shows that most offenders who opted in were male (77 percent) and most victims were female (75 percent). The average offender was thirty-seven years old with just under ten previous charges and 4.7 previous convictions.

Table 8.1 compares some of these characteristics with those of individuals who opted out of the Pilot Project. The proportion of male offenders, and their average age, in each group was similar. The offenders also did not differ in the severity of the past charges or convictions. The groups differed on the number of charges and convictions they had in the past. The groups differed significantly on the average number of past charges and convictions. On average, individuals who opted in to the Pilot Project had faced fewer criminal charges in court in the past and had been convicted of fewer offenses than the individuals who opted out. Those who opted out of the Pilot Project seem to have been more chronic, and therefore possibly higher-risk, offenders. They did not, however, have a history of more serious offending.

Table 8.1 also shows domestic violence related charges laid between June 2012 and December 2013 for both the opt-in and opt-out groups. In this regard, the two groups did not differ. Common assault, the least serious form of assault, and "being at large" constituted the majority of the charges for both groups. "Being at large" typically relates to having missed a court appearance on another domestic violence-related charge. Charges, and their severity, processed through the Pilot Project were quite similar to those processed outside the Pilot Project.

Table 8.1 Characteristics of Offenders, Victims, and Charges (June 2012 to December 2013)

	Opt Into the Pilot	Opt Out of the Pilot
Characteristics of Victims and Offenders	**153 people**	**325 people**
Percent female victims	75	no data
Percent male accused	77	75
Average age accused	37	38
Average number of previous charges*	9.92	19.25
Average number of previous convictions*	4.70	9.82
Average severity of past criminal charges**	53.0	51.7
Average severity of past criminal convictions**	53.5	55.6
Characteristics of Charges	**394 charges**	**860 charges**
Common assault: (s. 266)	32%	33%
Being at large (s. 145)	30%	24%
Threats/criminal harassment (s. 264.1 & s. 264(1))	13%	17%
Mischief (s. 430)	9%	10%
Breach of recognizance (s. 810)	1%	0%
Assault with weapon/bodily harm (s. 267)	3%	4%
Average severity of charge**	41.65	43.54

* Statistically significant difference between opt-in and opt-out groups.
** Higher numbers indicate more serious charges. We used weights from the Crime Severity Index to identify the severity of each charge (Statistics Canada, 2000).

Helping Victims

The Nova Scotia Pilot Project aimed to provide risk assessments and safety plans for victims but staff reported that few participated and only 15 percent of victims whose cases proceeded through the Pilot Project completed the Danger Assessment. Of those, only 17 percent scored higher than low risk. The hope was that Victim Services would offer more intensive support to victims and would, as a result, be better able to offer information about appropriate services. While staff have been available, victims have not taken advantage of this option. Contrary to the intent, as one key informant described, the traffic in Victim Services has actually decreased since the Pilot Project began. Furthermore, the program developed by the local transition house, specifically for victims whose cases were proceeding through the specialized court, stopped operating because victims lacked interest. This may reflect the low risk disclosed by most victims.

In spite of the low number of victims participating, our survey of twenty-one victims showed that most felt satisfied with the court process and had been referred to appropriate services. Interestingly though, victims from cases during the Pilot Project were equally satisfied with the outcomes of their cases as those who went through the system prior to specialization. In terms of safety, all victims reported an increased level of safety after the court process, however those whose cases went through the specialized court had a larger increase in sense of safety. We caution, however, that the small sample size limits any conclusions in this regard. In addition, as pointed out earlier, the cases that proceeded through the Pilot Project were associated with lower-risk offenders and they may have felt safer regardless of whether their case proceeded through the Pilot Project.

Helping Offenders Change

Assessing risk with more tools and delivering more treatment programs, with offenders assigned to programs based on risk, constituted the main activities for the Pilot Project and it succeeded in doing both. The implementation of the Pilot Project provided previously unavailable treatment to low-risk offenders and it added an intensive program for high-risk offenders.

All offenders who expressed interest in the program participated in two risk assessments: ODARA and LSI. Generally, those who opted in to the Pilot Project scored low risk on both assessments.

Table 8.2 shows that those with higher risk assessment scores were placed in longer programs. Those who had more charges were similarly referred to more intensive programming. These differences were statistically significant. We might have expected that those with more severe charges would receive more intensive programming but the relationship between severity of charges and level of program was not statistically significant and could be due to chance. It appears then that severity of charges is unrelated to level of programming.

Reduced re-offending was a key outcome associated with the NSDVCPP. We used police callback data to compare how many of those who opted in had contact with police, since the initial domestic violence charge, with those who opted out. Among a sample of thirty-five individuals who opted into the Pilot Project, none had a recorded police call relating to domestic violence between the date or their initial charge and when we pulled the data in winter 2014. In contrast, 53 percent of the 43 individuals who had opted out had a police call related to domestic violence and 19 percent had been charged again.

Police data has the potential to shed light on re-offending but, the individuals who opted in to the Pilot Project may differ in some significant way from those who opted out and this may explain differences in the police data rather than the effect of the Pilot Project. In other words, the opt-out group may have presented a higher risk in the first place making it unsurprising that they re-offended more often.

Table 8.2 Relationship between Program Level and Characteristics of Offenders

	Average LSI Score*	Average ODARA Score*	Average Danger Assessment*	Average Number of Charges*	Average Severity of Charges	Number of Cases
Level 1	1.04	2.40	1.05	1.83	36.05	62
Level 2	2.38	4.69	1.70	2.60	45.46	36

* Statistically significant relationship.

Table 8.3 Comparison of Outcomes for Charges Pre- and Post-Pilot

	Pre Pilot Project	Post Pilot Project
Final Disposition*	310 charges	1176 charges
Dismissed	50%	32%
Sentenced	23%	33%
Withdrawn	20%	30%
Other (including acquittal)	7%	5%
Conviction*	**342 charges**	**1475 charges**
Percent convicted	21	27
Custody	**342 charges**	**1475 charges**
Percent custodial sentence	6	7
Probation	**342 charges**	**1511 charges**
Percent probationary sentence	13	11

* Statistically significant.

Increased offender accountability was another outcome related to offenders and we explored various ways to measure accountability. As shown in Table 8.3, the Pilot Project produced different outcomes for domestic violence cases in the Sydney area before and after the implementation of the Pilot Project and some of these changes may have enhanced offender accountability. Since the pilot began, the proportion of cases being dismissed has decreased and more cases ended with a sentence or had charges withdrawn. The percentage of convictions also increased after the implementation of the Pilot Project. The percentage of offenders who received probation or custody did not change.

That fewer cases were dismissed, more sentenced, and more convicted, in the specialized court may have increased accountability for people who, in the past, may have walked away from court without any intervention, despite having actually committed and offense.

Accountability may also be achieved with increased monitoring of offenders. In the Pilot Project, service providers monitor most offenders while they participate in the treatment program. The probation officer also monitors the offenders while they participate in the treatment program. Offenders in the Level 3 program make progress reports to the court. Comparing the opt-in and opt-out groups, the opt-in cases have, on average, more appearances than the opt-out cases. These appearances enhance accountability.

Changing the Criminal Justice System

The Pilot Project designers perceived collaboration as a critical activity and stakeholders identified collaboration as key to achieving the objectives of the Pilot Project. The collaboration occurs at two levels. Locally, the Case Management Team (described earlier) includes representatives from government agencies who make collaborative decisions on each case. A local Working Group, that includes representatives from government and community agencies, address issues relating to the day-to-day operation of the court. A central Steering Committee includes senior management representatives from several government agencies who make decisions about "big picture" issues such as funding. Members of these groups worked collaboratively to establish the court in Sydney and improve services in the community. Community-based agencies deliver the treatment program mandated by the court, and victims can avail themselves of community-based services, including (at least at the outset) counseling at the local women's shelter. If court staff and community agencies had operated in isolation, the establishment of the court may have faced many more barriers.

While many of those involved with the Pilot Project thought that the collaborative work went well, we heard some concerns about the level of involvement of community agencies and whether the relationship would best be described as cooperative rather than collaborative. In our experience, government-community collaborations frequently face this critique. Even with the best of intentions, government tends to lead collaborative projects in consultation with community partners (Allen, 2005). In reality, the community partners often have no real say in how projects unfold. This leads to tensions in projects intended to be collaborative.

Based on our observations, the relationship between stakeholders involved with the Nova Scotia Pilot Project would best be described as cooperative. Collaboration may have characterized earlier phases in the development and implementation of the project but, with the exception of the agencies providing the treatment program, the community agencies have a diminished role in the day-to-day operation of the court. They are not, for example, represented on the Case Management Team.

The Pilot Project aimed to produce stakeholder endorsement, good working relationships, effective governing structure, shared goals, and reports/statistics about the court's operation. Our research found that the court generally produced these outputs. We found a high level of endorsement of the program among stakeholders who generally agreed on the goals of the program and felt that it had created positive working relationships. The governing structure worked well with the central Steering Committee addressing system questions, such as funding and long-term sustainability, and the local Working Group dealing with day-to-day operations. Staff produced reports on the cases proceeding through the court and kept good records of meeting.

Efficiency was a key outcome related to changes in the system, and like accountability, raises questions on what indicators reveal it. Looking at the pre-pilot control group and the post-pilot group we found no change in case processing time or number of appearances. Cases that proceeded through the Pilot Project took longer than the provincial average, for all criminal offenses, from the initial court appearance to the final disposition (not including the sentence). However, comparing case processing time may not be the best measure of efficiency for comparing the opt-in and opt-out groups. Individuals who opt in spend weeks in the treatment program in between their first appearance and their final court appearance, which is included in the case processing time variable. We might also argue that some efficiency has been gained if the opt-in cases take the same amount of time as the opt-out cases because many of the opt-out cases will require supervision after the court process has ended. In addition, those who have opted-in spend the time in a treatment program while those who have opted-out essentially just wait for their case to be processed without receiving any intervention. This more efficient access to treatment constitutes an improvement in the system.

Discussion

The Nova Scotia Pilot Project has focused on early intervention and treatment for almost any domestic violence offender who opts into the program regardless of their risk level. As noted earlier, most presented a low risk for re-offending according to the risk assessments used in the Pilot Project. While high-risk offenders could opt in, they typically did not. As a result, the court has provided previously unavailable treatment mainly to low-risk offenders and there has been little change, such as enhanced prosecution, for high-risk offenders or those who decline the treatment option.

While the Nova Scotia Pilot Project enhances opportunities for victims to receive support, few participated. Unfortunately, in spite of its best efforts, the Pilot Project had little effect on victims. Indeed, some researchers have begun to worry that specialized courts have failed to effectively increase safety for victims of domestic violence while noting that research on this issue has been lacking (Johnson & Fraser, 2011). Based on their research on whether specialized domestic violence courts enhance victim safety, Johnson and Fraser argue that "the primary goal of an 'effective' justice response to intimate partner violence should be to make victims safer" (p. 7). They also cite the body of research that suggests that changes made to the criminal justice system have not always enhanced victim safety (p. 8). While it may be easy to think that good work with offenders will have positive consequences for victims, the research does not bear this out.

Other specialized courts across Canada have struggled to address issues relating to victims. Indeed, to put this issue in context, criminal justice researchers and policy makers more generally have worked to address victim safety and ensure that criminal justice responses enhance victim safety. The problem is not, however, easily resolved, especially since the criminal justice system's mandate is to focus on those accused of committing criminal offenses. Further, victim safety can be achieved only with cross-sectoral collaboration among both criminal justice agencies and other sectors integral to responding to these cases. Specialized court programs provide an avenue for achieving improvement for victims but these programs need to be developed with a clear sense of how particular changes in process will trigger an improvement for victims.

Conclusion

As measured by whether the project did what it set out to do and had the effects it hoped to have, the Nova Scotia Domestic Violence Court Pilot Project succeeded. It worked well and accomplished many of its objectives. The project delivered pre-sentence treatment to a wide range of offenders based on their risk. The project expanded treatment options including an option for high-risk offenders. More domestic violence offenders in Sydney received early intervention and treatment than before the Pilot Project. The project enhanced cooperation between government and community agencies and offered opportunities for victims to receive more support than had been previously available.

In spite of these successes, the evaluation revealed several characteristics of an early intervention model that limited the impact of the Pilot Project. First, very little changed for most high-risk or chronic offenders. While the Pilot Project developed a treatment program for these individuals, few opted in. As a result, the Pilot Project had a limited effect on high-risk offenders and this may have limited its ability to enhance safety for victims at higher risk. Second, and related to the first point, the Pilot Project had a limited effect on changing how the justice system responds to domestic violence. While the Pilot Project provided an opportunity for some offenders to attend a treatment program prior to being sentenced, the justice system's response changed very little. The early intervention model is limited because it falls short of developing processes for vigorous prosecution and monitoring of chronic high-risk offenders. Third, most victims chose not to participate, which limited the staff's ability to enhance victims' safety and better meet their needs.

The early intervention model, with its focus on offenders who opt in, will have a narrower impact on victims, especially when the offenders who opt in are lower risk than those who opt out. Because of its focus on pre-sentence treatment, the early intervention model cannot radically change how we achieve justice for domestic violence offenders or victims.

Note

1. This chapter draws from an evaluation of the Nova Scotia Domestic Violence Court Pilot Project completed by Diane Crocker, Robert Crocker, and Myrna Dawson. The researchers would like to thank members of the Working Group and Steering Committee for their assistance with the development of this evaluation. Myrna Dawson provided extensive input on the current chapter and Robert Crocker compiled the statistics described in this chapter. Staff in Policy, Planning and Research, Bill Trask in particular, provided invaluable assistance with the court data. Valerie Jewkes, Pam Marche, Valerie Pottie Bunge, and Ken Winch offered support throughout the process. Miranda McInnis and Judy Conn contributed to the development of the dataset. Rene MacCandless compiled police call back data. Chloé Gagnon, Wayne Poisson, and Linda Smith provided research and clerical assistance. We consulted with several experts including Mike Boyes, Mary Ann Campbell, Carmen Gill, Verona Singer, Kevin McNichol, Leslie Tutty, and Jane Ursel.

Thanks also to Tod Augusta-Scott, Heather Paruch, Katreena Scott, Bill Trask, and Leslie Tutty for comments on an earlier draft of this chapter. The views expressed in this chapter belong to the authors and have not been endorsed by the Nova Scotia Department of Justice. The full evaluation report is available at: http://novascotia.ca/just/domestic_violence_court.asp.

References

Allen, N. (2005). A multi-level analysis of community coordination councils. *American Journal of Community Psychology, 35*(1/2), 49–63. doi:10.1007/s10464-005-1889-5

Andrews, D. A. & Bonta, J. (1995). *The level of service inventory—revised: User's manual.* Toronto, ON: Multi-Health Systems.

Campbell, J. (1995). *Assessing dangerousness.* Newbury Park, CA: Sage.

Cissner, A. B., Labriola, M., & Rempel, M. (2015). Domestic violence courts: A multisite test of whether and how they change offender outcomes. *Violence Against Women, 21*(9), 1102–1122. doi:10.1177/1077801215589231

Dawson, M. & Dinovitzer, R. (2001). Victim cooperation and the prosecution of domestic violence in a specialized court. *Justice Quarterly, 18*(3), 593–622. doi:10.1080/07418 820100095031

Gill, C. & Ruff, L. (2010). *Moncton Provincial Court-Domestic Violence Pilot Project: A comparative study.* Fredericton, NB: Muriel McQueen Fergusson Centre for Family Violence Research. Retrieved from: www.gnb.ca/0012/Womens-Issues/DomesticViolence Court/2010–03ViolencePilotProject.pdf.

Hilton, N. Z., Harris, G. T., Rice, M. E., Lang, C., Cormier, C. A., & Lines, K. J. (2004). A brief actuarial assessment for the prediction of wife assault recidivism: The Ontario Domestic Assault Risk Assessment. *Psychological Assessment, 16*, 267–275. doi:10.1037/ 1040-3590.16.3.267

Hoffart, I. & Clarke, M. (2004). *HomeFront evaluation: Final report.* Calgary, AB: HomeFront. Retrieved from: http://homefrontcalgary.com/main/assets/files/HomeFront%20 Evaluation%20Final%20Report.pdf.

Hornick, J. P., Boyes, M., Tutty, L. M., & White, L. (2008). The Yukon's Domestic Violence Treatment Option: An evaluation. In E. J. Ursel, L. M. Tutty, & J. LeMaistre (Eds.), *What's law got to do with it? The law, specialized courts and domestic violence* (pp. 152–171). Toronto, ON: Cormorant Press.

Johnson, H. & Fraser, J. (2011). *Specialized domestic violence courts: Do they make women safer?* Retrieved from: www.oaith.ca/assets/files/Publications/Criminal%20Law/DVC-Do-theyMake-Women-Safer.pdf.

Moyer, S., Rettinger, J., & Hotton, T. (2000). *The evaluation of the domestic violence courts: Their functioning and effects in the first 18 months of operation 1998–1999.* Toronto, ON: Attorney General of Ontario.

Russell, D. & Ginn, D. (2001). *Framework for action against family violence.* Halifax, NS. Retrieved from: https://novascotia.ca/just/publications/docs/russell/toc.htm.

Statistics Canada. (2000). *Measuring crime in Canada: Introducing the Crime Severity Index and improvements to the Uniform Crime Reporting Survey.* Retrieved from: www.statcan.gc.ca/ pub/85–004-x/85–004-x2009001-eng htm.

Tutty, L. M., Ursel, J., & Douglas, F. (2008). Specialized domestic violence courts: A comparison of models. In J. Ursel, L. M. Tutty, & J. LeMaistre (Eds.), *What's law got to do with it? The law, specialized courts and domestic violence in Canada* (pp. 69–94). Toronto, ON: Cormorant Press.

Tutty, L., Koshan, J., Jesso, D., Ogden, C., & Warrell, J. (2011). *Evaluation of the Calgary Specialized Domestic Violence Trial Court and monitoring the First Appearance Court: Final report.* Calgary, AB: RESOLVE Alberta. Retrieved from: www.ucalgary.ca/resolve-static/reports/2011/2011-01.pdf.

Ursel, J. & Hagyard, C. (2008). The Winnipeg Family Violence Court. In J. Ursel, L. M. Tutty, & J. LeMaistre (Eds.), *What's law got to do with it? The law, specialized courts and domestic violence in Canada* (pp. 95–120). Toronto, ON: Cormorant Press.

9 Shifting Toward a Trauma-Informed, Holistic Legal Service Model for Survivors of Violence

The Calgary Legal Guidance Family Law Program[1]

Kayla Gurski and Tiffany Butler

Terror, hopelessness, anxiety, and depression are only some of the symptoms that survivors of violence suffer because of being abused. These feelings, and even the abuser, can be difficult to escape completely after separation, particularly when it is necessary for parties to access the legal system. When survivors of violence participate in the legal system, for example, as a witness in criminal court or as a party to a family law issue, they most often do so with little to no choice. Often, they must attend court at the same time, in the same courtroom as their abusers on more than one occasion. As a result, the symptoms above are routinely present when survivors of family violence must navigate the legal system alongside their abuser. As will be discussed below, these symptoms may result in behavioral adaptations that can act as a barrier to accessing justice for a survivor of violence.

The Family Law Program (FLP) is one of five specialized programs within Calgary Legal Guidance (CLG), a non-profit legal clinic (other programs include immigration law, homeless outreach, social benefits, elder law, and criminal defense). The FLP team consists of a social worker, a legal assistant, and lawyers. The approach within the organization relies heavily on collaborative inter-disciplinary teamwork, in particular the marriage of social work and legal expertise.

The FLP is funded primarily to work with survivors of family violence (FV) in the areas of family, criminal, and civil law. The most common services the program provides assistance with are parenting orders, financial support orders, protection orders, and court preparation and orientation. While services are available to both male and female survivors of FV, the majority of clients seeking assistance from the FLP are women. Many clients are referred to the FLP from the various Victim's Assistance Units connected with police services located in and around Calgary. These clients are typically involved in a criminal procedure where their partner, or former partner, is being charged with an offense under the Criminal Code of Canada related to family violence, such as assault. Clients may self-refer to the program or are referred by partner agencies including women's shelters, mental health organizations, or immigrant service agencies.

Most FLP clients are ineligible for publicly funded or subsidized legal counsel (referred to as "legal aid" in Canada) but cannot afford private counsel due to low incomes or inaccessible funds. The FLP triages those seeking assistance based on the vulnerability of the client and case urgency. Clients accessing services may be thinking about leaving an abuser or they may already have left their abuser but are, nevertheless, still experiencing or are fearful of abuse.

At every stage during and after their relationship, FLP clients need to make difficult choices. Deciding to leave an abusive partner is complicated; fears for the safety of oneself and loved ones, along with systemic, socio-economic and emotional barriers, further complicate this decision (Brownridge et al., 2008). Unfortunately, even once a woman ends the relationship, she can seldom avoid her abuser completely, especially if they share children. Usually, at one point or another, one or both of the partners will turn to the legal system to assist with matters involving the family home, finances, children, and protection. The legal system involves numerous and varied types of service providers, professionals, and procedures. Accessing the legal system can be daunting and traumatic, especially for a woman who has experienced FV as it provides opportunities for their former partner to regain power and exert control over them.

This chapter explains the complicated context within which the FLP operates including some of the ways that abuse continues and is perpetuated within the legal system. It provides an overview of three different service delivery approaches and how the FLP service delivery model works to synthesize those approaches. Based on the firsthand experiences of the FLP professionals and their clients, it draws from case examples to demonstrate how the model addresses the unique client needs that arise as a result of FV, any resulting trauma, and the challenges that clients face within the legal system. We argue that a holistic service delivery model where a team of interdisciplinary professionals supports women's attempts to navigate a confusing legal system, while recognizing the unique client needs that arise as a result of FV, best serves FLP clients.

The Context within Which the Family Law Program Model Operates

Accessing the legal system can be overwhelming for survivors of violence attempting to find legal solutions to their family problems. In reality, it can be difficult for *any* individual to navigate the legal system. However, survivors of violence face additional barriers to accessing the legal system that non-survivors may not face. Indeed, as Randall (2013) comments:

> For women in particular, vulnerability to, knowledge of, and direct experiences of pervasive forms of gendered violence can be understood as a form

of broader trauma. Yet most lawyers, judges, court personnel, police, and even the majority of service providers within the social services, are unaware of the effects of trauma on human development and human behaviour. Instead, the legal system is premised on fairly simplistic and highly rationalist assumptions about human psychology and behaviour.

(Randall, 2013, p. 19)

The Partner's Use of the Legal System as an Extension of Their Abuse

When clients get to the stage where they must participate in court processes, these can be traumatizing for survivors of violence, as outlined above. This is because the legal system can become yet another avenue abusers use to continue the abuse survivors hoped they would leave behind in separating from their abusers. The abuser's extension of abuse into the legal system occurs in a variety of ways such as:

* threatening to use the legal system against the survivor to perpetuate violence;
* making numerous court applications that require the other party to be in court with the abuser each time;
* refusing to agree to reasonable terms in order to keep parties before the court;
* constantly making applications on short notice for adjournments of court dates;
* changing counsel repeatedly to prevent matters from being settled; and
* filing pleadings with unsubstantiated allegations that can be offensive and defamatory.

Miller and Smolter (2011) coined the term "paper abuse" to describe the abuse to which survivors are subjected by their partners when they access the legal system after separation:

This concept incorporates acts that are routinely used by batterers against their former partners to continue victimization and includes a range of behaviours such as filing frivolous lawsuits, making false reports of child abuse, and taking other legal actions as a means of exerting power, forcing contact, and financially burdening their ex-partners.

(Miller & Smolter, 2011, p. 638)

As FLP professionals, we commonly hear about abusers having established a pattern of control and violent behavior over the survivor *while in* the relationship, including using threats of the legal system prior to the relationship ending, but then *continuing* the abuse by manipulating, or taking advantage of, what we describe as a "non-trauma-informed legal system." This *extension* of abuse can take many different forms, including psychological and financial.

Psychological abuse is generally defined as "the systemic destruction of a person's self-esteem and/or sense of safety, often occurring in relationships where there are differences in power and control" (Doherty & Berglund, 2008, para. 2). When abusers threaten to do everything in their power to prevent survivors from spending time with their children or having access to family finances, survivors often feel overwhelming panic, anxiety, and fear. Survivors often share that former partners make threats such as, "You can't leave me—you'll be homeless," "I'll go to court for sole custody of the kids if you file for divorce," "You better do as I say, or I'll have you deported," "I can make you disappear," "I will prove you are unfit—mentally ill, and you'll never get the kids," or "You'll never see a cent of my money." Some women are told that they or their children may be abducted or even killed. Further, when these threats include ultimatums such as "unless you cooperate . . ." or "unless you drop the charges . . ." survivors feel trapped, hopeless, and confused. Such threats increase clients' fear and make it more difficult for them to leave abusive situations. Worries that they will not be able to afford basic needs or will be separated from children weigh heavily on top of other barriers faced when trying to leave violent partners. Many consider capitulating to such threats out of fear of what could happen if they do not. It is not a choice made of freewill but out of desperation.

Like psychological abuse, financial abuse can be exerted through the legal system. "[Financial abuse] keeps one dependent, isolated, and without power. Not power in the sense of 'authority,' but power as it relates to the ability to choose, make decisions, and maintain self-esteem" (Canadian Resource Centre for Victims of Crime, 2011, p. 4). When abusers make numerous court applications, refuse to agree with reasonable terms in court applications, or constantly contact the survivor's lawyer, the abuser continues the pattern of financial abuse knowing that these actions increase the survivor's legal costs. These actions result in financial strain for the survivor and the abuser maintains some control over their former partners. Unfortunately, survivors have shared with us that financial stress from legal costs can be a factor in their decision to return to or stay with their abusers. When the legal process is drawn out, either due to an abuser's unreasonable behavior or due to standard procedures, a significant financial burden is placed on the survivor. This burden can include costs associated with court fees, lawyer fees, childcare, or time away from paid employment. By using the court system in this way, the abuser undermines the survivor's financial stability and also dictates when the survivor must appear in court and under what circumstances.

According to Statistics Canada (Williams, 2010), single mothers earn incomes much lower than single fathers. Many FLP clients stay at home to look after children or the home and earn no income during their relationships. Isolating a woman from friends, family, and other supports is a common control tactic used by abusers (Canadian Resource Centre for Victims of Crime, 2011). Women who are newcomers to Canada often have an even greater reliance on their abusers (Ahmad, Ali, & Stewart, 2005). More often than not, our clients tell us that their abusers strongly discouraged or otherwise prevented them from achieving any independence through gainful employment, education, or community groups. Income disparity coupled with limited opportunities to gain work experience places our clients at significant disadvantages when trying to access a system that most often requires the services of a highly trained, high-cost professional.

As Przekop (2011) outlines in her work on the experiences of domestic violence survivors in the American court system, abusers are more likely to apply to be the primary parent for children, but are less likely to abide by conditions in court orders or to see applications through. Therefore, survivors must attend court to address applications made by the abusers, despite many abusers' apparent lack of interest in parenting on a primary basis.

This scenario is worsened when women represent themselves because they cannot afford legal counsel to advocate for faster resolutions, to appear on their behalf, or to argue for costs for unreasonable court applications. Further, when one or more of the common trauma responses discussed later are present, it is even more difficult for women to represent themselves in court successfully. As Nicolas Bala points out:

> Divorce and family law is "civil law" with an onus on parties to hire their own lawyers (or represent themselves), marshal their evidence and present it in court. This may pose special challenges for women who have been abused, and lack self-esteem and resources. Women with limited resources may be eligible for a lawyer paid by legal aid . . . But there are still delays in getting legal aid, and the funding for these cases is limited, sometimes affecting the nature or amount of representation that may be provided.
> (Bala, 1999, para. 71)

In cases where criminal charges have been pursued against the man, the woman may be required to testify in a trial as a witness. Often, women must take time away from work to attend court only for the trial to be adjourned or for the matter to be dismissed. In cases where the trial is adjourned, the woman will often be subpoenaed to attend the next court date, requiring another missed day of work. Taking time away from work for both criminal and family law matters can place a strain on a woman's employment and finances. One client estimated that, over a twelve-month span, she had taken approximately three weeks away from work due to obligations to attend family and criminal court.

The abuser's extension of abusive acts into the justice system spans many areas of law, including criminal, immigration, and civil (family and other). Even when a matter is seemingly resolved, an abuser can often start a new application, forcing the survivor into court yet again. An illustration of how this extension of abuse can be manifested is provided further below relating specifically to parenting orders. Before that, though, it is important to understand the foundations of FLP's service delivery approaches, discussed in the next sections.

Holistic Service Delivery Approaches

Holistic approaches to service delivery are present in a variety of settings including schools, health care facilities, and social service agencies. A holistic approach to the delivery of legal services gained international recognition as a result of the service model created and implemented by the Bronx Defenders based in New York City. In that public defender's office, the lawyers and social workers realized that their clients' criminal cases resulted in, or were from, a wide range of other legal and non-legal problems. This realization inspired the founders to innovate and pioneer what was, at the time, a novel model of public defense coined "holistic defence" (Steinberg, 2013).

The Bronx Defenders' holistic defense model is founded upon four pillars, all of which are considered necessary to embody "true" holistic service (Steinberg, 2013). First, there must be seamless access to legal and non-legal services that meet client needs. Pillar one is about "recognizing that clients have a range of legal and nonlegal social support needs" (Steinberg, 2013, p. 8). Second, there must be dynamic, interdisciplinary communication among professionals, both in and out of the office, as well as between professionals and the client. The end goal here is to enable the professionals, "To think and strategize more effectively and to assist clients with collateral consequences and social service needs in a more efficient manner" (Steinberg, 2013, p. 991). Third, the clients must have access to professionals with an interdisciplinary skill set. In addition to working on interdisciplinary teams, newly hired lawyers at a holistic defenders office should receive basic interdisciplinary training in several legal disciplines, in the complexities of the social services sector, and on different types of addictions and mental illnesses. Fourth, the service provider must have a robust understanding of, and connection to, the community served. Pillar four involves establishing relationships with community organizations, performing community outreach, community legal education, spirited commitment to law reform, and participating in advocacy and establishing connections with local schools, non-governmental organizations, and community organizations.

According to Robin Steinberg, Executive Director of the Bronx Defenders, that model is now "widely recognized as the most effective model of public defense in the country" (Steinberg, 2013, p. 963). She describes it as, "The only current model of public defense that addresses the real-life consequences of criminal justice involvement—the consequences that are often more dire than the criminal case itself—and addresses the underlying issues driving clients into the system" (p. 1017).

Trauma-Informed Approaches

Specific to FV, "trauma-informed services" refer to services in which the delivery is based on an understanding that interpersonal violence and victimization can affect an individual's life and development (Elliot, Bjelajac, Fallot, Markoff, & Reed, 2005). Importantly though, as Jennings (2008) notes, trauma-informed services are not designed to treat symptoms related to domestic violence. Rather, these services are informed about and sensitive to issues resulting from domestic violence in survivors. Realizing that "traumatic events make people feel unsafe and powerless, trauma-informed practice seeks to create programs where clients . . . feel safe and empowered" (Smyth, 2012, para. 5). With this in mind, one of the FLPs goals is to ensure that, regardless of the level of formal program support available, in every meeting with the team the client feels heard and respected.

An important part of the FLP's approach is for the professionals to recognize and understand trauma survivors' responses. These responses may include turning to drug/alcohol use to numb some of the pain felt as a result of experiencing trauma, presenting as highly anxious, feeling triggered as a result of a perceived power imbalance in working with professionals, untrusting, especially of those in authority, presenting as distracted, disinterested, hyper, defiant, or irritable, or presenting with no affect. Regardless of trauma response, practicing from a trauma-informed perspective entails recognizing that clients use the coping mechanisms (i.e. the trauma-response) available to them and in doing so exhibit strength and resilience.

In practice, this understanding is displayed through patience, thoughtfulness, and a non-confrontational approach with all clients. This means being understanding despite having to repeat oneself several times, staying calm when a client appears agitated, and allowing a client to share details of their experience that may not be relevant to the legal matter at hand. In our experience, taking the time to listen to client stories, practicing empathy, validating feelings, and offering clients choices, our clients are treated with dignity and can begin regaining control and power in their own lives. While this approach may take more time, it is necessary in trauma-informed practice.

Client-Centered Approaches

To best meet clients' legal and social needs we adopt a client-centered approach. The client-centered approach involves "having the client actively participate in identifying their problems, formulating potential solutions, and making decisions . . . [it] emanates from a belief in the autonomy, intelligence, dignity and basic morality of the individual client" (Steinberg, 2013, p. 976). For us, this means looking through a trauma-informed lens at the whole client.

Many FLP clients accessing services for the first time are contemplating leaving abusive partners and considering the many factors that influence their decisions to stay or leave. In some cases, after having left, the woman is contemplating returning to her partner. The role of FLP staff is not to convince the woman what to do, regardless of personal beliefs about the woman's situation. What seems "best" from a professional's perspective may not be what the woman herself deems best for her or her family. Rather, the appropriate role for a FLP professional is to provide the woman with all the information she needs in order to make an informed decision that works for her. In doing so, the FLP takes a client-centered approach and helps create space for the woman to regain control and exercise choice. This also aligns with the trauma-informed approach.

The Family Law Program Model

With our growing understanding of the above highlighted approaches, a survivor's experience, and what we coin a "non-trauma-informed legal system," the FLP has adapted the holistic legal defense model to offer holistic, trauma-informed legal services in the family law sector. Uniquely, the FLP heavily incorporates its awareness of client-centered and trauma-informed approaches under each of the four pillars adapted from the Bronx Defender's holistic defense model (Steinberg, 2013).

Pillar One: Seamless Access to Services That Meet Clients' Legal and Social Support Needs

The holistic approach "accepts the challenges of addressing those issues by going beyond [the legal case] to the whole person" (Steinberg, 2013 p. 987). As Rachel Shepherd, CLG Homeless Outreach program advocate aptly observes, often the legal issues a client brings to CLG are symptoms of some greater social issue the individual faces. She maintains that the legal issues that our clients face never exist in a vacuum (personal communication, 2016). The FLP model applies a tandem approach to service so that professionals can work with clients to identify the impact the client's legal and social issues could have on each other. This is often done over the course of one meeting rather than meeting with a different professional at a later time, resulting in a seamless assessment of the intersecting needs. For example, when a relationship breaks down, FLP clients may face, among other challenges, the loss of stable housing, economic destitution, mental health struggles, or encounters with the regional child welfare authority.

While some of these challenges can be addressed through legal remedies, legal remedies do have limitations. For example, child or spousal support orders can assist clients with their financial struggles, however, such remedies may be limited based on the payer's income. Social resources such as income support and government subsidies may supplement available legal remedies. Similarly, an order for exclusive possession of the family home can assist someone struggling with a housing issue, but this remedy may not adequately consider a survivor's safety needs, and it may not be realistic as a long-term solution if the survivor cannot afford the monthly rent or mortgage payment. Subsidized housing or a woman's shelter could provide a more appropriate alternative depending on the client. Many short-term and long-term solutions to a client's problems will not come from the legal sector alone but, when legal options are coupled with social options, the client has a closer to seamless array of choices.

With this consideration in mind, we address common myths or misunder-standings of clients and service providers regarding what legal remedies are avail-able and the extent to which those legal remedies alone can "solve the problem." Approaching problem-solving through a trauma-informed lens provides a level of transparency to the client from the onset—preparing them for what to expect and to make difficult choices. For example, a protection order is a civil remedy available to individuals who fear for their safety, however it is not always the best option for survivors of violence. When meeting with a client looking for information about protection orders, the lawyer discusses the pros and cons of applying for a protection order from a legal perspective while the social worker assists the client in assessing safety and when necessary accessing women's shelters. If the abuser's aggression toward the woman escalates as a result of a court application being filed, the woman could be in considerable danger, as the abuser knows where the woman is living and how to gain access to the home. In these situations, the woman should consider obtaining safe and secure housing prior to making any court applications. We always consider safety to be the most important factor when supporting clients while tempering that with the client-centered approach reminding clients that the case ultimately belongs to them.

Pillar Two: Dynamic, Interdisciplinary Communication

When professionals do not engage in interdisciplinary communication or have an interdisciplinary skill set, it makes sense that these professionals would not have an understanding or connection to the community served. Women who have survived FV may display behavior that can be viewed negatively by those with whom she interacts who do not understand the effects of trauma on behavior and brain health. While a traumatized survivor may have a difficult time presenting evidence, gathering her thoughts, or appearing calm in court, it is not uncommon that her abuser will present (and be presented by his counsel) as charismatic, together, and stable. For example, on several occasions we have heard of legal professionals not having a strong understanding of the supports available to women living at domestic violence shelters. One woman shared with us that the judge she appeared before declared that a woman's shelter is "no place for children"; while it is clear to anyone with a basic understanding of the DV sector that it is a perfectly acceptable, if not optimal, place for children to live given the security and social supports available to the family.

In the FLP, lawyers and advocates engage in constant, fulsome dialogue and brainstorming on client files. Through regular joint meetings and ongoing com-munication, the legal professional is able to gain insight into the social systems impacting clients just as the social worker is able to learn about the legal sys-tem impacting clients. Because of this interdisciplinary approach, both the social worker and the lawyer can identify potential issues more effectively. For example, the lawyer and social worker can collaborate to prepare submissions that properly inform the court of the benefits and appropriateness of a woman's shelter as a primary residence for a child. Additionally, FLP professionals have the benefit of working in an interdisciplinary multi-program environment, and regularly consult with the professionals in the other program areas (such as immigration) as need be.

Pillar Three: Professionals with an Interdisciplinary Skill Set

The strength in an interdisciplinary approach lies with the specialized skillset that each profession brings to client work. Professionals with formal education in the social services field learn a very different skill set from individuals with a legal education. As a result, a legal service provider focusing narrowly on the legal issue at hand may not be seeing the "whole" picture. As Randell and Haskell (2013, p. 6) observe:

> Although the law is deeply involved with regulating and responding to human behaviour, legal professionals are virtually never exposed to formal or informed psychological literature, research, or professional knowledge about human behaviour in their legal education or ongoing professional training.

Many lawyers work with clients experiencing some distress as a result of criminal charges, the breakdown of a relationship, navigating the immigration system trying to sponsor loved ones, or stay in a country that makes them feel safe, settling a family member's estate, etc. Despite this reality, it is up to individual lawyers to learn, through experience or other formal training outside of law school, how to engage with clients in these difficult contexts. In contrast, social workers learn many different skills to support clients experiencing a multitude of barriers or life circumstances. During joint FLP client meetings, the lawyer and social worker have opportunities to shadow each other and incorporate new skills into their daily practice.

It is not necessary to become an expert in a new field to incorporate new skills into daily practice. For example, while an FLP advocate would never give any legal advice or provide representation at court, they can provide legal information and attend court as an emotional support or to assist with navigating what can be a very confusing system, which they learn through experience working with legal professionals. Alternatively, a lawyer need not be able to conduct a danger or suicide assessment but can implement tools, such as grounding techniques to maladaptive responses, learned from observing an advocate assist a client to de-escalate or drawing from lessons learned through trauma-informed training in order to best support survivors. Sharing knowledge across disciplines underlies trauma-informed practice, where professionals are taught that anyone at any organization can be trauma-informed when working with clients.

Pillar Four: A Robust Understanding of and Connection to the Community Served

The FLP has developed several outreach legal clinics serving women living in family violence shelters. FLP professionals sit on various community committees, allowing high-level participation in policy discussions and interdisciplinary networking at the community level. The program also provides public legal education to community members and service providers throughout the city and in surrounding areas at no cost. Further, the FLP social worker is able to make high-quality referrals when FLP services are otherwise limited, connecting survivors to specialized counseling services and support through family violence outreach workers and other community members.

The "Non-Trauma-Informed" Client Experience: Setting the Context

Without incorporating the service delivery model specific to the FLP at CLG, as outlined above, the typical FV client experience can be described as being "non-trauma-informed." To illustrate this, the following example focuses on orders that pertain to the delineation of parenting responsibilities. Parenting and custody orders outline how to distribute the powers, responsibilities, and entitlements of parents in relation to their children (Alberta Justice and Solicitor General, 2015; *Family Law Act*, 2003, s 32(2)(a)). According to Landau, Landau, and Wolfson (2009), custody and parenting orders outline who can control the physical person of the child and who has the right to make decisions about the child's upbringing, including decisions regarding the child's education, religion, and lifestyle and the right to grant or withhold consent to the marriage of an underage child. These orders also establish each parent's responsibilities for taking care of the child both physically and morally, as well as providing for the child's basic needs.

Custody and parenting orders also address access rights (for ease, the writers use the term access to mean visitation, parenting time and/or contact), which allow the non-custodial (or non-decision-making) parent to visit with the child. Orders can include a schedule allocating access time between the parents. The purpose of access is to encourage the continuation of a parent-child relationship after a marriage breakdown (Landau et al., 2009); however, the parent with access does not necessarily have the same rights or responsibilities over the life of the child.

The overall goal of the courts in making a parenting or custody order is to act in the best interests of the child (Wilson, 2015, at I(a)(ii)). The courts may consider factors such as: the love, affection, and emotional ties between children and parents or family members; the parent's ability and willingness to provide for the child; the stability of the family unit; the parent's ability to act as a parent; and any prior abuse (*Family Law Act*, 2003, c F-4.5).

These orders can be useful tools for co-parenting. The terms of the order vary depending on individual family situations. They can include terms for dropping off and picking up children, each parent's weekly access time, how parents are to communicate about the children (i.e. via email, text message, or phone), and can even dictate that neither party speak ill about the other in front of the children. However, in cases of family violence, obtaining an order can be difficult due to the use of abusive tactics by abusers described earlier. Unfortunately, abusers can turn negotiations over even simple terms into fights for power. Complications can also arise after a parenting order has been granted, despite the inclusion of specific terms. For example, although both parties may be abiding by the conditions of a parenting order, an abuser may make false claims about the other parent's conduct in relation to the order. Further, often the only way to address this breach is to return to court. The police rarely become involved in civil matters such as parenting orders unless the order contains a police enforcement clause. Even police enforcement clauses are generally limited to enforcing visitation time and do not apply to other types of breaches. Enforcement may not take precedence when police have competing emergency calls concerning crimes and public safety, and so response and enforcement is delayed. Therefore, unless a criminal act has been committed, such as child abduction, parties most often must return to family court.

In situations where abusers have or try to have their children engage in behaviors that advance the abuser's goal of controlling the other parent, survivors are put in a situation where they must remain the appropriate parent. An appropriate parent does not discuss the relationship between the abuser and the survivor or the matters before the court with the children except in a way that is age appropriate and supported by a professional with expertise in child development. When the abuser uses the children to manipulate the survivor, children are left with a picture of the survivor or the family's situation that has been painted exclusively by the abuser.

In our experience, unless there is a record of significant abuse against the other parent or toward the children, judges seldom deny or limit the abuser's access to children. Many clients and other service providers believe the common myth that access will be limited with ease. In many cases, survivors connect with the FLP in the hopes of obtaining a parenting order that prevents or limits the abuser's access to the children. Often other professionals, such as child protection workers, who sometimes misunderstand family law or common practice in family court, refer these clients to the FLP. Unfortunately, obtaining a parenting order where one parent's visitation is supervised is often easier said than done.

Survivors may be at risk for physical, emotional, or psychological damage when they abide by a parenting order that does not consider the survivor's safety or acknowledge the previous abuse. As Bala (1999, paras. 93–94) states:

> Sometimes an abusive father will be denied the right to visit his children after separation, though some judges appear to accept that even an abusive husband has the right to visit his children, posing a risk to mothers . . . The exercise of access rights can be used to control a former partner.

Unfortunately, "while research-informed expertise on domestic violence has been available to policy makers, service providers, judges and lawyers, for decades, the expertise has not resulted in significant change in the legal system" (Nielson, 2014, p. 2). This lack of change, coupled with a lack of awareness on the traumatizing effects domestic violence has on survivors by professionals, within the system perpetuates trauma either inadvertently through systemic inefficiencies or by providing a platform for abusers to continue patterns of psychological and financial abuse. This context informs our efforts to provide a trauma-informed, holistic legal service to our clients in the family law sector. The FLP attempts to address the typical non-trauma-informed experience, by offering supportive trauma-informed services and preparing survivors for the limitations that arise due to the current structure of the legal system.

The Family Law Program Model Client Experience: Case Examples

The case example of Ms. Lola Garcia illustrates this collaboration (personal details are disguised to ensure confidentiality). Ms. Garcia first accessed the FLP through the social worker after her child's daycare told her that she needed a parenting order stating her child's father was not allowed to pick the child up from daycare. Daycare staff told Ms. Garcia that if she did not provide this order to them and the child's father subsequently came to pick the child up from daycare, they would release the child to the father. Ms. Garcia went on to explain that her former partner had been extremely violent to her resulting in criminal charges against him and child protection involvement. The child protection worker involved also urged Ms. Garcia to obtain a parenting order preventing her former partner from having access to the child. As their conversation continued, the social worker in the FLP wondered whether or not the child's father even had any legal rights to the child; it was clear that Ms. Garcia would need legal advice and the social worker arranged for her to meet with the FLP lawyer at CLG.

Subsequently, both the FLP social worker and the lawyer met with Ms. Garcia. The lawyer determined that the client's former partner did not meet the legal test for guardianship under provincial legislation and, thus, did likely not have legal rights to the child. A parenting order was not necessary, and Ms. Garcia could apply for sole guardianship instead. When an application for sole guardianship is made, the other party must be notified and has the right to respond. However, Ms. Garcia's former partner had not seen the child in years, did not know where she was living, and had expressed no interest in being involved in the child's life. In applying for sole guardianship, the client ran the risk of involving the abuser in her life yet again, and she could find herself in a dangerous situation should he respond to the application.

Rather than assisting her with an application for sole guardianship, with Ms. Garcia's consent, the social worker phoned the daycare and the child protection worker. She explained to the daycare that the father was not a guardian and that releasing the child to the father would be equivalent to releasing the child to a stranger. She further advised the daycare that the FLP lawyer agreed to represent Ms. Garcia should the child's father make an application for guardianship or for contact with the child. The interdisciplinary team engaged in safety planning with Ms. Garcia around what she should do if her child's father served her with any court application, made any attempts to contact her, or posed any kind of threat, physical or otherwise.

In another case that illustrates the importance of trauma-informed legal services, Ms. Brown was being abused by her current partner and experiencing a host of associated mental and physical health challenges. She was apprehensive about seeking legal assistance and remained fearful and anxious after initiating a meeting with a legal professional at a shelter outreach clinic about potentially leaving her abuser. She was afraid that she would not be able to support herself, to relocate, or to raise her children on her own.

Ms. Brown became visibly upset each time the lawyer canvassed legal solutions and discussed the pros and cons of each option. From Ms. Brown's perspective, her concerns about leaving her partner were validated, and she appeared to be losing hope quickly. As it rarely is in these cases, it became clear that a purely legal approach would not be sufficient to assist Ms. Brown.

At a second meeting, Ms. Brown met with the lawyer and the social worker, who identified various sources of social assistance for which Ms. Brown might qualify. At the same time, the lawyer provided information and advice on the legal remedies of child and spousal support, as well as the division of matrimonial property. In the end, Ms. Brown had a comprehensive overview of the social and legal options available to her if she decided to leave her abuser, resulting in a holistic service, provided in a trauma-informed manner making the prospect of decision-making less daunting to her.

If the FLP social worker and lawyer had worked in silos rather than together, important opportunities to support clients would be missed. The social worker would likely not be aware that a legal test for guardianship exists, would be unclear about daycare legislation, or even the difference between parenting, contact, and guardianship orders. Similarly, the lawyer would not be versed in assessing for risk in family violence situations, practicing trauma-informed service delivery, safety planning, or interdisciplinary solutions to assist clients with their varied needs. Working together is truly the best way to practice holistically.

Conclusion

Through the experiences highlighted in this chapter, it is obvious that the legal system is complex and difficult to navigate. The difficulty of obtaining satisfactory recourse within this system is exacerbated for survivors of family violence. The FLP at CLG seeks to support survivors in managing their experiences in relation to the legal system.

By integrating social work and legal practice over the past eighteen months, the FLP has adapted the Bronx Defender Defense Model and adopted a more trauma-informed, client-centered and holistic approach based in current trauma-informed research and best practices. CLG is a small non-profit organization with limited resources. Thus, the FLP's ambition to adopt a truly holistic and trauma-informed model is tempered by institutional limits and intra-agency program mandates. While small organizations have some challenges in adopting a truly interdisciplinary approach, adaptations are possible. For example, as the organization itself moves toward a more holistic model, agency-wide interdisciplinary trainings in suicide awareness, domestic violence, crisis intervention, trauma-informed service, privacy legislation, public legal education, court diversion programs, and the holistic service model have been provided. Rooted in experience, the FLP approach allows professionals (and intra-program professionals) to collaborate to manage client expectations, thus reducing the element of surprise and retraumatization that survivors may feel throughout the legal experience. Fortunately, leadership at CLG supports the FLP's vision of representation and there has been an organizational shift that supports this preferred service delivery model.

Note

1. The writers would like to thank Ramsha Shafaq and Kyle Isherwood for their assistance in writing this chapter and Natalie Simpson and Margaret Keelaghan from Calgary Legal Guidance office who suggested edits and revisions.

References

Ahmad, F., Ali, M., & Stewart, D. E. (2005). Spousal-abuse among Canadian immigrant women. *Journal of Immigrant Health, 7*(4), 239–246. doi:10.1007/s10903-005-5120-4

Alberta Justice and Solicitor General. (2015). *What are parenting orders and contact orders under the Alberta Family Law Act?* Retrieved from: https://justice.alberta.ca/programs_services/families/Common_Questions_Library_Families/ParentingOrdersContactOrdersUnderAlbertaFamilyLawAct.aspx/DispForm.aspx?ID=6.

Bala, N. (1999). Legal responses to domestic violence in Canada and the role of health care professionals. *Syrtash Collection of Family Law Articles* (SFLRP/2000–004).

Brownridge, D. A., Chan, K. L., Hiebert-Murphy, D., Ristock, J., Tiwari, A., Leung, W. C., & Santos, S. C. (2008). The elevated risk for non-lethal post-separation violence in Canada: A comparison of separated, divorced, and married women. *Journal of Interpersonal Violence, 23*(1), 117–135. doi:10.1177/0886260507307914

Canadian Resource Centre for Victims of Crime. (2011). *Spousal abuse.* Prepared by the Canadian Resource Centre for Victims of Crime. Retrieved from: http://crcvc.ca/docs/spousalabuse.pdf.

Doherty, D. & Berglund, D. (2008). *Psychological abuse: A discussion paper.* Ottawa, ON: Public Health Agency of Canada. Retrieved from: www.phac-aspc.gc.ca/sfv-avf/sources/fv/fv-psych-abus/index-eng.php.

Elliott, D. E., Bjelajac, P., Fallot, R. D., Markoff, L. S., & Reed, B. G. (2005). Trauma-informed or trauma-denied: Principles and implementation of trauma-informed services for women. *Journal of Community Psychology*, *33*(4) 461–477. doi:10.1002/jcop.20063

Family Law Act, Statutes of Alberta (2003 c F4.5) at s 32(2)(a-b). Retrieved from: www.qp.alberta.ca/documents/Acts/F04P5.pdf.

Jennings, A. (2008). Models for developing trauma-informed behavioural health systems and trauma-specific services. United States National Center for Trauma-Informed Care. Retrieved from: www.ct.gov/dmhas/lib/dmhas/trauma/TraumaModels.pdf.

Landau, B., Landau, N., & Wolfson, L. (2009). *Family mediation, arbitration and collaborative practice handbook* (5th ed.). Markham, ON: LexisNexis Canada.

Miller, S. L. & Smolter, N. L. (2011). "Paper abuse": When all else fails, batterers use procedural stalking. *Violence Against Women*, *5*, 637–650. doi:10.1177/1077801211407290

Neilson, L. C. (2014). Enhancing safety: When domestic violence cases are in multiple legal systems (Criminal, family, child protections): A family law, domestic violence perspective. Ottawa, ON: Department of Justice. Retrieved from: www.justice.gc.ca/eng/rp-pr/fl-lf/famil/enhan-renfo/neilson_web.pdf.

Przekop, M. (2011). One more battleground: Domestic violence, child custody, and the batterers' relentless pursuit of their victims through the courts. *Seattle Journal for Social Justice*, *9*(2), 1052–1106.

Randall, M. (2013). Restorative justice: Restorative justice and gendered violence? From vaguely hostile skeptic to cautious convert: Why feminists should critically engage with restorative approaches to law. *Dalhousie Law Journal*, *36*, 461–464.

Randall, M. & Haskell, L. (2013). Restorative justice: Trauma-informed approaches to law: Why restorative justice must understand trauma and psychological coping. *Dalhousie Law Journal*, *36*, 501–533.

SLT v AKT, 2009 ABQB 13 (Alberta Queens Bench 2009) at para. 7.

Smyth, N. (March 20, 2012). *Trauma-informed social work practice: What is it and why should we care?—Opinion piece by Dr. Nancy Smyth*. Retrieved from: https://swscmedia.wordpress.com/2012/03/20/trauma-informed-social-work-practice-what-is-it-and-why-should-we-care-opinion-piece-by-dr-nancy-smyth/.

Steinberg, R. (2013). Heeding Gideon's call in the twenty-first century: Holistic defense and the new public defense paradigm. *Washington and Lee Law Review*, *70*(2), 962–1017. Retrieved from: http://scholarlycommons.law.wlu.edu/wlulr/vol70/iss2/6.

Williams, C. (2010). Economic well-being. *Statistics Canada Catalogue* (89–503-X) Retrieved from: www.statcan.gc.ca/pub/89–503-x/2010001/article/11388-eng.pdf.

Wilson, J. (2015). *Children and the law*. Markham, ON: Butterworth.

Part IV
Restorative Justice

10 Creating Safety, Respect, and Equality for Women

Lessons from the Intimate Partner Violence and Restorative Justice Movements

Tod Augusta-Scott, Pamela Harrison, and Verona Singer[1]

Almost twenty years ago in Nova Scotia a significant rift occurred between feminists in the Intimate Partner Violence (IPV) movement and feminists in the restorative justice (RJ) movement. This fracture resulted in the IPV movement successfully establishing a moratorium on restorative justice programming for intimate partner violence being processed in the criminal justice system. The split created such a division among those involved that no parts of the criminal justice system have since embraced restorative approaches on any issues connected to domestic violence, except for programming run by Nova Scotian Mi'kmaw communities (Archibald & Llewellyn, 2006; Clairmont & Waters, 2015; Rubin, 2010). The moratorium remains, as do the deficiencies of the criminal justice system's response to women who experience intimate partner abuse. The pressure created by the inadequacies of the current system, and further developments in both fields in this province have encouraged IPV professionals to begin to dialogue in search of better interventions.

This chapter focuses on the common ground for this dialogue, drawing on the strengths of both IPV and RJ movements in addressing intimate partner violence. Various authors have addressed the value of combining these strengths (Frederick & Lizdas, 2010; Goodmark, 2012; Hopkins, 2012; Pennell & Francis, 2005; Ptacek, 2010a; Strang & Braithwaite, 2002). This chapter examines some of the lessons learned within each movement with respect to how to better serve women. We also review the commonality of interests of the movements such as making interventions victim-centered; addressing issues of safety; focusing on men being responsible for their violence; engaging the local community to take responsibility to support the individual to change; and engaging the wider community to take responsibility to address broader social issues of men's violence against women.

The authors have all been in the IPV movement for many years as executive directors of a provincial women's shelters association (Pamela), an urban victim services unit (Verona), and a men's intervention program (Tod). In this chapter, we observe the strengths of the IPV movement and its commonalities with RJ principles. As the authors became more confident of the extent of the common purpose in the practice and values of the two movements, a two-day workshop was provided to women's shelter directors, men's program directors, RJ practitioners and academics. Could the fractures begin to be mended? Could more profound reforms begin in the criminal justice system?

The two-day workshop provided IPV staff with the first formal opportunity to talk about restorative justice since the moratorium was established. Many who attended were nervous about discussing the topic, in part, because previous discussions had concluded that any approach that did not punish men to the full extent of the law or *might* involve facilitating contact between some women and their partners or ex-partners was dangerous for women. The two-day session involved consultants who are recognized as feminists and also experts in restorative justice. The experts who acted as consultants for the group were Jennifer Llewellyn, Schulich Law School, Dalhousie University; Lori Haskell, Department of Psychiatry, University of Toronto; Melanie Randall, Department of Law, University of Toronto (Randall, 2013; Randall & Haskell, 2013); and Lisa Teryl, Senior Legal Counsel, Nova Scotia Human Rights Commission. The group participants asked questions of the consultants and each other as they considered how both fields could help each other effectively address intimate partner violence.

While the participants were interested in talking more about the possibility of using restorative justice to address intimate partner violence within and among their own organizations, they were not interested in lifting the moratorium on using restorative justice within the current criminal justice system. For many, there would need to be numerous changes in the system that were consistent with the values shared among both the IPV and RJ communities. Some of these values include principles such as a victim-centered approach to justice, defining justice as repairing harms, listening to women, focusing on women's safety and men's responsibility. The themes discussed in the two-day workshop are presented in the context of a published literature review, forming the core discussion in this chapter.

A Victim-Centered Approach

The IPV movement provides to the restorative justice movement a clear focus on the interests of women who have been victimized, and demands that the complexity and subtleties of these dynamics be understood by any system of justice. IPV practitioners prioritize women's safety and work toward restoring their dignity, respect, and equality. While Braithwaite (2002) and Zehr (2002) argue that restorative justice is victim-centered, in practice, however, restorative justice in the Unites States and Canada remains primarily focused on the offender. Restorative programming primarily focuses on rehabilitating youth, the offender, which replicates the offender-focus of the traditional criminal justice system. While restorative practices stem from Indigenous communities in North America and New Zealand starting in the 1970s, the contemporary field developed from the Mennonite communities in Canada and later the United States (Fernandez, 2010). Faith-based victim-offender reconciliation programs were the first to use the term "restorative justice." The process focused on repairing the harm caused by the crime and bringing about reconciliation and forgiveness through face-to-face interaction. Mark Yantzi, a Mennonite probation officer, in Kitchener, Ontario in 1974, created the first program. The success of these programs with youth soon spread throughout Canada and the Unites States (Ptacek, 2010c; Zehr, 1990).

Similar to the global context, in Nova Scotia restorative justice has been primarily applied to youth crimes (Ptacek, 2010b) and young offenders. The victims of these crimes are often adults who attend sessions with the youth to help rehabilitate them. For example, the person who has been victimized could be, in fact, representing a department store from which the youth has stolen. While the (adult) victim's needs are ostensibly the focus of the session, often the victim is part of a process that attempts to persuade the youth to see the error of their ways and encourages them to take responsibility.

When using a restorative approach to address violence against women was first proposed in Nova Scotia, the proposal paralleled the model of restorative justice that is used with youth. Clearly, from the perspective of the IPV movement, this process would fall short with cases of intimate partner violence (Archibald & Llewellyn, 2006). Victims should not be responsible for rehabilitating the men that have hurt them. Women do not want to be in a position where they are trying to convince their male partners of their responsibility and of the seriousness of the effects of their abuse. Moreover, unlike a majority of youth crime, intimate partner violence cases need to account for issues of safety and power that may stem from a history of abuse and possible ongoing abuse. Also in intimate partner violence cases, the woman often has a history of being repeatedly victimized by the same person and may be dependent on the man financially or sharing other responsibilities such as co-parenting.

IPV advocates were understandably cautious about systemic restorative justice programming given the focus on the offender and not the victim. For example, the criminal legal process for victims provides minimal support. Defense counsel represents the accused in a well-defined role. The victims, however, are unrepresented in the system. The Crown or District Attorney represents the interest of the state not the woman. Within this traditional legal framework, the crime is considered a violation of state law—and only indirectly, a violation of a particular victim. A victimized woman, then, is singularly used by the legal system as a witness to garner a conviction. Further, the state pays for men's incarceration and rehabilitation, yet most often does not pay for services to help restore women after being abused. In Nova Scotia, criminal justice services offered to women are limited to the provincial Department of Justice Victim Services, which assists women to navigate the legal process and refers women to outside agencies for other support. This traditional process, however, does not engage the victim as a central principle of the justice.

A restorative victim-centered approach would command fundamental change in the current criminal justice goals and processes. Again, from the perspective of both advocates of the IPV and the restorative justice movement, the legal system would have to move away from defining "just outcomes" as simply convictions, to defining these as repairing and healing the harms done to victims. Restorative approaches to intimate partner violence have been adopted by some community-based programs in Nova Scotia such as men's programs, using the victim-centered approach of the IPV movement (Augusta-Scott, 2008). These programs have engaged in restorative practices without a change in the criminal justice system to adopt a restorative approach. This restorative engagement happens with men who have volunteered to attend programs or have been mandated to attend programs for domestic violence. These approaches ensure that the process focuses on healing and repairing the harms done to women, and restores women's safety, respect, and dignity. The maturity of these community-based programs provides a model for how restorative justice could be applied to interpersonal violence in the criminal justice system.

Listen to Women

To center women in the process, women need to be consulted about not only what happened but also about what they want to repair the harms that have been done to them and their relationships (Archibald & Llewellyn, 2006; Frederick & Lizdas, 2010; Goel, 2000, 2010; van Wormer, 2009). While this may involve women accessing housing, counseling, finances, and childcare, it may also include what women want from their partners or ex-partners. As a result of a commitment to women's agency, a restorative approach would also invite women to choose what process will help address the harms. Some women may decide that they want to achieve a conviction through the court system, others want to address the harms in a pre-charge restorative process outside the court system, and some may want the opportunity to engage in restorative processes post-conviction. Whatever their choice, women may still want their needs and the needs of their family and community to be the primary focus of justice. Women can decide if and how they want to connect with the men who hurt them. With a restorative approach, women can decide if they want to address the issues with men on their own or with the help of professionals.

While the authors have been committed to listening to women and their self-determination, in retrospect we also recognize how our earlier support of the mandatory state intervention introduced in the mid-1990s of pro-arrest, pro-charge, pro-prosecution in IPV did not result in listening to many women. Such an approach resulted in the legal authorities arresting and prosecuting men regardless of what women wanted. This mandated response was designed to support women who wanted charges laid against their partners but would not do it on their own because they were afraid their partners might retaliate. The reality of this policy, however, is that many women do not want their partners to have criminal record convictions (Coker, 2002; Frederick & Lizdas, 2010;

Grauwiler & Mills, 2004; Mills, 2008; van Wormer, 2009). With a restorative response, one possible intervention could include a woman's counselor or advocate working with women to assess over time whether women want to have criminal charges laid or not or whether a woman wants to cooperate with the Crown Prosecutor or District Attorney. The staff can assist women to make informed choices, providing women with information about the current process of having the Crown or District Attorney take over. This process respects that women may have other ideas about what would achieve just outcomes for themselves and their families other than criminalizing their partners or ex-partners.

A restorative approach resists the gender essentialism that has significantly influenced those of us working in the IPV movement (Augusta-Scott, 2007; Goodmark, 2012; Mills, 2008; Singer, 2012). Within the IPV movement, women were typically defined uniformly as being terrorized, powerless to stop the violence, and all wanting to or should want to leave their partners. These uniform assumptions about women who have been abused prevented us from hearing the varied ways women were defining just outcomes. My (Verona) PhD research helped disrupt the essentialist assumptions I was making about women who are abused (Singer, 2012). While emphasizing that women are not responsible for men's choices to abuse is important, the women I interviewed commented that they were not simply helpless, passive victims. They often sincerely wanted to stay with their partners because they knew there was more to him than his choice to abuse. Often women did not identify safety as their primary concern. In retrospect, women had been telling me these stories previously; however, I did not listen to them. Having only one acceptable script for women in abusive situations—that they are helpless, powerless victims who want to leave or should want to leave—prevented me from truly listening to them and decreased the likelihood of me helping women find solutions that best fit their particular circumstances.

Similarly, when I (Tod) began also to talk with women I heard that the violence was often not "high risk" or even never high risk in their particular relationships (Johnson, 2008). Rather than wanting to leave their partners, women indicated that they wanted to stay with their partners and for them to be given educational and economic opportunities to help stabilize their family. Other women wanted nothing more to do with their ex-partners. However, regardless of whether women stay with the men or not, whether men are charged or not, most wanted the men to take responsibility and acknowledge what they had done. Most women wanted to be assured that the men were not going to hurt other women. Most remained connected to the men because they lived in the same small community or they shared children. The women remained invested in the help they wanted for and from their partners or ex-partners.

While I (Pamela) had also supported the pro-arrest, pro-charge, pro-prosecution policy to support abused women, as I visited shelters across the province and worked with both their executive directors and frontline staff, their frustrations with the current criminal justice system became very evident. I listened to women who resented the pro-arrest, pro-charge, pro-prosecution policy, and many who genuinely loved their partners, and just wanted the abuse to stop. I began to think about that policy from the perspective of choice, and realized that, with the best of intentions, the IPV movement had inadvertently taken away their choices and had been instrumental in developing a policy that has, essentially, failed many women.

As a result of listening to individual women and recognizing that women define just outcomes in a variety of ways, many community responses have moved away from the uniformed response of groups for men and safety plans for women. Lagging behind, the traditional legal system is criticized as being inflexible and unresponsive to women (Goodman & Epstein, 2008; Goodmark, 2012; Grauwiler & Mills, 2004; Mills, 2008). Restorative justice principles support a more subtle, contextualized justice and cannot be defined by any particular procedure. To understand its principles is to understand it is not a one-size-fits-all approach and cannot be manualized as such (Coker, 2002). The practices of restorative justice can be varied, while the principles are consistent and make far-reaching demands of all the participants when applied in a system of justice (Llewellyn, 2011; Teryl, 2015; Zehr, 2002).

A number of participants from the IPV movement who attended the two-day workshop expressed relief that a restorative approach would not simply replace the current one-size-fits-all legal response with another one-size-fits-all approach. Inevitably, any one-size-fits-all approach is wrong for women, regardless of how well thought out it is. The workshop participants were pleased that a restorative approach would investigate what individual women want and how they might define fairness and just outcomes. The staff want the interventions to be responsive to individual women and what they want for their families. In this way, a restorative approach is a principled approach rather than a manualized approach to the work. A restorative approach recognizes that the number and combination of conversations, whether group, individual, family, couple, and so forth will change from case to case. As one participant stated:

> I don't have any concerns if RP [restorative practice] is done properly. If we were to roll something out without thoughtful consideration, that would be problematic. However, I don't see that as being a concern here. I would be concerned if we saw this as a blanket approach or a one-size-fits-all.

Women's Safety

The IPV movement makes an important contribution to addressing intimate partner violence by prioritizing the safety of women who have been abused. Those in the IPV movement have studied the various ways in which men can abuse and control their female partners. Sometimes the abuse can be subtle. This awareness about safety issues is essential in being able to manage any possible formal contact between the men and the women they have harmed. In conjuction with those working with men, IPV staff can manage these situations in a restorative process to ensure women are not being pressured by men for contact or not at risk of retaliation by men after contact. Shelters pro vide residential and non-residential services such as shelter, crisis intervention, safety planning, and counseling. Because of the leadership of the IPV movement on this issue, those who already use or simply advocate for using restorative alternatives to address intimate partner violence also prioritize women's safety (Fernandez, 2010; Frederick & Lizdas, 2010; Goodmark, 2012; Hayden, 2012; Mills, 2008; Pennell & Francis, 2005; Strang & Braithwaite, 2002). In addition to supporting the efforts of the IPV movement, restorative approaches can also engage men who have done the harm and others to help create safety for women. Working with men can contribute to both stopping the abuse and repairing the harms by respecting the distance women want or by taking responsibility in front of women. When men engage in these initiatives they often lead women to feel safer.

Many who participated in the two-day conversation prioritized concerns for women's safety, particularly in cases where a woman and a man may talk in person. One participant stated, "Learning about a restorative approach helped me to understand that the victim would not be re-victimized. I saw the different ways that would ensure the victim would be in a safe place. That was eye-opening for me."

There remained concerns about the possibility that some men would better be able to manipulate a restorative approach than the current punitive legal system. One participant was of the opinion that, "There needs to be some pretty frank discussions. People need to understand that some men manipulate the system and consider whether this situation can be managed or not."

Others who worked with men shared this concern, however, they also thought that many men wanted to make amends and were sincere in their efforts. They also indicated that, with proper collateral contacts, the process of identifying men who are not sincere is not difficult. Participants in the two-day conversation welcomed the possibility of men participating in processes that could lead to their partners and ex-partners feeling safer.

Men's Responsibility and Accountability

Both IPV and RJ approaches want men to take responsibly to stop their violence and to be held accountable for their choices (Frederick & Lizdas, 2010; Hayden, 2014; McMaster, 2014; Pence & Paymar, 1993). The IPV movement has sought to have the legal system force men to take responsibility by having abuse against women constituted as a crime through pro-arrest, pro-charge, and pro-prosecution. A segment of the IPV movement also advocated for pro-gramming for men to help stop their violence. Men taking responsibility means not only stopping the violence but also men healing and repairing the effects of the violence.

An important part of these men's programs has involved not working with men in isolation, that is, without contacting their partners or ex-partners. Many of these programs sought to be accountable to the women and women's advocates to ensure the man and the interventions were actually contributing to women's safety. The practice of men's programs contacting partners or ex-partners seems to have eroded and more agencies are working with men in isolation (Frederick & Lizdas, 2010; Scott, Heslop, David, & Kelly, 2017, Chapter 4, this volume). Restorative approaches have the possibility of reinvigorating the principle of not working with men in isolation from their partners or ex-partners. These approaches are also focused on men taking responsibility to stop the abuse and be responsible not only to a judge, who represents the broader communities' norms, but to men's families, friends, and their community.

To create a social response to intimate partner violence that treated it as seriously as other assaults, the rhetoric of the early IPV movement adopted the same punitive tone and objectives as the traditional criminal justice system. This definition of justice was the only option most people knew. This punitive approach supported the traditional legal system's way of operating. Men who are guilty are presumed not to want to take responsibility to stop their violence and repair the harms. With this premise, the remedies move directly to punishment, never asking men what they can do to fix the wrongs. The retributive system punishes men as a way of holding them accountable. However, this approach encourages men to minimize and deny responsibility since, to do otherwise, will necessarily inflict harm on themselves.

In contrast, a restorative system does not assume that men want to avoid responsibility. While many men find that taking responsibility is challenging; while many men are unclear about what taking responsibility means beyond saying, "I did it"; while many men need to be mandated initially to do the right thing, eventually, with the right support, many men believe that the process of taking responsibility and repairing the harms they have created is rewarding. Such an approach is reflected in some of the specialized domestic violence courts (Tutty, Ursel, & Douglas, 2008). If he does not accept responsibility and correct the wrong, restorative justice imposes justice but does it in ways that reflect restorative principles. For example, it focuses on repairing and healing the victim and asks what will make it better for women despite his lack of responsibility.

In terms of creating these opportunities for men to take responsibility, a restorative approach would support a pro-arrest policy because it ensures men take responsibility since a lack of cooperation from the men would escalate from arrest to charges. However, automatic charge and prosecution, which is the current protocol, may not be helpful in achieving just outcomes for the woman. If men are taking responsibility and women do not want their partners or ex-partners to have criminal records, an outcome that produces a criminal record for their partners may cause women further harms economically and otherwise to their family units.

Of course, if men are unable or unwilling to take responsibly, the state may have to have a remedy to uphold the community's values and to restore women's safety and respect. Restorative justice is justice. It seeks, however, to tailor justice closely to the context and to allow an opportunity for a wrongdoer to voluntary make it right. If that does not happen, justice must then be imposed (Braithwaite, 2002). Therefore, if there are reasonable grounds for the arrest and men refuse to engage a restorative pre-charge process, the men are charged.

Restorative justice processes also happen without a legal mandate by a woman or a man contacting a restorative domestic violence program, such as the work conducted at the Bridges Institute and New Start Counselling (Augusta-Scott, 2017, Chapter 12 this volume). These kinds of restorative programs can be tapped for pre-charge, pre-trial, and pre-sentencing processes. They can be integrated into criminal justice domestic violence protocols if the IPV movement makes a demand for their work to have a role in the justice system.

The IPV movement participants in the two-day workshop emphasized the need for men and men's programs to be responsible to and in dialogue with women who have been abused, and their advocates. They also saw how women benefit from women's shelters and men's programs working closer together. Along with the women's shelter staff, most of the staff who work with men were also feminist women with years of experience in the IPV movement. Some programs for men work closely with shelters in the province while others do not. Part of the two-day workshop involved the women's shelter staff learning more about the men's programming. All of the men's programs have contact with partners of the men, some offer women's counseling as well. Many of the women whose partners attend the men's programs have not accessed shelter services, whether in-house or outreach. As a result of recognizing that many men change, one participant in the two-day conversation stated that there needs to be more work done in partnership with organizations supporting men:

> Engaging men in case conferencing and in the process more because we have [historically] focused our work primarily on the victim and we put men in a box and isolate him. So we need to take a look at families and how do we help those that want to reconcile and keep safe.

As trust grew over the two-day workshop, another staff commented, "It was interesting watching the two groups—men's programs and the women's shelters—on how they were going to work together because some hadn't really connected before. That is building bridges."

Most participants recognized that a restorative approach would not only involve how they were engaging women and men who consult them but also how staff engage with each other as colleagues. One individual noted:

> So much has gone on between some shelters and men's programs and I openly discussed the disconnect between my shelter and men's program in the area. We said we would both like to work on it but the trust factor is still a key issue. Let's try to use a restorative approach to mend what has happened between us.

Both movements identify that men and the programs that help them need to be accountable to the women they have harmed and their advocates. Working with men should not be done in isolation from their families.

Change is Possible

Restorative justice focuses, in part, on how men can change their choices, stop their violence and how they can successfully work to heal and repair the effects of the violence. To implement a fully restorative justice system, one must accept that men can change and participate in a responsible manner in restoring women's safety, respect, and equality. Staff from both shelters and men's programs have been cynical that men would actually change, that men could be part of the solution to women's safety, equality, and healing. The movement had defined men's violence solely in terms of it "working" for men and primarily resulting in "privilege" and "power and control." This narrow analysis of men's violence left many of us wondering why men would want to change.

Part of the IPV movement advocated for services for men in an effort to stop their violence against women. However, even this element was cynical that men would change. Women's advocates helped establish funding for men's intervention programs in Nova Scotia. However, they advocated for men's programs with the sole intent to make women safer. At that time, the women's movement had very little concern for the men themselves. I (Pamela) was skeptical about men's ability or desire to change their behavior, and solely focused on supporting women and their children. However, by engaging with those involved with men who abuse, I developed a strong respect for the careful and respectful way they worked with men, not only to change their behavior but also to give them the space to understand and acknowledge the harm they had done. I began to see that men could participate in helpful conversations supported by a restorative process.

Similarly, while I (Tod) had worked exclusively with men for many years, I always assumed that they only wanted power and control and would not change and, in fact, did not want to change (Augusta-Scott, 2003, 2006, 2009). When I started to have direct conversations with women, I realized there was more to the men than simply wanting power and control. Many men did want their violence to stop but many men really considered their partners as responsible for the men's abuse. I heard stories from women, not only of the men being controlling, but also about how they were good partners and caring fathers at various times in the relationship. As a result, I began to ask men about what they valued and preferred in relationships (Augusta-Scott, 2003; Brown & Augusta-Scott, 2007). They reported that they preferred different types of relationships with their partners and children than their use of violence suggested. I found that many men wanted loving, caring harmonious relationships with all their family members. Often their violence was not only a means of establishing control but also a (misguided) way of trying to live these positive values. For example, many men yelled at their children to try and teach them about respect.

At the same time, another segment of the IPV movement did not concern itself with men. This part was influenced by a separatist approach to social justice that emphasized strategies that were "of women, by women, for women." I (Verona) was in the IPV movement for years and never considered work with men as a part of the solution for women. I did not begin to consider how men might contribute to women's healing until I conducted research on intimate partner violence for my PhD (Singer, 2012). I interviewed women who had been designated as "high risk" on what would be helpful to them. While the women did not wish to reunite with their ex-partners, they believed that men needed to take responsibility for their abuse and get help to stop the violence. The women inquired whether I would be interviewing men who abused for my research. My initial response was, "Goodness no, why would I do that? How could interviewing men possibly contribute to my research?" I was not interested in them or their experiences; I didn't see how talking with men about their violence could be in the best interest of women. As I listened to the women, however, almost all of them indicated that what would help them is for the men to get help, be it treatment for addictions, mental health, access to education, and employment opportunities, or counseling to stop the violence. The women believed men could change. They wanted the men to take responsibility for their actions and become accountable if they were given the support.

Because of my conversations with these women, I realized that, in much of my efforts in the domestic violence field, I had relegated men to the sidelines. By focusing policy and program discussions primarily on women, the field inadvertently placed too great a burden on the woman—she becomes responsible for escaping the violence, rather than the man being held responsible for ending it. While interventions with men should not supersede, or be developed in isolation from supports directed at the abused woman, it makes sense that a societal problem as complex and widespread as violence against women should be tackled from more than one angle. I now realize that intervention programs for men can facilitate profound acknowledgement for women of the existence and significance of the abuse.

Social Justice/Social Change

The IPV movement and the restorative movement are both movements for social justice and social change. They are both feminist movements that seek to challenge how issues of sexism, racism, and class serve to support men's violence against women. As a result, both movements are aware of how violence and oppression in a relationship creates a power imbalance in relationships that must be accounted for in interventions with intimate partner violence (Frederick & Lizdas, 2010). For some, the intent behind pro-arrest, pro-charge, pro-prosecution strategies was to address the imbalance of power between women and men in the context of intimate partner violence. The intent was to have the state support women against the power of their partners.

Both movements also recognize that the power imbalance is created not only through the fear men create by using or threatening to use violence against their partners. The power imbalance is also supported by patriarchy. Societal gender expectations encourage the idea for both partners that men are supposed to have power and control in their relationships. The power imbalance is supported further by social expectations that women are supposed to focus on what others want—not themselves. Further, women are expected to make others feel better, even when the women themselves have been harmed. Women are expected to be forgiving and not angry. As a result, after a conflict, women are pressured by these social expectations to forgo taking care of themselves and, instead, continue to take care of others.

These social expectations need to be accounted for in conversations with women before possible contact with partners or ex-partners about taking responsibility to stop the violence and repair the harms. IPV staff need to ensure that women are aware of these dynamics and are making choices to participate in conversations because of their own free will and not because they feel pressured by fear or by patriarchal expectations. For example, women need to be invited to not feel obligated to relinquish their anger over injustice or to forgive their partners or ex-partners as men seek to take responsibility for the harm they have done (Curtis-Fawley & Daly, 2005; Frederick & Lizdas, 2010; Ptacek, 2010c). Interventions to stop men's violence against women need to address the patriarchal forces that shape this issue of social injustice.

As a result of the social justice analysis informing both the IPV and RJ movements, the strategies they adopt for change include not only work with individual men or families but change within the wider community (Braithwaite, 2002; Coker, 2002, 2006; Frederick & Lizdas, 2010; Zehr, 2002). These movements want to engage the wider community to change cultural values and norms that support stopping men's violence against women. The process of creating justice needs to meaningfully include the community. Along with the man, the community needs to take responsibility to support the woman and man in an effort to ensure just outcomes; to ensure the man stops his violence and that respect, safety, trust, and equality are restored. This process moves beyond the current legal system where the community allows a judge to decide on just outcomes. For men, these communities can involve groups of men, family members, or community-based services both supporting men and reminding them of their values of taking responsibly and having respectful relationships. The community and the men also need to challenge the wider community to change the social forces that supported men's violence against women.

To contribute to social change and for the public to be confident justice is being done, the interventions with intimate partner violence cannot be completely confidential. Private justice does not safeguard the public good. At the same time, the earlier the issue is removed from the state justice system, the greater the privacy that can be afforded while still balancing out the public interest. For example, a woman or man may engage a community program to initiate a restorative process and choose which family or community players they want involved. Alternatively, if the police were involved, a matter that is referred to a restorative process post-arrest and pre-charge, need only have the arresting officer involved representing the broader public good in developing the plan that helps heal and repair the victims harm. If a matter proceeds to charges and community restorative domestic violence programs are involved, then the Crown or District Attorney is involved representing the state's interest in the plan that helps to heal and repair the victim's harm. Similarly if the matter is sent to trial and a conviction entered, a judge would need to be involved in the restorative sentencing plan. At this stage, the restorative justice processes are fully open to the wider public, which is consistent with liberal democratic principles of open courts (Dagenais v. Canadian Broadcasting Corp., 1994 CanLII 39 (SCC)).

The issue of privacy can be important to women in resolving these cases. Depending on the stage of the process (self-referred or referred after pre-charge, post-charge etc.), to address this issue, some interventions do not need to make public the intimate details of women's relationships. At the same time, in conjunction with the women, those involved in the process could collectively communicate their values and commitments to those outside the process. Through these values and commitments, these restorative processes cannot only be transparent to the wider community but transform it. Such processes can demonstrate how men can take responsibility for stopping their violence and building respectful relationships. The public can also be made aware of how men are living up to these values by completing agreements set out by the restorative process. In this way, the men are confirmed to be responsible to not only to their immediate community but the wider community as well.

Commonalities between the Movements

Those within the IPV movement who attended the two-day workshop recognized the resonance between their feminist values and practices and the restorative approach being explored. Rather than restorative justice principles and ideas being foreign, many identified that they also valued giving women more voice and choices; creating greater accountability for men; engaging community and defining the issue as a social problem. For many in the discussion, the restorative approach offered them another way to talk about values and practices that have long been important to them. Several people noted:

> I always like to have conversations where people realize that we are doing some of the stuff in our own work around restorative principles. We are not at ground zero and we can build on what we are doing and move forward.
>
> A restorative approach is a way of articulating what we value and are committed to in the work we currently do. It offers us a theoretical framework for what we have been practicing. We identified that this approach wasn't really different, it just offers a politically powerful [way] to articulate our practices.

One participant clarified that the shelter has been trying to restore women's safety, equality, and respect for a long time. Another mentioned that there has also been a long history of a segment of the IPV movement that advocates for men's services:

> Restorative language leads people to think it is something new but I suspect it is not. There has been a general support in the province for working with men. A restorative approach has given us a way of describing and affirming that guys can be part of the solution to restore respect and equality.

In terms of future conversations, most participants of the two-day workshop wished to continue; some with a regional conversation, while others wanted to invest more in their immediate local conversations. One shelter staff member indicated that the process led her to realize how committed the men's counselors also were to women's safety:

> We can get caught up in the fearfulness of our position: women's safety is our turf. We need to let that go, as we cannot do everything. The two-day conversation was fruitful and would like to continue meeting with all those people.

These themes were reflected in a number of participant's comments about the possibility of coordinating the work with women and men more closely to benefit women. Many participants mentioned that they have valued and worked on such coordination for many years.

Conclusion

Interventions with intimate partner violence are better when they draw on both the wisdom of the IPV movement and the restorative movement. Such an approach can create more safety for women and greater accountability of men and men's programs. Further, some women will have the option of having contact with their partners or ex-partners that will lead to men healing and repairing the harms they have created. This approach could also create new strategies for social change focused on inequality as a result of gender, race, and class and may engage the immediate community and the wider community. The community is challenged to examine the larger social forces such as sexism, racism, and poverty that contribute to men's violence against women in relationship. Members of the community are invited to take responsibility to restore safety, equality, and respect for women. The reflections of those in the IPV movement in Nova Scotia show promise for developing new possibilities for women and their families after abuse. Toward this end, the community conversations involving both IPV and RJ movements in Nova Scotia continue. The conversations are both supporting the restorative work already being done in communities and creating a vision for how a criminal justice system could work with community-based agencies to create just outcomes for women who have been abused.

Note

1. Names appear alphabetically.

References

Archibald, B. & Llewellyn, J. (2006). The challenges of institutionalizing comprehensive restorative justice: Theory and practice in Nova Scotia. *Dalhousie Law Journal, 29,* 297–343.

Augusta-Scott, T. (2003). Dichotomies in the power and control story: Exploring multiple stories about men who choose abuse in intimate relationships. In Dulwich Centre Publications (Eds.), *Responding to violence: A collection of papers relating to child sexual abuse and violence in intimate relationships* (pp. 204–224). Adelaide, AU: Dulwich Centre Publications.

Augusta-Scott, T. (2006). Talking with men who have used violence in intimate relationships: An interview with Tod Augusta-Scott. *International Journal of Narrative Therapy and Community Work, 4,* 23–30.

Augusta-Scott, T. (2007). Conversations with men about women's violence: Ending men's violence by challenging gender essentialism. In C. Brown & T. Augusta-Scott (Eds.), *Narrative therapy: Making meaning, making lives* (pp. 197–210). Thousand Oaks, CA: Sage.

Augusta-Scott, T. (2008). *Narrative therapy: Abuse intervention program. A group facilitator's manual.* Truro, NS: Bridges – a domestic violence counselling, training and research institute.

Augusta-Scott, T. (2009). A narrative therapy approach to conversations with men about perpetrating abuse. In P. Lehmann & C. Simmons (Eds.), *Strengths-based batterers intervention: A new paradigm in ending family violence* (pp. 113–135). New York, NY: Springer.

Augusta-Scott, T. (2017). Preparing men to help the women they abused achieve just outcomes: A restorative approach. In T. Augusta-Scott, K. Scott, & L. Tutty (Eds.), *Innovations in interventions to address intimate partner violence: Research and practice.* New York, NY: Routledge.

Braithwaite, J. (2002). *Restorative justice and responsive regulation.* New York, NY: Oxford University Press.

Brown, C. & Augusta-Scott, T. (2007). *Narrative therapy: Making meaning, making lives.* Thousand Oaks, CA: Sage Publications.

Clairemont, D. & Waters, K. (2015). *The Nova Scotia Restorative Justice Program: Assessment of current status and future directions.* Halifax, NS: Atlantic Institute of Criminology, Dalhousie University. Retrieved from: https://dalspace.library.dal.ca/bitstream/handle/10222/64610/Assessment%20of%20the%20NSRJ%20Program%202015.pdf?sequence=1&isAllowed.

Coker, D. (2002). Anti-subordination processes in domestic violence. In H. Strang & J. Braithwaite (Eds.), *Restorative justice and family violence* (pp. 128–152). New York, NY: Cambridge University Press.

Coker, D. (2006). Restorative justice, Navajo peacemaking and domestic violence. *Theoretical Criminology, 10,* 67–85.

Curtis-Fawley, S. & Daly, K. (2005). Gendered violence and restorative justice: The views of victim advocates. *Violence Against Women, 11*(5), 603–638. doi:10.1177/1077801205274488

Fernandez, M. (2010). *Restorative justice for domestic violence victims: An integrated approach to their hunger for healing.* London, UK: Lexington Books.

Frederick, L. & Lizdas, K. (2010). The role of restorative justice in the battered women's movement. In J. Ptacek (Ed.), *Restorative justice and violence against women* (pp. 39–59). New York, NY: Oxford University Press.

Goel, R. (2000). No woman at the centre: The use of the Canadian sentencing circle in domestic violence cases. *Wisconsin Women's Law Journal, 15,* 293–334.

Goel, R. (2010). Aboriginal women and political pursuit in Canadian sentencing circles: At cross roads or cross purposes? In J. Ptacek (Ed.), *Restorative justice and violence against women* (pp. 60–78). New York, NY: Oxford University Press.

Goodman, L. & Epstein, D. (2008). *Listening to battered women: A survivor-centred approach to advocacy, mental health, and justice.* Washington, DC: American Psychological Association.

Goodmark, L. (2012). *A troubled marriage: Domestic violence and the legal system.* New York, NY: New York University Press.

Grauwiler, P. & Mills, L. (2004). Moving beyond the criminal justice paradigm: A radical restorative justice approach. *Journal of Sociology and Social Welfare, 31*(1), 49–69.

Hayden, A. (2012). Safety issues associated with using restorative justice for intimate partner violence. *Women's Studies Journal, 26*(2), 4–16.

Hayden, A. (2014). Reflections on family violence and restorative justice: Addressing the critique. In A. Hayden, L. Gelsthorpe, V. Kingi, & A. Morris (Eds.), *A restorative approach to family violence: Changing tack* (pp. 211–220). Farnham, UK: Ashgate.

Hopkins, Q. (2012). Tempering idealism with realism: Using restorative justice processes to promote acceptance of responsibility in cases of intimate partner violence. *Harvard Journal of Law & Gender, 35,* 312–355.

Johnson, M. P. (2008). *A typology of domestic violence: Intimate terrorism, violent resistance, and situational couple violence.* Boston, MA: Northeastern University Press.

Llewellyn, J. (2011). Restorative justice: Thinking relationally about justice. In J. Downie & J. Llewellyn (Eds.), *Being relational: Reflections of relational theory and health law* (pp. 89–108). Vancouver, BC: UBC Press.

McMaster, K. (2014). Restoring the balance: Restorative justice and intimate partner violence. In A. Hayden, L. Gelsthorpe, V. Kingi, & A. Morris (Eds.), *A restorative approach to family violence: Changing tack* (pp. 93–108). Farnham, UK: Ashgate.

Mills, L. (2008). *Violent partners: A breakthrough plan for ending the cycle of abuse.* New York, NY: Basic Books.

Pence, E. & Paymar, M. (1993). *The Duluth Model: Education groups for men who batter.* New York, NY: Springer Press.

Pennell, J. & Francis, S. (2005). Safety conferencing: Toward a coordinate and inclusive response to safeguard women and children. *Violence Against Women, 11,* 666–692. doi:10.1177/1077801205274569

Ptacek, J. (Ed.) (2010a). *Restorative justice and violence against women.* New York, NY: Oxford University Press.

Ptacek, J. (2010b). Introduction. In Ptacek, J. (Ed.), *Restorative justice and violence against women* (pp. ix–xviii). New York, NY: Oxford University Press.

Ptacek, J. (2010c). Resisting co-optation: Three feminist challenges to antiviolence work. In J. Ptacek (Ed.), *Restorative justice and violence against women* (pp. 5–38). New York, NY: Oxford University Press.

Randall, M. (2013). Restorative justice and gendered violence? From vaguely hostile skeptic to cautious convert: Why feminists should critically engage with restorative approaches to law. *Dalhousie Law Journal, 36*(2), 461–499.

Randall, M. & Haskell, L. (2013). Taking a trauma informed approach to law: Why restorative justice must understand trauma and psychological development. *Dalhousie Law Journal, 36*(2), 501–533.

Rubin, P. (2010). A community of one's own? When women speak to power about restorative justice. In J. Ptacek (Ed.), *Restorative justice and violence against women* (pp. 79–102). New York, NY: Oxford University Press.

Scott, K. L., Heslop, L., David, R., & Kelly, T. (2017). Justice-linked domestic violence intervention services: Description and analysis of policy and practice across Canada. In T. Augusta-Scott, K. Scott, & L. Tutty (Eds.), *Innovations in interventions to address intimate partner violence: Research and practice.* New York, NY: Routledge.

Singer, V. E. (2012). *Tensions in the dominant domestic violence discourse and the high risk case coordination protocol.* PhD thesis, Dalhousie University. Retrieved from: https://dalspace. library.dal.ca/bitstream/handle/10222/21403/Singer-Verona-IDPhD-May%20 2013.pdf?sequence=5.

Strang, H. & Braithwaite, J. (Eds.) (2002). *Restorative justice and family violence.* New York, NY: Cambridge University Press.

Teryl, L. (2015). A restorative adjudication process shows promise. *The Society Record, 33*(2), 31–32. Retrieved from: http://cdn2.nsbs.org/sites/default/files/cms/publications/ society-record/nsbssrvol33no1fall2015.pdf.

Tutty, L., Ursel, J., & Douglas, F. (2008). Specialized domestic violence courts: A comparision of models. In J. Ursel, L. Tutty, & J. LeMaistre (Eds.), *What's law got to do with it? The law, specialized courts and domestic violence in Canada* (pp. 69–94). Toronto, ON: Cormorant Books and RESOLVE.

van Wormer, D. (2009). Restorative justice as social justice for victims of gendered violence: A standpoint feminist perspective. *Social Work, 54*(2), 107–116. doi.10.1093/ sw/54.2.107

Zehr, H. (1990). *Changing lenses: A new focus for crime and justice.* Scottsdale, PA: Herald Press.

Zehr, H. (2002). *The little book of restorative justice.* Intercourse, PA: Good Books.

11 Restorative Justice, Domestic Violence, and the Law

A Panel Discussion

Tod Augusta-Scott, Leigh Goodmark,
and Joan Pennell

This chapter is based on the transcript of a panel discussion presented on June 2015 for the Canadian Domestic Violence Conference 4, among three strong proponents of developing a restorative justice response to domestic violence. Each of the panelists followed her or his unique pathway into a restorative justice framework for understanding and addressing domestic violence. Nuances in views among the three panelists are influenced by their backgrounds in the domestic violence field, legal system, and child protection work. Nevertheless, they came to hold in common the idea that restorative practices applied to domestic violence offer a viable alternative to the traditional, patriarchal, punitive justice system. Their combined experience affirms the unfolding possibilities that have been and can yet be realized by working restoratively.

Specifically, they focus on how restorative justice can create an opening for the voices of women who have been abused to be heard. This process can create opportunities for men who have abused to make amends and to work to restore the women's safety and dignity. The process can engage the family and community in responding to harms, thus enlarging the circle to prevent further domestic violence. The panelists contrast a restorative justice process to the prevailing paradigm in which a judge defines just outcomes and women's voices are largely ignored; men are urged not to take responsibility by their criminal lawyers; families and informal supports are sidelined and handicapped in lending their caring and resources; and community members are invited to abdicate any responsibility for addressing domestic violence by ceding the responsibility for determining what constitutes just outcomes to a judge.

Journey Toward Listening to Women and Restorative Justice

The panelists each had different starting points for their involvement with the battered women's movement: Joan with establishing places of refuge for women and children, Tod with batterer interventions, and Leigh with representing abused women in court. Only gradually did they come to frame their work as restorative interventions.

JOAN: I was one of the people who helped to found the first shelter for abused women in the Canadian province of Newfoundland and Labrador. I know we did the right thing. Twenty years later women would run up to me and say that coming into shelter was the best thing that ever happened to their families. They were in a situation that they would never have been able to get out of without the transition house for abused women and their children. It confirmed to me that shelter was where we needed to start. But it wasn't enough.

As I facilitated support groups for abused women, I heard that the participants wanted safety for themselves and their children, but they also wanted to be part of a family and community. They did not want to be alone. And this is something that I have heard over and over in working with women, whether of European, Indigenous, or African descent.

The shelter offered sanctuary from male violence, links to needed services, and, importantly, a place to be with other women and make choices about future life directions. What we did *not* do was engage the extended networks of the women and children in helping them heal and transition into the community. At the time, we were characterized as trying to "break up families" (Pennell, 1987, p. 114), even though we were, in effect, creating an alternative child welfare system in which mothers and children stayed together (Callahan, 1993). Reflecting the disparate views of the founding shelter members and the larger debates among feminists, our original Statement of Philosophy wavered between two visions: (a) gender separation, in which empowered women join together and live apart from men and (b) gender integration, in which men and women live together and form non-oppressive relationships (Pennell, 1987, p. 118).

My understanding of the centrality of families and their cultures in peace-making within the home and community deepened when I co-facilitated in Manitoba a support group for Indigenous abused women. This group was guided by the spiritual traditions of the Medicine Wheel (Perrault, Hudson, & Pennell, 1996). Listening to an Ojibway elder give teachings on men and women walking side by side in harmony, I came to respect, all the more, Anishinabe cultures and to connect all the more to my own beliefs as a Quaker on the spiritual equality of women and men. This reawakening helped me to reposition strategies for ending domestic violence within people's cultural heritage.

On returning to Newfoundland, my colleague Gale Burford told me about the passage in Aotearoa New Zealand of legislation on family group conferencing. By this stage, I was open to engaging the wider family group in stopping intergenerational family violence (Pennell & Burford, 1994) and so were women's advocates in the province who envisioned conferencing as increasing the number of eyes monitoring the safety of abused women. Gale and I did not initially use the framework of "restorative justice" to conceptualize the Family Group Decision Making Project. Such terminology was not used in Aotearoa New Zealand at the time. The link to the project was made by representatives from Justice Canada. In other words, I did not search out a framework of restorative justice. Instead I was enveloped by restorative justice. It fit so well with my own roots as a Quaker and with my understanding of lasting solutions to violence within the family.

TOD: I have worked at the Bridges Institute with men who have been violent and their families for the last twenty years (Augusta-Scott, 2001, 2006, 2008, 2009; Augusta-Scott & Dankwort, 2002; Brown & Augusta-Scott, 2007). I was trained initially by Ellen Pence and Michael Paymar, both of whom developed the Power and Control wheel, in Duluth, Minnesota (Pence & Paymar, 1993). Since that time I have incorporated other approaches. Their work remains important, however: the gender analysis, coordinated community response, focusing on accountability, and responsibility. Then I got introduced to narrative therapy, a social justice approach to therapeutic conversations (Jenkins, 1990, 2009; White, 2007). More recently, I've found restorative justice helpful to describe work that I have been doing for years (Braithwaite, 2002; Goodmark, 2012; Llewellyn, 2011; Pennell & Francis, 2005; Strang & Braithwaite, 2002).

A significant part of the reason the workers at Bridges moved toward a restorative approach was we heard repeatedly from women how dissatisfied and, often, traumatized they are from the state intervention in their lives after they phone 911. Women are often shocked to learn they have no control over the process after they make a phone call to 911 to ask for help. I really can't think of too many women who have been pleased with state intervention. Even if the state gets convictions, I don't find women achieve a sense of just outcomes, feeling that respect and safety have been restored. The current system, how it got set up, how it screens women's voices out; it's not a victim-centered process (Smith, 2010).

LEIGH: I am a lawyer who has represented people subjected to abuse, primarily women, for the last twenty years. I came to restorative justice because of my concern about the lack of space for women's voices in the legal system. The criminal justice system is the primary systemic means of responding to domestic violence in the United States. And in the criminal justice system, women are frequently denied the opportunity to decide how they want cases involving their partners to proceed, regardless of the impact that prosecution might have on them. For those women who want retributive justice, the criminal justice system is a good option. But I don't believe that the state should have the right to intervene on behalf of someone who says she doesn't want to participate in prosecution, even if we believe she is coerced or misguided in some way. If I'm going to err, I'm going to err on the side of the client, of the woman telling me what it is that she wants out of this system. Restorative justice could provide a viable option for those women who do not want to be part of a criminal prosecution.

I believe that the ideal response is a hybrid system, one that allows for both incapacitation through incarceration and other forms of justice. We should try to leverage all of the tools that we have to give people the best possible just outcomes that meet their goals as they articulate them. For so many years we've dictated what women's goals are supposed to be: safety and accountability. But for some women, physical safety is not actually their primary goal. They may get hit from time to time, but stopping that violence isn't their priority. Instead, their priority is economic security, or keeping a father in their children's lives, even if he's a lousy father. They have other goals. The criminal justice system substitutes its goals, particularly punishment for physical violence, for women's goals. Restorative justice honors those other goals.

TOD: Similarly, I want to have an individualized approach that is focused around how the individual woman defines just outcomes, defines the harms, and provides what she believes is going to be helpful to heal those harms. In this way she remains at the center of the process. One difference between a restorative approach and the present legal system is the role of women in defining just outcomes. In the courtroom, just outcomes are not defined by asking women to identify the harms and what will be helpful to address these harms. In the current system, from the advocate's perspective, just outcomes are defined by whether or not the state gets a conviction—regardless of whether she wants her partner to be convicted or not.

In the traditional current system, women are not given the chance to define what would be helpful for their partners and others to do to repair the harms. Instead, a judge simply sentences the man to counseling and probation, without regard to how and if the terms of this sentence will address the harms to herself and her family. Women are not given a voice beyond giving a victim impact statement to help secure a conviction and punishment. In the courtroom, rather than women contributing to the definition of just outcomes, the judges alone define just outcome. Women are not even given a lawyer in the courtroom. The Crown lawyers primarily represent the state— as though the state has been violated, not the woman (Llewellyn, 2011). Clearly the specialized domestic violence courts are trying to address the issue of listening to women beyond victim impact statements.

JOAN: To include people who have suffered so much, the process needs to take place within a community of caring that they trust. And even if those who have been abused can't acknowledge harms that have happened to them, there are those around them whom they trust who can identify the harms and speak about their impact. One of the family group conferences that we did in Newfoundland involved a stepdad who intimidated everyone in the family. So only he and the eldest son, who was also abusive, were at the table. But the mother's sister came and a woman who helped out in the house came, and these two women were able to present the absent family members' concerns. Now you could well ask why others did not take part? The stepdad warned the relatives to stay away from the conference. His threats mobilized the extended family group to say that this abuse had gone on far too long. So after the conference, the mother and most of children had the needed family and agency support to leave this incredibly abusive, coercive man. But it had to be a process in which the mother was truly cared for and in which her children were cared for.

TOD: Prior to the pro-arrest, pro-charge, pro-prosecution policies, in the early days of the work, I always thought when a woman dropped charges, that they were somehow acquiescing to him. In the early days I also thought that justice simply meant prosecution and conviction. As a result, when she didn't want to press charges, I thought, "She's doesn't want to prosecute him and give him a criminal record? Why doesn't she want justice?" Now I see some of those women actually didn't define prosecution as justice. She wanted support, she wanted help, she didn't want to drag herself and her partner through a court system. And I pathologized her for making that decision, assuming she was too afraid or unable to go after justice. I now recognize that many of these women were defining and continue to define justice differently than the patriarchal legal system.

Women Advocates and Women's Safety

The three panelists identified the important role of many women advocates in developing a community-based restorative process for responding to domestic violence. For example, given the co-occurrence of domestic violence with child maltreatment (Black, Trocmé, Fallon, & MacLaurin, 2008), Joan highlighted how women's advocates help to create safety at child welfare conferences that include fathers who commit domestic violence. The safety measures used in child welfare can be applied to restorative practices addressing domestic violence in other systems.

JOAN: In the child welfare arena, the worker is usually responsible for making a referral to a coordinator to organize a family group conference. The coordinator then works with the family to figure out whom to have present at their meeting. In situations of domestic violence, it is crucial that the coordinator assess, particularly with those who have been victimized, whether it is safe to proceed and if so, under what conditions. It is also so very helpful to invite women's advocates to speak at the conference about the dynamics of coercive control and its impact on child and adult family members (Pennell, 2005). There are good methods available for ensuring that women and children's voices are heard at a conference and for engaging men who abuse safely in the deliberations (American Humane Association, 2010; Burford, Pennell, & MacLeod, 1995; Pennell & Koss, 2011). One strategy is forming a community panel with which the coordinator consults on culturally respectful and safe approaches. In Aotearoa, New Zealand, care and protection, these advisory groups are referred to as resource panels (Fraser & Norton, 1996). I had the opportunity to observe a resource panel with representation from the Maori and Samoan communities as well as the domestic violence field.

LEIGH: Although domestic violence advocates have raised cautions about restorative practices (Ptacek, 2010), they also have been more open to restorative justice than many others, particularly lawyers. The advocates were seeing the same things I was seeing in my work in the legal system: the legal system, particularly the criminal justice system, often doesn't work well for their clients. Since the inception of mandatory arrest, the rates of arrests of women and of dual arrests have increased significantly (Durfee, 2012). Women who initially seek help through the legal system but later change their minds about testifying have been jailed for refusing to testify and prosecuted for perjury. Women who come to court alleging harm to themselves and their children are sometimes blamed for that harm, held responsible for failing to protect their children, and some even lose their children to the child protection system as a consequence of coming forward. Undocumented women who call police for help have faced deportation of their partners and themselves as a consequence (Goodmark, 2012). The criminal justice system imposes separation on people who simply wanted help in disrupting a violent incident in the moment, entering no contact orders that operate as "de facto divorces" (Suk, 2011). Turning to the legal system is often harmful for people subjected to abuse and their children. When you look at the social science research on openness to restorative justice in the context of domestic violence, it is domestic violence advocates who are most open to having this conversation, because they recognize how limited the legal system really is (Curtis-Fawley & Daly, 2005).

I've said consistently that we—domestic violence advocates—are the people who should be doing restorative justice work. Given the many concerns that have been raised about engaging in restorative practice in the context of domestic violence, whom else are we going to trust? Those of us with experience with and a desire to find other options to address domestic violence, and who believe that women need a broader range of options, need to get trained, to be a part of the process. That may be the commitment that we need to make restorative justice a viable option for women subjected to abuse.

TOD: When I think of a restorative legal system that is integrated with the community, I envision the shelter worker or the woman's advocate at the center of that process because of their expertise around women's safety (Augusta-Scott, Harrison, & Singer, 2017, Chapter 10 this volume). To gauge a man's level of taking responsibility, there needs to be an experienced men's worker engaging him. And then I think there needs to be a third person— a restorative justice worker. I get nervous when I think that the roles of those three people are expected to be met by one facilitator. Or that the community is going to give the responsibility for this issue to just one agency and one person to navigate all the safety issues, all the power issues, all the process issues. I would be nervous if that was going to be my job description. There needs to be a collaboration between a restorative justice agency, a women's shelter, and a men's program, and in the background there needs to be a legal system that's making sure this process happens appropriately. It's those three agencies coming together to monitor these cases. We need to have the assurance that the safety issues are being addressed by the people who are the experts on safety in the domestic violence context within our community.

Discerning what women want in these situations is a process. That's why I want women's advocates on the front line with her from the very beginning, even at the arrest stage. So the women's counselor is thinking about what she wants, is asking those questions of her. A shelter worker is next to her as a social worker, not a police officer. Beyond ensuring there is immediate safety, I'm not envisioning a state response in which a police officer is given the responsibility to go in and assess what the woman wants. I want the woman's advocate in there doing that work, helping the woman to have the confidence that this intervention can go somewhere that's going to be helpful. So it's not only people in the department of justice doing the work, its women's advocates in the community.

LEIGH: But I don't think we want people in a moment of trauma making decisions about engaging in restorative justice versus other options. Victims often want more time to make decisions about arrest, about prosecution, and about alternatives. How do we build time into this system? One concern that is often raised is the use of restorative justice as a pre-trial diversion from the criminal justice system. I think those concerns may be valid, if only because at that point in the process, the woman may not have had sufficient time to consider her options. One thing we have to think through is how and when the restorative option is presented. For example, does it get presented at arraignment? Could you have a victim advocate at arraignment explaining the various options that are available to the victim? These are the kinds of questions we will need to address.

The larger context for this conversation for me is about how we make the legal system itself work better, because I want that system to work for those women who choose to use it. The two essential ideas here are time, as mentioned above, and information. The legal system does a poor job of giving women information. We should provide information that gives women a sense of what the legal process will entail. If, for example, he's arrested, he's going to be held for a certain number of hours and they're going to take him to Central Booking. He's likely going to be charged with this crime and then he's most likely going to be released. When he is released, there may be a stay away order, but there may not be a stay away order. This is what you're going to have to do if he's arrested and if he's charged. This is what your responsibilities will be to assist in prosecution. Building a more detailed and specific process will help victims to understand their options and make informed choices about how to proceed, whether that's via prosecution or restorative justice.

Contextualized Approaches

The panelists emphasized shaping domestic violence responses to the particular situations and cultural settings rather than fitting people into pre-set approaches. Any approach has to be flexible to use a combination of conversations—individual, group, couple, or family—as well as varying number of conversations depending on the needs of each individual case.

JOAN: Restorative justice is about working together to create peace in a way that respects human rights and culture. People want to be in community and family, which are sites of oppression but also sites of belonging, identification, and safety. Sometimes there is a tension between safety and belonging to a family or community culture. How do we find safety within groupings that have reinforced violence against women and violence against children?

What we learned from interviewing family group conference participants in North Carolina is the importance of cultural safety. The term cultural safety comes from Maori nursing in Aotearoa, New Zealand. The Indigenous care providers criticized Eurocentric health systems as culturally unsafe and harmful to their people (Ramsden, 1993). For family group conferencing participants, cultural safety means inviting the right people to the conference, holding it in a manner that feels right to the family group, convening it in a place that feels right to the family group, and, notably, ensuring enough supports and protections are in place (Pennell, 2004). In other words, fitting the conference to the cultural practices of families is linked to a sense of emotional and physical safety.

For conferencing to work it needs to be contoured not only to the family but also to the unique setting in which it is used. The process is developed around the individual families and communities involved. What we found in Canada and the United States was that it was so important that the diverse communities taking part shaped the program, figured out where it should be located, and guided it throughout (Pennell & Weil, 2000). For example, one woman in an Inuit community stressed that in her community, "You can't hold a conference at the police station, you can't hold it in Social Services, you've got to have it at the Inuit Health Commission. Then we will take part."

TOD: I also think that services need to be tailored to each situation. I want to be clear when I'm talking about a restorative/narrative therapy process, I am not talking about a manualized, one-size-fits-all approach to the work. There is no fixed practice; particularly, there is no suggestion that requires a woman and the man who hurt her to meet face-to-face. The woman determines with the workers if and how she wants to have contact: through letters, email, video, other people, and so forth. I'm talking about a principled approach, that is, a variety of practices that are guided by ideas (Llewellyn & Philpott, 2014; White, 2007). These ideas or principles guide the conversations that I'm having with men and women who are in these kinds of situations.

The goal of a restorative approach is not restoring intimate relationships either (Frederick & Lizdas, 2010; Llewellyn, 2008, 2011). There are lots of repairs that men can make even if they don't have direct contact with the partner. And repair not only to her, but also to community, to her family; so moving it outside of the immediate relationship in terms of looking at what the harms are in different contexts.

LEIGH: I had a woman call me not too long ago and she said, "I've read your work, I'm really interested in restorative justice, I think that it would be so great for my family if we could get engaged in a restorative practice, can you send me somewhere?" I asked, "Do you think that your husband is ready to accept responsibility?" She responded, "Absolutely not. He denies it, he says he didn't do it but I really think it would be good for us." And I said, "I think you have a problem if you want to use restorative practices because reputable restorative justice practitioners are not going to start with you until he's willing to accept responsibility."

This is probably the biggest concern domestic violence advocates have about restorative practice: How can I know he's really accepted respon-si-bility? I want to create a victim-centered process, but even in a victim-centered process, it seems that you need to start with determining whether offenders are ready to engage. So one starting point might be to talk with offender intervention providers to ask if they are working with offenders who might be ready to engage in such a process. Then, instead of telling the offenders about restorative justice, we might go to their partners and say,

> We think your partner might be ready to engage in this process, but we'll only do it if it's something you're interested in doing. Is this something you might want to do? Here's what the process might look like, here's how it might play out.

If she says, "No, thank you, I have no interest," the process doesn't go any further. If, however, she says, "Yes, I might be ready to do this, and it sounds like a good thing to me, let's get him engaged," then you go to him. There's a lot of work that must go into those initial conversations with both parties. Restorative justice is labor intensive in ways that the current system is not. It requires numerous conversations before you have a victim who is in a position where she might be ready to say, "I'm ready now to start this process," whether it's face to face or not.

TOD: Of course, women need to decide whether or not they want any involvement in a restorative process. I'm defining a restorative approach as giving a man the opportunity to take responsibility to heal and repair the harms he has caused not only to his (ex) partner but also to other family members and the community. I want the state to engage him restoratively to repair what he has done whether she wants to punish him or not (and of course, he always has the option to go to court and plead not guilty). I want a shelter worker there to participate in the restorative process as a member of the wider community, even if the woman involved doesn't want to be there, so that we can collectively work with him on not hurting other women in the future. In presenting a restorative approach to the female partner, I would say, "He is going to be assisted to take responsibility for what he has done. Are there any harms he has caused to you or others that you want him to address?" That engages her in the process, but the process doesn't necessarily require her to meet with him or others.

JOAN: I agree. A restorative process with the man and his family and community can proceed as long as the former partner is not coerced into participation. In New Zealand, for example, child welfare conferences can be held without the parents present. Another strategy used in North Carolina is to have staggered meetings with the mother and father attending at different times, at least initially (Pennell & Kim, 2010; Pennell & Koss, 2011). It is crucial, though, to update both parents on the deliberations in order to minimize suspicion, keep the process open and inclusive, and continue to figure good plans to safeguard child and adult family members.

LEIGH: At the same time, if a woman decided not to get involved further in the process, I would want her to be able to receive updates about the progress or lack of progress when and if she wants them. I'm also wary of engaging a man in a restorative process that his partner actively opposes. I agree that he has a responsibility to his children, other family members, and to the wider community and that we want that restoration, whether or not she wants to be a part of it. There may be issues, however, with the process proceeding without her involvement. For example, two people from the same small religious or ethnic community are engaged in a relationship and he is violent. She does not want to be part of the restorative process and does not necessarily want him restored to that community, for whatever reason. Is that a conference that should go forward? That's a harder conversation. I can absolutely envision a process that engages the shelter worker and that is focused on preventing future harm to others. I think that the key is to define the community to which he's being restored carefully.

TOD: If a process proceeds without the woman so the man can still take responsibility to repair what he can with his children, family, and the community and work not to harm any future partners, the participants would have to be careful that she is not being further harmed as a result.

Men's Responsibilities

The panelists did not presume that abusive men would change. Instead they saw restorative processes as offering an opportunity for the men to take responsibility not only to stop their violence but to repair what they have done.

LEIGH: One of the central tenets in restorative justice is the man has to accept responsibility first. One obvious question about this work is how do you know he's taking responsibility? The inability to answer that question to the satisfaction of those involved with the legal system may prevent us from providing restorative justice as an option.

There are many other violent offenders with whom restorative practices are being used successfully. And I don't know why it's easier to figure that they've genuinely accepted responsibility than it is for us to determine that acceptance of responsibility has been genuine in a domestic violence case, except that we're more afraid of being wrong than most people. We work so closely with the victims of domestic violence, we know what they go through, and we seem to be much more worried about bad outcomes than any other group of victim advocates. We don't have a screening tool that can tell us with absolute certainty that someone has accepted responsibility. No risk assessment is solid enough that I could feel, with 100 percent or even 95 percent confidence, that having used that tool I know that someone has really accepted responsibility. That uncertainty makes this work very hard, and causes us to limit our options in ways that are particularly damaging for people who do not want to engage with state systems to get assistance.

TOD: I have become much more hopeful now that I have seen many men not only stop their violence but work to repair the harms they have created. I now see men in conversations with their partners where men are working to take responsibility to heal and repair the harms their violence has done to their partners and others. I have seen many men acknowledging that they, not their partners, were and are fully responsible for their choices. I have seen men give this message directly to their partners. These conversations are often very powerful for women. While I have been trying to convince women for years they are not responsible for their male partners' choices, hearing their male partners say that has a much greater impact.

I thought those type of conversations were impossible, because it would never be safe, because he would never change. We were really cynical about the men changing. I never thought the men wanted to change (Augusta-Scott, 2001, 2006). Over the years, I came to realize that the dominant domestic violence discourse was actually preventing me from noticing changes men were making. The only story I knew was they got power and privilege from their violence, so why would they want to change? I only saw how men wanted power and control and never noticed that, at the same time, they also want loving, caring, respectful relationships. I never noticed change because I always just pathologized any positive change as the "honeymoon stage" of the cycle of violence (Walker, 1984). I was also afraid to hope that change was possible because hope is dangerous for *some* women. Sometimes hope that men will change keeps women in dangerous relationships. I thought the only real way to stop the abuse was for her to leave. As a result, for many years, I inadvertently smothered *all* women's hope over the possibility that he and their relationships could change. This practice was unhelpful for many women.

There are ways the traditional legal system fosters men's irresponsibility (Jenkins, 1991). In the criminal justice system where punishment is a likely outcome, men are expected to get a criminal lawyer and the criminal lawyer is going to counsel them to take as little responsibility as possible. A lot of the men I work with want to say, "I'm guilty" and their lawyers say, "Definitely do not say that!" No lawyer will invite their client to take responsibility, the system is not designed for men to take responsibility and to be thoughtful about what they've done and how they're going to heal and repair what has happened. The system is designed to have men minimize their responsibility—regardless of the truth—so they can avoid "justice," that is, being punished. Again, the specialized domestic violence courts are trying to address this issue.

Community Taking Responsibility

The panel discussion also focused on the need not only for men to take responsibility for ensuring safety and respect and restoration but also investigating how the community can be helpful toward this end.

TOD: In conjunction with listening to women, a restorative approach also enables men to respond in a helpful way to the harms they've created so they can become part of the solution of restoring her respect, safety, integrity, and so forth in the relationship. And community engagement is so important. The process invites the community to take responsibility for becoming part of the solution. A restorative approach engages the community to become part of the conversation around restoring her safety and respect and integrity.

In terms of community, we've abdicated responsibility for participating in justice. The community gives the judge all of the responsibility to protect the community's interest. But in terms of accountability, it may be better if I can help the man create a plan with input and accountability to his parents, his grandparents, his minister, and whomever else he has in his life that is important to him. A restorative process can create accountability through him creating a contract with those people he cares about. While the man may not care about disappointing strangers, such as a judge or probation officer, he might care about disappointing his mother or his in-laws. In cases where the community is willing and able to come forward and play an active role in working to support both partners, and we can create a contract within community, the man's family and others in his informal network are in a much better position to be able to monitor issues of safety: people he can call for support, or whom she can call and other resources rather than simply a probation officer monitoring issues of safety. In some cases, the community has already tried to hold the man accountable for his behavior, and failed; restorative justice is probably not a good option for those men. But in other situations, the community can support families and find out what needs to happen so that we can all take responsibility in restoring her safety and the quality of the relationship and respect.

Responding to High-Risk Cases: Responsive Regulation

The panelists agreed that a range of possible responses, including restorative approaches, should be considered for cases that are at high risk of repeated serious violence or lethality. A framework of responsive regulation guided their discussion of options.

JOAN: Restorative justice needs to be placed within a larger framework of responsive regulation. Responsive regulation is often depicted as a pyramid with different levels of regulation that respond flexibly to the situation (Braithwaite, 2002). At the broad base of the pyramid are educational and supportive responses. At the next tier are restorative practices that engage people directly in decision making. Above these two lower levels are coercive approaches such as protective orders or incarceration. Importantly the regulatory response does not necessarily escalate up the pyramid because of the extent of risk. Instead, determining the response depends on what is most effective at the time to counter coercive control with the possibility of climbing up or down the pyramid at a later time.

We must always pay attention to the level of lethality. With a shelter director in North Carolina, I conducted focus groups with women who had been severely abused (Pennell & Francis, 2005). They had escaped from very violent men. All three of them had nearly died from the abuse. We asked them to reflect on what family group conferencing would mean in their lives. They knew that they could not have conferencing for themselves and their children if it were to include any family, even those they truly trusted, because their partners could come and find them. Together, we created an alternative called "safety conferencing" in which a circle of care is constructed around them and their children.

TOD: I also want to be clear that, when I'm talking about a restorative approach, incarceration is still an option. While I'm sure victim impact statements do influence incarceration levels, I actually think if we adopted a restorative approach, incarceration might be used more often. If we were actually listening to the terror that some of these women experience, if we actually listened to women and centered the woman's experience in the process, we wouldn't be as reluctant to use incarceration as an option. At the same time, incarceration wouldn't be used to punish or degrade the man. The idea behind incarceration within this framework would be the community taking responsibility to restore safety by incapacitating the man until the man can live safely in the community.

Sometimes people suggest a restorative approach could and should only be used for less serious violence and not for higher-risk situations. In part, I think such caution arises from people erroneously thinking that a restorative approach always involves the woman and man talking face to face. Again, a restorative approach is not a manualized, one-size-fits-all approach. I'm defining a restorative approach as listening to women and helping men to respond in a helpful manner to the harms they have created. Because I'm defining a restorative approach as workers consulting with women about what they want, I want a restorative approach to be available to all women, regardless of the level of risk. I want women who are at a high level of risk to be thoroughly consulted about what they want. Women who are at high risk often have the most investment in having a say about what is going to happen in their lives, with their families, and their relationships. In high-risk cases, I suspect many intervention programs for men that have close relationships with the female partners and their advocates already implement components of what I'm defining as a restorative approach.

LEIGH: Some women who choose to use restorative processes instead of turning to the criminal justice system may be killed. But women who use the traditional legal system also get killed. There are stories every single day of women who did everything "right." They prosecuted, they got protective orders, they did all the things they were told to do and they also got killed. Professor Martha Mahoney once called them the women who die with protective orders in their pockets (Maguigan, 2003). We need to be realistic about the fact that if somebody really wants to kill somebody else, they're likely to do so. We can't prevent all of those kinds of incidents, short of keeping those people in jail for the rest of their lives, which we almost never do in cases involving domestic violence and which we do only after they've already done the thing that we were afraid they were going to do.

We have no guarantees. I empathize completely with prosecutors and judges. I understand why they're so concerned about bringing these cases to court, even when women are reluctant or unwilling. I think that's got to be the hardest thing in the world, when you fail to issue a protective order or secure a conviction, and someone is killed in the aftermath. But we don't control any of those horrible outcomes. Arrest and prosecution don't guarantee safety. There's only one person who really controls what happens in situations where someone is determined to harm someone else, and there's not one of us in the room who controls him.

And so then the question becomes whether we allow this fear to motivate everything we do. Do we use the fear to justify denying other options to women who are perfectly capable of telling us what they want? Or do we trust what the social science literature tells us, that the people who are best placed to assess the risk they face from their partners is the women themselves? Studies have repeatedly shown that women understand the risk posed by their partners better than any of us (Gondolf & Heckert, 2003; Goodman, Dutton, & Bennett, 2000; Weisz, Tolman, & Saunders, 2000). And do they make mistakes? Yes, tragically, absolutely. But they make those same mistakes after they do everything we tell them to do.

Restorative justice is not the cure-all for everything that's wrong with the criminal justice system. There are some people who are so dangerous that they need to not be walking among us. The top of Braithwaite's pyramid still uses incapacitation and incarceration when other methods of changing behavior have failed. Incarceration needs to exist as the thing against which we measure all of our other actions. In some situations, incarceration can serve as the ultimate failsafe. But even a system that allows incarceration as the ultimate response could be oriented differently. We could move from having a retributive criminal justice system, one that is based on the idea that people should be punished, to a restorative criminal justice system. We could make incapacitation more constructive, less punitive, less likely to provoke further violence (Gilligan, 2001). We could change the entire orientation of the system, and that's where our focus needs to be.

Conclusion

Adopting a restorative approach to work with domestic violence challenges assumptions that many make about the field. A restorative approach creates the possibility of listening to women who have experienced abuse. The process allows her to define how she has been affected by the abuse and what she believes will be helpful to address these impacts. A restorative approach can give a man and the community the opportunity to make the situation better for the woman, and to restore her sense of safety, integrity, and respect. The process can move beyond attempts to simply stop violence to healing, and taking away the causes of harm.

References

American Humane Association and the FGDM Guidelines Committee. (2010). *Guidelines for family group decision making in child welfare*. Englewood, CO: Author. Retrieved from: www.ucdenver.edu/academics/colleges/medicalschool/departments/pediatrics/subs/can/FGDM/FGDM_Resources/Documents/FGDM%20Guidelines.pdf.

Augusta-Scott, T. (2001). Dichotomies in the power and control story: Exploring multiple stories about men who choose abuse in intimate relationships. *Gecko: A Journal of Deconstruction and Narrative Ideas in Therapeutic Practice, 2*, 31–54.

Augusta-Scott, T. (2006). Talking with men who have used violence in intimate relationships: An interview with Tod Augusta-Scott. *International Journal of Narrative Therapy and Community Work, 4*, 23–30.

Augusta-Scott, T. (2008). *Narrative therapy: A group manual for men who have perpetrated abuse.* Truro, NS: Bridges Institute.

Augusta-Scott, T. (2009). A narrative therapy approach to conversations with men about perpetrating abuse. In P. Lehmann & C. Simmons (Eds.), *Strengths-based batterer's intervention: A new paradigm in ending family violence* (pp. 113–135). New York, NY: Springer.

Augusta-Scott, T. & Dankwort, J. (2002). Group work with partner abuse: Lessons from constructivist and educational approaches. *Journal of Interpersonal Violence, 7*(7), 783–805.

Augusta-Scott, T., Harrison, P., & Singer, V. (2017). Creating safety, respect and equality for women: Lessons from the intimate partner violence and restorative justice movements. In T. Augusta-Scott, K. Scott, & L. Tutty (Eds.), *Innovations in interventions to address intimate partner violence: Research and practice* (pp. 157–173). New York, NY: Routledge.

Black, T., Trocmé, N., Fallon, B., & MacLaurin, B. (2008). The Canadian child welfare system response to exposure to domestic violence investigations. *Child Abuse & Neglect, 32*, 393–404. doi:10.1016/j.chiabu.2007.10.002

Braithwaite, J. (2002). *Restorative justice and responsive regulation.* New York, NY: Oxford University Press.

Brown, C. & Augusta-Scott, T. (2007). *Narrative therapy: Making meaning, making lives.* Thousand Oaks, CA: Sage Publications.

Burford, G., Pennell, J., & MacLeod, S. (1995). *Manual for coordinators and communities: The organization and practice of family group decision making (Revised).* St. John's, NF: Memorial University of Newfoundland, School of Social Work. Retrieved from: http://faculty.chass.ncsu.edu/pennell//fgdm/manual.

Callahan, M. (1993). Feminist approaches: Women recreate child welfare. In B. Wharf (Ed.), *Rethinking child welfare in Canada* (pp. 172–209). Toronto, ON: McClelland & Stewart.

Curtis-Fawley, C. & Daly, K. (2005). Gendered violence and restorative justice: The views of victim advocates. *Violence Against Women, 11*(5), 603–638. doi:10.1177/10778012 05274488

Durfee, A. (2012). Situational ambiguity and gendered patterns of arrest for intimate partner violence. *Violence Against Women, 18*(1), 64–84. doi:10.1177/1077801212437017

Fraser, S. & Norton, J. (1996). Family group conferencing in New Zealand child protection work. In J. Hudson, A. Morris, G. Maxwell, & B. Galaway (Eds.), *Family group conferences: Perspectives on policy & practice* (pp. 37–48). Annandale, AU: The Federation Press.

Frederick, L. & Lizdas, K. (2010). The role of restorative justice in the battered women's movement. In J. Ptacek (Ed.), *Restorative justice and violence against women* (pp. 39–59). New York, NY: Oxford University Press.

Gilligan, J. (2001). *Preventing violence.* New York, NY: Thames and Hudson.

Gondolf, E. W. & Heckert, D. A. (2003). Determinants of women's perceptions of risk in battering relationships. *Violence and Victims, 18*(4), 371–386.

Goodman, L., Dutton, M. A., & Bennett, L. (2000). Predicting repeat abuse among arrested batterers: Use of the Danger Assessment scale in the criminal justice system. *Journal of Interpersonal Violence, 10*, 63–74. doi:10.1177/088626000015001005

Goodmark, L. (2012). *A troubled marriage: Domestic violence and the legal system.* New York, NY: New York University Press.

Jenkins, A. (1990). *Invitations to responsibility: The therapeutic engagement of men who are violent and abusive.* Adelaide, AU: Dulwich Centre Publications.

Jenkins, A. (1991). Intervention with violence and abuse in families: The inadvertent perpetuation of irresponsible behaviour. *Australian and New Zealand Journal of Family Therapy, 12*(4), 186–195.

Jenkins, A. (2009). *Becoming ethical: A parallel, political journey with men who have abused.* Dorset, UK: Russell House Publishing.

Llewellyn, J. (2008). Bridging the gap between truth and reconciliation: Restorative justice and the Indian Residential Schools Truth and Reconciliation Commission. In M. B. Castellano, L. Archibald, & M. DeGagné (Eds.), *From truth to reconciliation: Transforming the legacy of residential schools* (pp. 183–201). Ottawa, ON: Aboriginal Healing Foundation Research Publications. Retrieved from: http://speakingmytruth.ca/?page_id=701.

Llewellyn, J. (2011). Restorative justice: Thinking relationally about justice. In J. Downie & J. Llewellyn (Eds.), *Being relational: Reflections of relational theory and health law* (pp. 89–108). Vancouver, BC: UBC Press.

Llewellyn, J. & Philpott, D. (Eds.) (2014). *Restorative justice, reconciliation, and peacebuilding.* New York, NY: Oxford University Press.

Maguigan, H. (2003). Wading into Professor Schneider's "Murky middle ground" between acceptance and rejection of criminal justice responses to domestic violence. *American University Journal of Gender Social Policy and Law, 11*(2) 427–445.

Pence, E. & Paymar, M. (1993). *Education groups for men who batter: The Duluth Model.* New York, NY: Springer Publishing.

Pennell, J. (1987). Ideology at a Canadian shelter for battered women: A reconstruction. *Women's Studies International Forum, 10*(2), 113–123. doi:10.1016/0277-5395(87)90020-3

Pennell, J. (2004). Family group conferencing in child welfare: Responsive and regulatory interfaces. *Journal of Sociology and Social Welfare, 31*(1), 117–135.

Pennell, J. (2005). Safety for mothers and their children. In J. Pennell & G. Anderson (Eds.), *Widening the circle: The practice and evaluation of family group conferencing with children youths, and their families* (pp. 163–181). Washington, DC: National Association of Social Workers Press.

Pennell, J. & Burford, G. (1994). Widening the circle: The family group decision making project. *Journal of Child & Youth Care, 9*(1), 1–12.

Pennell, J. & Francis, S. (2005). Safety conferencing: Toward a coordinated and inclusive response to safeguard women and children. *Violence Against Women, 11*(5), 666–692. doi:10.1177/1077801205274569

Pennell, J. & Kim, M. (2010). Opening conversations across cultural, gender, and generational divides: Family and community engagement to stop violence against women and children. In J. Ptacek (Ed.), *Restorative justice and violence against women* (pp. 177–192). New York, NY: Oxford University Press.

Pennell, J. & Koss, M. P. (2011). Feminist perspectives on family rights: Social work and restorative justice processes to stop women abuse. In E. Beck, N. P. Kropf, & P. B. Leonard (Eds.), *Social work and restorative justice: Skills for dialogue, peacemaking, and reconciliation* (pp. 195–219). New York, NY: Oxford University Press.

Pennell, J. & Weil, M. (2000). Initiating conferencing: Community practice issues. In G. Burford & J. Hudson (Eds.), *Family group conferencing: New directions in community-centered child and family practice* (pp. 253–261). Hawthorne, NY: Aldine de Gruyter.

Perrault, S., Hudson, B., & Pennell, J. (1996). Having a balance. In J. L. Ristock & J. Pennell, *Community research as empowerment: Feminist links, postmodern interruptions* (pp. 24–32). Toronto, ON: Oxford University Press.

Ptacek, J. (Ed.), (2010). *Restorative justice and violence against women*. New York, NY: Oxford University Press.

Ramsden, I. (1993). Kawa Whakaruruhau: Cultural safety in nursing education in Aotearoa (New Zealand). *Nursing Praxis in New Zealand, 8*(3), 4–10.

Smith, A. (2010). Beyond restorative justice: Radical organizing against violence. In J. Ptacek (Ed.), *Restorative justice and violence against women* (pp. 255–278). New York, NY: Oxford University Press.

Strang, H. & Braithwaite, J. (Eds.) (2002). *Restorative justice and family violence*. New York, NY: Cambridge University Press.

Suk, J. (2011). *At home in the law: How the domestic violence revolution is transforming privacy*. New Haven, CT: Yale University Press.

Walker, L. (1984). *The battered woman*. New York, NY: William Morrow.

Weisz, A., Tolman, R., & Saunders, D. G. (2000). Assessing the risk of severe domestic violence. *Journal of Interpersonal Violence, 15*(1), 75–90.

White, M. (2007). *Maps of narrative practice*. New York, NY: Norton.

12 Preparing Men to Help the Women They Abused Achieve Just Outcomes

A Restorative Approach

Tod Augusta-Scott[1]

A restorative approach defines just outcomes primarily in terms of repairing and healing the effects of the men's violence on women, restoring women's safety, respect, and equality. This approach is a principled approach rather than a particular practice. The principles can be practiced in a variety of ways depending on the moment-to-moment assessment of those involved in a particular case. Therefore, the approach cannot be a fixed, manualized, one-size-fits-all practice. Depending on the people involved, restorative conversations often involve a combination of conversations with individuals, couples, families, and communities.

Two principles of a restorative approach are collaboration and communication with those impacted by the harm. Restorative justice (RJ) focuses on consulting with women about the harms and what they think will be helpful to address these harms. Within this framework, the work of shelter movements can be considered a component of restorative justice work. Similarly, the work of men's intervention programs, as they are directed toward restoring the safety, respect, and equality of women, can also be considered restorative.

Often other family or community members who are supportive of both parties are involved in the process, many of whom have also been harmed indirectly by men abusing their partners or ex-partners. The community involves people in the men and women's lives who care about them—parents, in-laws, friends, neighbors, cousins, co-workers, counselors, spiritual leaders, and so forth. Community members also include men's counselors and women's counselors or advocates. If either of the couple is involved with the legal or child welfare system, currently the child protection worker and probation officer will also be involved (Pennell, 2005; Pennell, Sanders, Rikard, Shepherd, & Starsoneck, 2013). This approach works in a restorative manner with all these parties engaged in the repair plan.

Much of the domestic violence field is focused on restoring safety for women, in part, by having men stop their violence. However, often women want much more from the men than just stopping the abuse. Some women also want to witness their partners or ex-partners taking responsibility and being accountable.

They wish them to acknowledge what they have done and the effects of the abuse. Women often want to hear directly from the men about the men's relapse prevention plans (Takano, 2017, Chapter 6 this volume). These women report that hearing men relay their relapse prevention plans helps deepen their sense of safety and increase their assurance the men will not abuse them or other women again. Women also want to hear how the men will help heal and repair the effects of their abuse (Herman, 2005). A restorative justice approach is designed to help women achieve these and other just outcomes by assisting men to take responsibility and to be accountable for their behaviors (Augusta-Scott, 2003, 2009; Braithwaite, 2002; Goodmark, 2012; Jenkins, 1990, 2009; Llewellyn & Howse, 1998; Mills, 2008; Ptacek, 2010; Strang & Braithwaite, 2002; White, 2007).

In an effort to achieve just outcomes for women, this chapter outlines a restorative engagement of men that prepares them to repair the harms they have created for their (ex) partners. This chapter focuses only on the initial conversations with men, drawing on the work of the Bridges Institute and New Start Counselling over the last twenty years (Augusta-Scott, 2008). This work has been conducted primarily with men who are mandated by courts to attend a community-based domestic violence intervention program. The men's and women's quotations in this chapter are used with permission and are taken from either their written evaluations or transcribed from video.

Many of these men will work on restoring the harms they have created for their partners or ex-partners, their children and the wider community. Some will have the opportunity to connect with their partners or ex-partners and some will not. In some cases, women have moved on or they are not interested in "counseling" or the workers deem that any contact is unsafe. Even if a man does not have contact with his ex-partner, the individual conversations with men and conversations between men and others are still restorative.

The Restorative Process

Restorative justice processes are not conducted to reinstate intimate relationships, although this may happen for some couples (Frederick & Lizdas, 2010; Llewellyn, 2008, 2011). Again, the intent is to restore the women's respect, equality, and safety. Some women want to either continue or re-establish their relationships with their partners and are deeply invested in this restorative process. However, even if women never want a relationship with their partners again, they often want these men to take responsibility and commit to not harming any other women. Further, even after a divorce, many women remain connected to the men who harmed them because they are co-parents or live in the same small community. Many of these women are genuinely invested in the men taking responsibility and repairing the harms of the men's violence.

The woman and the counselors jointly determine *if* contact should happen within the program setting. They also determine *how* contact should happen: through email, discussions with the man's counselor, through telephone calls, pre-recorded video or in person. Before any contact between the woman and man, the man needs to be prepared to engage women responsibly. Before addressing these issues with his (ex) partners, a man must already be engaged in the process of taking responsibility: he needs to have a plan for stopping further violence, he needs to want to hear about the effects of their violence and desire to repair and heal the harms he has created. The preparation may involve a man attending both individual conversations with a counselor or group counseling with other men and a counselor. For some, the process of preparation takes weeks before contact begins, for others it takes many months. For some, the program never allows contact. If attempts are made for men and women to discuss these issues before the men are prepared to respond responsibly, the men will likely further harm their (ex) partners through minimizing the seriousness of the abuse, blaming the women for it or denying it.

Establish Values/Identity

For the contact to be helpful to women, the men themselves need to be willing to address the effects of their violence on their partners or ex-partners. Rather than being cajoled by the court or a counselor, men need to want to repair the effects of their violence because they think such a process would fit with their own values. Men need to be clear about their own values and why they would wish to take responsibility for the harms they have created. Toward this end, men are invited to consider their values for taking responsibility, respect, and safety before being invited to consider how they might be able to live these values through a restorative justice approach. Because of the influence of patriarchal expectations on men, many have not seriously considered what is important for themselves in relationships. Prior to being asked about his values and what was important to him in relationships, one man stated that:

> I just wanted to be with her and the kids to be happy and that was it. None of the rest was even on my mind. It's just, I want to be together with my family, basically to be happy instead of depressed. But now I sit here and think about that [what he values in relationships]. Yeah, this is what I wanted. Since I met her, this is what I wanted but it has never worked out that way. It is getting worse.

As a counselor, I was trained initially only to notice men's value and desire for having power and control over their female partners (Pence & Paymar, 1993). These values and how they are supported by patriarchy are important to address. While men often desire power and control, many of them also value fairness and justice. Their values are often contradictory (Augusta-Scott, 2003; Jenkins, 2009). I want to invite men to notice and amplify their value for equitable, respectful, and safe relationships to create a foundation for men to confront their own use of violence.

Numerous lines of inquiry can invite men to consider their values in relationships. Initially, men are simply asked: "What kind of relationship do you want? What do you value in relationships? What is important to you? What type of relationships would you prefer?" (Augusta-Scott, 2008; Jenkins, 1990, 2009; White, 2007). In this process, I often state, "Some men say that respect in relationships is important to them. Is respect important to you? What do you mean by respect?"

To disrupt men from blaming their partners for the men's choices, I often ask if they want to live these values even if their partners are not. For example,

> Do you want to respect your partner even during times when she might get off track and get on the disrespect path? Do you want to hold on to your own values or would you be prepared to abandon them and just go down the disrespect path after her?

Such questions allow men to interrupt blaming their partners for the men's own choices. These lines of inquiry can also help solidify men's commitment to living these values and avoid being distracted from their own values even if their partners may not be practicing these same values (Augusta-Scott, 2007a).

Part of exploring men's values involves asking them if they value "taking responsibility." I ask,

> Some men say that "taking responsibility" is important to them in a relationship, is that important to you? What do you want your children to learn from you about taking responsibility? What do you want them to learn about how to respond to the consequences of their own poor choices?

Often men are initially confused about who is responsible for their abusive *behavior*. They often blame others. However, men are often clear about who is responsible for their *choices*. The discussion of responsibility begins with men acknowledging that people are responsible for their *choices* (Frederick & Lizdas, 2010; Pence & Paymar, 1993). I also ask men about the dangers of blaming others for their choices:

> If men are blaming others, what effect does this have on the men? Does blaming others lead men to feel more in control over time or less in control? Does it lead men to feel more powerful or less powerful? Does it lead men to take greater responsibility for their choices over time or less responsibility?

Men often blame their partners for their abusive behaviors when they comment, "It takes two." I often agree with men saying, "It does 'take two' to make a relationship work" but also ask whether it makes sense that, "It only takes one person to stop yelling—the person who is yelling." I continue to clarify that men can only decide for themselves if they are going to choose to escalate with their partners or not. While their partners may choose to escalate, they do not have to choose to escalate as well. Again, I affirm that, "It does take two" to make a relationship work. The man alone will not be able to save the relationship. If he stops yelling but she does not, the relationship may not be able to be saved. At the same time, he can take responsibility to stop yelling and be respectful even if she does not. There is no excuse for abuse. If the situation does involve both parties using abuse in the relationship, men can be invited to take leadership for taking responsibility in the relationship for themselves, on the basis of their own values, for their own self-respect. Again, men need to take responsibility whether she does or not.

Sometimes, men can be asked to build their own definition of "taking responsibility" by focusing on their partner's need to take responsibly for her choices. I invite men to build a definition of "taking responsibility" by asking, "Who is responsible for your partner's choices?" (He is often clear about the response: "She is.") What would she have to do to take responsibility? What difference would it make if she slowed down to consider how to stop her behavior? What difference would it make if she was putting herself in your and the children's shoes? What difference would it make if she would consider what needs to happen to repair and heal the harms she has created?' Through this line of inquiry, a man creates a definition of taking responsibility. Then I can ask if it is also important for him to take responsibility by asking, "Who is responsible for your choices? What would you want to do to take responsibility for your choices?" Men rarely argue for a double standard in which she is responsible for her choices but he is not responsible for his own.

Evidence of men's values can also be found in their protest against any injustices they may have experienced in their lives (Jenkins, 2009). Implicit in men's stories of their responses to oppression and trauma, there are often values for justice and fairness. By accessing these stories and the values associated with them, men are better able to make sense of why they would want to protest and confront their own use of violence. For example, as children, it is common for these men to have protected their mothers from their father's violence. I invite men to tell me what that might say about their values as a child that they took such a stand? What does it tell them about what was important to them in terms of fairness and taking stands against abuse? Then, I might ask about the connection between what they valued back then and how they may be the same values they are considering as they think about standing up against their own use of abuse.

Traditionally, I seldom asked men directly about their own experiences of injustice because such an inquiry might lead men to justify or excuse their behavior because they were victimized or oppressed. The reality for most men is that they have been both powerful and powerless, oppressed and oppressive, however, they are still fully responsible for their choices. Victimization does not excuse individual responsibility for choosing abuse (Augusta-Scott, 2003, 2007b, 2007c). Men are often able to acknowledge this complexity when I ask them:

What is it like to be asked to take responsibly for hurting others when no one is taking responsibility for hurting you? What does it require of you to stay focused on what you have done, rather than get caught up on what was done to you?

(Jenkins, 2009, p. 116)

Asking questions about this tension allows men to acknowledge that other people are responsible for oppressing them, while still affirming the men are responsibility for oppressing their (ex) partners. Victimization and oppression do not justify or excuse victimizing and abusing others. Again, there is no excuse for abuse. Inviting men to consider their values and bring forward stories of their commitment to these values, creates a foundation for men to take responsibility by acknowledging their violence, creating relapse prevention plans to stop it; studying the effects of their abuse and working to heal and repair these effects.

Respect for Self through Repairing Harms

The process of men stopping their violence and repairing the harms they created needs to lead men to self-respect rather than self-defeat. If the process leads to self-defeat, men are much *less* likely to engage in the journey of taking responsibly. The process of taking responsibility needs to lead men to feel shame for using abuse and self-respect for stopping it and repairing the effects of it. Men need to know that their identities are not reduced to and conflated with the abuse. By allowing men to articulate their preference for loving, caring, respectful relationships, counselors implicitly communicate that they know there are more stories about them than simply the story of them perpetrating violence. After men share stories about themselves and the values that they are proud of, they are much more willing to talk about the stories of behavior about which they are ashamed.

If men are only allowed to build stories about themselves as problems, they often continue to act accordingly. For men to develop self-respect by taking responsibly, I inquire, "Which path is tougher—taking responsibility or blaming others and making excuses? Which path takes more courage: facing mistakes and taking responsibility or running from problems?" Men are often clear that facing problems takes more courage and strength than avoiding them. I then ask, "Would you respect yourself more for facing up to and taking responsibility for your own choices or for blaming other people?" Many men are clear they would respect themselves more for taking responsibility rather than running from it. Men often report: "I've been running from it for too long."

To move the process toward self-respect, I also invite men to consider the values that might be implicit in their shame over perpetrating abuse (Jenkins, 2009). Men frequently have contradictory experiences of their violence. Men feel a sense of entitlement when they use violence to control their partners, which is supported by patriarchy. At the same time, men often experience shame for perpetrating violence against those they love, feeling like failures as partners and fathers (Augusta-Scott, 2003; Augusta-Scott & Dankwort, 2002; Jenkins, 1990). I ask men, "If you feel bad about these harms, what does that say about your values?" Often men respond initially by saying, "I don't know." Then I ask, "If you could hear about the effects of your violence and not feel ashamed, what would that tell you?" Men are typically clear that not feeling any shame would mean that they do not care; they would be monsters and heartless. Then I return to the question, "What does it say about you that you do feel ashamed?" Men respond, "Feeling shame means I care; that I want respectful relationships; that I do not want to hurt anyone; that violence is not alright with me."

Inviting men to consider their shame as evidence of their value for respectful, caring, and equal relationships is important in setting the stage where they can acknowledge the pain they have caused others. The intensity of their shame often reflects the intensity of their commitment to these values. Without addressing the meaning of men's shame in the context of violence, men often experience their shame and violence as simply evidence of how bad they are. In turn, such an association makes it very difficult for men to hear about the effects of their abuse, to experience their shame, and respond to women in a helpful manner. As a result of establishing the men's values and ensuring the experience the process leads men to self-respect, men are then ready to study their own violence to create a relapse prevention plan to ensure it stops.

Create a Relapse Prevention Plan

I feel safer knowing my partner is working toward understanding and controlling his abuse. I know counseling makes him a better listener and it allows me to express past hurts and to work on healing those wounds. It allows for honesty between us. It allows me to see my partner taking responsibility for his actions and thoughts.

(Woman after RJ sessions with partner)

Many women do not simply want men to say that they know they were violent and that they will never do it again. Rather, they want to hear that the men fully understand why they used violence and their detailed plan to stop it. To stop the abuse, men develop relapse prevention plans (Augusta-Scott, 2008). Often relapse prevention plans are referred to as "time outs," "anger logs," or "control logs" (Pence & Paymar, 1993). Developing a plan involves men studying past incidents of abuse so that they are better able to make different choices in the future. Men need to be practicing their relapse prevention plans and women need to be reporting that they feel safer before they discuss on their own or have formal contact with each other to address past violence.

Initially, men often report, "I don't know why I abused her but I know it won't happen again." Such statements do not reassure many women. By the time men address the issues with their (ex) partners, they need to express a significant understanding of why they perpetrated abuse. Further, men need to be able to be clear how they will navigate similar situations or stressors in the future. By men taking responsibility in front of their (ex) partners, women begin to gain trust, safety, and respect. As one woman reported, "For once I see my partner being vulnerable. By acknowledging the abuse, it's like he's telling on himself. It's okay to tell. This is the message we can give our children."

An important part of a relapse prevention plan involves men considering the effects of the violence on their partners. Often abuse happens, in part, because of the men's self-absorption and minimizing the seriousness of the abuse or denying the effects of it. As a result, men studying the actual effects and costs of the violence on their partners is important in the process of stopping the violence.

Prepare to Acknowledge the Effects

Sometimes it's just so much easier to talk by myself to a stranger or counselor. But so often the stuff I'm saying and feeling needs to be shared with my partner in order to understand and heal, to not let history repeat itself. But this kind of communication just wasn't possible between us with so much pain and shame—yet it is necessary! And can be done with the counselors.

(Woman after RJ sessions with partner)

I know that I affected people in my family in a bad way with my abuse, but having my partner sit there and talk about it to other people makes me realize just how bad it really was. Taking responsibility for the abuse is a big step in healing yourself and your family.

(Man after RJ sessions with partner)

For the restorative process to be healing for them, women want the men who hurt them to acknowledge their experiences through the men listening to and acknowledging these. When men (finally) listen to and acknowledge the harms they have created, women often feel understood and validated. If men are not prepared to hear the effects of their abuse, they will likely be defensive, minimize the seriousness of the abuse, blame their partners for the abuse or deny it. These irresponsible stories will re-victimize the women trying to share their stories.

To prepare men to listen to and acknowledge women's experiences of men's violence, men are invited to consider *why* they would want to hear these effects. They need to realize how listening to the effects of their choices fits with their own values to take responsibility to heal and repair the harms they have created. To uphold men's values for taking responsibility for the consequences of their abuse, I ask men, "Would you want to repair the effects of your abuse or would you be prepared to simply allow your (ex) partner and children to try and heal and repair the effects of it on their own?" Further, I ask, "How might it be helpful to hear from your partner how the abuse affected her? What difference do you think it would make to her if you were able to hear about her experience? How might hearing about these effects make you better able to heal and repair these effects?" Men will often respond, "She might feel understood." I then ask, "How would listening and acknowledging the effects fit with the man, partner and father you want to be?" (Jenkins, 2009, p. 120).

Before men can participate in healing the effects of their violence, they need to know that change is possible; repair is possible. For many men, the idea that they could repair what they have done is novel. Initially, men often say that they do not want to hear about the effects of the abuse because, "What is done is done and nothing can be done about it now." Many men say this, in part, because they do not realize that healing and repair of the effects is possible. I often agree with the men that there is nothing that can be done to change the fact that they abused their (ex) partners. At the same time, I introduce men to the idea that healing, repair, and restitution could still happen.

Men also need to be aware that their partners' experiences are likely very different from their own. This difference does not necessarily mean that one of them is wrong; they simply experience it differently. Men often do not realize or intend all of the effects their violence has on their partners. In this manner, men can adopt a posture of curiosity rather than debating or thinking they need to determine whether or not they agree with their (ex) partners' experiences.

Men are also invited to contrast this responsible engagement with irresponsible engagement. I ask, "How might a man minimize the seriousness of his abuse or deny his partners experience? What would happen if you denied or minimized the effects of the abuse on her—where would that lead?" (Jenkins, 2009, p. 120). This process helps men identify the irresponsible responses they want to avoid when listening and responding to their partners and can help men respond in accordance to how they prefer to be.

Women often want to express their anger at their partners' choices to perpetrate abuse and the effects of his abuse on her, the children and the family relationships. Women want to feel safe to share their anger without risk of further abuse. Men need to be prepared to hear their (ex) partners' anger. An important part of the preparation process involves inviting men to anticipate that their (ex) partners will want to express their anger over the violence (Ptacek, 2010). In the preparation process, men are invited to consider what values are implicit in their partners' anger and how their partners' anger is often related to men violating the trust, respect and fairness in the relationship. Often women's anger is the result of them taking a stand against the injustice of men choosing to perpetrate abuse. Through this line of inquiry, men often realize that their (ex) partner's anger is connected to the same values the men have. Men are often angry with themselves for violating these values as well. Their partners' anger can connect them as a result of their shared values rather than as a source of divisiveness.

Without preparation to hear and acknowledge their partners' anger, men can become defensive and oppositional with their partners, which can serve to re-victimize women. Men can be asked, "What might happen if you tried to close down her anger? Where would that lead?" Men may realize that women's anger over the effects of the abuse is not in opposition to their own values. In fact, rather than becoming defensive in the face of women's anger, men are invited to take the opportunity to join with the women's anger over the men's choices to abuse, thereby demonstrating that the men share the same values and are also angry that they violated their own values. Further, the woman's willingness to express her anger (sometimes for the first time) can be seen, in part, as evidence of the man's success in leading her to feel safe enough to express her anger.

After women talk about their experiences of various incidents or time periods in the relationship, many are interested to hear from the men about the men's experiences. As a result, men are prepared for these conversations by being invited to consider their sense of entitlement, their self-absorption, and how they often did not think significantly about the women's feelings. Men often talk about taking their partners for granted. Another man talked about starting to listen to his partner at home:

> We're talking about stuff that I never really gave a shit about before. She's wanting more respect instead of her walking on eggshells because I yell all the time. She's starting to talk with me. She's saying, "This is what I want. When we go to our [restorative] meeting together, this is what I am going to say because this is what I feel." And it's good she's saying that because we never talked that way before. Before I was too busy with me and I didn't even think she had any feelings. I don't mean that in a bad way but that was the last place my head was.

Women often find hearing men acknowledge that they took them for granted very powerful. Hearing men acknowledge that they were wrong to blame the women for the abuse is also very important.

Remedies: Healing and Repairing the Harm

> Attending these sessions together certainly made me feel safer. The sessions provided a time for both of us to reflect on the abuse. For myself, having him hear and learn about the effects of his abuse and take responsibility is very important. In order for me to begin to trust him . . .It was great to have him know my feelings on the topic!
>
> (Woman after RJ sessions with partner)

After men are invited to consider the effects of the abuse, they are often in a better position to consider what they can do to heal and repair these effects. By taking responsibility to think of what might address the abuse, men share their ideas with women rather than simply relying on women to think of ideas. Women often do not want the burden of dealing with the effects of his violence on themselves and others. Of course, women are encouraged to evaluate men's ideas about what will be helpful and to change them according to what women actually think will be helpful.

The seriousness with which men evaluate the harms is reflected in the significance of the remedies that he suggests might be helpful. When men commit to significant actions to address the effects of the abuse, they communicate to women the seriousness with which they take the abuse. The best-case scenario is when the remedies that men suggest are more significant than the women believe are necessary to address the harms. To ensure the men's plans to take responsibility are helpful, after the men first consider possible plans individually, the plan is eventually developed collaboratively with the women and community members.

Sometimes women want men to repair or pay to repair any damage to property; to pay financial compensation for other costs incurred because of the assault; to share the domestic load and parenting responsibilities; to spend less time on the internet and more time with the family; to maintain distance—separate bedrooms or separate residences—until she decides how she wants to proceed. They may be separated and only connected through their children or both just continue to live in the same small community. As a result, men might consider what women might want from the men to live in these situations. For example, men are invited to question whether they should initiate any contact or should they rely on the women to initiate contact.

Apology and Forgiveness

Nothing we wanted to say got said at home. Families in our position don't want to hear, "I'm sorry" one more time! Or "I didn't mean to." Apologies are old. This process is much deeper than that. We need to understand each other. Understanding and making sense is what we needed to do. It does not excuse things or make them okay; it just helps with the healing process.

(Woman on RJ sessions with partner)

In preparation for addressing the harms they have created, men are invited to consider issues of apologies and forgiveness (Randall, 2013). Processes that mandate apologies and forgiveness after violence create "cheap justice" (Coker, 2002). Men have often employed unhelpful apologies in a manner that is insincere, manipulative, and meaningless (Busch, 2002; Stubbs, 2007). Men are invited to consider, "What is the difference between a sincere apology and hollow promises and apologies? What is the difference between the apologies you made in the past and the process you are engaged in now?" One man responded:

Before I never did anything about it and now I'm going to. It's as simple as that. Oh yeah, it's got to change . . . I guess basically I took her for granted.

Some women will want to hear an apology while others will not. Men need to consider the potential effects of the timing of an apology. Men are asked, "What would happen if you tried to apologize before you fully realized what you have put her through? Would you be apologizing for her or only for yourself?" Men are often clear that they apologized many times in the past to simply pacify an incident of having perpetrated abuse rather than working at fixing it.

Men are also invited to consider how they and others may have pressured women to forgive (Coker, 2002; Stubbs, 2002) by asking, "What is the difference between an apology that is freely given and one in which the person who has been harmed feels obligated to forgive? Which is more helpful for the person? Why?" The process of apology and forgiveness does not necessitate women relinquishing their anger over injustice (Jenkins, Hall, &Joy, 2002;Jenkins, 2009). To prevent men from inferring that they are requesting or obligating women for forgiveness, men are invited to frame their reparation simply in terms of their *realizations* and their remorse (Jenkins, 2009).

Conclusion

This restorative approach is about women achieving just outcomes after being abused by their (ex) partners. The chapter has elaborated on preparing men to address the effects of their abuse on the women they have harmed. Conversations with men are one component of many different conversations with women, family, and community members in a larger restorative process. These preparation conversations most often involve men taking responsibility by acknowledging the abuse; developing relapse prevention plans to stop it; studying the effects of the abuse and considering how they may participate in healing and repairing these effects. Men listening to women may also lead to conversations to include men's choices beyond women's immediate experiences of abuse. For many women, reparation also involves men taking responsibility for their life choices generally in relation to their own well-being and the well-being of others (Tanako, 2017, Chapter 6 this volume). This restorative process raises the community expectations of what women and others can expect from men after they abuse. Patriarchal expectations of men in relationships are often very low: men are seldom expected to take responsibility to address the emotional and physical harms they have created for others. These restorative processes increase expectations of men so they can and will be part of the process of creating justice for women.

Note

1. I want to acknowledge that the restorative and narrative approach outlined in this paper developed with Marilee Burwash-Brennan, Bridges Institute; Jane Donovan, New Start Counselling; and Debbie Van Horne, Canadian Armed Forces.

References

Augusta-Scott, T. (2003). Dichotomies in the power and control story: Exploring multiple stories about men who choose abuse in intimate relationships. In Dulwich Centre Publications (Eds.), *Responding to violence: A collection of papers relating to child sexual abuse and violence in intimate relationships* (pp. 204–224). Adelaide, Australia: Dulwich Centre Publications.

Augusta-Scott, T. (2007a). Conversations with men about women's violence: Ending men's violence by challenging gender essentialism. In C. Brown & T. Augusta-Scott (Eds.), *Narrative therapy: Making meaning, making lives* (pp. 197–210). Thousand Oaks, CA: Sage.

Augusta-Scott, T. (2007b). Challenging anti-oppressive discourse: Uniting against racism and sexism. In C. Brown & T. Augusta-Scott (Eds.), *Narrative therapy: Making meaning, making lives* (pp. 211–228). Thousand Oaks, CA: Sage.

Augusta-Scott, T. (2007c). Letters from prison: Re-authoring identity with men who have perpetrated sexual violence. In C. Brown & T. Augusta-Scott (Eds.), *Narrative therapy: Making meaning, making lives* (pp. 251–268). Thousand Oaks, CA: Sage.

Augusta-Scott, T. (2008). *Narrative therapy: A group manual for men who have perpetrated abuse.* Truro, NS: Bridges Institute. Retrieved from: www.bridgesinstitute.org/?portfolio= narative-therapy.

Augusta-Scott, T. (2009). A narrative therapy approach to conversations with men about perpetrating abuse. In P. Lehmann & C. Simmons (Eds.), *Strengths-based batterers intervention: A new paradigm in ending family violence* (pp. 113–135). New York, NY: Springer.

Augusta-Scott, T. & Dankwort, J. (2002). Group work with partner abuse: Lessons from constructivist and educational approaches. *Journal of Interpersonal Violence, 7*(7), 783–805. doi:10.1177/0886260502017007006

Braithwaite, J. (2002). *Restorative justice and responsive regulation.* New York, NY: Oxford University Press.

Busch, R. (2002). Domestic violence and restorative justice initiatives: Who pays if we get it wrong. In H. Strang & J. Braithwaite (Eds.), *Restorative justice and family violence* (pp. 223–248). New York, NY: Cambridge University Press.

Coker, D. (2002). Anti-subordination processes in domestic violence. In H. Strang & J. Braithwaite (Eds.), *Restorative justice and family violence* (pp. 128–152). New York, NY: Cambridge University Press.

Frederick, L. & Lizdas, K. (2010). The role of restorative justice in the battered women's movement. In J. Ptacek (Ed.), *Restorative justice and violence against women* (pp. 39–59). New York, NY: Oxford University Press.

Goodmark, L. (2012). *A troubled marriage: Domestic violence and the legal system.* New York, NY: New York University Press.

Herman, J. (2005). Justice from the victim's perspective. *Violence Against Women, 11*(5), 571–602. doi:10.1177/1077801205274450

Jenkins, A. (1990). *Invitations to responsibility: The therapeutic engagement of men who are violent and abusive.* Adelaide, AU: Dulwich Centre Publications.

Jenkins, A. (2009). *Becoming ethical: A parallel, political journey with men who have abused.* Dorset, UK: Russell House Publishing.

Jenkins, A., Hall, R., & Joy, M. (2002). Forgiveness and child sexual abuse: A matrix of meanings. *The International Journal of Narrative Therapy and Community Work, 1,* 35–51.

Llewellyn, J. (2008). Bridging the gap between truth and reconciliation: Restorative justice and the Indian Residential Schools Truth and Reconciliation Commission. In M. B. Castellano, L. Archibald, & M. DeGagné (Eds.), *From truth to reconciliation: Transforming the legacy of residential schools* (pp. 183–201). Ottawa, ON: Aboriginal Healing Foundation Research Publications. Retrieved from: http://speakingmytruth.ca/ ?page_id=701.

Llewellyn, J. (2011). Restorative justice: Thinking relationally about Justice. In J. Downie & J. Llewellyn (Eds.), *Being relational: Reflections of relational theory and health law* (pp. 89–108). Vancouver, BC: UBC Press.

Llewellyn, J. & Howse, R. (1998). *Restorative justice. A conceptual framework.* Ottawa, ON: Law Commission of Canada. Retrieved from: https://dalspace.library.dal.ca/bitstream/ handle/10222/10287/Howse_Llewellyn%20Research%20Restorative%20Justice%20 Framework%20EN.pdf?sequence=1.

Mills, L. (2008). *Violent partners: A breakthrough plan for ending the cycle of abuse.* New York, NY: Basic Books.

Pence, E. & Paymar, M. (1993). *Education groups for men who batter: The Duluth Model.* New York, NY: Springer Publishing.

Pennell, J. (2005). Safety for mothers and their children. In J. Pennell & G. Anderson (Eds.), *Widening the circle: The practice and evaluation of family group conferencing with children youths, and their families* (pp. 163–181). Washington, DC: National Association of Social Workers Press.

Pennell, J., Sanders, T., Rikard, R. V., Shepherd, J., & Starsoneck, L. (2013). *Family violence, fathers and restoring personhood. Restorative Justice, 1*(2), 268–289.

Ptacek, J. (Ed.) (2010). *Restorative justice and violence against women.* New York, NY: Oxford University Press.

Randall, M. (2013). Restorative justice and gendered violence? From vaguely hostile skeptic to cautious convert: Why feminists should critically engage with restorative approaches to law. *Dalhousie Law Journal, 36*(2), 461–499.

Strang, H. & Braithwaite, J. (Eds.) (2002). *Restorative justice and family violence.* New York, NY: Cambridge University Press.

Stubbs, J. (2002). Domestic violence and women's safety: Feminist challenges to restorative justice. In H. Strang & J. Braithwaite (Eds.), *Restorative justice and family violence* (pp. 42–61). New York, NY: Cambridge University Press.

Stubbs, J. (2007). Beyond apology? Domestic violence and critical questions for restorative justice. *Criminology and Criminal Justice, 7*(2), 169–187.

Tanako, Y. (2017). Existential self-responsibility: Critical elements of change processes in male domestic violence offenders. In T. Augusta-Scott, K. Scott, & L. Tutty (Eds.), *Innovations in interventions to address intimate partner violence: Research and practice.* New York, NY: Routledge.

White, M. (2007). *Maps of narrative practice.* New York, NY: Norton.

Part V

Broadening the Lens

Integrating Interventions for Domestic
Violence Across Systems

13 Strengthening Families

An Evaluation of a Pilot Couples Program for Situational Intimate Partner Violence and Substance Abuse[1]

Leslie M. Tutty and Robbie Babins-Wagner

Intimate partner violence (IPV), primarily male-perpetrated against women, is a significant social problem across North America (Johnson, 2007). In addition to the important institutional responses to protect victims (i.e. violence against women shelters) and to hold perpetrators accountable (i.e. police primary aggressor policies and specialized domestic violence courts), a number of IPV-specific counseling approaches have emerged. Most commonly offered are groups for men who perpetrate violence (i.e. Augusta-Scott & Dankwort, 2002; Scott, King, McGinn, & Hosseini, 2011) and support or therapy groups for women (Abel, 2000; Tutty, Babins-Wagner, & Rothery, 2015). Each of these are directed at either the victim or the perpetrator of the violence, but aside from a seldom-used option of the men and women concurrently attending groups, if a couple wishes treatment as a unit, this is rarely offered.

One challenge for clinicians in considering how or whether to assist couples when IPV is an issue has been the range of abusive behaviors used by male perpetrators, with some physically beating and threatening the lives of women partners and others using psychological control to coerce their partners (Johnson, 2005). While neither end of the spectrum is acceptable, some researchers suggest that these men are different. With respect to the conceptualizing "minor" from more serous intimate partner violence, in studies conducted in shelters for intimate partner violence, women are much more likely to report experiencing severe violence, including violence that causes significant injuries, sexual assaults, sadistic denigration, and death threats, termed "intimate partner terrorism" by Johnson (2005). In contrast, "situational couple violence," the form of violence disclosed by the majority in national incidence studies, is less likely related to significant control issues, fear, or injury and more likely involves mutual, "low-level" violence, although one must always be cautious about using this term because even a push can be fatal. Situational violence entails minor aggressive acts by both men and women, sometimes termed "mutual violence." The distinction between terroristic and situational violence is important because the needs of victims and the focus of services differ (Johnson, 2005).

Substance abuse has long been associated with higher risk for intimate partner violence. Clinical intervention with couples is a common approach in treating substance abuse since, while the non-abusing partner is not seen as responsible for the substance abuse issues, improving partner interactions are considered important in assisting the individual with the substance abuse problem (Fals-Stewart, Klostermann, Yates, O'Farrell, & Birchler, 2005).

Recently clinicians have experimented with conjoint couples therapy that addresses both situational intimate partner violence and substance abuse, with the caveat that both issues must be appropriately understood and addressed. This chapter reviews research with respect to couple's interventions for IPV, the impact of substances on IPV and relatively new interventions that address both issues using a couple's therapy format. The chapter then describes a pilot program, Strengthening Families, offered by the Calgary Counselling Centre in Calgary, Canada that addresses both situational IPV and substance abuse by one or both partners. We conclude with an evaluation of the program.

Couples Intervention to Address Intimate Partner Violence

While some consider couples therapy to be an appropriate method for addressing spousal violence, this has been debated for decades (i.e. Bograd, 1984). Traditional family systems theorists view individual problems as caused by family dynamics and addressing these issues entails the premise of equal power in relationships (McCollum & Stith, 2007). This viewpoint moves responsibility and accountability away from the individual and instead holds the dyad responsible, which in essence, blames the victim for her part in the "couple dynamics."

Nevertheless, more recently, couples therapy specific to IPV has been offered with the caveat that the violence be minor, as in the case of situational violence, and that the power imbalances become a central focus of the intervention (Stith, Smith, Penn, Ward, & Tritt, 2004). One important aspect of this approach is the therapist abandoning the family system's notion of neutrality when it becomes apparent that one partner is behaving abusively toward the other. Other suggestions include assessing not only the severity of the IPV acts but also fear of the partner and fear of the consequences of joint therapy sessions, such as fears that disclosures during counseling could lead to violent retaliation by a perpetrating partner (Stith & McCollum, 2011).

With such important caveats, recent evaluations of couple intervention specific to IPV report positive results (LaTaillade, Epstein, & Werlinich, 2006; McCollum & Stith, 2008). Similarly, Johannson and Tutty (1998) evaluated a twelve-week couples group offered after each member of the couple had successfully participated in twenty-four weeks of gender-specific IPV groups. Notably though, while the pretest/posttest analysis reported significant improvements in couple-relationship issues and a continued lack of violent incidents, at one-year follow-up, two men had re-assaulted their partners and another had kidnapped their child. Clearly, challenges remain in working with men who abuse partners.

Intimate Partner Violence and Substance Use/Abuse

While alcohol and substance abuse are not typically seen as direct causes of partner violence (Galvani, 2004), for many couples they are associated (Leonard, 2001). When men abuse their intimate partners, alcohol use/abuse increases the likelihood of the violence occurring (Coker, Smith, McKeown, & King, 2000) and being more dangerous (Thomas, Bennett, & Stoops, 2013). A number of researchers have examined the effects of both drugs and alcohol on intimate partner perpetration. In a meta-analysis of eighty-five studies, Stith et al. (2004) found a large effect of illicit drug use on emotional abuse, forced sex, attitudes condoning marital violence and marital satisfaction, and a moderate effect of alcohol use on traditional sex-role ideology, anger/hostility, history of partner abuse, depression, and career/life stress. Researchers suggest that alcohol use is involved in 40 to 60 percent of episodes of intimate partner violence (Chermack, Walton, Fuller, & Blow, 2001) and substance abuse, regardless of type, predicts domestic violence (DV) perpetration and victimization by persons of both genders (Stuart et al., 2008) and binge drinking is more common among perpetrators (Langenderfer, 2013). In summary, considerable study of substance abuse and perpetrating intimate partner violence has found many associations, leading to the conclusion that treatments for domestic violence and those for substance abuse should, at minimum, assess for the other clinical issue, while others advocate the joint treatment of these two significant clinical problems.

Treatment Approaches for Partner Abusers with Substance Misuse Issues

Although researchers have documented relatively high proportions of men and women in substance abuse programs with intimate partner violence issues (Chermack et al., 2001) and relatively high numbers of men and women in batterer intervention programs with substance abuse problems (Langenderfer, 2013; Thomas et al., 2013), until recently, few programs addressed both issues (Humphreys, Regan, River, & Thiara, 2005). Further, "few men entering substance abuse treatment accept referrals to batterers treatment, and among those who do, the majority drop out very early" (Fals-Stewart & Clinton-Sherrod, 2009, p. 258).

Behavioral Couples Therapy (BCT), the model used to develop the Strengthening Families program, which is the focus of the current evaluation, is conjoint treatment for couples in committed relationships in which one partner has an alcohol and/or substance abuse disorder. BCT invites the non-substance-abusing partner into treatment to support abstinence for the substance abuser, while improving the relationship, which has likely been negatively affected by the substance abuse (Fals-Stewart & Clinton-Sherrod, 2009). Within this framework, it is important to acknowledge that the IPV will not necessarily cease when substance abuse is controlled, but must be directly addressed as a separate issue.

BCT has received extensive empirical support for its clinical and cost effectiveness as for alcoholism and drug abuse for both male (Fals-Stewart et al., 2005; O'Farrell & Schein, 2011) and female alcoholics (Fals-Stewart, Birchler, & Kelley, 2006). While BCT did not originally address intimate partner violence, recent modifications added domestic violence content (Fals-Stewart & Clinton-Sherrod, 2009) including weekly check-ins regarding any violence, and the use of IPV strategies such as time-outs. Although the major clinical focus remains on the substance abuser's inappropriate use of violence against his partner, "Partners are taught certain coping skills and measures to increase safety when faced with a situation where the likelihood of IPV is increased" (p. 258), such as him not drinking or using time-outs and her developing a safety plan.

The Calgary Counselling Centre's Domestic Violence Programs

The Calgary Counselling Centre was founded more than fifty years ago in 1962. A batterer intervention program for partner abuse has been offered since 1981; the revised group programs, "Responsible Choices for Men" (McGregor, Tutty, Babins-Wagner, & Gill, 2002), "Responsible Choices for Women" (Tutty, Babins-Wagner, & Rothery, 2009), and "You're Not Alone" (Tutty, Babins-Wagner, & Rothery, 2015) are for those who use and who have been the victims of physical, psychological violence, or control tactics by their intimate partners.

As a general counseling agency, couples commonly access the Calgary Counselling Centre requesting therapy together. With the specialized knowledge of the dynamics of intimate partner in the agency, the counselors routinely assess the couple dynamics first in a conjoint interview, then with separate segments to speak with each partner individually, to address safety if violence were a factor. Although no standardized measures differentiate different forms of violence, general assessment principles for IPV have been developed (Tutty, 2012).

If intimate partner abuse were identified, the couple would first be referred separately to the specialized DV programs for perpetrators and victims. Once the group interventions were completed, the couple would meet with their primary therapist to discuss the need for and advisability of couple counseling. However the risk to saying no to a request for couple's therapy is that the couple do not access any support.

The current pilot program, Strengthening Families, is based on the previously described BCT that concurrently addresses intimate partner violence and substance abuse (Fals-Stewart & Clinton-Sherrod, 2009). The program was developed to address a gap in the services offered in the community for couples with concurrent low levels of IPV and substance abuse. International experts on similar programs (Sandra Stith and Eric McCollum, William Fal-Stewart and Keith Klostermann) were consulted. In addition, representatives from local agencies such as Children and Family Services (Child Welfare), Police Services, substance abuse treatment agencies and HomeFront, an agency offering support to victims of domestic violence, were consulted and participated in a project advisory team throughout the pilot (Tutty, 2014). The agency also held two community meetings to raise awareness of the proposed program.

The majority of couples were referred from sources different from those eligible for the group interventions for perpetrators and victims of intimate partner violence. None were court-referred but came primarily from Children and Family Services (Child Welfare) and from HomeFront's special program for "low-risk" IPV couples (police attended but did not lay charges).

Couples were typically seen for twelve weekly outpatient conjoint sessions over a three to six month period, although treatment length also depended on the number and severity of problems. The program was designed to help couples work effectively as a team toward open, agreeable, and attainable goals, including decreased incidents of intimate partner violence, the abuser accepting responsibility for their behaviors, decreasing distress and increasing empathy toward the victim, and decreased substance use.

The program is highly structured, following a predictable format in each session, typically concluding with the introduction of new skills. The therapist is active, directive, and focused on recovery first. At times, the therapist functions as an instructor, explaining and modeling the session's skill. Couples rehearse the skills in-vivo, while exploring feelings related to relationship and substance abuse issues. A manual guides the sessions but the therapist has the flexibility to focus on what is most pertinent to each couple: Significant crisis or emotionally laden issues take precedence over manual topics.

As a pilot program, the funders required an evaluation to assess how well the program addressed the joint concerns of IPV and substance use, the focus of the remainder of the chapter. In addition to looking at the clinical outcomes, we were also interested in identifying the characteristics of the couples who attended and those who started but did not complete, which could influence how the program is marketed or the content or structure of sessions.

Method

The current evaluation examined the Strengthening Families pilot project, both by comparing the characteristics of those who completed the program and those who dropped out and analyzing whether program completers made statistically significant improvements pre- and post–treatment. Couples answered an extensive package of outcome measures. Mental health symptoms were assessed by the Outcome Questionnaire (OQ-45.2) (Lambert et al., 1996) with three subscales (symptom distress, interpersonal relations, and social role); depression by the Generalized Contentment Scale (Hudson, 1992); anxiety by the Index of Clinical Stress (Hudson, 1992); and self-esteem by the Rosenberg Self-Esteem Index (Rosenberg, 1965).

Problematic personality traits were assessed using the Personality Assessment Screener (PAS) (Morey, 2007). To account for potential biases in reporting the short form of the Marlowe Crowne Social Desirability Test (Andrews & Moyer, 2003; Reynolds, 1982) was included. The Family Assessment Measure (FAM-III: Dyadic Relationship) (Skinner, Steinhauer, & Santa-Barbara, 1983) was used to assess couple interactions including one's perception of the relationship with one's spouse with seven subscales: task accomplishment, role performance, communication, affective expression, involvement, control, and values and norms. The T-scores have a clinical cut-off of seventy or higher.

Levels of intimate partner violence were assessed by four abuse of partner scales (Hudson, 1992) that assess self-reported abusive behaviors toward one's partner and vice versa. The physical abuse scales contain items on physical and forced sexual assault, while the non-physical abuse scale items reflect psychological abuse or coercive behavior. Suggested clinical cut-off scores are two for the physical abuse scales and fifteen for the psychological abuse scales (Attala, Hudson, & McSweeney, 1994).

Substance abuse was assessed using the Substance Abuse Subtle Screening Inventory (SASSI-3) (Miller, Roberts, Brooks, & Lazowski, 2003) that identifies the likelihood of a substance dependence disorder, even if the individual does not acknowledge misuse. Ten subscales include: FVA: acknowledged use of alcohol; FVOD acknowledged use of other drugs; SYM Causes, consequences and correlates of substance abuse; OAT Obvious Attributes: Characteristics commonly associated with substance misuse; SAT Subtle: Basic personal style similar to substance dependent people; DEF Defensiveness that may or may not be related to substance misuse—may reflect an enduring character trait or a temporary reaction to a current situation; FAM Family versus Control subjects: similarity to family members of people who misuse substances; COR Correctional: similar to people with extensive legal difficulties. The subscale scores were translated into T-scores with a sixty representing the 85th percentile (of concern) and seventy being at the 98th percentile (the clinical cut-off).

Although the sample sizes are small, they are large enough to warrant statistical tests; Pearson's chi-square for categorical data and independent t-tests for the scores comparing completers versus non-completes and repeated measures ANOVAs for pretest/posttest comparisons. As this was an evaluation of a pilot program, a probability level of .05 to signify statistical significance was adopted (in future, a more stringent probability level could be used). When the ANOVA scores are statistically significant, the effect sizes documented is eta-squared. The University of Calgary Conjoint Research Ethics Committee approved the ethics components of the research. Ethical considerations included confidentiality, informed consent and the right to withdraw at any time in the research process.

Results

Over a two and a half year period between 2010 and 2013, 108 couples were referred or self-referred to the Strengthening Families program. For forty-four of these couples (40.7 percent), it is not known whether they came to the agency for an intake session or not. A further twenty-two referred couples (20.4 percent) did not materialize for their first appointment and eight (7.4 percent) did not meet the Strengthening Families criteria. Nine couples (8.3 percent) considered appropriate by the agency did not start the SF program. Of the total 108 referrals, then, twenty-five couples (23.1 percent) started the program and nine couples completed.

The demographics of the eighteen individuals (from nine couples) who completed the Strengthening Families program are compared to twenty-eight individuals from fifteen couples (men from two couples did not complete the pretests) who started but did not complete the program (see Table 13.1). The agency defines completion as ten sessions or more. As can be seen, there were almost no statistically significant differences between these two groups.

Table 13.1 Comparison of Demographics of Non-Completers and Completers

Variable	Category	Non-Completers (N = 28)	Completers (N = 18)	Chi-Square
Marital Status by couple	Married	5 (31.3%)	2 (22.2%)	0.23, p = .63 n.s.
	Common-law	11 (68.8%)	7 (77.8%)	
Education	High school or less	17 (58.6%)	10 (58.8%)	1.0, p = .60 n.s.
	Technical/vocational	8 (27.6%)	3 (17.6%)	
	University	4 (13.8%)	4 (23.5%)	
Income for couple	$0 to 29,999	3 (20%)	1 (11%)	1.7, p = .64 n.s
	$30,000 to 59,999	1 (6.7%)	2 (22.2%)	
	$60,000 to 89,999	7 (46.7%)	3 (33.3%)	
	$90,000 and above	4 (26.7%)	3 (33.3%)	
Children by couple	No children	3 (18.8%)	0 (0%)	3.1, p = .21 n.s.
	One or two children	10 (62.5%)	5 (55.6%)	
	Three or more children	3 (18.8%)	4 (44.4%)	
Child welfare involvement	No	5 (31.3%)	1 (11.1%)	0.4, p = .52 n.s.
	Yes	11 (68.8%)	8 (88.9%)	
Referral source	Child & Family Services	7 (43.8%)	6 (66.7%)	1.3, p = .54 n.s.
	Legal/HomeFront/ probation	2 (12.5%)	1 (11.1%)	
	Counsellors/self	7 (43.8%)	2 (22.2%)	
Previous counseling	Yes	23 (82.1%)	9 (50%)	5.4*; p = .02*; phi = .34
	No	5 (17.9%)	9 (50%)	
Number of sessions completed	One to three sessions	5 (31.3%)	0	N/A
	Four to six sessions	4 (25%)	0	
	Seven to nine sessions	7 (43.7%)	0	
	Ten or more sessions	0 (0%)	9 (100%)	

All twenty-five couples were heterosexual. The individuals ranged in age from nineteen to fifty-three years with an average of 33.4 years (s.d. = 8.1 years). Of the forty-five individuals who disclosed their racial backgrounds, the majority were Caucasian (88.9 percent), four were East Asian and one was Filipino. The majority (72 percent of twenty-five couples) were in common-law relationships.

With respect to the education levels of the clients, a little more than two-fifths (42 percent) have more than a highschool education. The income levels of the majority of couples were over $60,000 per year (70.9 percent) considering income from both parties. The oldest child was a preschooler for half of the twenty-two couples with children, 41 percent were aged six to twelve years and 18.1 percent were teens. Considering the total number of children, over half (60 percent) had two or more offspring. Neither this variable nor child welfare involvement (ever) differentiated completers from non-completers. However, a high proportion of both (76 percent) had child welfare involvement at some point, although not necessarily at present. Referrals from Child and Family Services (child welfare) made up slightly more than half of the total, however these were about as likely to complete as not. Almost half of the couples (43 percent) who did not finish, nonetheless completed seven to nine sessions, a respectable time in treatment that could have impacted their relationships.

Interestingly, there was a statistically significant difference in Strengthening Families completers as compared to non-completers such that more individuals who completed had not previously had any form of counseling (a moderate effect). Of those who had previous counseling, over half (eighteen of thirty-two) had clinical interventions for issues besides domestic violence, substance abuse, or couples counseling. These included counseling for bereavement, sexual assault, issues with parents, and mental health concerns. Four individuals had previous interventions for domestic violence either as victims or perpetrators, four had previous counseling from the Calgary Counselling Centre, and three had previous couples counseling. Two individuals had previous addictions counseling and one had both addictions and domestic violence intervention prior to attending the Strengthening Families program.

With respect to recent police interventions, the majority of the couples (four-fifths) had police intervention at some point, although not all of this resulted in charges but with no statistically significant difference between completers or non-completers. Of the eleven couples, eight self-reported that the police had been called and three noted that charges had been laid.

Strengthening Program Completers versus Non-Completers on Standardized Measures

The data in Table 13.2 provide important information describing the characteristics of all of the couples referred to the Strengthening Families program at pretest whether they completed or not. As can be seen in Table 13.2, few variables differentiated clients who completed the program compared to those

Table 13.2 Comparison of Measures for Non-Completers and Completers at Pretest

Measure	Non-Completers (n= 30)	Completers (n = 18)	t-test
Marlow-Crowne Social Desirability	6.4 (s.d. = 3.2)	6.9 (s.d. = 3.2)	0.5 n.s.
Personality Assessment Screener	56.5 (s.d. = 29.9)	51.2 (s.d. = 37.6)	0.50 n.s.
OQ-45 Symptom Distress	26.9 (s.d. = 13.4)	25.4 (s.d. = 18.1)	0.33 n.s.
OQ-45 Interpersonal Relations	15.2 (s.d. = 8.4)	12.7 (s.d. = 6.8)	1.1 n.s.
OQ-45 Social Role	9.6 (s.d. = 3.7)	8.4 (s.d. = 5.5)	0.86 n.s.
OQ-45 Total	51.7 (s.d. = 24)	46.4 (s.d. = 28.4)	0.68 n.s.
Rosenberg Self-Esteem	30.9 (s.d. = 6.1)	31.8 (s.d. = 6.3)	.46 n.s.
Generalized Contentment Scale	29.0 (s.d. = 15.7)	28.8 (s.d. = 27.4)	.04 n.s.
Index of Clinical Stress	32.9 (s.d. = 20.6)	30.8 (s.d. = 20.3)	.35 n.s.
Conflict/Partner Abuse Scales			
Physical Abuse of Partner Scale	1.4 (s.d. = 2.6)	4.9 (s.d. = 7.7)	1.8 n.s.
Non-Physical Abuse of Partner	10.8 (s.d. = 9.5)	12.2 (s.d. = 9.2)	.51 n.s.
Partner Abuse Scale – Physical	3.5 (s.d. = 5.2)	6.0 (s.d. = 7.7)	1.4 n.s.
Partner Abuse Scale – Non-Physical	19.9 (s.d. = 20.4)	16.8 (s.d. = 11.9)	0.68 n.s.
Couple Relationship Scales			
FAM-III Task Accomplishment	60.4 (s.d. = 13.4)	56.2 (s.d. = 8.7)	1.2 n.s.
FAM III Role Performance	59.0 (s.d. = 11.4)	55.0 (s.d. = 13.3)	1.1 n.s.
FAM III Communication	62.1 (s.d. = 13.0)	58.4 (s.d. = 12.7)	0.95 n.s.
FAM III Affective Expression	56.5 (s.d. = 13.8)	54.8 (s.d. = 12.6)	0.44 n.s.
FAM III Involvement	58.7 (s.d. = 14.1)	54.1 (s.d. = 13.7)	1.1 n.s.
FAM III Control	78.6 (s.d. = 69.8)	57.8 (s.d. = 13.2)	1.3 n.s.
FAM III Values and Norms	56.8 (s.d. = 14.0)	48.7 (s.d. = 16.9)	1.8 n.s.
Substance Abuse Scales			
PAS Substance Abuse Subscale	67.2 (s.d. = 63.6)	52.8 (s.d. = 19.3)	0.92 n.s.
SASSI-Face Valid Alcohol-T	63.3 (s.d. = 15.7)	61.7 (s.d. = 17.5)	0.38 n.s.
SASSI-Face Valid Other Drugs-T	60.5 (s.d. = 15.9)	65.0 (s.d. = 18.6)	−0.89 n.s.
SASSI-Symptoms Substance Misuse-T	61.6 (s.d. = 13.6)	61.5 (s.d. = 14.3)	0.36 n.s.
SASSI-Obvious Attributes-T	58.0 (s.d. = 10.2)	55.6 (s.d. = 12.3)	0.71 n.s.
SASSI-Subtle Attributes-T	51.9 (s.d. = 10.2)	52.2 (s.d. = 10.6)	−0.12 n.s.
SASSI-Defensiveness-T	50.6 (s.d. = 8.8)	49.2 (s.d. = 11.3)	0.47 n.s.
SASSI Response Set Subscales-T			
SASSI-Family versus Controls-T	47.2 (s.d. = 10.2)	47.7 (s.d. = 12.7)	0.15 n.s.
SASSI-Correctional-T	54.0 (s.d. = 16.8)	59.4 (s.d. = 13.0)	−1.1 n.s.

who did not. On measures with clinical cut-off scores, the average scores on most were in the area of concern, though not in the clinical range; perhaps explained by the program criteria screening out couples with severe intimate partner violence, and the fact that referrals from addictions agencies were rare.

The scores on the Personality Assessment Screener for both groups at pretest were above the clinical cut-off of forty-seven, indicating significant problems. In contrast, mental health issues assessed by the average OQ-45 total score (Lambert et al., 1996) for both groups was below the clinical cut-off of sixty-three, indicating that neither group was reporting significant clinical concerns at the start of the program.

Average scores on the Rosenberg Self-Esteem Index were above the clinical cut-off for both completers and non-completers, indicating high self-esteem. Similarly, the average scores on the Generalized Contentment Scale (depression) and the Index of Clinical Stress (anxiety) (Hudson, 1992) were not in the clinical range. There were no statistically significant differences between completers compared to non-completers at pretest on Hudson's two sets of domestic violence scales. With respect to using intimate partner violence, both completers and non-completers were in the clinical range of receiving physical and psychological abuse from their partners, suggesting their appropriateness for the program. While there were no statistically significant differences between problem completers and non-completers with respect to couple relationship factors (FAM-III), at pretest the average T-scores of the program completers were all non-clinical (below 60) (non-clinical), whereas program non-completers reported average scores in the "poor" region for Control, Task Accomplishment (how problems should be resolved), and Communication. The average scores on the substance abuse (SASSI) subscales were primarily in the "normal" or "of concern" range; none were above the clinical cut-off of seventy.

The Strengthening Families Program Client's Outcomes

The data in Table 13.3 illustrate statistically significant reductions in mental health issues (OQ-45 subscales and total score) for clients who completed the Strengthening Family program. The client's general mental health scores (OQ-Total) decreased (improved) on average more than the fourteen points considered to be a "Reliable Clinical Change," an additional standard of clinical significance (Lambert et al., 1996). That the social desirability scores (Marlowe Crowne) were not statistically significantly different is positive, indicating that the program clients did not present themselves in more socially desirable ways either before or after the program.

Congruent with the clinical improvements on mental health issues (OQ-45), the program clients statistically significantly improved their anxiety (Index of Clinical Stress) and self-esteem (Rosenberg Self-Esteem scale) but depression did

Table 13.3 Comparison of Pretest/Posttest Scores

Measure	Mean Pretest	Mean Posttest	F-score	Partial eta²
Marlow-Crowne Social Desirability (N = 16)	7.2 (s.d. = 3.2)	8.9 (s.d. = 2.7)	2.8 (p = .11) n.s.	
Personality Assessment Screener (N = 16)	48.7 (s.d. = 39.3)	27.7 (s.d. = 27.7)	3.8 (p = .07)	
OQ-45 Symptom Distress (N = 17)	**24.8 (s.d. = 18.4)**	**13.7 (s.d. = 16.7)**	**7.1 (p = .017)***	**.31**
OQ-45 Interpersonal Relations (N = 17)	**12.4 (s.d. = 6.9)**	**6.4 (s.d. = 7.0)**	**14.2 (p < .002)****	**.47**
OQ-45 Social Role (N = 17)	**8.3 (s.d. = 5.6)**	**4.7 (s.d. = 4.9)**	**6.7 (p = .02)***	**.30**
OQ-45 Total (N = 17)	**45.4 (s.d. = 28.9)**	**24.7 (s.d. = 27.8)**	**9.4 (p < .007)****	**.36**
Rosenberg Self-Esteem (N = 16)	**32.1 (s.d. = 6.3)**	**36.4 (s.d. = 4.4)**	**12.4 (p = .003)****	**.45**
Generalized Contentment (N = 15)	28.4 (s.d. = 29.1)	12.6 (s.d. = 5.4)	4.1 (p = .063)	
Index of Clinical Stress (N = 16)	**30.1 (s.d. = 21.2)**	**13.8 (s.d. = 10.5)**	**10.9 (p = .005)****	**.42**
Physical Abuse of Partner Scale (N = 16)	**4.9 (s.d. = 8.1)**	**0.0 (s.d. = 0.0)**	**5.9 (p = .028)***	**.28**
Non-Physical Abuse of Partner Scale (N = 16)	**12.1 (s.d. = 9.7)**	**3.5 (s.d. = 3.9)**	**11.4 (p = .004)****	**.43**
Partner Abuse Scale – Physical (N = 16)	**5.9 (s.d. = 8.1)**	**0.2 (s.d. = 0.5)**	**7.9 (p = .013)***	**.34**
Partner Abuse Scale – Non-Physical (N = 16)	**16.9 (s.d. = 12.5)**	**5.8 (s.d. = 7.6)**	**11.6 (p = .004)****	**.44**
Couple Relationship Scales				
FAM-III Task Accomplishment (N = 16)	**56.2 (s.d. = 9.2)**	**46 (s.d. = 10.6)**	**8.9 (p = .009)****	**.37**
FAM III Role Performance (N = 16)	**54.6 (s.d. = 14.0)**	**44.2 (s.d. = 8.8)**	**8.3 (p = .011)***	**.36**
FAM III Communication (N = 16)	**57.8 (s.d. = 13.2)**	**46.5 (s.d. = 11.3)**	**7.5 (p = .015)***	**.33**
FAM III Affective Expression (N = 16)	54.1 (s.d. = 13.2)	46.0 (s.d. = 14.0)	3.5 (p = .082)	
FAM III Involvement (N = 16)	**53.1 (s.d. = 14.1)**	**43.7 (s.d. = 11.0)**	**7.0 (p = .02)***	**.32**
FAM III Control (N = 16)	57.8 (s.d. = 14.0)	49.6 (s.d. = 14.0)	4.1 (p = .061)	
FAM III Values and Norms (N = 16)	48.0 (s.d. = 17.8)	43.5 (s.d. = 12.7)	0.9 (p = .36)	

continued . . .

Table 13.3 (Continued)

Measure	Mean Pretest	Mean Posttest	F-score	Partial eta^2
Substance Abuse Scales				
PAS Substance Abuse Subscale (N = 16)	53.1 (s.d. = 19.9)	47.3 (s.d. = 17.7)	0.9 (p = .34)	
SASSI-Face Valid Alcohol (N = 16)	60.4 (s.d. = 17.0)	52.9 (s.d. = 10.8)	2.9 (p = .11)	
SASSI-Face Valid Other Drugs (N = 16)	63.8 (s.d. = 19.0)	55.3 (s.d. = 11.6)	4.1 (p = .06)	
SASSI-Symptoms Substance Misuse (N = 14)	61.1 (s.d. = 13.6)	56.8 (s.d. = 15.2)	2.2 (p = .16)	
SASSI-Obvious Attributes (N = 14)	53.7 (s.d. = 12.1)	48.4 (s.d. = 15.7)	2.9 (p = .11)	
SASSI-Subtle Attributes (N = 14)	51.9 (s.d. = 10.9)	53.5 (s.d. = 9.5)	0.29 (p = .60)	
SASSI-Defensiveness (N = 14)	**48.7 (s.d. = 11.7)**	**57.2 (s.d. = 11.2)**	**9.9 (p = .008)****	**.43**
SASSI-Family versus Controls (N = 14)	47.2 (s.d. = 13.1)	49.1 (s.d. = 13.7)	0.69 (p = .42)	
SASSI-Correctional (N = 14)	58.0 (s.d. = 13.1)	53.0 (s.d. = 13.6)	2.8 (p = .12)	

Note: Bolded results indicate statistical significance.

Table 13.4 OQ-45 Comparison of Non-Completers and Completers

Measures	Non-Completers Pretest (n = 21)	Non-completers Posttest	Completers Pretest (n = 16)	Completers Posttest	F-Test pre versus post both groups	F-test Completers versus Non-completers
OQ-45 Symptom Distress	29.3 (s.d. = 12.5)	27.3 (s.d. = 13.3)	24.8 (s.d. = 18.4)	13.7 (s.d.= 16.7)	10.3 (p = .003)**; eta^2 = .23)	7.0 (p = .01)*; eta^2 = .17
OQ-45 Interpersonal Relations	16.9 (s.d. = 7.7)	16.2 (s.d. = 7.2)	12.4 (s.d. = 6.9)	6.4 (s.d. = 7.0)	13.9 (p = .001)**; eta^2 = .29	13.6 (p = .001)**; eta^2 = .28
OQ-45 Social Role	10.2 (s.d. = 3.8)	9.9 (s.d. = 5.3)	8.3 (s.d. = 5.6)	4.7 (s.d. = 4.9)	4.5 (p = .04)*; eta^2 = .12	7.7 (p = .009)**; eta^2 = .19
OQ-45 Total	56.5 (s.d. = 22.3)	53.7 (s.d. = 22.6)	45.4 (s.d. = 28.9)	24.7 (s.d. = 27.8)	10.5 (p = .003)**; eta^2 = .24	9.9 p = .003)**; eta^2 = .23

Note: * is p < .05; ** is p < .01.

not decrease to a statistical level (Generalized Contentment). Notably, however, neither self-esteem nor depression was in the clinical range either at program start or program completion.

Scores on the four Hudson partner abuse scales all improved to statistically significant degrees. Scores on physical abuse, both as received from partner and acted toward partner, improved from above the clinical cut-off of two to below the clinical cut-off to essentially zero, an additional standard that highlights the importance of the improvement (Jacobson, Follette, & Revenstorf, 1984). Similarly, the clients moved from receiving clinical levels of psychological abuse to below the cut-off of fifteen. Using psychological abuse tactics against their partners decreased significantly, though the average pretest scores were not at clinical levels. Similarly, the FAM-III subscale scores were all in the functional range both at pre- and at posttest. Four subscales also improved significantly: Task Accomplishment (problem-solving), Role Performance (expectations of performing central roles in the family), Involvement (closeness to spouse), and Communication.

No statistically significant improvements (reductions) were found for substance abuse (SASSI subscales), although the average SASSI scores were only in the level of concern not in the clinical range (T-score of seventy) either at pretest or posttest. The SASSI Defensiveness subscale was "worse" at posttest, indicating more defensiveness for clients at program completion.

Although couples who did not finish the program did not complete the entire posttest package of measures, they did answer the OQ-45 at every session. As such, it was of interest to compare all of the couples' pretest and posttest scores on this measure (see Table 13.4). Notably, the non-completers attended varied numbers of sessions.

A regression analysis assessed differences in the mental health symptoms (posttest subscale and Total OQ-45 scores) based on completing the program or not (with the pretest as a co-variate). The OQ-45 scores for the non-completers were from the last session attended. The results showed statistically significant differences for all four measures (with small to moderate effects sizes) such that, while both completers and non-completers significantly improved their mental health symptoms, program completers made significantly greater improvements than non-completers. Notably, though, almost half (43 percent) of the non-completers had attended seven to nine Strengthening Families program sessions, which could explain their improvements.

Discussion and Conclusions

The Strengthening Families pilot program offers a unique approach to address-ing the needs of couples in which one or both was perpetrating intimate partner abuse and using substances. While Fal-Stewart and Clinton-Sherrod's BCT program is essentially a substance abuse program with added domestic violence content, Calgary Counselling counselors had been working primarily in programs addressing intimate partner violence with little in-depth experience with substance abuse treatment. As such, although the Strengthening Families program used material from BCT (Fals-Stewart & Clinton-Sherrod 2009), the counselor's emphasis and deep understanding of intimate partner violence likely was reflected in the significant improvements with respect to mental symptoms, reduced partner abusive behaviors, and improved couple relationships.

Another program difference between Strengthening Families and BCT was that, to elicit sufficient referrals, the SF program did not insist on sobriety as part of intervention, which might be a factor in interpreting why the majority of the substance abuse variables did not reduce to a statistically significant degree. However, again, it must be noted that the majority of the substance abuse (SASSI) scales were not in the clinical level either at pretest or posttest. Few referrals were made from the community substance abuse treatment program and, based on their SASSI scores, the Strengthening Family clientele did not include individuals with severe substance abuse issues.

As highlighted previously, the safety of conjoint couple treatment has been much debated in the partner abuse literature (McCollum & Stith, 2008), however, couples in the Strengthening Families program fit the description of situational couple violence rather than intimate partner terrorism (Johnson, 2005), as noted in nineteen interviews with the agency staff and referring agencies. Also couples with more serious violence were screened out (Tutty, 2014). As one of the Strengthening Families counselors commented:

These couples would have been mutually combative; often both would have problems, but it was not high violence, even though the police had been called at some point. It was a more equal situation.

In response to questions about how the Strengthening Families program fits in the continuum of programs in Calgary to address intimate partner violence and the continuum of programs to address addictions, the key stakeholders all commented on the unique nature of the Strengthening Families program, both in dealing with these two issues concurrently and the benefits of offering the program conjointly to couples (Tutty, 2014).

While 108 couples were referred over two and a half years, a number were deemed inappropriate either because substance abuse or intimate partner violence was not of concern, or both partners were not available or willing to attend conjoint couples sessions. The proportion of couples that started the program (25 or 23.1 percent) was about twice as high as the start rate of 10 percent by Dr. Keith Klostermann (personal communication, 2012) from Fal-Stewart's Boston BCT program.

From a clinical perspective, it cannot be stressed enough that the Strengthening Families program criteria are complex and challenging. Intimate partner violence and substance abuse are both problems characterized by denial. Clients seldom present to counseling with these issues and, even when they are assessed, often minimize their importance. To insist that both members of the couple must attend complicates it that much further. The partners may be at different stages in acknowledging either problem, or the need to seek professional counseling conjointly. As such, entry into the program presented significant challenges. Despite similar starting rates with Fal-Stuart's Boston program, that a number of the referred couples did not materialize, were deemed inappropriate, or started but did not complete the program (two-thirds of twenty-five couples) is of concern.

As another aspect of the evaluation, every individual who was a client in the Strengthening Families program was invited to be interviewed about his or her perceptions of the program (Tutty, 2014). Seven interviews were conducted; five with program completers (including two couples from which both partners were interviewed) and two clients who started but did not complete. Two quotes from these interviews provide a sample of the client's perspectives of having participated in Strengthening Families.

> It was so positive for our relationship. I was proud that we had gone through it because it is pretty intensive. I had seen the changes from week to week so it didn't really feel any differently walking out from the last session. There was far more peace leaving the program than going into it. Proud of what I achieved and that we have these new tools for getting along. The process was great. It changed the direction of our marriage.
>
> (Male client, Strengthening Families)

> [*Did the program affect the conflict in your relationship?*] Yes, positively. Being able to listen better and word it better. Not blaming, not getting angry right away and trying to hear what the other person is saying versus hearing what you think they're saying or what you think you hear. The time outs; that was the biggest thing I took away from it.
>
> (Female client, Strengthening Families)

Only one demographic variable differentiated the Strengthening Families completers and non-completers: couples with less previous counseling experiences were more likely to complete. It is difficult to interpret this finding, which is somewhat counter-intuitive. The one variable that sheds some light on this is the URICA Stages of Change scale whereby a higher proportion of non-completing couples were in pre-contemplation (not acknowledging a problem) compared to completers (31 percent versus 11 percent). In addition, however, couples with previous counseling may have known earlier when they had reached their goals and stopped services at that point.

With respect to program completers, the comparison of the standardized measures at pretest and posttest for the sixteen Strengthening Families clients showed a number of significant improvements despite the relatively small sample size. The improvements were in the scales indicating less intimate partner abuse and addressing clinical symptoms such as improvements in self-esteem, reductions in anxiety, and improved relationships with spouse with respect to involvement, communication, role allocation, and problem-solving. The latter four interpersonal couple issues could be related to the abusers taking responsibility and being accountable to their partner for their previously abusive acts. Finally, comparing the mental health issues (posttest OQ-45 scores) for the entire sample at their last agency contact, those who finished the program reported significantly fewer symptoms compared to those who did not complete.

Overall, especially considering the relatively small sample size, the number of significant improvements for clients of the Strengthening Families program is impressive. The changes were with respect to individual issues such as decreases in depression, anxiety, and in couple relationship issues such as improved problem-solving, closeness, and working together as a couple unit. Importantly, both physical and psychological intimate violence behaviors were reduced to below clinical cut-off scores. While the majority of the scores on the substance abuse subscales did not improve from the start to the end of the program, these were primarily in the non-clinical range.

The concerns previously raised about offering couples therapy when IPV is identified remain important. Notably though, the Strengthening Families program is offered in an agency with a thirty-five-year history of addressing domestic violence and every precaution is taken to assure that the conjoint intervention is appropriate and safe for everyone. As such, the program is a promising option when couples wish to remain together and are willing to take part in counseling that assists individuals to accept responsibility for using partner violence and abusing substances.

Note

1. Acknowledgements: Funding for both the program and the evaluation was from the Government of Alberta Safe Communities Initiative. Thanks to the Strengthening Families Advisory Group, especially Christine Berry, Director of Family Violence Prevention Initiatives. The Strengthening Families Advisory group consisted of the following: Kevin McNichol and Maggie McKillop both with HomeFront; Patty McCallum and John Guigon from the Calgary Police Services; Christina Tortorelli, Child and Family Services Authority—Region 3; Dr. Nicole Sherren, Program Officer, Norlien Foundation; John Gulak, Prairie Merchant Corporation; Russ Moore, Alberta Health Services Alberta Alcohol and Drug Abuse; and Keith Klostermann, Project Consultant, Addiction and Family Research Clinic and the University of Rochester, New York. Thanks also to Sandy Berzins, CCC Research Manager, and to Stephanie Korol and Michelle McGrath who assisted with data entry. Most importantly, thanks to the couples who participated in the Strengthening Families Program.

References

Abel, E. M. (2000). Psychosocial treatments for battered women: A review of empirical research. *Research on Social Work Practice, 10*(1), 55–77.

Andrews, P. & Moyer, R. G. (2003). Marlowe-Crowne Social Desirability Scale and Short Form C: Forensic norms. *Journal of Clinical Psychology, 59*(4), 483–492.

Attala, J. M., Hudson, W. W., & McSweeney, M. (1994). A partial validation of two short-form partner abuse scales. *Women and Health, 21*(2/3), 125–139. doi:10.1300/J013v21n02_08

Augusta-Scott, T. & Dankwort, J. (2002). Partner abuse group intervention: Lessons from education and narrative therapy approaches. *Journal of Interpersonal Violence, 17*(7), 783–805. doi:10.1177/0886260502017007006

Bograd, M. (1984). Family systems approaches to wife battering: A feminist critique. *American Journal of Orthopsychiatry, 54*(4), 558–568. doi:10.1111/j.1939-0025.1984.tb01526.x

Chermack, S. T., Walton, M. A., Fuller, B. E., & Blow, F. C. (2001). Correlates of expressed and received violence across relationship types among men and women substance abusers. *Psychology of Addictive Behaviors, 15*(2), 140–151. doi:10.1037//0893-164X.15.2.140

Coker, A. L., Smith, P. H., McKeown, R. E., & King, M. J. (2000). Frequency and correlates of intimate partner violence by type: Physical, sexual, and psychological battering. *American Journal of Public Health, 14*(9), 829–838.

Fals-Stewart, W., & Clinton-Sherrod, M. (2009). Treating intimate partner violence among substance-abusing dyads: The effect of couples therapy. *Professional Psychology: Research and Practice, 40*(3), 257–563. doi:10.1037/a0012708

Fals-Stewart, W., Birchler, G., & Kelley, M. L. (2006). Learning sobriety together: A randomized clinical trial examining behavioral couples therapy with alcoholic female patients. *Journal of Consulting and Clinical Psychology, 74*(3), 579–591. doi:10.1037/0022-006X.74.3.579

Fals-Stewart, W., Klostermann, K., Yates, B. T., O'Farrell, T., & Birchler, G. R. (2005). Brief relationship therapy for alcoholism: A randomized clinical trial examining clinical efficacy and cost-effectiveness. *Psychology of Addictive Behaviors, 19*(4), 363–371. doi:10.1037/0893-164X.19.4.363

Galvani, S. (2004). Responsible disinhibition: Alcohol, men, and violence to women. *Addiction Research and Theory, 12*, 357–371. doi:10.1080/1606635042000218772

Hudson, W. (1992). *The WALMYR assessment scales scoring manual.* Tempe, AZ: WALMYR.

Humphreys, C., Regan, L., River, D., & Thiara, R. K. (2005). Domestic violence and substance use: Tackling complexity. *British Journal of Social Work, 35*(8), 1303–1320. doi:10.1093/bjsw/bch212

Jacobson, N., Follette, W., & Revenstorf, D. (1984). Psychotherapy outcome research: Methods for reporting variability and evaluating clinical significance. *Behavior Therapy, 17*, 308–311.

Johannson, M. A. & Tutty, L. M. (1998). An evaluation of after-treatment couple groups for wife abuse. *Family Relations, 47*(1), 27–35. doi:10.2307/584848

Johnson, H. (2007). Preventing violence against women: Progress and challenges. *International Prevention of Crime Review, 1*, 69–88.

Johnson, M. P. (2005). The differential effects of intimate terrorism and situational couple violence: Findings from the National Violence Against Women Survey. *Journal of Family Issues, 26*(3), 322–349. doi:10.1177/0192513x04270345

Lambert, M. J., Hansen, N., Umphress, V., Lunnen, K., Okiishi, J., Burlingame, G., Huefner, J., & Reisinger, C. (1996). *Administration and scoring manual for the Outcome Questionnaire (OQ45.2)*. Wilmington, DE: American Professional Credentialing.

Langenderfer, L. (2013). Alcohol use among partner violent adults: Reviewing recent literature to inform intervention. *Aggression and Violent Behavior, 18*(1), 152–158. doi:10.1016/j.avb.2012.11.013

LaTaillade, J. J., Epstein, N. B., & Werlinich, C. A. (2006). Conjoint treatment of intimate partner violence: A cognitive behavioral approach. *Journal of Cognitive Psychotherapy: An International Quarterly, 20*(4), 393–410.

Leonard, K. (2001). Domestic violence and alcohol: What is known and what do we need to know to encourage environmental interventions? *Journal of Substance Use, 6*, 235–247.

McCollum, E. E. & Stith, S. M. (2007). Conjoint couple's treatment for intimate partner violence: Controversy and promise. *Journal of Couple & Relationship Therapy, 6*(1/2), 71–82. doi:10.1300/J398v06n01_07

McCollum, E. E. & Stith, S. M. (2008). Couples treatment for interpersonal violence: A review of outcome research literature and current clinical practices. *Violence and Victims, 23*(2), 187–201. doi:10.1891/0886-6708.23.2.187

McGregor, M., Tutty, L., Babins-Wagner, R., & Gill, M. (2002). The long term impact of group treatment for partner abuse. *Canadian Journal of Community Mental Health, 21*, 67–84.

Miller, F. G., Roberts, J., Brooks, M. K., & Lazowski, L. E. (2003). *The Adult SASSI-3: A quick reference for administration and scoring*. Springfield, IN: The SASSI Institute.

Morey, L. C. (2007). *The Personality Assessment Inventory professional manual*. Lutz, FL: Psychological Assessment Resources.

O'Farrell, T. J. & Schein, A. Z. (2011). Behavioral couples therapy for alcoholism and drug abuse. *Journal of Family Psychotherapy, 22*(3), 193–215. doi:10.1080/08975353.2011.602615

Reynolds, W. (1982). Development of a reliable and valid short form of the Marlowe-Crowne Social Desirability Scale. *Journal of Clinical Psychology, 38*, 118–125.

Rosenberg, M. (1965). *Society and the adolescent child*. Princeton, NJ. Princeton University Press.

Scott, K. L., King, C., McGinn, H., & Hosseini, N. (2011). Effects of motivational enhancement on immediate outcomes of batterer intervention. *Journal of Family Violence, 26*(2), 139–149. doi:10.1007/s10896-010-9353-1

Skinner, H. A., Steinhauer, P. D., & Santa-Barbara, J. (1983). The Family Assessment Measure. *Canadian Journal of Community Mental Health, 2*, 91–105.

Stith, S. M. & McCollum, E. E. (2011). Conjoint treatment of couples who have experienced intimate partner violence. *Aggression and Violent Behavior, 16*(4), 312–318. doi:10.1016/j.avb.2011.04.012

Stith, S. M., Smith, D. B., Penn, C. E., Ward, D. B., & Tritt, D. (2004). Intimate partner physical abuse perpetration and victimization risk factors: A meta-analytic review. *Aggression and Violent Behavior, 10*(1), 305–318. doi:10.1016/j.avb.2003.09.001

Stuart, G. L., Temple, J. R., Follansbee, K. W., Bucossi, M. M., Hellmuth, J. C., & Moore, T. M. (2008). The role of drug use in a conceptual model of intimate partner violence in men and women arrested for domestic violence. *Psychology of Addictive Behaviors, 22*(1), 12–24. doi:10.1037/0893-164X.22.1.12

Thomas, M. D., Bennett, L., & Stoops, C. (2013). The treatment needs of substance abusing batterers: A comparison of men who batter their female partners. *Journal of Family Violence, 28*(2), 121–129. doi:10.1007/s10896-012-9479-4

Tutty, L. (2012). Identifying, assessing, and treating men who abuse and women abused by intimate partners. In R. Alaggia & C. Vine (Eds.), *Cruel but not unusual: Violence in Canadian families* (2nd ed.) (pp. 453–477). Waterloo, ON: Wilfrid Laurier Press.

Tutty, L. M. (2014). *An evaluation of Strengthening Families: The Calgary Counselling Centre's program for couples dealing with intimate partner violence and substance abuse.* Calgary, AB. University of Calgary. doi:10.13140/RG.2.1.4010.1605

Tutty, L. M., Babins-Wagner, R., & Rothery, M. (2009). A comparison of women who were mandated and non-mandated to the "Responsible Choices for Women" Group. *Journal of Aggression, Maltreatment and Trauma, 18*(7), 770–793. doi:10.1080/1092 6770903249

Tutty, L. M., Babins-Wagner, & Rothery, M. A. (2015). You're not alone: Mental health outcomes in therapy groups for abused women. *Journal of Family Violence, 30.* doi:10.1007/s10896-015-9779-6

14 Men Who Abuse Intimate Partners

Their Evaluation of a Responsible Fathering Program

Joan Pennell and Erika Brandt[1]

Strong Fathers is a fathering program for men with a history of committing domestic violence. Drawing upon a feminist framework of responsible fatherhood (Edleson & Williams, 2007; Scott & Crooks, 2007), Strong Fathers starts from the premise that some men who abuse their partners will be motivated to change by their desire to be closer to their children. Men's views on domestic violence, however, can impede such change, especially if they are further reinforced by cultural norms and local conditions constraining women's autonomy (Beyer, Wallis, & Hamberger, 2015; Koenig, Stephenson, Ahmed, Jejeebhoy, & Campbell, 2006).

Some men at least initially are not motivated by their children to change how they relate to intimate partners. The men may instead blame the women for provoking the violence (Lila, Gracia, & Murgui, 2013; Stanley, Fell, Miller, Thomson, & Watson, 2012), normalize women abuse as more prevalent than in actuality (Neighbors et al., 2010), and ignore the adverse impact on their children (Salisbury, Henning, & Holdford, 2009). Even when the men recognize the effects on children, this realization does not necessarily translate into intentions to change their behaviors (Rothman, Mandel, & Silverman, 2007). Post-separation from partners, the men may use their children to continue the abuse without regard to the impact on their families (Holt, 2015).

Men who abuse are not a homogenous population. Especially for low-income, non-resident fathers, the emotional attachment to their children may stand out as a significant source of pride (Featherstone, White, & Morris, 2014). The salience of the father-child relationship is supported by the research of a British social marketing campaign to convince men to stop abusing; consultations with local men about effective messages found highest rank given to fathers' worries about harming their children and being perceived as a "monster" in their children's eyes, with fears about losing intimate partners in second place (Stanley et al., 2012, p. 1312).

Few services are available for men who abuse their intimate partners to develop parenting skills; thus, knowledge in this field of practice is scarce. Batterer intervention programs may highlight the negative effects of domestic violence on children but do not offer training on caring for children. The inattention to parenting skills is especially problematic because the majority of men in batterer intervention programs are in some kind of fathering relationship (Salisbury et al., 2009). Child welfare agencies and available parenting programs tend to focus on mothers rather than fathers, even though the fathers may need and want help (Gordon, Oliveros, Hawes, Iwamoto, & Rayford, 2012).

Retention of the men is challenging in both parenting groups (Tiano & McNeil, 2005) and batterer interventions programs (Bent-Goodley, Rice, Williams, & Pope, 2011). As a result, the men do not have the opportunity to relearn how to relate to children or intimate partners. Moreover, fathering programs and batterer intervention programs alike have a poor track record of including men of color and low-income men (Jewell & Wormith, 2010; Julion, Breitenstein, & Waddell, 2012). Dropout is problematic because men who graduate from a batterer intervention program are at lower risk of re-assaulting partners (Bennett, Stoops, Call, & Flett, 2007; Gondolf, 2002). Even if the men are not motivated to change, group attendance in itself is a way to monitor for safety, including in high-risk situations (Juodis, Starzomski, Porter, & Woodworth, 2014). For instance, the group facilitators may conduct safety checks with the men's partners or former partners.

Fathering programs for men who abuse are relatively new and are limited in number. Nevertheless, they have elicited interest from men of diverse backgrounds (Edleson & Williams, 2007; Mederos, 2004) and have demonstrated that motivational techniques can effectively engage a population that is often hard to reach (Scott & Crooks, 2007). Most of these programs, however, have not evaluated their outcomes. A notable exception is a Canadian program called "Caring Dads," whose evaluators found a significant decrease in the men's overreacting to their children's behaviors and a significant improvement in communicating with and respecting the children's mothers (Scott & Lishak, 2012). Both these outcomes are in keeping with the original goals of the Caring Dads program to hold men accountable for their intimate partner abuse and to support men in learning how to empathically parent their children (Scott, Kelly, Crooks, & Francis, 2014).

The Strong Fathers program shares these aspirations to stop intimate partner abuse and to improve how fathers care for their children. Achieving these aims is jeopardized if men drop out. Accordingly, this chapter addresses three questions: Why are the men motivated to attend Strong Fathers? What do they see as the outcomes of their participation? How would they advise improving the program? In order to answer these questions, the authors draw upon the words of the men as they reflected on the program and its impact. Their responses are viewed within the context of the men's overall satisfaction with the group and the group facilitators' notes describing men's responses to the curriculum.

The Strong Fathers Program

The Strong Fathers program was developed in the southeastern US state of North Carolina for men who have committed intimate partner violence and whose families receive child welfare services. The goal of this psychoeducational and skills-building group program is to help the men relate to their family members in safe and caring ways. The program has two main messages: intimate partner violence detrimentally affects children, and fathers can work with their children's mothers to support healthy child development.

The North Carolina program was first delivered in 2009 in Winston-Salem, joined in 2012 by a second site in Durham. Compared to the state as a whole, Durham County and Forsyth County (where Winston-Salem is located) have higher percentages of non-White residents (NC: 28.3 percent, Durham: 46.9 percent, Forsyth: 32.2 percent) (US Census Bureau, 2015). In the state as a whole, the percentage of non-White children admitted to foster care is similar to their percentage in the general population, 45 percent versus 46 percent (Duncan et al., 2015; NC Child, 2013). In the two counties implementing Strong Fathers, there is disproportional placement of children of color. The percentage of non-White children admitted to care as compared to the percentage in the county child population is 83 percent versus 68 percent in Durham, and 64 percent versus 53 percent in Forsyth (Duncan et al., 2015; NC Child, 2013).

Referrals are made by the court or child welfare, and staff members from the program sites meet with the referred men to explain the program and assess their situation. Men are eligible if they had physically or emotionally abused an intimate partner, and they are screened out if they have committed child sexual abuse or if they have a court order of no contact with their children. A no-contact order would prohibit the men from applying parenting skills learned in group with their children. At times, the program sites redirect the referred men to a batterer intervention program because of concerns about the level of domestic violence.

The groups are usually co-facilitated by a man and woman in order to model respectful male-female interactions. Almost always the groups have at least one African-American facilitator to better reflect the group composition. The program uses a number of methods to encourage the men's attendance: scheduling meetings in the evening when men are more likely to be available, providing food, assisting with transportation costs, offering family incentives (e.g. a family pass to a local zoo), reaching out when participants miss sessions, and keeping the referring workers informed of the men's attendance so that they can follow up as necessary.

The curriculum is twenty sessions in length (Ake, Bauman, Briggs, & Starsoneck, 2012) and is, thus, somewhat briefer than the average of twenty-six sessions for batterer intervention programs in the United States (Bent-Goodley et al., 2011). Each session is two hours long, and the maximum number of participants is limited to twelve. This structure supports the men in processing new content, observing demonstrations by facilitators, practicing skills, setting goals, and assessing their achievement of these goals. Between group sessions, the participants are asked to reflect on learning from the group or to practice communication or parenting skills.

During the first five of the twenty sessions, the curriculum is devoted to orienting the group members to the program, establishing positive group norms, encouraging the men to reflect on their own family experiences as children and as adults, supporting them in setting positive goals as fathers, and reviewing stages of child development and positive ways of connecting with children and youth. With this foundation in place, Sessions 6 through 10 turn to examining abusive relationships and learning positive ways of relating.

Leading off this second section of the curriculum, Session 6 asks the men to identify an experience in which they felt powerless, for example, being disciplined as a child; define domestic violence and child maltreatment; and reflect on the impact of coercive control on children who may adopt aggressive or manipulative ways of relating. In Sessions 7 and 10, they learn parenting skills such as giving praise (to encourage positive behavior) and active ignoring (to discourage inappropriate behavior). Sessions 8 and 9 return to examining the impact of violence on child development and the capacity of partners to co-parent.

The final ten sessions look at ways to sustain the men's growth. This includes helping the men ask for support and use relaxation techniques (Sessions 11 and 17), identify tactics that undermine the children's mothers and model good ways of relating (Sessions 12, 14, and 16), hone previously covered parenting skills (Sessions 13, 15, and 18), and reflect on challenges and extend successes (Sessions 19 and 20).

Methodology

Interpretive Process

A hermeneutic approach was used to reflect on the men's views of their reasons for attending the group, the results of their participation, and the best ways of improving the program. Hermeneutic interpretation seeks to understand a discourse or web of meaning through an iterative process of moving between its whole and its parts and placing the discourse within layers of context (Hirsch, 1967). Validity, in hermeneutist Paul Ricoeur's words (1979), refers to the "dialectic of explaining and comprehending" to reach the most probable conclusion among possibilities but with the interpretation always open to revision (p. 87). The primary text is the men's responses on a brief participant feedback form. The contexts for interpreting the men's words are their associated responses on the same form, the commentary of other participants, the group facilitators' notes on the sessions, the curricular content, and the stages of the group process.

Research Participants

The men completed research consent forms. Data were de-identified prior to transmittal to the researchers and were securely stored. The study protocols were approved by the university's research ethics board. The seventy-three research participants are from Strong Fathers Groups 8 through 18, which began in the fourth year of program delivery after refinements had already been made to the curriculum. At the request of the group facilitators, the participant feedback form was introduced in Group 8. This meant that the participants' comments would reflect an established program rather than one under development. The forms were not connected to individual participants but were labeled with the respondents' group and session numbers.

Table 14.1 summarizes the demographic and program information on the research participants who attended at least one session of Groups 8 through 18. Enrolled men who did not attend at all would not have had the opportunity to complete the participant feedback form. Somewhat more men attended the program in Durham than in Forsyth. The sample shows a much higher percentage of non-White than White men: 78 percent non-White and 22 percent White. These percentages are relatively comparable to the percentages of non-White children with investigated child protection reports for each site's county in 2013–2014: 79 percent for Durham County and 64 percent for Forsyth County (Duncan et al., 2015). On average the men were in their early

Table 14.1 Demographic and Program Information of Research Participants (*N* = 73)

Demographics	
Race	*n (%)*
White	15 (22.4)
Non-White	52 (77.6)
Age, *M* (*SD, n*)	32.5 (8.7, 64)
Education	*n (%)*
Less Than High School	11 (16.4)
High School/GED	24 (35.8)
One or More Years of College	32 (47.8)
Employment	*n (%)*
Employed	81 (61.4)
Unemployed	51 (38.6)
No. of Children, *M* (*SD, n*)	2.5 (1.9, 73)
Program Information	
Program Site	*n (%)*
Winston-Salem	31 (42.5)
Durham	42 (57.5)
No. of Sessions Attended, *M* (*SD, n*)	14.1 (6.7, 73)
No. of Participants Per Group, *M* (*SD, n*)	6.6 (3.0, 73)

Note: Data from participants who attended at least one session of Groups 8–18 thirties and had two to three children. Many were limited in terms of their education and employment. The groups averaged seven members, who attended on average fourteen sessions.

Research Materials and Coding

Program participants who completed a feedback form at three points over the group were the primary source of research materials. The group facilitators who prepared notes after each group session were the secondary source. The participant feedback form, called "What do you think about Strong Fathers?" began by measuring the men's satisfaction with group. It had seven questions for which the men were asked to circle their level of agreement on a four-point Likert scale (Table 14.2). Then, the men were asked four open-ended questions: "Why did you come to the group?" "What made it hard to get to the group?" "How has the Strong Fathers helped you?" and "What would make Strong Fathers even better?" The feedback forms were filled out at the beginning of the session.

In Groups 8 through 18, the men completed 138 participant feedback forms: fifty-three from Time 1, forty-four from Time 2, and forty-one from Time 3. Most men in attendance filled out the form, with completion rates of 84 percent (53:63 men) at Time 1 (Session 3), 88 percent (44:50 men) at Time 2 (Session 11), and 85 percent (41:48 men) at Time 3 (Session 18; or in two groups, Sessions 15 and 19, respectively). The Time 3 variation coincided with the introduction of the forms at one program site. One group did not complete participant feedback forms at Time 3.

The facilitator notes first asked the facilitators to check if they completed each of the session's learning modules and if the module met its objectives. Then the facilitators were asked to comment on "Did anything really stand out to you about this session? Reflect on what happened at the session. How do you think this session went?" Each facilitator separately filled out the notes after each group session, with a total of 339 facilitator notes for Groups 8–18, of which 5.9 percent were recorded by a sole facilitator and 94.1 percent by two facilitators on the same group sessions. Serving as a measure of curricular fidelity, the facilitator notes indicated that, for the most part, each session covered its modules and these modules achieved their objectives. This meant that the participants' feedback reflected the same curricular content. The facilitator notes also demonstrated inter-rater reliability in that the co-facilitators might emphasize different aspects of same session but, overall, they shared similar perspectives on the group activities and dynamics.

A content analysis was first used to code the qualitative responses of the participant feedback forms into broad categories on the men's motivations, outcomes, and programmatic recommendations. One of the researchers coded the responses; the other researcher reviewed these codes and proposed some reassignments; and the two researchers reached consensus on the categorizations. Then one researcher used a hermeneutic process of interpretation to identify patterns and contextualize the texts and checked these interpretations with the other researcher. The qualitative analysis was conducted in ATLAS.ti, version 7.5.6.

Fathers' Perspectives

The interpretive process yielded four arching themes, each encapsulated by a quotation from a participant. The themes are embedded within the self-reflections of the participants and the group analyses of the facilitators. The quotations of the participants and facilitators are presented in the form in which they were originally written.

"Open My Eyes Up to a Different World"

The first theme reflected the overall high program satisfaction of the men and their expanded understanding resulting from participation. The men over-whelmingly reported satisfaction with the group on the seven Likert items. As seen in Table 14.2, the large majority of respondents said that they *strongly agree* with the items; this was the case at all three times of data collection. The one exception was a question on the length of the group. Here the majority said that they *agree* that the group was not too long.

Table 14.2 Participant Satisfaction Ratings ($N = 138$)

Item	n	Percentage				Mean (SD)
		Strongly Disagree	Disagree	Agree	Strongly Agree	
I felt respected in the group.	138	1.4	0.0	19.6	79.0	3.8 (.5)
I could be open and honest when I talked in group.	137	1.5	0.0	27.0	71.5	3.7 (.6)
The length of each group meeting was too long. (reverse coded)	135	4.4	11.9	52.6	31.1	3.1 (.8)
The group facilitators spoke to me in a way that I could understand.	138	2.9	3.6	25.4	68.1	3.6 (.7)
The group facilitators respected my beliefs.	132	0.0	0.0	34.1	65.9	3.7 (.5)
Strong Fathers helped me become a better father.	131	0.8	0.0	29.0	70.2	3.7 (.5)
I would recommend Strong Fathers to other men.	136	0.7	0.0	21.3	77.9	3.8 (.5)

Note: To interpret: Strongly Disagree = 1, Disagree = 2, Agree = 3, Strongly Agree = 4.

Over 70 percent of the men strongly agreed that they felt "respected in the group," could be "open and honest," were helped to "become a better father," and would "recommend" the program to other men. The ratings of *strongly agree* slipped under 70 percent for two items; these concerned the extent to which the facilitators spoke in a manner that the men could comprehend and the degree to which the facilitators respected the men's beliefs. None of the men, however, indicated that the facilitators did not respect their beliefs. Such was not the case for the facilitators speaking in a way that the men understood.

Disagreement about comprehending the facilitators' words only emerged after the Time 1 (Session 3) distribution of the feedback forms. In Time 2 (Session 11), five men disagreed that the facilitators spoke in a way that they understood, and in Time 3 (Session 18, one group in Session 15), four men disagreed. The curriculum before Time 1 focused on engaging the men in the group and helping them connect to their childhood experiences. By Time 2, the men would have explored the dynamics and impact of abusive relationships and practiced new ways of communicating and relating. These topics related to when some men exited the group.

Peak drop-out times for the twenty-session Strong Fathers occurred after three particularly challenging sessions: Session 6 ("What makes a relationship abusive"), Session 8 ("How children are affected by domestic violence"), and Session 18 ("How to give good directions to children"). The last session built on prior ones in which men learned about praising children and using active ignoring—two parenting skills that many participants found difficult to apply or, as the facilitators pointed out, were contrary to the men's cultural practices on parenting. After Session 10, a facilitator wrote,

> I do think participants enjoyed the role plays of active ignoring, although one father . . . repeatedly asserted that he would never ignore some of the behaviors (disrespect, swearing, etc.) depicted in the scenarios. He explained that ignoring these behaviors makes a child believe that they are acceptable.

None of the nine men who disagreed about understanding what the facilitators were saying was lodging a complaint. These men stayed with the group. Their ratings were about their own growth rather than failings of the facilitators. In their comments, they all acknowledged that the group, as one man put it, "open[ed] my eyes to a whole new world." Another man wrote that the group helped him "by seeing different ways"; and referring to changes in his fathering approach, a third man identified that the group helped him to "understand my kids' real need and not their wants!" In other words, the participants' willingness to recognize their lack of understanding within a supportive group milieu can be taken as a good sign that they are open to learning. This interpretation is backed by the facilitator notes. In one instance, a facilitator characterized a fourth session as a "Great Group" in that the participants "shared some of their experiences and confusions" about infant development and their fears that holding a crying baby was "equal to spoiling." The changes that the men were experiencing influenced how they framed their reasons for coming to the group.

"Well I Kinda Have To"

The men's comments reflected both the semi-involuntary nature of the program and solidification of their own reasons for taking part. All the men responded to the question "Why did you come to the group?" The participants' motivations for joining the Strong Fathers program fell into two broad categories—internal motivations and external motivations—which each contained several subcategories (see Table 14.3). Because a response could have more than one code, the number of coded themes (161) is greater than the number of forms completed (138). There were nearly twice as many internal motivations (107) identified by the men as external ones (fifty-four). The proportion of internal to external motivations remained relatively comparable across the three times at which the men completed the feedback forms.

The internal motivation category contained three subcategories: better relationship with child, better sense of self, and better relationship with intimate partner. Out of the 107 responses, 67 percent of the time the men indicated that they were motivated to attend because they wanted a better relationship with their child. In contrast, 27 percent of the time they aspired to have a better sense of self; and only 7 percent of the time they were seeking to improve their relationship with an intimate partner. Participants with motivations in the "better relationship with child" subcategory were focused on becoming better fathers and learning parenting skills (sixty-six responses) or reconnecting with their children (five responses). Of the fathers seeking to gain parenting skills,

Table 14.3 Self-Reported Motivations (N = 138) and Outcomes (N = 134)

	Motivation f	Outcome f
Internal		
Better relationship with child	71	66
Better sense of self	29	82
Better relationship with intimate partner (current or former)	7	16
Other	0	4
Total	107	168
External		
Court expectations	30	0
Child welfare expectations	18	0
Other	6	0
Total	54	0
TOTAL	161	168

Note: Totals greater than number of forms because a response could have multiple codes.

three were first-time parents, and three believed that they had previously been incompetent parents. Responses in the "better sense of self" subcategory included those expressing a desire to: be a better person (ten responses), get help working through personal problems (ten), learn to manage their stress or temper (seven), or learn more in general (two). Fathers seeking a "better relationship with intimate partner" wanted to be better husbands (four responses), improve their relationships with their children's mothers (two), or learn about domestic violence (one).

The external motivation category also contained three subcategories: court expectations, child welfare expectations, and other. Participants motivated by court expectations were court ordered to attend Strong Fathers (twenty-three responses), referred on judge recommendation (four), or seeking to look good for court (three). Fathers in the "child welfare expectations" subcategory were referred to the program by their workers (fifteen responses) or wanted to regain custody of their children (three). Responses in the "other" subcategory indicated non-voluntary attendance but did not specify further. Of the fathers externally motivated to attend the program, five noted that they were glad they took part.

The men's reluctance about attending and their hopes for the group are captured by one man who simply responded in Session 3 that he came to the group because "well I kinda have to." Unlike the majority of men, his ratings on the seven Likert items were *agree* rather than *strongly agree*. At the same time, he expressed gratitude that the program "very much makes me more calm." Reflecting back in Session 18, another man gave more ratings of *agree* on the Likert items than *strongly agree* and stated that he had felt compelled to participate as he came to realize, "I was an unfit parent." Comparing his parenting before and after attending, he concluded, "Now I am a better father."

The men recognized that the group gave the safety, support, and information necessary for their learning: "Other fathers needed answers and help and advice like me." The facilitators also recognized that the group process engaged men initially resistant to participating. At the end of Session 4, a facilitator observed that one man "started out in a very foul mood, saying he was only here because he had to be and that he didn't need to be in the group. Over time, though, he warmed up and really added a lot to the discussion." The men's identifying their own motivations for attending went hand in hand with their recognizing the personal benefits of their participation.

"I Could Finally Release the Pain Inside"

The men spoke of the program's benefits in terms of both a process of healing from trauma and of positive change in themselves and their family relationships. On the feedback form, nearly all the men responded to the question "How has Strong Fathers helped you?": fifty at Time 1, forty-three at Time 2, and forty-one at Time 3, for a total of 134 responses. As with motivations, the identified outcomes of the Strong Fathers program were self and relationship improvement (see Table 14.3). The order of the frequency of the responses, however, diverged.

With the motivations, the most cited reason was a "better relationship with child" (seventy-one), while the most cited outcome was a "better sense of self" (eighty-two). Although only seven men stated that a "better relationship with intimate partner" was a reason for attending, sixteen observed that the program had helped improve their relationship with their partner. A comparison of the Time 1 and Time 3 responses found that initially a lower percentage of men reported an improvement in their fathering relationship (Time 1: 30 percent; Time 3: 47 percent) while the reverse was the case for the partner relationship (Time 1: 15 percent; Time 3: 8 percent).

The responses of the fathers who gained a "better sense of self" included: appreciation for the peer support of the program and the opportunity to talk about their personal problems (fourteen responses); feeling empowered or better equipped to deal with personal problems (thirteen); change of perspective (on fatherhood, domestic violence, etc.) through the program (ten); improved stress or anger management (ten); increased skill with communication (eight); better self-understanding (eight); more patience (seven); more knowledge of program topics (six); and improved lives (five) and decision-making (one).

The "better relationship with child" category included responses where fathers reported increased parenting skills (fifty-three responses) or better understanding of/relationship with their children (thirteen). Fathers reporting a "better relationship with intimate partner" felt they were relating better with their partners or their children's mothers. In the "Other/None" category was a father whose only reported outcome was appreciating the gift card he received for participating, two fathers who felt it was too early in the program to report any outcomes (these responses occurred in Time 1), and one father who did not see any benefits.

Repeatedly the participants' self-reflections and the facilitators' notes identified that the men had experienced childhood trauma and that these experiences limited the men's capacity to relate in positive ways with their children and partners. In Session 18, one man affirmed, "I cam[e] to the group so I could finally release the pain inside I had been holding in." As a result, he stated, "[the program] has taught me other ways to rectify my problems." Multiple men welcomed having the opportunity to "vent," "get stuff off my chest," and "talk my stress out."

In their notes, the facilitators recorded the men's expressing "anger and fear" about their fathers, identifying "trauma . . . in their own childhood," and being "molested as kids." According to the facilitators, as the men expressed their own pain they began to recognize that abuse could not only be physical but also emotional and to acknowledge their own acts of coercive control. After Session 6, a facilitator wrote that the group members identified "behaviors . . . [they] have used in relationships" and considered "alternative behaviors to power and control." Given that only a minority of the men on their feedback forms identified improvements in their partner relationships, it is not surprising that their most substantive recommendations for program improvement centered on involving women and women becoming "strong mothers."

Strong Mothers

The most common recommendation was to keep Strong Fathers as it is. Those who made suggestions often differed on what changes to make. When asked "What would make Strong Fathers even better?" the large majority of men responded (forty-nine at Time 1, thirty-nine at Time 2, and thirty-eight at Time 3, for a total of 126 responses). Participants' suggestions touched on several major areas: session format (twenty-six), attendance and transportation support (sixteen), program curriculum (fifteen), and involving women (fifteen). Overwhelmingly, though, the men concluded that Strong Fathers was already an effective program that did not need improvement (fifty-three responses). As one father summed up, the program should "stay the same."

To improve the session format, participants requested longer sessions (eight responses), shorter sessions (five), more sessions per week or more flexible/ ongoing class (six), weekend sessions (three), smaller groups (two), shorter total length of program (one), and online sessions (one).

Regarding attendance and transportation support, twelve respondents indicated the belief that more men should attend the program; whether this meant the men desired larger class sizes or that they believed others would benefit from Strong Fathers was sometimes unclear. Other comments included requests to provide transportation (two responses), require better attendance from participants (one), and allow men to bring their children (one). The recommendations reflect the struggles of a number of men in attending the program. In a separate question, the men were asked, "What made it hard to get to the group?" Their responses pertained largely to pragmatic factors such as transportation and scheduling problems.

Curriculum improvement suggestions included requests for more individualized attention from facilitators (five responses), more time for participants to vent feelings (three), bringing in past participants to share their experiences (three), more Biblical basis in curriculum (two), stronger focus on men's relationships with their partners (one), and teaching men to communicate better with their families (one).

Fifteen recommendations were focused on involving women in some manner: two in Time 1, eleven in Time 2, and two in Time 3. Their disproportionate occurrence in Time 2 may have reflected the intensive examination during the preceding sessions of the dynamics and impact of women abuse. Among the Time 2 responses, five recommended including partners, family, or a women's perspective in the group sessions. For instance, one man thought the group would be enhanced, "If our wives could be here with us"; a second man, using the language of granting permission, offered, "Maybe allow the spouse to come by once a month and participate; and a third proposed, "A mediation session" between the mothers and fathers. Particularly, this last recommendation raises questions about the safety of the women to engage in the process (Ptacek, 2010).

Having women present was proposed only once in Time 3 and, in this case, by a respondent who wanted to limit the partners' involvement to "one time."

Over Sessions 11 through 17, the curriculum covered ways for the men to lower their stress, gain support, and work with their children and partners. By the end of program, some men may have felt less need to have their partners present as they explored together other ways of relating with women. The facilitator notes indicated that the men had made strides. Summarizing Session 12, which focused on supportive co-parenting, a facilitator wrote, "[The] discussion about how their motives and mindset affected behavior in working with and support [of] mother of children. Participants looked at their own situation and found example[s] of how they could have approached their child's mother differently."

Recognizing the benefits of Strong Fathers, seven recommendations from all three data collection times focused on providing a similar program to the women. This was envisioned as offering "mom support" and ensuring a "balance" between what the women and men received. Three responses used the term "strong mothers" to refer to the women's program. One father elaborated, "Knowing that there was a Strong mothers program. So mom and dad both get professional help, guidance, support, encouragement, and lesson."

Only in Time 3 did two participants express a deep sense of injustice about having to attend the group, and these were framed in terms of male-female relationships. One man recommended, "Some focal points on the relationships between the mother and father," and continuing, he asserted, "Overall the class is good for people who have issues with domestic violence but it is unfair to push people into this class who do not have a history of/for domestic violence." A second man disclosed that he was motivated to come to group "to have some type of good mark on the parental report card, because women have put me in a bad situation." He rated himself as "already [having] great fatherhood capabilities." Gendered tensions were most overt in his statement. All the recommendations to involve women, nevertheless, point to cultural norms about female and male roles as partners and parents.

Social Determinants and Responsible Fathering

The majority of respondents reported simultaneous advances in parenting and self-worth. The men's gains in how they viewed themselves are noteworthy given that so many participants had multiple indicators of economic instability—low formal education, unemployment, and transportation problems. As Featherstone et al. (2014) surmised, for low-income men, a positive relationship with their children may be especially crucial to their sense of self-pride. And such is all the more evident for this predominantly African-American group, whose families and communities had historically endured enslavement and then segregation and today continue to encourage fathers, whether or not they live with their families, to offer support and care to their children (Cole & Green, 2010).

Maintaining family connections of White and non-White men, however, poses challenges in the context of a US state influenced by the patriarchal practices of the Anglican plantation elites and the Presbyterian backcountry settlers (Fischer, 1989). By 2010, among the states forming the original thirteen British colonies, North Carolina had the highest reported lifetime prevalence of physical violence, stalking, and rape against women by their intimate partner, and among all states, North Carolina had the fourth highest percentage (Black et al., 2011). In regards to corporal punishment of children, North Carolina along with South Carolina had notably higher rates than the rest of the country. In 2002, according to parents surveyed, half of children ages eight and nine in the Carolinas were hit with an object (Zolotor, Theodore, Chang, & Laskey, 2011).

Not surprisingly then, the Strong Fathers participants struggled with what appeared to them as overly permissive child-rearing practices such as praising children and actively ignoring misbehavior. After connecting to their own traumatic childhood experiences, many of the men worked to develop alternative parenting skills. Progress on relating with partners was far more limited. Compared with feedback responses at the beginning of the program, fewer at the end claimed to have improved their relationships with partners.

The responses may have reflected the men's reactions to a curriculum that, over time, concentrated increasingly on holding men accountable for their abuse of women. Their proposals for involving the women directly in the men's group or separately providing re-education to the women redirected the responsibility to change to the women.

A second and more optimistic interpretation is that the men who persevered with the program rather than exiting early had developed a more realistic appraisal of their partner relationships. Likewise, a prior study of the first six Strong Fathers groups found that the men made strides first on fathering and only later on partner relationships (Pennell, Sanders, Rikard, Shepherd, & Starsoneck, 2013). Both interpretations point to the necessity of helping the men move away from relying on women to set their families right and of supporting the men to become strong fathers.

Conclusions

This study examined the participants' feedback on the Strong Fathers program after it had moved beyond its early formative stages, and the facilitators' notes indicated that the curriculum was carried out as intended. This curricular fidelity means that the men's feedback can be attributed with greater confidence to the program itself. Attesting to the benefits of curricular fidelity, the men gave high marks to the curriculum, which most thought should remain unchanged but with some recommendations related to adjusting the format and assisting the men so that they could attend. Asking fathers about their preferences is one strategy for improving the curriculum and preventing dropout (Frank, Keown, Dittman, & Sanders, 2014). Participant perception of a program as helpful in meeting their goals is another motivator to attend.

Overall, the men's feedback showed high satisfaction with their experience in the program even if they initially enrolled to meet external expectations and only later developed personal reasons for participating. The program ratings testify to the success of the program in helping the men recognize the adverse impact of child maltreatment and domestic violence, first in their own childhoods and then in the lives of their children. Almost invariably, the respondents agreed that the program helped them become better fathers, and in their written comments, 60 percent of the respondents credited the program with enhancing their sense of self.

In their self-reflections, the participants described the group sessions as an opportunity to share their own traumatic experiences and open their eyes to alternative ways of parenting. These group processes were also documented in the facilitators' recordings of the sessions. In relating to women, however, progress was far more limited. A substantial minority of men recommended that the program involve or change their children's mothers. Although the men's reports of progress were overwhelmingly positive, questions remain about the program's capacity to redirect the focus beyond the father's parenting their children to co-parenting with the children's mothers. Development of positive co-parenting may, however, depend upon the men gaining greater stability in their own lives. Nevertheless, the men's affirmations point to potential of this fathering program to change the lives of men and their families for the better.

Note

1. The three collaborating organizations in North Carolina are: lead organization, Family Services, Inc., in Winston-Salem; curriculum developers, Center for Child and Family Health in Durham, and evaluators, Center for Family and Community Engagement at NC State University. The Strong Fathers project was funded by the North Carolina Department of Health and Human Services, Division of Social Services from 2009–2014 and by the North Carolina Council of Women for 2014–2015, prime Family Violence Prevention and Services Act, US Department of Health & Human Services. Corresponding author is Joan Pennell: jpennell@ ncus.edu.

References

Ake III, G. S., Bauman, K., Briggs, E. C., & Starsoneck, L. (2012). *Strong Fathers curriculum & facilitators manual.* Durham, NC: Center for Child & Family Health.

Bennett, L. W., Stoops, C., Call, C., & Flett, H. (2007). Program completion and re-arrest in a batterer intervention system. *Research on Social Work Practice, 17*(1), 42–54. doi:10.1177/1049731506293729

Bent-Goodley, T. B., Rice II, J., Williams, O. J., & Pope, M. (2011). Treatment for perpetrators of domestic violence. In M. P. Koss, J. W. White, & A. E. Kazdin (Eds.), *Violence against women and children: Navigating solutions* (Volume 2) (pp. 199–213). Washington, DC: American Psychological Association.

Beyer, K., Wallis, A. B., & Hamberger, L. K. (2015). Neighborhood environment and intimate partner violence: A systematic review. *Trauma, Violence, & Abuse, 16*(1), 16–47. doi:10.1177/1524838013515758

Black, M. C., Basile, K. C., Breiding, M. J., Smith, S. G., Walters, M. L., Merrick, M. T., Chen, J., & Stevens, M. R. (2011). *The National Intimate Partner and Sexual Violence Survey (NISVS): 2010 summary report.* Atlanta, GA: National Center for Injury Prevention and Control, Centers for Disease Control and Prevention. Retrieved from: www.cdc. gov/ViolencePrevention/pdf/NISVS_Report2010-a.pdf.

Cole, R. L. & Green, C. (2010). *The myth of the missing black father.* New York, NY: Columbia University Press.

Duncan, D. F., Kum, H. C., Flair, K. A., Stewart, C. J., Vaughn, J., Bauer, R., & Reese, J. (2015). *Management assistance for Child Welfare, Work First, and Food & Nutrition Services in North Carolina (vol. 3.1).* Chapel Hill, NC: University of North Carolina at Chapel Hill. Retrieved from: http://ssw.unc.edu/ma/.

Edleson, J. L. & Williams, O. J. (Eds.). (2007). *Parenting by men who batter: New directions for assessment and intervention.* New York, NY: Oxford University Press.

Featherstone, B., White, S., & Morris, K. (2014). *Re-imagining child protection: Towards humane social work with families.* Bristol, UK: Policy Press.

Fischer, D. H. (1989). *Albion's seed: Four British folkways in America.* New York, NY: Oxford University Press.

Frank, T. J., Keown, L. J., Dittman, C. K., & Sanders, M. R. (2014). Using father preference data to increase father engagement in evidence-based parenting programs. *Journal of Child and Family Studies, 24*(4), 937–947.

Gondolf, E. W. (2002). *Batterer intervention systems: Issues, outcomes, and recommendations.* Thousand Oaks, CA: Sage.

Gordon, D. M., Oliveros, A., Hawes, S. W., Iwamoto, D. K., & Rayford, B. S. (2012). Engaging fathers in child protection services: A review of factors and strategies across ecological systems. *Children and Youth Services Review, 34,* 1399–1417. doi:10.1016/j.child youth.2012.03.021

Hirsch, E. D. (1967). *Validity in interpretation.* New Haven, CT: Yale University Press.

Holt, S. (2015). Post-separation fathering and domestic abuse: Challenges and contradictions. *Child Abuse Review, 24,* 210–222. doi:10.1002/car.2264

Jewell, L. M. & Wormith, J. S. (2010). Variables associated with attrition from domestic violence treatment programs targeting male batterers: A meta-analysis. *Criminal Justice and Behavior, 37*(10), 1086–1118. doi 10.1177/0093854810376815

Julion, W. A., Breitenstein, S. M., & Waddell, D. (2012). Fatherhood intervention development in collaboration with African American non-resident fathers. *Research in Nursing & Health, 35,* 490–506. doi:10.1002/nur.21492

Juodis, M., Starzomski, A., Porter, S., & Woodworth, M. (2014). What can be done about high-risk perpetrators of domestic violence? *Journal of Family Violence, 29*(4), 381–390. doi:10.1007/s10896-014-9597-2

Koenig, M. A., Stephenson, R., Ahmed, S., Jejeebhoy, S. J., & Campbell, J. (2006). Individual and contextual determinants of domestic violence in North India. *American Journal of Public Health, 96*(1), 132–138. doi:10.2105/AJPH.2004.050872

Lila, M., Gracia, E., & Murgui, S. (2013). Psychological adjustment and victim-blaming among intimate partner violence offenders: The role of social support and stressful life events. *The European Journal of Psychology Applied to Legal Context, 5,* 147–153. doi:10.5093/ejpalc2013a4

Mederos, F. (2004). *Accountability and connection with abusive men: A new child protection response to increasing family safety.* San Francisco, CA: Family Violence Prevention Fund. Retrieved from: www.futureswithoutviolence.org/userfiles/file/Children_and_Families/Accountability_Connection.pdf.

NC Child. (2013). *KIDS COUNT data center*. Retrieved from: www.ncchild.org.

Neighbors, C., Walker, D. D., Mbilinyi, L. F., O'Rourke, A., Edleson, J. L., Zegree, J., & Roffman, R. A. (2010). Normative misperceptions of abuse among perpetrators of intimate partner violence. *Violence Against Women, 16*(4), 370–386. doi:10.1177/1077 801210363608

Pennell, J., Sanders, T., Rikard, R. V., Shepherd, J., & Starsoneck, L. (2013). Family violence, fathers, and restoring personhood. *Restorative Justice, 1*(2), 268–289. doi:10. 5235/2050472.1.1.2.1

Ptacek, J. (Eds.). (2010). *Restorative justice and violence against women*. New York, NY: Oxford University Press.

Ricoeur, P. (1979). The model of the text: Meaningful action considered as a text. In P. Rabinow & W. M. Sullivan (Eds.), *Interpretive social science: A reader* (pp. 73–101). Berkeley, CA: University of California Press.

Rothman, E. M., Mandel, D. G., & Silverman, J. G. (2007). Abusers' perceptions of the effect of their intimate partner violence on children. *Violence Against Women, 13*(11), 1179–1191. doi:10.1177/1077801207308260

Salisbury, E. J., Henning, K., & Holdford, R. (2009). Fathering by partner-abusive men: Attitudes on children's exposure to interparental conflict and risk factors for child abuse. *Child Maltreatment, 14*(3), 232–242. doi:10.1177/1077559509338407

Scott, K. L. & Crooks, C. V. (2007). Preliminary evaluation of an intervention program for maltreating fathers. *Brief Treatment and Crisis Intervention, 7*(3), 224–238.

Scott, K. L. & Lishak, V. (2012). Intervention for maltreating fathers: Statistically and clinically significant change. *Child Abuse & Neglect, 36*, 680–684. dx.doi.org/10.1016/ j.chiabu.2012.06.003

Scott, K., Kelly, T., Crooks, C., & Francis, K. (2014). *Caring dads: Helping fathers value their children* (2nd ed.). Bloomington, IN: Trafford.

Stanley, N., Fell, B., Miller, P., Thomson, G., & Watson, J. (2012). Men's talk: Men's understandings of violence against women and motivations for change. *Violence Against Women, 18*(11), 1300–1318. doi:10.1177/1077801212470547

Tiano, J. D. & McNeil, C. B. (2005). The inclusion of fathers in behavioral parent training: A critical evaluation. *Child & Family Behavior Therapy, 27*, 1–28. doi:10.1300/J019 v27n04_01

US Census Bureau. (2015, May 29). *State & county QuickFacts: North Carolina*. Retrieved from: http://quickfacts.census.gov/qfd/states/37000.html.

Zolotor, A. J., Theodore, A. D., Chang, J. J., & Laskey, A. L. (2011). Corporal punishment and physical abuse: Population-based trends for three-to-11-year-old children in the United States. *Child Abuse Review, 20*, 57–66. doi:10.1002/car.112

15 Preventing Homelessness for Women Who Leave Abusive Partners

A Shelter-Based "Housing First" Program

Monique Auffrey, Leslie M. Tutty, and Alysia C. Wright[1]

Since the plight of women whose partners abused them first became acknowledged, the most common response has been, "Why doesn't she just leave?" What has since become clear, however, is that when women and children leave their homes due to violence, at least for a while, they become essentially homeless, even if staying with friends, in a hotel or a violence for women (VAW) emergency shelter (Sev'er, 2002; Tutty et al., 2009).

Wherever women stay after leaving partners, finding a new safe and stable place to live will be a priority. The importance of access to stable housing for women abused by intimate partners and their children should not be underestimated (Clough, Draughon, Njie-Carr, Rollins, & Glass, 2014; Ponic et al., 2011). Rollins et al. (2011) recently found that, while danger from the partner was significantly associated with PTSD symptoms, the number of housing instability characteristics (i.e. evictions, multiple moves, difficulties with landlords) were equally correlated with poor health outcomes.

This chapter describes potential housing options and the experiences of homelessness for women who have left abusive intimate partners. The network of first and second-stage VAW shelters in Canada, both of which commonly do their utmost to assist women to find stable housing, is described as well as other housing options. These are briefly contrasted to women's experiences in homeless shelters.

Housing First programs are a relatively new homeless sector initiative designed to house individuals (not specifically for women or women abused by partners) who have become homeless for a variety of reasons such as mental health and substance abuse. Housing First programs have been rapidly adopted for homeless individuals (primarily men) with a variety of serious issues such as mental health and substance abuse. The final section describes a unique program, the Community Housing Program (CHP) specific for women leaving abusive partners that builds on the Housing First principles, whose offices are housed at Discovery House, a second stage VAW shelter in Calgary, Alberta, Canada. The chapter ends with a critical assessment of the challenges and opportunities of this program for women abused by intimate partners.

The Risks of Homelessness for Women Abused by Intimate Partners

Homelessness has become a social issue of increasing concern across North America. While the stereotypical face of homelessness is a man on the streets with obvious mental health or substance abuse problems, women make up an increasing number of homeless individuals (Gaetz, Scott, & Gulliver, 2013). Moreover, identifying how many abused women become homeless is difficult, since women are often reluctant to access formal resources and, as such, are often among the ranks of the "hidden homeless," living in overcrowded conditions, couch-surfing or having sufficient money for shelter, but not for other necessities (Gaetz et al., 2013; Novac, 2006).

Intimate partner violence (IPV) is considered a major cause of homelessness for women. Homeless women are commonly former VAW shelter residents who could not find adequate and/or safe housing (Baker, Cook, & Norris, 2003; Charles, 1994). In Baker and colleagues' study of 110 women who had been abused by partners, 25 to 50 percent reported housing problems and 38 percent were or had been homeless at some point.

Women are especially vulnerable to becoming homeless because of interpersonal conflict. As women are often in relationships in which they are economically dependent upon a partner, if a significant disruption occurs, the woman's home is often at stake (Tessler, Rosenheck, & Gamache, 2001). In Tessler and colleagues' study, homeless men more often perceived their homelessness as caused by loss of work, discharge from an institution, mental health problems, or substance abuse. In contrast, homeless women more often reported becoming homeless because of eviction, interpersonal conflict, or having no one who was willing or able to assist them.

Fear of becoming homeless may also influence women's decisions to remain with or return to an abusive partner. Sev'er (2002) noted that, "For some women, their escape means long durations of unacceptable living conditions or homelessness. According to Canadian shelter statistics, the wait for subsidized housing is anywhere from three weeks to five years" (p. 320). Over half of the thirty-nine women in Sev'er's study stayed in their abusive relationships because they were afraid they could not access decent accommodation.

Abused women of Aboriginal or visible minority backgrounds or those with children are often discriminated against by landlords who refuse to rent to them (Tutty et al., 2009). As a further complication, a study by Canada Mortgage and Housing Corporation (CMHC, 2006) suggested that women might also be discriminated against by landlords who become aware that they are fleeing partner abuse. In this scenario study, landlords commonly raised concerns regarding the women's ability to pay the rent, and/or had concerns about her abusive partner's potential for further violence. A small number of landlords were described as "openly hostile" (p. 3) toward battered women, blaming them for the abuse and stating that they would not rent to them under any circumstances.

Housing Options for Women Leaving Abusive Partners

Some question why women should have to leave their homes at all because their partners abuse them. A number of Canadian provinces and American states have civil legislation so that women may obtain emergency protection orders that include provisions for her to remain in the home, while he is removed from it but how often such provisions are used has not been well documented. In an evaluation of Alberta's PAFVA legislation, over a two and a half year period, 64 percent of applications were granted exclusive occupation of the residence (508 of 796) (Tutty, Koshan, Jesso, & Nixon, 2005), however, the extent to which the women stayed safely in their own homes was not available. Further, women who fear their partners would likely not feel safe even if the provision was granted and, thus, may be more likely to leave to seek safer accommodation.

Most women leaving violent partners do not go to VAW shelters for abused women. Statistically, only 11 percent of abused women access VAW shelters and only 7 percent actually reside in VAW shelters (AuCoin, 2005). Most women first seek help from their informal support system, relying on friends or family for a place to stay (Miller & DuMont, 2000; Novac, 2006; Tutty, 2015). Thus, as mentioned earlier, they are often part of the hidden homeless rather than being counted in the absolute homeless statistics.

Canada has a network of shelters and transition homes specifically developed to serve women abused by intimate partners and their children. The Transition House survey conducted in 2014 by Statistics Canada (Beattie & Hutchins, 2015) reported that, in the year ending March 31, 2014, 60,341 women were admitted to 627 shelters (mostly VAW specific) in the country. In addition to fleeing IPV, housing issues were another common reason for women seeking shelter: 30 percent of women identified being unable to find affordable housing as among their reasons for seeking shelter, while 17 percent of women cited short-term housing problems, and 10 percent reported housing emergencies as reasons for their admission. On a one-day snapshot in 2014, 539 women and children were turned away from Canadian shelters, 56 percent of these because the shelter was full. This number represents 0.07 percent of the total number of 7,969 women and children who were sheltered that day (Beattie & Hutchins, 2015). Though a small proportion, the risk of becoming homeless should not be ignored.

Stays in VAW emergency shelters are typically short, from three to six weeks depending on the province, with much of that time spent finding resources to address post-shelter basic needs such as employment, welfare, schools for children and stable, accessible permanent housing. In a cross-Canada study of

YWCA emergency shelters with 368 respondents (Tutty, 2006) reported that, on shelter entry, 136 women wanted assistance finding accommodation and, on exit, forty-nine found the shelter very helpful, another forty-six "somewhat helpful" and a final nineteen, "not very helpful." An additional forty-nine women stated that they did not need help with housing and five mentioned that housing assistance was not offered to them.

It is important to note that with short VAW emergency shelter stays and with increasingly unaffordable housing prices and low vacancy rates, especially in large urban centers, finding housing can be a major challenge. Thus, on exiting VAW shelters, women are often faced with inadequate housing and financial support that leaves them with a choice between homelessness and returning to their abusive partner. Many shelters have follow-up or outreach programs to continue providing support to residents post-shelter with respect to critical issues such as housing. Funding for these can be difficult as they are sometimes seen as "extras" rather than as essential outgrowths of shelters (Tutty, 1996).

Second stage shelters offer longer-term (three to twelve months) secure housing with support and referral services designed to assist women while they search for permanent housing. Generally, women live with their children in their own apartment; but the units have enhanced security measures to address the families' safety needs as well as programs, services and/or supports. In 2013/2014, Canada had 123 second-stage shelters (Beattie & Hutchins, 2015). Thus, while second-stage shelters are an attractive and secure solution for many women, fewer are available and, because residents stay longer, they tend to be reserved for women facing significant risks from partners.

Other VAW programs offer housing to women once they return to the community. Although the names are different, the philosophies are similar. "Transitional housing" programs are a US model that attempts to serve the immediate needs of housing and security for from three months to three years by offering counseling, housing and employment assistance (Melbin, Sullivan, & Cain, 2003). Similarly, a program in Edmonton, Alberta, described as a "third-stage shelter," provides outreach to women who live in social housing. Another similar program in the province of Manitoba offers "interim housing" and support in social housing units while women wait for more permanent accommodation (Tutty et al., 2009). Thus, while safety could be of concern, women are housed in "normal" community settings and provided support and referrals to resources when needed. As noted, though, what women want is permanent, safe, affordable housing. Some US states (Botein & Hetling, 2010) and Canadian provinces such as Ontario (Tutty et al., 2009) have legislated preferred access to social housing for women fleeing abusive partners.

In contrast to shelters specific to abused women, homeless shelters are perhaps best seen as a final resort for women who have used up their resources and have no other housing options. Women also use homelessness shelters, comprising an estimated one-quarter of residents in Canada; males: 73.6 percent, females: 26.2 percent (Segaert, 2012, p. 14). Few homeless shelters are gender-specific for women, most have limited residency, usually over-night, and women have commonly raised significant issues about their safety, some preferring to live rough rather than use homeless shelters (DeWard & Moe, 2010; Tutty et al., 2009).

The Housing First Model

Housing First programs are a relatively new strategy from the homeless sector developed to house chronically homeless individuals, many of whom have severe mental health and substance abuse problems. Housing First has been applied all over the world, including Canada, France, Holland, the United Kingdom, and the United States (Gaetz et al., 2013; Macnaughton et al., 2015; Tsemberis, 2011). The primary principle is that the first step to positively address the issues of individuals who become homeless is to provide permanent and stable housing that supports their unique needs (Baker, Billhardt, Warren, Rollins, & Glass, 2010). Supports are usually provided by a specialized team of caseworkers, mental health professionals, housing liaisons, and case managers. Evaluations of the Housing First model, primarily with men with chronic homelessness, have yielded consistently positive findings (Adair et al., 2016; Gaetz et al., 2013; Tsemberis, 2011; Waegemakers Schiff, 2014).

The basic tenets of Housing First are quite simple and are comparable to what we understand to be basic human rights, social determinants of health and Maslow's hierarchy of needs (1943). It accepts that every individual requires food, shelter, and clothing to sustain them. Housing First models encourage participants to hold their own rental lease in the general housing market. Ideally, a fair rent is negotiated. If rental costs exceed income support, rental subsidies are provided. The model acknowledges "Intensive Case Management" as the precursor to successful self-sufficiency. Intensive case managers work closely with clients in their own homes from a strengths-based perspective, often applying harm reduction principles. They model behaviors to assist clients retain their housing, mitigate against eviction, work with landlords, advocate for fair rents and tenancy agreements, educate the community of the unique needs of survivors of domestic violence (DV), and encourage clients to address their mental, physical, and financial needs.

Notably though, the homeless shelter and VAW shelter sectors developed from different needs and with different primary focuses; VAW shelters on the risk and consequences of intimate partner violence and homeless shelters on housing gaps primarily for individuals with mental health and addiction issues. At times, these differences could be seen as a reluctance of the homeless sector to identify women staying in a short-term VAW shelter as being homeless. Further, the approaches to housing are different, with homeless shelters offering primarily one-night accommodation compared to the VAW shelter sector offering much longer-term support and assistance in accessing housing and other basic needs so that women can successfully transition back into the community (Tutty, Ogden, & Weaver-Dunlop, 2007). From this perspective, programs such as Housing First that offer longer-term support to assist homeless individuals to remain housed are arguably "catching up" with the VAW sector philosophy of providing significant supports.

Applying a Housing First model as a response to intimate partner violence could address concerns about transitional and temporary shelter arrangements. This requires a unique relationship between Housing First providers and VAW shelters in order to reduce any gaps between shelter exit and entry into Housing First residences. It is also important to consider that Housing First is not a one-size-fits-all strategy; women fleeing intimate partner violence may require additional security and safety measures that may not be available in a standard Housing First model, necessitating the continued use of transitional housing or adapting existing Housing First structures to meet the needs of survivors of intimate partner violence. The Washington State Coalition Against Domestic Violence (Strategic Prevention Solutions, 2011) is one example of a US coalition that has implemented a Domestic Violence Housing First approach, including the use of wrap-around social services and support while clients rebuild their lives.

Best practice recommendations for ending homelessness for women and girls include establishing comprehensive discharge plans that include placement into permanent housing that will support self-sufficiency and the development of independent living skills (van Berkum & Oudshoorn, 2015). The Housing First model also addresses the issue of providing adequate housing for women and their children so that mothers are not forced to live in subpar housing that could put them at risk for community violence or involvement with child protective services (Guo, Slesnick, & Feng, 2016). Nevertheless, little has been written about Housing First models specific to women abused by intimate partners.

The Discovery House Family Violence Prevention Society

Discovery House was established in 1980 as a long-term shelter facility for women with children fleeing domestic violence. It was the first "second-stage" facility for women and children dealing with the consequences of domestic violence in Calgary and one of the first of its kind in Canada. The inaugural location provided seven furnished units in an apartment building. In four short years it doubled its capacity by moving to a larger building and, by 2004, Discovery House opened its doors to a brand new facility through government funding and corporate donations. Since its initiation, the organization has held to a strong commitment of increasing its' capacity to meet the needs of the community. While the mission of the organization is to put an end to domestic violence, the need for service continues to grow.

As stated earlier in the chapter, second stage facilities exist to help women transition from a "first-stage" or initial emergency shelter point where accommodation is limited and available only for a short period of time to independence. In recognition of the many stressors affecting women abused by intimate partners, including safety risk, financial and legal needs, and the trauma associated with domestic violence, second-stage shelter facilities can provide women more time to get settled and to adapt to life on their own, thereby reducing the likelihood of returning to an abusive partner. It accepts that if a woman can be supported financially and emotionally during the stressful period immediately following escaping from an abusive partner she is much more likely to successfully find her way to independence. In other words, a second-stage facility provides the stability required for women and their children to begin putting their lives back together.

Today, Discovery House provides shelter and support to more than 600 women and children each year. The "shelter" provides nineteen independent apartment units in a secure, confidential location. The apartments range in size from two to four bedrooms. Rents are subsidized and tenancy is for a twelve-month period. Typically, a woman in financial need will begin the process of applying for income support while staying in an emergency shelter. Rents at Discovery House are consistent with the rental amounts provided for by provincial income support. Admission to Discovery House is not dependent on provincial government support although financial hardship is a determinant of admission.

Women participate in an intake interview, are given a tour, and offered a unit as space becomes available. Group work and counseling are offered but are not a requirement for admission. Case managers, child and youth workers, children-center workers, and volunteers make up the panoply of front-line staff. Recently, trauma-informed specialists, a nursing clinician, yoga, and meditation have been introduced to the residents of the shelter. The building is shaped in the form of the letter U allowing each apartment unit a view into a garden courtyard.

After their residency at Discovery House, women are given twelve months of post-exit case management and outreach support, as the psycho-social needs of women and their children do not disappear at the end of a year. The goal is to retain an arms-length approach to service, allowing clients to remain connected and, should they require outreach support, are at risk of losing their tenancy or risk returning to an abusive relationship, staff are a phone call away and will engage in community and family conferencing if requested. Staff may support women and their children by accompanying them to family court, attending school visits, and assisting in whatever way they can to build self-sufficiency in the community. The overarching goal is to ensure that women are provided with housing stability and are able to live successfully in the community without returning to either homelessness or abuse.

The Housing First Community Housing Program at Discovery House

The CHP was launched in 2009 as a collaborative pilot project between other shelters and community organizations including the Calgary Homeless Foundation (CHF). Through a joint funding proposal, Discovery House became the lead agency in the implementation of what we might call a "third-stage" housing model or an access point to finding shelter pre or post-emergency shelter admission. With offices at Discovery House, CHP is an accredited program funded primarily by the CHF (2015). It applies a Housing First philosophy positing that, once an individual is housed, they can then begin a process of healing, addressing the issues that led to homelessness in the first place.

Questions arose early on within the domestic violence sector in Calgary as to whether a Housing First model could be used for women fleeing domestic violence. Two significant questions around applying this model to the sector were related to safety—would women feel safe in their own home in the community? Second, funder requirements related to data collection—would women's information into the database systems be "identifiable" and, therefore, pose a threat?

When the program launched in 2009, the Calgary shelter community was able to house additional women and children directly in "a home of their own," thereby reducing wait times for VAW shelters, significantly reducing demand for shelter space and providing an opportunity to avoid entering a shelter in the first place. Today, the Discovery House Community Housing Program receives funding to support more than 350 women and children in the community each year. The program funding model provides for moving costs, damage deposits, rental subsidies, transportation costs, utilities, and groceries. Originally, clients were referred to the program by Calgary area domestic violence specific emergency shelters. Referrals could also be taken from other human service organizations including second stage shelters, family shelters, and other organizations such as Alberta Health Services.

The Community Housing Program Case Management Model

The team currently comprises a Program Manager who also acts as the associate director of clinical services for Discovery House, a Program Coordinator who looks after the more administrative functions of the program such as looking after budgets, Intensive Case Managers, and Mental Health Specialists, a nursing clinician and a Housing Liaison, sometimes referred to as a "Housing Advocate." Clients of the CHP have access to other Discovery House programs and staff support, programs, and groups.

The program uses a case management matrix to inform its practice that incorporates elements of critical time intervention and provides a framework to guide the activities of case management. The matrix speaks to intensity, duration, and the focus of services. Case managers focus on facilitating services to support women with children in maintaining safe and affordable housing in the community. As such, case managers work primarily as facilitators, linking clients to resources in the community. They also provide direct service by way of crisis intervention and collaborating with clients to develop the likes of budgets and safety plans.

Upon receipt of a referral, staff travel to the location of the client and conduct an in-depth interview. The Housing Liaison locates housing according to the client's stated preferences and together they coordinate viewings as well as paying the damage deposit and first month's rent. Women leaving abusive partners have unique and heightened safety concerns when it comes to safe and secure housing, which may be experienced differently from others in the homeless serving sector. Women with children fleeing intimate partner violence require specialized coordination between local emergency shelters and their Housing First housing liaisons. In locating appropriate housing, housing locators must ensure secure entrances and consider other factors that may pose certain safety risks such as in basement apartments with unbarred windows and no proper escape route.

Once the client is housed, the Community Housing staff commence program specific service such as needs and risk assessments, such as the Danger Assessment for risk of lethality (Campbell, Webster, & Glass, 2009), goal setting, planning, and monitoring activities to support families in maintaining safe and sustainable housing in the community. Staff engage in ongoing evaluation activities to ensure that the needs of families are being met.

After the ninth month of program support, staff begin the process of transition planning and ensuring that the family is connected to the necessary community supports. Funder compliance requires however that no client be exited into homelessness. In other words, if a client continues to need the program support at or near the twelve-month period, staff are required to continue supporting the client. Ideally through an intensive case management approach, staff assess and work with the client's needs consistently and over time so that immediate needs are met and longer-term needs are addressed either through the program or through community referrals. For example, once income and rental supports are in place and the client is stabilized, the case manager will ensure that the long-term supports required can be accessed in the community, therefore, dependence on intensive supports is reduced. In addition, once their housing is considered stable, a clients' level of acuity is also reduced. The case management model is seen as successful when a client finds the balance between independence, community integration, and housing stability.

Since 2009, CHP has successfully housed over 500 women and over 1,000 children in the community. In 2012, 52 percent of the women were Aboriginal, 22 percent visible minorities, and 26 percent Caucasian, although in 2016, there were fewer Aboriginal and Caucasian women (34 and 27 percent respectively) and more visible minority women (40 percent). On average, women participating in the CHP program are between thirty-three and thirty-six years of age; over the last four years the percentage of women younger than thirty-five years has increased. Many of the women have not finished high school (40 percent). In 2012, 85 percent remain stably housed; 96 percent reported a stable income; 26 percent with an active Child Protective Services files had their files successfully closed; 43 percent of those with unmanaged mental or physical health concerns have engaged with appropriate health care professionals; 20 percent with an active addiction have voluntarily engaged with drug and alcohol treatment centers.

These statistics highlight both the success of the CHP program and that the populations served represent vulnerable women with complex and significant needs for support. Discovery House believes that together with our partners, we can continue to find ways to enhance service delivery, work collaboratively within the community and find pro-active solutions that will best serve women fleeing intimate partner violence.

Discussion and Critical Analysis

As mentioned, the VAW sheltering system has always been starkly different from the homeless sheltering sector. Women's VAW shelters offer longer-term stay and considerable opportunities for emotional support and follow-up compared to more traditional homeless shelters, which are primarily overnight beds with no attached resources (Tutty et al., 2007). Both types of shelters were developed in response to different social problems and, only recently, has there been recognition of a potential overlap in clientele by looking at hidden homeless populations and considering prevention strategies.

Housing First models have been applied to almost every specialized population at risk of homelessness, including women and children (van Berkum & Oudshoorn, 2015). While evaluations have been generally positive, these have been focused on initiatives with homeless populations other than IPV. In an intensive literature search, few descriptions of Housing First programs specific to women whose partner abused them were found, and no published evaluations. The Washington State Coalition Against Domestic Violence program, mentioned previously, conducted a case study evaluation of four HF programs (Strategic Prevention Solutions, 2011). One conclusion of interest from their report was that, "Within just five or six months of working with the Family Resource Center, survivors experienced a level of change or growth that was on a deep, psychological level, and related to a feeling of dignity or self-worth" (p. 30).

Nonetheless, several authors have raised concerns about applying Housing First programs to women in general. Fotheringham, Walsh, and Burrowes (2014) note that, because of their trauma histories, Housing First many not be the best model for women at risk of homelessness as, "Unfortunately, in most permanent housing arrangements, residents have little control over who is allowed into the building, potentially leading to feelings of insecurity and fear for survivors of abuse and, in some cases, further victimization" (p. 14). Mosher (2013) raised the need for gender comparisons across Housing First initiatives to assess that these meet women's needs as well as those of men. It is critical that funding for Housing First programs not jeopardize funding for women-specific homeless programs. Further, Housing First programs require that housing and services are available, both of which are in short supply across Canada, especially in rural and northern locations. Finally, Mosher reiterates concerns about the lack of security in public housing, noting that transitional housing and second-stage shelters remain more appropriate for many women, especially those who have left high-risk abusive partners (although these are admittedly time-limited).

Other key indicators of housing stabilization and long-term success are fair market rentals and affordable housing. Housing First models cannot control for external factors such as income supports and financial stability. Clients may experience an immediate sense of security once they have been placed in housing, but if they do not have the financial means to support themselves or maintain permanent housing after their tenancy ends, they risk losing the progress they have made during their stay.

On the positive side with respect to the CHP program, the funding comes from the homelessness sector, a welcome influx of financial support when provincial funding for post-shelter housing beyond social housing (with no emotional support services) is essentially non-existent. The two concerns mentioned previously by the Calgary domestic violence sector, would women would feel safe in the community and whether confidentiality would be maintained, were both answered in the affirmative.

However, despite the successes of the Calgary CHP program, systems are rarely static. Whereas in the first years of the program, 70 percent of the referrals from the community were immediately housed, today, admission into the program is overseen by the CHF funder triage system and centralized intake process. Now, funder compliance means that only 50 percent of the community referrals will be considered and those women must first go through the centralized intake. The triage assessment tool does not include a trauma/VAW/Danger lens, so women referred by VAW shelters typically do not score as high as those who present with double axis mental health diagnoses. Further, more and more women being triaged in by CHF have some history of DV but are not "immediately" fleeing DV, as would be the case if they were in a VAW women's shelter. The triage system assigns acuity ratings to clients with the expectation that the most highly acute clients will be offered service first, while those with mid to lower acuity will either find alternative placements or must wait for a spot to become available.

Advocates from the IPV-specific Housing First program from Washington State argue that the highest long-term housing retention rates for survivors of domestic violence are those with lower acuity levels, thus, also ensuring the application of a "prevention lens" (Strategic Prevention Solutions, 2011). The question remains to what extent women post-shelter in Calgary will be able to access the CHP with the new CHF triage model, or be forced to find housing on their own that will lack the supports offered by HF.

Some of the most significant obstacles faced by clients on the road to independence and self-sufficiency are systemic and economic. Lack of safe, accessible affordable housing continues to be a problem. We often hear of clients returning to shelters for reasons associated with a lack of financial means to sustain their housing. Issues related to family court, custody and access, child welfare, lack of affordable child-care contributes to the difficult and sometimes contradictory systems that perpetuate women's oppression.

Women from diverse backgrounds, new Canadians and Aboriginal and Indigenous women face additional barriers in the support networks described in this chapter. One specific example of the ongoing debate is confidentiality controls within data management systems that require disclosures with which some clients are not comfortable. We have heard from some clients that being "tracked in a system" is reminiscent of the "Residential School" system where Indigenous People were monitored over time.

Conclusion

The Calgary CHP offers important emotional and instrumental support to women who are at risk of homelessness after fleeing partners who abused them. While any woman who meets the criteria can be assessed to enter the program, the DV community hoped the program would provide an important new resource after women have resided in a VAW emergency or second stage shelter. The CHP staff's understanding of intimate partner violence is an essential component for assisting women to establish safe and affordable housing as well as providing support if necessary. The program complements the need for emergency and second stage VAW shelters. Unfortunately, access to both second-stage shelters and the CHP remains limited.

In 2008–2009, when Housing First options for women fleeing domestic violence were first introduced in Calgary, DV sector workers were hesitant because of concerns for women need to feel safe. While shelter services and second-stage VAW shelters focus on women feeling safe, for many women these places can still be scary places. While emergency and second-stage VAW shelters provide on-site staffing, some women and children still feel unsafe because of lack of privacy, the required sharing of personal information, intrusive child welfare policies, the potential close proximity with others who may be exhibiting behaviors foreign to some, cultural factors, and social exclusion (Dewey & St. Germain, 2014; Glenn & Goodman, 2015; Tutty, 2017, Chapter 1 this volume).

As an alternative to homelessness, shelter spaces (whether emergency or second stage) are needed and appreciated by many. Providing a woman an opportunity to have safe housing when leaving an abuser is necessary and may even help to establish a sense of community and solidarity. The Housing First model provides yet another housing option; it gives women choices. A Housing First placement, whether permanent supported housing in the community at large or place-based, is effective at preventing homelessness for women fleeing domestic violence. Once market (community) housing is found for those ready to live in a community, housing can be offered immediately, bypassing a shelter entirely. For those who require more intensive support in the short-term and are comforted by the shared space afforded by a shelter, Housing First is a great next step before complete independence.

Note

1. Brigitte Baradoy, former ED of Discovery House presented the program at the Toronto Canadian Domestic Violence Conference 4 in 2015. Thanks also to Trevor Baxter for providing CPH program statistics.

References

Adair, C. E., Streiner, D. L., Barnhart, R., Kopp, B., Veldhuizen, S., Patterson, M., ... & Goering, P. (2016). Outcome trajectories among homeless individuals with mental disorders in a multisite randomised controlled trial of Housing First. *The Canadian Journal of Psychiatry/La Revue Canadienne de Psychiatrie.* doi:10.1177/0706 743716645302

AuCoin, K. E. (2005). *Family violence in Canada: A statistical profile 2005* (85-224-XIE 2005000). Ottawa, ON: Canadian Centre for Justice Statistics Retrieved from: www.statcan.gc.ca/pub/85-224-x/85-224-x2005000-eng.pdf.

Baker, C. K., Cook, S. L., & Norris, F. H. (2003). Domestic violence and housing problems: A contextual analysis of women's help-seeking, received informal support, and formal system response. *Violence Against Women, 9*(7), 754–783. doi:10.1177/1077 801203009007002

Baker, C. K., Billhardt, K. A., Warren, J., Rollins, C., & Glass, N. E. (2010). Domestic violence, housing instability, and homelessness: A review of housing policies and program practices for meeting the needs of survivors. *Aggression & Violent Behavior, 15*(6), 430–439. doi:10.1016/j.avb.2010.07.005

Beattie, S. & Hutchins, H. (2015). *Shelters for abused women in Canada, 2014.* Retrieved from: www.statcan.gc.ca/pub/85-002-x/2015001/article/14207-eng.htm.

Botein, H. & Hetling, A. (2010). Permanent supportive housing for domestic violence victims: Program theory and client perspectives. *Housing Policy Debate, 20*(2), 185–208. doi:10.1080/10511481003738575

Calgary Homeless Foundation. (2015). Calgary's plan to end homelessness. Calgary, AB: Author. Retrieved from: http://calgaryhomeless.com/who-we-are/history/10-year-plan/.

Campbell, J., Webster, D. W., & Glass, S. (2009). The Danger Assessment: Validation of a lethality risk assessment instrument for intimate partner femicide. *Journal of Interpersonal Violence, 24*(4), 653–674. doi:10.1177/0886260508317180

Canada Mortgage and Housing Corporation (CMHC). (2006). *Housing discrimination against victims of domestic violence.* Ottawa, ON: CMHC. Retrieved from: www.cmhc-schl.gc.ca/odpub/pdf/65096.pdf.

Charles, N. (1994). The housing needs of women and children escaping domestic violence. *Journal of Social Policy, 23*(4), 465–487.

Clough, A., Draughon, J. E., Njie-Carr, V., Rollins, C., & Glass, N. (2014). "Having housing made everything else possible": Affordable, safe and stable housing for women survivors of violence. *Qualitative Social Work, 13*(5), 671–688. doi:10.1177/14733250 13503003

DeWard, S. L. & Moe, A. M. (2010). "Like a prison": Homeless women's narratives of surviving shelter. *Journal of Sociology and Social Welfare, 37*(1), 115–135.

Dewey, S. C. & St. Germain, T. S. (2014). Social services fatigue in domestic violence service provision facilities. *Affilia: Journal of Women and Social Work, 29*(4), 389–403. doi:10.1177/0886109914528700

Fotheringham, S. F., Walsh, C. A., & Burrowes, A. (2014). "A place to rest": The role of transitional housing in ending homelessness for women in Calgary, Canada. *Gender, Place & Culture: A Journal of Feminist Geography, 21*, 834–853. doi:10.1080/0966369X. 2013.810605

Gaetz, S., Scott, F., & Gulliver, T. (2013). *Housing First in Canada: Supporting communities to end homelessness.* Toronto, ON: Canadian Homelessness Research Network Press. Retrieved from: www.homelesshub.ca/sites/default/files/HousingFirstInCanada.pdf.

Glenn, C. & Goodman, L. (2015). Living with and within the rules of domestic violence shelters: A qualitative exploration of residents' experiences. *Violence Against Women*, *21*(12), 1481–1506. doi:10.1177/1077801215596242

Guo, X., Slesnick, N., & Feng, X. (2016). Housing and support services with homeless mothers: Benefits to the mother and her children. *Community Mental Health Journal*, *52*, 73–83. doi:10.1007/s10597-015-9830-3

Macnaughton, E., Stefancic, A., Nelson, G., Caplan, R., Townley, G., Aubry, T., . . . & Goering, P. (2015). Implementing Housing First across sites and over time: Later fidelity and implementation evaluation of a pan-Canadian multi-site Housing First program for homeless people with mental illness. *American Journal of Community Psychology*, *55*, 279–291. doi:10.1007/s10464-015-9709-z

Maslow, A. H. (1943). A theory of human motivation. *Psychological Review*, *50*, 370–396.

Melbin, A., Sullivan, C. M., & Cain, D. (2003). Transitional supportive housing programs: Battered women's perspectives and recommendations. *Affilia*, *18*(4), 445–460. doi:10.1177/0886109903257623

Miller, K. L. & Du Mont, J. (2000). Countless abused women: Homeless and inadequately housed. *Canadian Woman Studies/Les Cahiers de la Femme*, *20*(3), 115–122.

Mosher, J. (2013). *Housing First, women second? Gendering Housing First. A brief from the Homes for Women campaign*. Toronto, ON: Homes for Women & YWCA Canada. Retrieved from: http://ywcacanada.ca/data/documents/00000382.pdf.

Novac, S. (2006). *Family violence and homelessness: A review of the literature*. Ottawa, ON: Public Health Agency of Canada. Retrieved from: www.phac-aspc.gc.ca/sfv-avf/sources/fv/fv-homelessness-itinerance/summary-sommaire-eng.php.

Ponic, P., Varcoe, C., Davies, L., Ford-Gilboe, M., Wuest, J., & Hammerton, J. (2011). Leaving ≠ moving: Housing patterns of women who have left an abusive partner. *Violence Against Women*, *17*(12), 1576–1600. doi:10.1177/1077801211436163

Rollins, C., Glass, N. E., Perrin, N. A., Billhardt, K. A., Clough, A., Barnes, J., . . . & Bloom, T. L. (2011). Housing instability is as strong a predictor of poor health outcomes as level of danger in an abusive relationship: Findings from the SHARE study. *Journal of Interpersonal Violence*, *27*(4), 623–643. doi:10.1177/0886260511423241

Segaert, A. (2012). *The National Shelter Study: Emergency shelter use in Canada 2005–2009*. Ottawa, ON: Homeless Hub. Retrieved from: http://homelesshub.ca/sites/default/files/Homelessness Partnering Secretariat 2013 Segaert_0.pdf.

Sev'er, A. (2002). A feminist analysis of flight of abused women, plight of Canadian shelters: Another road to homelessness. *Journal of Social Distress and the Homeless*, *11*(4), 307–324. doi:10.1023/A:1016858705481

Strategic Prevention Solutions. (2011). *The missing piece: A case study analysis of the Washington State Domestic Violence Housing First Project*. Retrieved from Seattle, WA: http://wscadv.org/wp-content/uploads/2015/06/casestudyanalysisofDVHF.pdf.

Tessler, R., Rosenheck, R., & Gamache, G. (2001). Gender differences in self-reported reasons for homelessness. *Journal of Social Distress and the Homeless*, *10*(3), 243–253. doi:1053-0789/01/0700-0243

Tsemberis, S. (2011). Housing First: The pathways model to end homelessness for people with mental illness and addiction manual. *European Journal of Homelessness*, *5*(2), 235–240.

Tutty, L. M. (1996). Post shelter services: The efficacy of follow-up programs for abused women. *Research on Social Work Practice*, *6*(4), 425–441. doi:10.1177/104973159600600402

Tutty, L. M. (2006). *Effective practices in sheltering women leaving violence in intimate relationships: Phase II. Final report to the YWCA Canada.* Retrieved from Toronto, ON: http://ywca canada.ca/data/publications/00000013.pdf.

Tutty, L. M. (2015). Addressing the safety and trauma issues of abused women: A cross-Canada study of YWCA shelters. *Journal of International Women's Studies, 16*(3), 101–116.

Tutty, L. M. (2017). "A place to go to when I had no place to go to": Journeys of VAW emergency shelter residents. In T. Augusta-Scott, K. Scott, & L. Tutty (Eds.), *Innovations in interventions to address intimate partner violence: Research and practice.* New York, NY: Routledge.

Tutty, L. M., Koshan, J., Jesso, D., & Nixon, K. (2005). *Alberta's Protection Against Family Violence Act: A summative evaluation.* Calgary, AB: RESOLVE Alberta. Retrieved from: www.ucalgary.ca/resolve-static/reports/2005/2005-03.pdf.

Tutty, L. M., Ogden, C., Giurgiu, B., Weaver-Dunlop, G., Damant, D., Thurston, W. E., . . . & Solerno, J. (2009). *"I built my house of hope": Best practices to safely house abused and homeless women.* Calgary, AB: Resolve Alberta. Retrieved from: www.ucalgary.ca/resolve-static/reports/2009/2009-01.pdf.

Tutty, L. M., Ogden, C., & Weaver-Dunlop, G. (2007). *Feasibility study for a national network of women's shelters and transition houses.* Prepared for the Housing and Homelessness Branch, Department of Human Resources and Social Development, Ottawa. Calgary, AB: RESOLVE Alberta. Retrieved from: www.ucalgary.ca/resolve-static/reports/2007/2007-01.pdf.

van Berkum, A. & Oudshoorn, A. (2015). *Best practice guideline for ending women's and girls' homelessness.* London, ON: All Our Sisters & Women's Community House. Retrieved from: http://londonhomeless.ca/wp-content/uploads/2012/12/Best-Practice-Guideline-for-Ending-Womens-and-Girls-Homelessness.pdf.

Waegemakers Schiff, J. (2014). *Comparison of four Housing First programs.* Calgary, AB: University of Calgary. Retrieved from: www.homelesshub.ca/sites/default/files/Comparison%20of%20Four%20Housing%20First%20Programs%20-%20v%201.2.pdf.

Index

Locators for tables are in **bold** and those for figures in *italics*.

abuse: acknowledgement 192, 197–200;
emotional 26–27, 41; extension via
legal system 141–143; financial
142–143; psychological 6, 142, 220;
range of 6, 207–208; reasons for
76–78, 197–198; strategies for dealing
with 7, 19, 39; *see also* leaving abusive
partner; remaining in abusive
relationships; responsibility for abuse
abuse scales 212–220, **217–219**;
see also safety planning tool
abusers: demographics 130, 227;
demographics in Nova Scotia case
study **131**; impact of childhood abuse
76, 79, 85, 87; IPV movement
163–166, 167; male perceptions
research 96–101; responsibility for
actions 78–80, 85–86, 88; responsibility
perspectives research **96**; victim-only
narratives 81; *see also* amending ways;
coordinated community responses;
justice-linked intervention;
responsibility for abuse; Strong Fathers
program; trauma-informed narrative
therapy; victim-only narratives
accountability for abuse: to community
185; coordinated community responses
118; IPV movement 163–166; research
study 98–99, 104, 105; restorative
justice movement 163–166
acknowledging effects of harm 192,
198–200
acknowledging the abuse 197–198
addictions 23; *see also* substance abuse
advocacy: battered women's movement
108; Family Law Program 146, 147,

148; IPV movement 159, 163–164,
166, 170; justice-linked intervention 53,
67, 69; restorative justice approach
178–180
affordable housing 254
agencies: coordinated community
responses 115–118; peer-led groups
46
Alberta, shelters 247
alcohol: dominant masculinity 77, 81;
justice-linked intervention 65; response
to trauma 145; safety planning 21, *24*,
24; Strengthening Families program
209–210, 215
amending ways: acknowledging abuse
197–198; acknowledging the effects
of harm 192, 198–200; apology and
forgiveness 201–202; 'change of heart'
94; female perceptions research 95,
103, 105; healing harm 200–201;
male perceptions research 95, 96–97,
99–101; restorative justice 183–184;
values 193–196
anger (victims) 199–200
apologising 201–202; *see also* amending
ways
app, safety planning tool 29
arousal, hyper 76, 82–86
arrests 179
ashamed (sense of shame) 88, 197
assumptions: justice-linked intervention
53–54; leaving abusive partner 19,
161; male perceptions 80, 82, 84;
victims 161
attachment, trauma-informed narrative
therapy 85

bail 115, 117
basic needs assistance 7, 9, 14, 246–247, 248
battered women's movement 108, 174–175
batterer intervention: collaboration 109, 112; justice-linked intervention 61, 64; restorative justice approach 175, 209, 210
Before Everything Escalates (BEEP) 113, 115, 116–117
Behavioral Couples Therapy (BCT) 209–210, 220
blame: perspectives research study 93; restorative justice 194–195; taking responsibility 97–98; victims 101
Bronx Defender Defense Model 144, 152–153

Calgary Community Housing Program 250–253, 254–255
Calgary Counselling Centre 210–211
Calgary Homeless Foundation (CHF) 250–251, 252–253, 254
Canada: emergency shelters 3, 4, 14, 246–247; justice-linked intervention 53; law courts 55–60, **56**; specialised courts 126
Canadian Domestic Violence Conference 174, 187; contextualised approaches 180–183; high-risk cases 185–187; responsibilities of community 184–185; responsibilities of men 183–184; restorative justice 174–178; safety 178–180; women advocates 178–180
Caring Dads program 228
case management: courts 127–128, 133–134; Discovery House 251–252
'change of heart' 94; *see also* responsibility for abuse
charges (criminal justice) 127, 130, **131**, **133**, 143
charity, housing 248–249; *see also* Family Law Program
child abuse: amending ways 100; impact on becoming abusers 76, 79, 85, 87; justice-linked intervention 65–66; Strong Fathers program 237
child-rearing practices 240
children of abuse victims: control issues 11; after emergency shelter 12–13; emergency shelter support 9; in emergency shelters 8; financial support

11, 12, 142–143; legal custody 149–150, 151–152; making amends 100–101; single parent families 142–143; women advocates 178; *see also* parenting; Strong Fathers program
chronic abuse 34
civil law 143
client-centered services, Family Law Program 145–146
coalitions 109; *see also* coordinated community responses
cognitive-behavioral therapy 63–64
collaboration: coordinated community responses 109, 111–113, 116, 118; councils 110; criminal justice system 133–135; government 134; justice-linked intervention 55–60; restorative justice 191; *see also* couples intervention; homelessness prevention; Strong Fathers program
communication: justice-linked intervention 68–69; legal information 180; restorative justice 191
community: accountability 104, 185; agencies 134; barriers to leaving abusive partner 25–26; homelessness prevention 252; restorative justice 184–185, 191; safety 181; social changes 168–169; taking responsibility 104, 184–185; women advocates 178; *see also* coordinated community responses
complex trauma 76–78
confidentiality: coordinated community responses 116; housing support 255; interventions 169; peer-led groups 40
contact with partners, after emergency shelter 9–11; *see also* couples intervention; remaining in abusive relationships
content analysis 232–233
continuing in abusive relationship *see* remaining in abusive relationships
control issues: after emergency shelter 11; IPV movement 166; legal system 141–142
coordinated community responses (CCR) 108–111, 117–119; collaboration 109, 111–113, 116, 118; evaluation study 115–117; innovative continuum of services 113–115
corporal punishment 240
councils, coordinated community responses 110

counselling *see* Strengthening Families program; therapy
couples intervention: Behavioral Couples Therapy 209–210, 220; Calgary Counselling Centre 210; mothers and fathers 238–239; range of abusive behaviors 207–208; referrals 211; restorative justice 191, 192–193, 197–202; safety of 221, 223; *see also* Strengthening Families program
courts: coordinated community responses 114–115; justice-linked intervention 55–60, **56**; Nova Scotia Domestic Violence Pilot Project 125–129, 133–135; specialised 55–60, **56**, 125–129, 131, 133
criminal justice system: abuse extended via 141–143; charges 127, 130, **131**, **133**, 143; Nova Scotia Domestic Violence Pilot Project 125–129, 133–135; police 7, 109–110, 114; responses to abuse 157; responsive regulation 185–187; restorative justice 176–177; sentencing 128–129; specialised courts 125–129, 131, 133; *see also* courts; justice-linked intervention; restorative justice movement
criminal records 160–161, 164
crisis-oriented approaches: coordinated community responses 109–110; housing 247; safety planning 18–19
cultural safety 181
custody 149–150, 151–152

Danger Assessment: Discovery House 252; emergency shelter residents 5; and safety planning 22
dating, peer-led group discussions 42
death threats 6; *see also* lethality risk
Discovery House 249–253
dissemination of information *see* information sharing
Domestic Abuse Intervention Project 108–109
Domestic Violence Action Plan 126
Domestic Violence Treatment Option Court (DVTO) 59
dominant masculinity 77, 78, 80, 81–82, 86
drugs *see* substance abuse
Duluth model 53–54, 63, 108–109
Durham County, Strong Fathers program 229

early intervention: Before Everything Escalates 113, 115, 116–117; courts 126; Nova Scotia Domestic Violence Pilot Project 135, 136
economic support *see* financial support
efficiency, Nova Scotia Domestic Violence Pilot Project 134–135
emergency protection orders 246
emergency shelter residents 3–4; contact with partners 9–10; demographics 5–7; experiences 7–9; life as better or worse 12–13; ongoing abuse 10–11; after the shelter 9; study context 4–5; study discussion 13–15; support services use 11–12
emergency shelters 3–4; battered women's movement 175; Canada 3, 4, 14, 246–247; homelessness prevention 244, 246–247, 253–255; IPV movement 165, 170; peer-led group discussions 8, 34; responsive regulation 185–186
emotional abuse 26–27, 41
emotions: of abusers 81, 82, 86; female perceptions research 102–103; male perceptions research 97; Strong Fathers program 237
enforcement: coordinated community responses 110; police 150; *see also* criminal justice system; justice-linked intervention
equality, gender 158, 166, 170, 192

fairness *see* justice
family *see* children of abuse victims; couples intervention; Strengthening Families program
Family Assessment Measure (FAM) 211–212
Family Law Program (FLP) 139–140, 152–153; abuse extended through legal system 141–143; client experience examples 151–152; client-centered services 145–146; context 140–141; holistic service approaches 144; model 146–149; non-trauma informed context 149–151; trauma-informed services 144–145
fathers *see* parenting; Strong Fathers program
feedback: emergency shelters 14, 15; safety planning 25, 27; Strong Fathers program 232, **233**, 233–234, 235–236, 241

feminism: IPV movement 169; justice-linked intervention 63; peer-led group discussions 36
financial abuse 142–143
financial support: affordable housing 250, 254; children of abuse victims 11, 12, 142–143; after emergency shelter 12–13, 14–15; homeless women 245, 247; legal issues 146; responsibility of men 102–103
follow-up services, emergency shelters 11–12
forgiveness 201–202; *see also* amending ways
Forsyth County, Strong Fathers program 229
Framework for Action on Family Violence 126

gay offenders 54
gender equality 158, 166, 170, 192
gender integration 175
gender separation 175
government: collaboration 134; councils 110
group discussions (for offenders): Before Everything Escalates 113–114; justice-linked intervention 60–66; responsibility for abuse perspectives 94, 98; Strong Fathers program 228–229; trauma-informed narrative therapy 82
group discussions (for victims): emergency shelters 8; indigenous communities 175; responsibility for abuse perspectives 95; *see also* peer-led groups
group-modality programs 62–63
Growth Circles 36–37, 40, 43–45, 46
guardianship 149–150, 151–152
guilt 88

healing harm 200–201; *see also* amending ways
helpful guilt 88
hermeneutic interpretation 230, 232–233
high-risk cases, Canadian Domestic Violence Conference 185–187
holistic approaches, Family Law Program 144
homeless shelters 247–248
homelessness prevention 244–245, 255; Discovery House 249–253; after emergency shelter 15; in emergency

shelters 244, 246–247, 253–255; Housing First Model 248–249, 250–251, 253, 255; housing options 246–248; management model 251–253; risks of 245–246
homicide *see* lethality risk; suicide threats
honesty, taking responsibility 97–98
housing assistance: emergency shelter support 9, 14; Family Law Program 146–147; *see also* homelessness prevention
Housing First Model 248–249, 250–251, 253, 255
Hudson partner abuse scales 216
hyper-arousal 76, 82–86

identity: restorative justice outcomes 193; trauma-informed narrative therapy 81, 87–88; victim-only narratives 81
incapacitation 187
incarceration 186, 187
indigenous communities: community programs 181; coordinated community responses 117; Inuit 62–63, 65, 181; justice-linked intervention 62–63, 65; support group 175
information sharing: justice-linked intervention 68–69; legal system 180; safety planning tool 28–29
innovative continuum of services for domestic violence (ICS-DV) 113–115
integrated interventions *see* collaboration
interdisciplinary professionals 144, 147–148
interventions: confidentiality 169; IPV movement 170–171; restorative justice movement 170–171; safety planning 18–19; support groups 34–35; *see also* coordinated community responses; couples intervention; justice-linked intervention services; Strengthening Families program; Strong Fathers program; trauma-informed narrative therapy
Inuit: community programs 181; justice-linked intervention 62–63, 65
IPV movement 157–158, 170–171; comparison to restorative justice movement 157–158, 169–170; listening to women 160–162; making change 166–167; responsibility for abuse 163–166; safety 162–163; social justice 167–169; victim-centered approach 158–160

jurisdictions 55–56, **56**
just outcomes *see* restorative justice
    outcomes
justice: retributive 176; social 167–169;
    social response 164–165; taking
    responsibility 195; *see also* restorative
    justice
Justice Enterprise Information Network
    (JEIN) 129
justice-linked intervention services 53–54,
    67–69; associated services for victims
    66–67; integration with broader
    response 55–60; programs for 54,
    60–66, 67; risk factors 57, 58–60, 66

landlords 245–246
law courts *see* courts
leaving abusive partner: assumptions 161;
    barriers 25–26; female perceptions
    research 102–104; legal issues 140,
    152; lethality risk 21; ongoing abuse 9,
    10–11; restorative justice movement
    161–162
legal issues: custody 149–150, 151–152;
    domestic violence advocacy 179;
    emergency protection 246; information
    sharing 180; interdisciplinary
    professionals 144; leaving abusive
    partner 140, 152
legal system *see* criminal justice system;
    Family Law Program; Nova Scotia
    Domestic Violence Pilot Project;
    police
lethality risk: death threats 6; housing
    252; leaving abusive partner 21;
    responsive regulation 185–187
LGBTQ offenders 54

masculinity, dominant 77, 78, 80, 81–82,
    86; *see also* patriarchy
men as abusers *see* abusers; dominant
    masculinity; patriarchy; Strong Fathers
    program
mental health: leaving abusive partner 34;
    Strengthening Families program
    222–223; *see also* emotional abuse
minority groups 62–63; *see also* indigenous
    communities; race
mobile phones, safety planning tool 29
modality programs 62–63
mortality *see* lethality risk; suicide threats
mothers, support for 238–239; *see also*
    children of abuse victims; parenting
mutual violence 207

narrative approaches: justice-linked
    intervention 63–64; responsibility
    perspectives research 94–95; *see also*
    trauma-informed narrative therapy
nature of violence 6, 33–34, 39, 207–208
networks 109; *see also* coordinated
    community responses
New Brunswick, safety planning 20–21,
    29
non-trauma informed services 149–151
North Carolina: cultural safety 181;
    lethality risk 185–186; restorative
    justice approach 182–183; Strong
    Fathers program 228–229, 240
Nova Scotia: advocacy 166; restorative
    justice movement 159, 160; specialised
    courts 131, 133
Nova Scotia Domestic Violence Pilot
    Project (NSDVCPP) 125, 136;
    criminal justice system 133–135;
    research discussion 135; research
    findings 130–133; research methods
    129–130; specialised courts
    125–129

offenders *see* abusers
ongoing abuse (after leaving partner) 9,
    10–11; *see also* remaining in abusive
    relationships
Ontario: coordinated community
    responses 110; justice-linked
    intervention 55, 59, 61, 62; Sudbury
    collaboration case study 111–112, 113,
    114, 118–119
Ontario Domestic Assault Risk
    Assessment (ODARA) 59
outreach, bail 115
outreach, Family Law Program 149

paper abuse 141
parenting: justice-linked intervention
    65–66; legal custody 149–150,
    151–152; strong mothers 238–239; *see
    also* children of abuse victims; Strong
    Fathers program
Partner Assault Response (PAR) 112,
    114–115, 117
partnerships 109; *see also* coordinated
    community responses
patriarchy 168, 193
peer-led groups 33; agency response 46;
    curriculum 40–42; demographics 37,
    38; interventions 34–35; nature of
    violence 33–34, 39; organizational

challenges 44–45; research discussion
45–46; research overview 36–37;
research results 37, **38**; Sagesse 36;
structure 40–45; support services use
35–36
personal relationships 93–94
Personality Assessment Screener (PAS)
211–212, 214–216
personality traits 211–212
perspectives research *see* responsibility
for abuse; Strong Fathers program
physical abuse 6, 39, 65–66, 212, 216
Pilot Project *see* Nova Scotia Domestic
Violence Pilot Project
police: coordinated community responses
109–110, 114; strategies for dealing
with abuse 7; *see also* justice-linked
intervention services
post-traumatic stress disorder (PTSD):
abusers 80; danger 244; victims 34
power relations 79, 166, 167–168
privacy *see* confidentiality
problem-solving courts 55
professional support: Family Law
Program 146, 147–148; group
discussions 35–36, 43–44, 46; legal
issues 144; trauma-informed narrative
therapy 81–88; *see also* support services
programs *see* Calgary Community
Housing Program; coordinated
community responses; Family Law
Program; Housing First Model; justice-
linked intervention; restorative justice
outcomes; Strengthening Families
program; Strong Fathers program
prosecution: restorative justice 177–178;
restorative justice movement 160–161;
sentencing 55–60, **56**, 128–129,
177–178, 186–187
prosecution streams 57–60
psychoeducation 63–64
psychological abuse: emergency shelter
residents 6; legal system 142;
Strengthening Families program 220
psychological explanations (abusers) 80,
84

Quebec, justice-linked intervention 62

race: emergency shelter resident
demographics 5–6; homelessness 245,
254–255; Strong Fathers program
229, **231**, 239–240; *see also* minority
groups

reconciliation 10, 158–159; *see also*
amending ways
relapse prevention 207
relapse prevention plans 197–198
relationships *see* leaving abusive partner;
ongoing abuse; remaining in abusive
relationships
remaining in abusive relationships:
homelessness prevention 245; lethality
risk 21; nature of violence 39; reasons
for 19, 39; safety planning tool 22–24,
22–24, 26, 28; *see also* couples
intervention
remedies (restorative justice sessions)
200–201
re-offence: coordinated community
responses 114–115; justice-linked
intervention 58, 65; Nova Scotia
Domestic Violence Pilot Project
132–133, **132–133**; relapse prevention
plans 197–198
repairing harm 200–201; *see also*
amending ways
research studies *see* coordinated
community response; emergency
shelters; Nova Scotia Domestic
Violence Pilot Project; peer-led
groups; responsibility for abuse; safety
planning tool; Strengthening Families
program
resistance to abuse 88
respect for self 196–197, 239
Respectful Relationships program 59–60
responsibility for abuse: Canadian
Domestic Violence Conference
183–185; co-constructing meaning
93–94, 104; community 184–185;
female perceptions research 101–104;
IPV movement 163–166; male
perceptions research 96–101;
perspectives research study 94–95, *96,*
104–106; restorative justice 163–166,
181–185, 192, 194–195; trauma-
informed narrative therapy 78–80,
85–86, 88
responsive regulation 185–187
restorative justice approach 174, 187;
Canadian Domestic Violence
Conference 174–178; community
184–185, 191; contextualised
approaches 180–183; high-risk cases
185–187; responsibilities of community
184–185; responsibilities of men
163–166, 183–184, 192, 194–195;

safety 178–180; women advocates 178–180
restorative justice movement 157–158, 170–171; comparison to IPV movement 157–158, 169–170; listening to women 160–162; making change 166–167; responsibility for abuse 163–166; safety 162–163; social justice 167–169; victim-centered approach 158–160
restorative justice outcomes 191–192, 202; acknowledging the effects 192, 198–200; apology and forgiveness 201–202; healing harm 200–201; identity 193; processes 192–193; relapse prevention plans 197–198; respect for self 196–197; sentencing 177–178; values 193–197, 199
restorative practice 162, 174
retributive justice 176
returning to abusive partner: Family Law Program 145–146; restorative justice 192
risk, needs, responsivity (RNR) model 58
risk assessment 28; *see also* Danger Assessment; safety planning tool
risk factors: courts 126; justice-linked intervention 57, 58–60, 66; Nova Scotia Domestic Violence Pilot Project 131–132, 135; responsive regulation 185–187; safety planning 18, *22–23*, 22–24, 27–28; *see also* lethality risk
risk management, coordinated community responses 117
role plays, Strong Fathers program 234
RP (restorative practice) 162, 174
rural areas: barriers to leaving abusive partner 25–26; New Brunswick Context 20–21; safety planning tool 20

safety: Canadian Domestic Violence Conference 178–180; couples intervention 221, 223; cultural 181; emergency shelters 8; Family Law Program 147; IPV movement 162–163; justice-linked intervention 66–67; Nova Scotia Domestic Violence Pilot Project 135; peer-led groups 40; restorative justice 191–192; restorative justice movement 161, 162 163, 164–165; *see also* lethality risk
safety planning 18–19
safety planning tool: New Brunswick Context 20–21, 29; research overview 19–20, 29–30; research results 25–29; research validation 25, 29; self-assessment 22–24, 27, 30
Sagesse, peer-led groups 36
second-stage shelters 247, 249–250
self-assessment: abuse scales 212–220, **217–219**; safety planning tool 22–24, 27, 30; Strong Fathers program **235**, 235–236
self-esteem: emergency shelter residents 13; emotional abuse 26–27; peer-led group discussions 41; Rosenberg Self-Esteem Index 216
self-respect 196–197, 239
sentencing: prosecution 160–161, 177–178; restorative justice 177–178, 186–187; specialised courts 55–60, **56**, 128–129
separation *see* leaving abusive partner
services *see* support services
sexual abuse 6, 98
shame 88, 197
shelters *see* emergency shelters; homeless shelters; second-stage shelters; third-stage shelters
siloization 111–112, 116, 152
single parents 142–143
situational couple violence 207
social assistance *see* support services
social changes 168–169
social issues: homelessness 245; responsible fathering 239–240
social justice 167–169; *see also* restorative justice movement
South Carolina, Strong Fathers program 240
Spousal Assault Risk Assessment (SARA) 59
staff: Calgary Community Housing Program 251, 252, 255; coordinated community responses 116–117; emergency shelters 4, 8–9; homelessness prevention 252; IPV movement 165, 166; specialised courts 127–128; Strong Fathers program 234
staying in abusive relationship *see* remaining in abusive relationships
strategies for dealing with abuse 7, 19, 39
strategies for preventing relapse 197–198, 207
Strengthening Families program: Calgary Counselling Centre 210–211;

demographics **213**, 213–214, 222;
research discussion 220–223; research
methods 211–212; research outcomes
216–220; research results 212–216,
215; substance abuse 209–210
substance abuse: female perceptions
research 102; justice-linked
intervention 65; response to trauma
145; self-reporting 212;
Strengthening Families program
209–210, **215**, 221
Sudbury collaboration case study
111–112, 113, *114*, 118–119
suicide case, Nova Scotia 126
suicide threats 6
support groups *see* group discussions
support services (for abusers) *see*
coordinated community responses
(CCR); Strengthening Families
program; Strong Fathers program;
trauma-informed narrative therapy
support services (for victims): after
emergency shelter 11–12; in
emergency shelters 9, 14; housing 252;
justice-linked intervention 66–67;
peer-led group discussions 35–36;
see also homelessness prevention

taking responsibility *see* responsibility for
abuse
terroristic violence 207
therapy: Behavioral Couples Therapy
209–210, 220; cognitive-behavioral
63–64; group discussions 34, 35;
justice-linked intervention 59, 62, 63;
philosophies 63, 64; *see also* trauma-
informed narrative therapy
third-stage shelters 247, 250–251
threats, suicide/death 6
time-outs 197, 210
trauma: Family Law Program 140–141,
143, 144–145; post-traumatic stress
disorder 34, 80, 244; reasons for abuse
76–78; responses to 145
trauma scales 5; *see also* abuse scales;
safety planning tool
trauma-informed narrative therapy
75–76, 89; dominant masculinity 77,
78, 80, 81–82, 86; hyper-arousal 76,
82–86; identity 81, 87–88; reasons for
abuse 76–78; responsibility for abuse

78–80, 85–86, 88; victim-only
narratives 75, 77–78, 79–86
trauma-informed services: Family Law
Program 144–145; non-trauma
informed context 149–151
trial process 143, 169; *see also* criminal
justice system
trust, amending ways 100–101

UK, justice-linked intervention programs
61
unhelpful shame 88
USA: criminal justice system 176;
intervention programs 229; justice-
linked intervention programs 61;
restorative justice approach 181

values of abusers 193–197, 199
VAW shelters *see* emergency shelters;
second-stage shelters; third-stage
shelters
victim-centered approach: IPV
movement 158–160; restorative justice
movement 158–160
victim-only narratives: male perceptions
research 98; restorative justice
195–196; trauma-informed narrative
therapy 75, 77–78, 79–86
victims: aid in Nova Scotia Domestic
Violence Pilot Project 131–132, 135;
assumptions about 161; female
perceptions research 101–104; IPV
movement 159–162, 166–167;
response to trauma 145; responsibility
perspectives research 95, **96**, 101–104;
restorative justice movement 158–162;
see also emergency shelter residents;
peer-led groups; safety; safety planning
violence against women (VAW) shelters
see emergency shelters; second-stage
shelters; third-stage shelters

weapons, safety planning tool *23*, 26
who to inform: barriers 39, 45; safety
planning tool *22*, 22–23
Winnipeg, specialised courts 126
women advocates *see* advocacy
women as victims *see* victims

Yukon: early intervention 126; law courts
57, 60